Patrizia Norelli-Bachelet

the Gnostic Circle

a synthesis in the harmonies of the cosmos

Æon Books

By the same author:

Symbols and the Question of Unity
The Magical Carousel
September Letters
The Hidden Manna
The New Way
The Tenth Day of Victory

ISBN 0-87728-411-3

Acknowledgements :

The Sri Aurobindo Ashram Trust, for permission to publish the writings of
Sri Aurobindo and the Mother included in this volume

Æon Books
P.O. Box 396
Accord, New York 12404
(914) 687-0639

CONTENTS

9 The Transcendent

1 ESSENTIAL PURPOSE OF THE STUDY OF COSMIC HARMONIES 3
   The Ideal 6
   The Goal 8

2 THE SUN AND THE CIRCLE DIVIDED INTO THREE PARTS 12

3 THE CIRCLE DIVIDED INTO FOUR 14

4 THE TWELVE MANIFESTATIONS AND THE GREATER CIRCLE 18

5 THE TWELVE MANIFESTATIONS 32
   Rama, the 7th Avatar and the 7th Manifestation 33
   Krishna, the 8th Avatar and the 8th Manifestation 37

6 THE NINTH MANIFESTATION 42
   The Fire Trinity and the Evolution 51
   The Gunas 54
   The Indian Yugas 61

7 SAGITTARIUS AND AQUARIUS 70
   The Body Transformation and the Earth Atmosphere 70

8 THE AGE OF PISCES 75

9 THE AQUARIAN AGE 86
   The Descent and the Ascent 100

6 The Cosmic

10 THE CIRCLE DIVIDED INTO NINE 105
    Saturn (Kāla), the Time-Spirit 111
    The Planets and the Circle of 9 118

11 THE ENNEAGRAM 123
    Transformation of Matter: The New Body 127

12 THE NEW PLANETS, THE SIGNIFICANCE OF THEIR DISCOVERY
    AND THE CALENDAR YEARS 137

13 THE GNOSTIC CIRCLE *159*
    The Leap Years 168
    Use of the Gnostic Circle 169

14 TIBET: ITS DESTINY IN THE GNOSTIC CIRCLE *173*

15 THE UNITED STATES OF AMERICA AND INDIA *181*
    Examples in the Gnostic Circle 181
    The Sacrifice in Matter 188
    *A Gnostic Community in Formation : the 6 Point Sacrifice
    and Intervention 190*
    Re-establishing Order and the Process of Renewal 194
    East and West Rapprochement 197

3 The Individual

16 THE GNOSTIC DEVELOPMENT OF THE INDIVIDUAL *205*
    The Four Cords 209
    The Zodiac and the Creation 225
    A Gnostic Pattern in Life 232

17 THE TRIAD OF UNITY AND THE INITIATION OF BEING *238*
    The Great Pyramid and the Mutation of Consciousness 239
    The Great Pyramid and the Mutation of Matter 243
    Into the Dimension of Simultaneous Time 247

18 THE EARTH *259*

0 The Centre

MATRIMANDIR AND THE COSMIC TRUTH *265*
    The 12th Latitude, and the Radius of the Earth 266
    The Inner Chamber 284
    The Central Portion 292
    The Core 294
    The Geometry of Time 295
    The Outer Shape of the Temple 298
    Conclusion 305

INDEX

In Matter shall be lit the spirit's glow,
In body and body kindled the sacred birth;
Night shall awake to the anthem of the stars,
The days become a happy pilgrim march,
Our will a force of the Eternal's power,
And thought the rays of a spiritual sun.
A few shall see what none yet understands;
God shall grow up while the wise men talk and sleep;
For man shall not know the coming till its hour
And belief shall be not till the work is done.

Savitri

the Father **9**
the seed
the vast

The Transcendent

"... *We shall see that what exists is not world at all but simply this infinity of spirit in which move the mighty cosmic harmonies of its own images of self-conscious becoming ...*"

Essential Purpose of the Study
of Cosmic Harmonies

IN SPIRITUAL CIRCLES of late it has been argued that the study of astrology and its sister arts is of no value in the unfolding of the spirit, and in most cases is a distraction and a deviation from the right path and leads the disciple in a direction away from the Goal. Because such an opinion is widespread today it is our purpose here to speak of some of the essential reasons why the knowledge has been contained and transmitted in the zodiac and the structure of the solar system, so that the student of these arts may not be discouraged by such considerations. Moreover, it is our intention to give as clear a picture as possible of the true purpose of astrology, and in which way it can be an asset in the development of the spirit.

First of all we must be clear as to what cosmic harmonies really are, for only then can we understand their true purpose. Cosmic harmonies give us the understanding of the movement of *progression within the eternal*. The art in its totality is transmitted so that man may have a clear vision of the process of evolution, and above all, of its ultimate goal for any particular Age. That is, these designs and patterns which are based on the deep understanding of the workings of the Cosmos, contain the history of the evolution, past, present and future. But to be able to understand this in its fullest sense, certain points must be explained. One is that it is indispensable for the student to realise that the movement of evolution in its most physical aspects is determined by a 'subtle essence', the Spirit, which upholds the movement, and is the support of the outer play, of which evolution is the mechanics. Therefore, in order to understand this play, we must first realise that the ultimate aim of creation is to be an ever more direct manifestation of the upholding and underlying Spirit.

The zodiac gives us a picture of this outer movement of evolution which has as its support the inherent spirit. It represents the aspect of the unique Energy in a state of *movement*, as opposed to the aspect of the unique Energy in a state of *rest*. The purest example of the former is Matter, and the purest example of the latter is Spirit. These two poles represent two aspects, apparently contradictory and opposite, of the One Unique Energy, working itself out into its fullest manifestation.

Thus, with this understanding we can proceed to unravel the mystery of creation and the map of evolution, which the zodiac and the structure of the solar system present to us. Without the understanding of the upholding Spirit, the study is rendered impossible, for it is this Spirit that determines the forms to be taken in the more dense realms, and the whole of creation and its evolution do nothing more than organise themselves and weave their 'substances' according to this upholding essence.

Since cosmic harmonies are concerned with the movements of evolution, or the workings of the manifest divinity, it is understood that those who do not look upon creation as real, who regard it as 'illusion', or who attempt to withdraw from participation in the progressive movement of evolution, seeking for salvation in a heaven beyond this material world, rather than an ever more perfect union of these two poles, cannot engage themselves in this study. It is an art for those who have had the inner experience of the utter reality of creation, and who have understood its unity with the upholding spirit, their essential Oneness,—and moreover, who have seen the necessity to become progressively more conscious in this creation in order to assist in the work of our present Age. In a word, this study is for those who have had the experience of *Śakti*, the Divine Mother, who herself determines the course of evolution which is nothing more than the play of her consciousness-force.

For those who cannot recognise the Mother and who do not see the reality of creation, this study is pointless.

Thus it can easily be understood why astrology has fallen into a degraded condition over the last two thousand years—something which appears to have never occurred before. On the contrary, it always occupied a foremost place in the organisation and development of past gnostic societies. Only during the last era, the Piscean Age, did the darkening of its light take place—which corresponded to the rise of Buddhistic, Mayavadist and similar thought that pulled the evolution *away* from the understanding of the reality of Creation, and advocated an escape from the pains and travails of its transformation as the only means by which a being could realise God and become free from the bondage of Matter. This movement therefore created a tremendous conflict in the evolution, as the two currents were then pulling in opposite directions. The very symbol of Pisces ♓ shows us the duality and struggle, but at the same time it points to the joining and fusion of these two currents.

In India the effects of such a split of spiritual force are especially noticeable. It is a land where most of the culture is rooted in and grows from a basic understanding of the Cosmos. Astrology in India occupied the same important position—perhaps an even greater one—than it did in all other ancient civilisations. And because the knowledge of this art was so profound in India and more deeply rooted in the structure of its societies, to this day, in spite of the opposite current, traces of it are still found; the Hindu Temple and the organisation of the Hindu religion reflect this long-lost knowledge. In particular, Tantrism, with its worship of the Shakti, has served to preserve and transmit the knowledge of the union of Spirit and Matter, or the equality of Brahman and Shakti.

Hence, when Buddhistic philosophy planted its seeds and took sway over the hearts and minds of men, the art of astrology fell into decadence, more so in India than elsewhere, though its essential meaning was preserved in Tantrism—because it was strongest in India and had progressed farthest in that land. It appears that the lost knowledge from the remote civilisation which we call Lemurian was transplanted and preserved on Indian soil. It is therefore on this very soil that the art will rise once more to its rightful place.

But this rise is not an isolated occurrence, having meaning only for the few who are especially interested in the Cosmos and its workings. Its rise indicates that just now the entire evolution is awakening to the oneness of spirit and matter, and ultimately to the understanding of the goal of evolution which is to divinise matter, or spiritualise the creation. For this reason we give so much importance to the study, because by reinstating it we assist mankind in its approach to the true path and purpose of the evolution. Cosmic harmonies reflect the will of the Transcendent, a Will of which we must become fully aware.

We find that even the most ardent worshippers of Shakti, namely those of the Tantric tradition, look upon the Cosmos as essentially equal to the Ignorance. It is rare to find schools today which are capable of perceiving the true will of the Transcendent in the workings of the Cosmos. They separate the basic trinity of Transcendent, Cosmic and Individual Divine, and anything below the Transcendent is for most spiritualists a part of the Ignorance and the Illusion; the Cosmic Truth is far from being apparent to the uninitiated eye as yet. But the evolution moves toward this very achievement and in the teachings of Sri Aurobindo the first attempt has been made to reawaken man to the unity of the essential Trinity and the perfection of all levels of the Manifestation, down to the individual. Only in his teachings do we find one who has the boldness to say not only that the Cosmos itself is a perfection, but that man with his very body is a mirror of the perfection of the Transcendent and will one day unveil his Light.

We can see the effects the division of spirit and matter has caused in the Indian nation, how it has cloaked the land in a blanket of inertia, depleted it of its force and power and the true understanding of its destiny as a nation. But at the same time we can also see that this covering made it possible for the knowledge to be preserved in the country, awaiting the day when the light would reappear to illumine the deep and profound mysteries of the Divinity Manifest.

We shall attempt to go into this matter as deeply as permissible on paper, hoping that these lines will awaken the student to the actual inner experience and realisation of what is here written, because the understanding of these things comes only with the direct experience in the soul. We can work with numbers, with diagrams, with symbols, but the real understanding, or *seeing*, comes through an opening in the psyche and the inner perception of the truths here put forth.

This brings us to another relevant point: the question of *seeing*. The study of cosmic harmonies is concerned mainly with helping mankind to see. People have believed throughout the Ages that astrology can be a tool and can be used as some sort of weapon, or that it can confer power on an individual. It must be stated here that the only power it confers is that which arises out of the action of *true seeing*. This has not been fully accomplished as yet in astrology and therefore the power certain individuals pretend or may believe themselves to possess through this study is an illusion. Astrology is a means of knowledge, the highest and fullest knowledge, but in order to grasp this it is essential for man to see properly, and this seeing comes only with an intense and dedicated work for purification. Its truest mysteries are only made evident to those who have undergone this purification; and the outcome of such a purification is the profound understanding that we are merely instruments of the Supreme, made to see when She wills, to know when She wills us to know, and to do or act when and as She wills. All sense of individual power vanishes with the deep knowledge of cosmic harmonies; to use astrology as a tool for acquiring power over others or over the workings of destiny, shows a great misunderstanding of the matter. The power this knowledge brings is simply the Power of Truth. We pray that this may be sufficient for the accomplishment of the Task.

Therefore, in this present study, it is hoped we can bring man to the point of seeing, and nothing more. As such, we also understand that the process of seeing rightly assists in the translation of the reality of the spirit into the realms of the more dense material creation. For this reason we feel it is vitally important to put forth the truths we have been allowed to see regarding these harmonies, because in their revelation we may assist the evolution in lessening the distance between the high ideal that is reflected as the Goal of the Age, and the actual condition of the race.

The Ideal

Cosmic harmonies deal essentially with Ideals; that is, they present mankind with the clearest possible image of the Supreme's will with regard to creation. In its purest essence, therefore, this study does not judge things as being positive or negative, something which often characterises the more superficial approach to astrology. In viewing the harmonies in the fullest and most unified manner, we see that all elements are part of the whole, and that in this sense neither one nor another is better or worse, but simply a necessary ingredient for the full manifestation. The falsity in the concept of positive and negative influences can be fully shown as we penetrate in our study, in particular when we unravel the mysteries of the Gnostic Circle.

The Ideal, or the Will, of the Supreme is written in the harmonies of the solar system and the symbols of the zodiac, and this we can understand through the study of astrology. We can say that the essence of astrology is the ideal, and we know that the art falls under the rulership of the 11th House of the mundane wheel, or the sign Aquarius, which governs the Ideals of man. It shows us the highest possibilities and the essential purpose of our quest, on a collective and individual scale. But between the realm of the Ideal and the regions of dense material creation where this fine substance is to be planted and to fructify, there are other planes which often interfere in the translation or intercept it, and therefore we are faced with the fact that much of what we see as possible in the purest terms of our vision, does not take shape in the physical plane, or if it does this may be after terrific destruction or great lapses of time. Hence people reject astrology and say that its truth is limited and there is much error in its workings.

Actually the problem lies elsewhere. In the first place we can say that cosmic harmonies will only be understood in their true value when man becomes fully conscious of the planes that exist between the vast upholding reality wherefrom the Ideal stems and takes its initial form, ephemeral though it may be, and the denser planes of material creation. When he becomes acquainted with these realms he will understand how in those planes there are forces which intercept and, shall we say, swallow up or dilute that which is offered as a possibility to the individual or the collectivity. We can further state that the more conscious man becomes of these intermediate planes, the more effective will his action be therein so that the power to deviate and distract the Ideal from translation into the substance of our Earth life will be radically lessened. These lower fields correspond to the domain of the Ignorance, and the forces working there take their nourishment from the powers of the Ignorance. They are a part of the Cosmos, but certainly not an essential part, in the same way that the ego is not the essential part of man but only acts to impede the direct action of the spirit, or else to veil the perfection of his existence. In this manner also to the uninitiated the planes of Ignorance act to clothe the Cosmos in a blanket made of ignorance. It can be understood that the more we progress toward a Truth-Consciousness, toward an existence which feeds on Truth, on Life, and not on Ignorance and Death, the greater will our possibilities be to understand the universal harmonies and then to directly translate them into the forms of material creation, thereby substituting ignorance with truth. Astrology and cosmic harmonies are born of Truth, and all that which does not correspond to this Truth is a part of the inferior existing planes which interfere with the manifestation of Truth.

As yet a wide gap exists between the essence of cosmic harmonies, the Ideal, and the planes of Earth life where the essence is to take root and flower. But it is known that we are in the Aquarian Age; we are passing through the portion of the Great Circle which corresponds precisely to the sign that rules astrology and the Ideal. Therefore, during our present Age we shall be engaged in lessening the gap between these two poles, in erasing the Ignorance and effacing the power of the interfering forces of falsehood.

The Goal

Our goal during this Age therefore is to enlighten the masses and render them capable of seeing the Reality. We are faced with the task of eliminating the Ignorance, and this can be done only by first *seeing* properly.

The last three signs of the zodiac, Capricorn, Aquarius and Pisces, are the trinity Sat-Chit-Ananda. Of these, Aquarius is Chit, or the aspect of Consciousness. At the same time it is Knowledge. We are therefore in the period of evolution which shall bring forth this aspect of the Divine, and this prepares the way for the Capricorn Age which is Sat, or the condition of Being. In order to enter that phase we must now discover how to *see*, for only then can the actual materialisation of the Ideal become accomplished.

Thus, the purpose of our times, and therefore the purpose of the study of astrology, is to give man a means by which he can learn to perceive integrally—that is, to gain a view of the total movement, but at the same time of the fragments which make up the whole. All of this can be accomplished in a very simple manner. The entire study of astrology and cosmic harmonies is founded on the understanding of the Circle, and this symbol represents the *unified multiplicity*. By the living experience of the Circle we can come to know the play of the Multiple as the indispensable ingredient in the question of Unity. We can say the Circle represents unity for us, but only because it is at once the representation of multiplicity; without this, its aspect of unity would be impossible to realise.

To be more precise, the study of cosmic harmonies can be contained in its entirety in one symbol, the Circle with the Dot or Point in the centre, ⊙ which is the symbol of our Sun. It is for this reason that we say: 'Look to the Sun always, for it is He who gives you your light.' In this symbol, all the secrets of the universe are contained; likewise, in the physical sun the secrets of the material universe and their correspondence to the Spirit are contained.

This brings up the question of total seeing and fragmentary vision: identified with the Earth consciousness one perceives only from the point located on Earth, therefore there is the sensation that one is at the centre of a revolving universe; one has only the consciousness of singular perception, the first dimension, and is limited and sees everything as transitory, changeful, where only the ego is steady and stable and through this ego one perceives the unending swirls of the universe.

But there is the possibility, and necessity, of acquiring another greater capacity of perception which would be positioning oneself on the sphere of the Moon from where one sees that one is a part of a more total movement, a global dance, and is a fragment on that sphere of the Earth which is not at all static but which itself revolves and thus gives rise to the apparent revolution of the universe around *it*. One acquires with this first 'detachment' a greater stability. Placing one's consciousness on the Moon, so to speak, is the first step toward a more unified vision. One sees oneself as a fragment spinning through space, whereas from the Earth one seemed to be static and the heavens alone to be spinning.

There is a further possibility, and this is to place one's consciousness on the Sun and from there realise the vision of the true centre of the movement, which sees that not only is this first vision fragmentary, but so too is the second, while in fact both these movements are the necessary ingredients for the principal one to occur. Thus from the Sun one sees the totality: one sees the Earth spinning on its axis, and at the same time the Earth rotating around a centre with the Moon, and these two creating an already complete movement. But the fuller scope is the positioning of the consciousness at the centre which carries the two in orbit around itself. It is the true centre because it is apparently steady and unmoving. This is the symbol of the Sun ⊙, and for this reason we say it is our symbol of the Divine in the physical manifestation.

However, there is yet the fourth movement: the positioning of the consciousness in the greater centre from where we see the motion of the Sun as well. In all we have then four dimensions. The first is the line, the vision from the Earth; the second is the plane, the vision from the Earth as well as the Moon; the third is the cube, from the Sun, which gives depth, width and height; and the last, the fourth, is the upholding and sustaining dimension, from the centre of the Galaxy.

In this realisation, the most important factor is the capacity for simultaneous perception. That is, it is not enough to place oneself in these positions (from the standpoint of consciousness) and subsequently put them together. Already with the third dimensional movement we have a greater possibility of unity; yet it is only with the fourth one that we touch the real substance and the simultaneous experience of all the dimensions and possibilities together.

We are all these things at one time. We are the Earth, the Moon, the Sun and the Centre, the *bindu*.[1] By turning to the Sun we can find the way because it is the Sun that opens the doors to the fullest dimensional perception.

These movements are related to time and space, but the simultaneity of the multi-dimensional experience is what carries us apparently beyond the limits of time, beyond the limitations of space. We are constantly breaking through these barriers in order to experience these dimensions, and this can only be done in the realm of consciousness: it is only consciousness that is *all*-pervading, therefore offering the possibility for such experiences. This is the Divine Mother, Consciousness-Force, the Circle that carries us to the experience of the Supreme Lord, the *bindu*—the point—together making up the symbol of the Sun.

In the discipline of yoga, in one way or another, one school or another, this is the experience one attains, progressing gradually until one achieves the position of the Sun, so to speak. In the world of science the same experiences are being had but in a slightly different manner: the astronauts are physically following the same path and most of them have had glimpses of higher states of consciousness when on the Moon or simply out of the gravitational pull of the Earth; free of the weight that pulls one ever downward, their bodies have experienced a greater freedom and through this bodily experience the state of consciousness has been affected. Seeing the Earth from beyond it has produced in most of these men radical changes in their thinking and feeling and a greater possibility of a more unified perception. Most interesting of all is that not only have they undergone these experiences with regard to consciousness, but their bodies themselves are experiencing these states. This is the fundamental and formidable difference now. A yogi may sit in his room and pass through the different states of consciousness that ultimately bring him to the experience of the Centre, but his body is not participating essentially, unless he is doing a particular yoga that concentrates precisely on expansion of the body consciousness for the purpose of carrying the physical as well to the experience of the fullest Light, a yoga such as has been envisioned and practised by Sri Aurobindo and the Mother. In the Mother's case, her last years were dedicated precisely to opening up the cells of the body to the *supramental light*, carrying them through the many dimensions, which will one day signify the concrete transformation of the body into a more perfected instrument. The body of man is at a transitional point at this time, caught between two tendencies which we can describe in symbol form: Man's body is in transition between the Square and the Circle. What actually must take place is that what the Circle represents, the divine manifestation,

[1] Sanskrit: *point or dot*.

must be pulled down to the realm of the Square, our actual condition on this planet. To be more exact, it is a question of the Square and the Circle becoming one. Matter must be divinised; the divine light must be unveiled therein. Leonardo Da Vinci's drawing-symbol of a man in a square and circle is an accurate prophecy of this process; in it we find that the navel is the central pivot of the man in the circle, and that the sex centre is the central pivot for the man within the square. Thus the problem for Earth beings is revealed: birth through sex and attachment to the lower nature is the eternal obstacle on the path to a greater spiritualisation of this life in all of its manifestations. But consciousness holds the key to all the work, the transformation of matter as well; thus *expansion of consciousness* is the imperative necessity of our times, and the circle as a symbol speaks to us of the many different aspects of the one all-pervading consciousness.

Therefore we learn that however we approach the subject of cosmic harmonies we begin and return always to one element: the realisation of the Circle, or the Sphere. Hence all our studies will be centered on the various manners of dividing the circle.

The Sun and the Circle Divided into Three Parts

AT THE OUTSET we must establish certain facts, which then shall constitute our particular language. The first is that symbols are related to numbers and can only be understood in this way. For example, when there is the realisation of the Circle there is a simultaneous realisation of the number Nine—because this is its number. And when there is the understanding of the Dot or Point, one then can comprehend the Zero.

Thus, in the symbol of the Sun the point is o and the circle is 9. These two therefore, 9 and o, are the numerical essence of the symbol of the Sun. In fact, all the workings of the Cosmos which we can capture in symbol form can also be captured in numbers. Thus number is our link with the Cosmos, because it is by means of number that we relate the movement of the spheres to the time periods of Earth. Number is the key to Time, and the study of astrology and cosmic harmonies is essentially connected with Time. If this element is abstracted we have no study, nor do we have a cosmos or a manifested divinity. And there are various levels of perception of Time. The denser and the more ignorant the material creation, the more divided is our perception of Time; closer to Truth and the spiritualisation of the denser realms, the perception of *simultaneous time* becomes possible, nay, inevitable, which does not exclude Time but only brings the experience of this element into the field of Unity. The past, present and future are not eliminated, but are perceived as three elements of one whole and are experienced simultaneously.

The Indians call the Time-Spirit, *kāla*. The feminine form is Kali, the Mother, who devours and gives birth to all things. In the solar system this is Saturn, *Kronos*, Father Time; and as astrology is linked to the sign Aquarius it must be remembered that the ancient ruler of this sign is Saturn, and is ever joined to it. Uranus is a later addition, indicating a newly manifested element in the possibility of understanding these harmonies and the workings of the System. It is Uranus that makes it possible for us to come to a greater and more integral understanding of Time (Saturn); by its appearance in the scheme of the solar system we know that the point has been reached to break certain barriers and enter into another dimension in our studies.

Therefore, it is to Saturn, the ancient ruler of Aquarius, that we turn our gaze, because this planet, by its very physical appearance and position in the system, tells us much. Physically Saturn is a unique planet because of its beautiful rings, three in number, and we understand then that *three* is a basic number in the comprehension of the structure of the universe and its unfoldment in time. Moreover, Saturn is at the sixth orbit, and thus the number *six* is a primary factor in the division of Time and the Circle. Therefore from ancient times the Seal of Solomon was considered a sacred symbol (two interlaced equilateral triangles), especially since in the old system there were six planets and the central Sun.

Thus, we have three numbers which are most important in our study and are the fundaments of this cosmic language: 3, 6 and 9. To these we must add the 0, without which the others could not have their being.

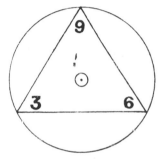

If we want to translate these numbers into symbol form we can do so by putting an equilateral triangle within a circle, and placing a number at each angle. The 9, then, is the apex of the Triangle because it is the number that is equivalent to the entire circle; the 6 is at one angle of the base, and the 3 is at the other. These latter two together equal the apex. The 9 is positive, 6 is negative, and 3 is neutral. The 0 is placed in the middle, and in this manner the symbol of the Sun is the centre.

The symbol constructed here is the basis of what we have called the Gnostic Circle. It represents the foundation in that the entire unfoldment of the evolution in time and space is balanced upon this triangle, or, we can say, the whole of creation bears in its essence the Trinity, and the evolution moves toward an ever more total and perfect revelation of the inherent triune Godhead. The symbol as such is the closest in essence to the Ideal, or, better said, it is only one step removed from the Ideal, which we may consider to be the total Circle. The Trinity therefore carries the Ideal in its bosom, and being the basis in the structure of the universe as well as in the structure of man, the Ideal is occultly lodged in the intimacies of all created things.

The Circle Divided into Four

FOR THE PURPOSE of understanding the structure of material life and the history of evolution on the planet, perhaps the most important and meaningful division of the Circle is into four parts. In this way we have the four Cardinal Points of the zodiac. It must be remembered that the *square,* which is derived from the *cross* or the division of the Circle into four, represents Matter, or material creation. The 360° thus divided present us with segments of 90° each, or numerologically, 9,[1] the number that represents material creation, the cell, or matter—the opposite pole of the spirit, the 0. Thus, in this manner of division we can come to understand and unravel the secrets of our evolution in matter. This is the basis we can say for discovery in the material, as the triangle is the basis for the understanding of our inherent divine part. The Circle divided into four as here reproduced is the symbol of the Earth.

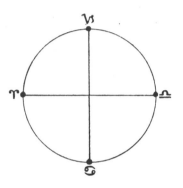

In this division, the aspect most obvious to the ordinary vision is the organisation of the seasons of Earth. The Cardinal Points represent the division of the four seasons, spring, summer, autumn, winter. But before continuing on this point it must be stressed that this cross sectioning is not concerned with the outward manifestation of the seasons as we know them, but rather with separation in four quarters of the three energy flows, Cardinal, Fixed and Mutable. We prefer to call these Creation, Preservation and Destruction or Dissolution, because these terms offer a clearer visual image of the action of the energy flows, or *qualities,* as they are called in astrology. In such a manner, each season as we know it consists of three months, each month corresponding to one of the energy flows; and thus in the final analysis we have the full circle divided into four, and each quarter divided into three, making twelve parts in all, the twelve signs of the zodiac.

The physical aspects of the seasons as are experienced on Earth only corres-

---

[1] For the study of cosmic harmonies the method of *theosophical addition* or 'cabbalistic reduction' is essential. It consists of simply adding all the numbers in a digit until one reaches the unit, i.e., 360=3+6+0=9.

pond to the energy of these three forces, and each season, no matter what its outward appearance: hot, cold, wet, dry, etc., is simply an effect of the three causes. It is only because we remain in the realm of outer physical perception and do not relate to the force behind the external manifestation that we speak of winter and summer, spring and autumn. In the study of astrology, the Earth, the globe, is taken as a whole, and what is relevant for the northern hemisphere is equally relevant for the southern.

The first Cardinal Point is 0° Aries, the first zodiacal sign, and it belongs to the *Fire* element. The second is Cancer, of the *Water* element; the third is Libra, of the *Air* element, and the fourth is Capricorn, of the *Earth* element. Thus through the four Cardinal Points we are shown the play of the four elements in creation, four aspects of the divinity manifest, the four faces of Brahma of the Hindu Trinity. These, *in their symbolic sense*, can be visualised as the seasons of the northern hemisphere, for Fire, the first point, which is the element that relates to Spirit, can be understood as the spark that sets the creation to action and the powerful impulse of creation to manifest and flower, due to the spark of spirit that quickens matter; this is energy in its purest and most potent state, the symbol of springtime. Cancer, the second point, can be symbolically understood by summer, because Cancer is the Life Principle or the appearance of organic matter in evolution, the cell, and we can visualise the process as taking place in a sort of 'hot house', where the summer heat represents the ingredient necessary for this life principle to evolve, since the element Water has been unveiled in the process of evolution.

The third season corresponds to the Air element and Libra; again we find the autumn winds characteristic of the force that uplifts the evolution by the principle of Mind unfolding at this time. The shedding of the leaves of the trees is symbolic of this third quarter, or season, which indicates the rise into a higher manifestation, or the emergence of the evolution from the 'lower hemisphere',—therefore the falling leaves are representative of the 'death' to the lower half that the evolution experiences, the shedding of the elements that hinder the passage to a higher manifestation, of which Mind is the means.

At the fourth point there is Capricorn, winter and the Earth element, whereby the full gamut is achieved as Matter is fully manifested and redeemed, and all the other sections of elements are *jelled*, or crystallised in the density of form. This is the symbol of winter, which hides in its bosom all the possibilities of the unfolding of creation, freezes them into the Earth's breast or core, only so that they may blossom one day. Thus we have at this time the growing light, the legendary *Festival of Light*, the Saviour's birth. This fourth pillar of creation which mediaeval astrology symbolically allocated to winter, shows us that in matter the divine light is inherent and awaits the moment of its epiphany.

These are some of the symbolic meanings of the seasons, but the true meaning of the physical action of the solstices and equinoxes is to be understood by the three flows, Cardinal, Fixed and Mutable, irrespective of the outer manifestation.[1] The essential point in this division of the celestial sphere is the beautiful image of the evolution or Creation reposing on the four cardinal points, which gives us the understanding of the development of the evolution, first by the appearance of matter or the physical, then life, the vital or emotional, then mind, and finally the quarter that contains all these and is for us the period of Sat-Chit-Ananda, the three last signs, Capricorn, Aquarius and Pisces, the unified, integral man, the divine or gnostic being.

Therefore we can present the following diagram, showing the quarters to be manifestations of one of the four primary components of the evolution. We relate this to the life of an individual or a community, a nation or a society or class or caste, so that the student can be brought closer to the purpose of our study, which is to show the gnostic development of being.

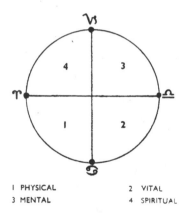

1 PHYSICAL	2 VITAL
3 MENTAL	4 SPIRITUAL

The understanding of the Circle divided into four is very enlightening because not only does it show us the structure of the Cosmos and the time periods on Earth, but it gives us the vision of the development of creation on the *individual* and *collective* scale. We see that man has essentially four 'bodies', or sheaths. The first is the physical, the second is the vital, the third is the mental, and the fourth is the spiritual or divine body. Of particular interest is the fact that the divine body corresponds to the last quarter, which refers to the fourth Cardinal pole of the Earth element, and therefore we know that the ultimate goal of creation is the unveiling of the Divine in matter. Creation does not progress toward the more ethereal manifestation, but rather it evolves toward making the densest part the visible tabernacle of divine light, because it is this part that contains the light in a 'jelled' form, the particular attribute of Saturn mentioned earlier, the ruler of Capricorn or the fourth pillar. It is only the most dense element that has the capacity to resist and hence contain or crystallise the highest vibration or the purest light. The other 'bodies' do not have this capacity of resistance, and were it not for

---

[1] The Equinoxes give us equal days and nights, equal division of time; they belong to the signs Aries and Libra, the Fire and Air elements which have affinity with the manifestations of spirit and mind. The solstices give us unequal time division, and belong to the signs Cancer and Capricorn, the Water and Earth elements which are connected to matter and its more dense manifestation.

the Earth element their manifestation would be impossible.

With respect to the collectivity or the structure of society, this division again holds the key to the understanding of both the ancient and modern organisation of civilisation. The four sections of the circle correspond to the four ancient castes of India: servers (physical), merchants (vital), warrior-kings (mental), and priests or Brahmins (spiritual). In modern times the same division prevails: the labour class, the economic or trade class, the governments and military, and the priests or inspired body. However, what is lacking today and has not as yet manifested is the part the divine body is to play. Of all the four classes this latter is the only one that has not as yet come fully forth from behind the veil; and it is a curious fact that according to the precession of the equinoxes which determines the point we are on in the spiral of evolution, we are now proceeding through the fourth section which tells us that though the appearances are contrary, everything now taking place on Earth, this great churning of all the powers and forces, is nothing more than the means to fully bring to the fore the divine rule or the appearance of the gnostic being and the unity of man and of mankind—for unity can only come about when the individual as well as the collectivity have centered themselves in the divine, or have realised *and manifested* their essential and inherent divinity. The evolution proceeds through this portion which indicates that the time has come for the spiritual force to take possession of the hearts, minds and bodies of men.

We shall go into this in much greater detail as we penetrate in our studies. To do this it is necessary to speak of the *Map of the 12 Manifestations*. But before concluding our study of the division of the circle into four parts the movement must be mentioned that is the most powerful and relevant indication of the importance of the fourth and last Cardinal Point: the orbit of the Earth around the Sun, which is an ellipse, and comes slightly closer to the Sun at the time of the Festival of Light (early January), moving farther away from the luminary at the time of the 'fall', the entry into Cancer. The latter is the Cosmos cloaked in the veils of Ignorance, hiding the light of the Supreme, and working from behind these veils: Maya, who casts the spell of 'illusion' over the entire manifestation; the former, Capricorn, is the Cosmic Truth,—the Earth moves closer to the Sun, and in the play of evolution this is the period when the light returns once more and the Cosmic Ignorance is redeemed. It is this 'redemption' that is now to take place, where mankind shall see that the Cosmos is the translation of that very Truth it aspires to but places *out* of the manifestation; that is, the Cosmos is nothing but a projection of that Truth, and it is only our veils, our ignorance, that impede us from seeing and revealing this Reality in the dense realms of the Creation.

4

The Twelve Manifestations and the Greater Circle

SATURN IS THE 6 point of the Triangle as we have stated, the angle that represents the *Cosmic Divine*, or the sixth orbit away from the Sun; it is the Time-Spirit. The number 6, therefore, helps us in our understanding of time, and by the physical appearance of Saturn we know that the sphere or circle with three rings around it is the key to the progression of the Ages and their relation to Time. It is in this manner, therefore, that we divide the circle; that is, we combine the elements studied thus far, and by so doing we come to the key of evolution. Taking the Circle divided into four parts, we place three circles around it, and extend the cross through these rings, beginning at 0° Aries, the Equinox, (diagram opposite).

In order to give the proper understanding of the movement the circles are drawn in a spiral, since this is the motion in space of the universe, reflected in the very structure and movement of our galaxy. Then, each of the sections of the spiral corresponding to a quarter of the Circle is given a number, going backwards, or clockwise, through the spiral as the precession of the equinoxes moves. These are called the Manifestations. When they are all numbered we find that there are twelve, and if we count the number of zodiacal signs included in this triple spin, there are found to be thirty-six in all. The same diagram could be drawn not using the spiral, as shown on page 21.

In this manner we find that our spiral is really a reproduction of what some astronomers and archaeologists consider the oldest existing astrological documents on Earth, the 'astrolabes' of Mesopotamia, which as yet they are unable to decipher.

This Map of the 12 Manifestations, as we have termed it, becomes dynamic when we add to it the factor of Time, and this is accomplished by the Precession of the Equinoxes. It takes 25,920 years for the Precession to make one complete round of the Circle, or to pass through the twelve signs of the zodiac once, taking us through four Manifestations. The completion of the entire three circles on the spiral takes then 77,760 years (3 × 25,920), and this we call one *Great Circle*. A full period for the development of a civilisation would be approximately this amount of time. That is, the seeds planted in the first Manifestation would take close to 80,000 years to bear the intended fruit. Thus, as we enter the final round in any

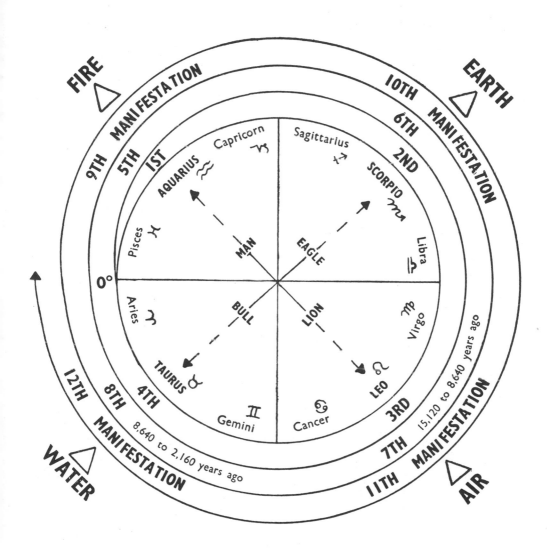

THE 12 MANIFESTATIONS

Map of the Evolutionary Ages
(Dynamic)

1 Age (1 sign)	=	2,160 years
1 Manifestation (3 signs)	=	6,480 years
1 Complete Round (12 signs)	=	25,920 years
1 Great Circle (12 Manifestations or 36 signs)	=	77,760 years

given Great Circle we know that the point has been reached where the civilisation is nearing its culmination and its destiny is pressing to be fulfilled.

By knowing the date of the beginning of the Age, or the '0' point of this great cosmic clock, we can insert ourselves into the Wheel with great precision and, moving backwards through the signs with the aid of all the sub-influences of the zodiac, in particular the individual degrees of the circle, or what the Indians call the *triṁśāṁśa*, 360 in all, the influence for any given year, month and day, and hour even can be known.

It has often been suggested that the Atlantean civilisation existed between 50,000 to 80,000 years ago. This mighty and apparently advanced civilisation reached a peak and then suffered the inevitable decline. There has been much speculation as to the reasons for the decline; some believe that because of incorrect use of occult knowledge the forces of destruction turned back upon the society and tremendous natural catastrophes began, finally bringing the total disappearance of the civilisation and the submergence of the continent into the waters of the Atlantic.

There have been many theories put forth regarding Atlantis, and Lemuria, another legendary civilisation, but as yet nothing precise and accurate has been found. It is a fact, however, that as archaeologists and scientists advance in their knowledge and probe with greater skill through the strata of time, they come closer and closer to the conclusion that not only is our civilisation much older than has been believed, but that long before ours came into being there may well have been civilisations which existed, flourished in a manner undreamt of today, and then were apparently completely demolished. Obviously scientists do not care to publicise such facts or give them too much credit, because man as he is presently constituted prefers to believe he is the sole and only possibility for humanity to evolve any further, and his ignorance of past accomplishments seems to be a necessary ingredient for his present evolution. Up to the present point it appears that for various specific reasons knowledge of the past would have hindered the effort needed to pull the evolution forward. In like manner, a clear knowledge of the future would also have hindered the development. In order for the knowledge of past and future to be beneficial and not harmful for the evolving race, it is necessary that a new capacity awaken in man, one which allows him the vision of the totality which will in turn show him the rightful place of Creation and Preservation, as well as *Destruction*, in the true scheme of things.

In man's present condition he cannot have this knowledge because he abides within the ignorance. With the dawn of a consciousness of Truth, it will naturally become easier for the entire race to learn of its full being in Time, without this resulting in an obstruction of the work that is to be accomplished. In fact, we are approaching the point where ignorance is now the obstacle, where ego is the element

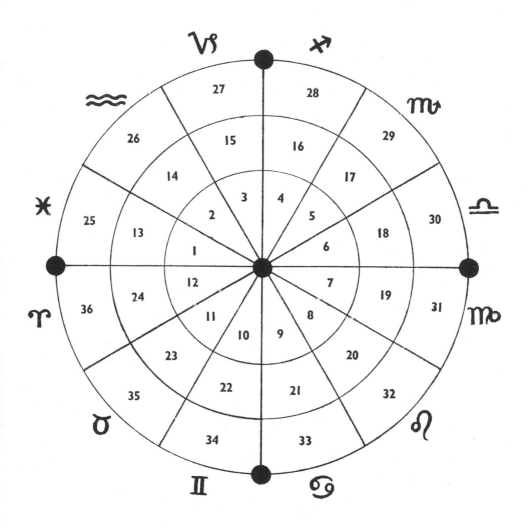

MAP OF THE 12 MANIFESTATIONS

(Static)

of disintegration, and mind is the organ of the perpetuation of falsehood. These must now be erased and surpassed if the race is to move into its rightful place in the unfolding of the Manifest Divine. Once, and for a long, long time, it was necessary to be limited, because limitation was the element safeguarding the gestation of the Light. This being born, the veils can finally be shed.

We are now in the 9th Manifestation, equivalent to the ninth month when the child is born. On this position of the three-fold spiral, it is the time of the birth of that which was conceived some 54,000 years ago. But it must be pointed out that if man would know the past and future, he must be master of himself. If the time has come when the race as a whole is being given certain knowledge hitherto reserved for the enlightened, it is a sign that mankind on a collective scale has reached the point where it must become another more perfected species. If certain truths are handed to man it is because he must now become responsible and act in accordance with this greater knowledge.

The precession of the equinoxes is what determines the movement of the Ages backwards through the constellations; and we know that one of the principal determinants in this movement is the Moon which, by its gravitational pull on the Earth, creates a wobble, resulting then in the precession or the shifting of the equinoctial points with respect to the stars, so scientists say. This is not to be confused with the movement of the Earth respective to the ecliptic of the Sun that occurs every year around March 21st, a movement that ever recurs on that date. What is here spoken of is the greater circle upon which the 'ascendant of the Earth', so to speak, is traced, and which coincides with the annual equinoctial point every 25,920 years.

We can see therefore that as for a woman the Moon is the determining factor in her cycles, which make it possible for her to conceive and bring forth a child, so too the Earth becomes the Woman, and by the Moon's pull the Divine Spirit is gestated within her womb and is born during the period of the 12 Manifestations. After the 9th it 'lives' for three Manifestations, what for the Cosmos would be something close to three days.

It is only when we can perceive the planet in this way, as a being itself, a part of the Divine Mother, that we can come to unravel the mysteries of this wide and vast universe we inhabit. All mythologies of old have given us this image of our planet in their tales of the Earth Mother, Isis, Demeter, Durga and many others, and it is time to understand that these myths are not abstract concepts but pertain to the reality of our creation, and in particular that they are descriptive of what we are now living, what is taking place in our very times.

As we proceed in our studies it will become ever more evident to the student that in order to grasp the unity underlying the magnificent order of the universe the capacity must be cultivated to view man, the solar system, the galaxy, and finally the whole of the universe as one being. He must come to see that in the rhythms of Earth and those of its inhabitants the very same movements and the same order and goal are seen as in the entire body of the manifest Divine. He must realise, and in no abstract way, that within him is a universe like unto the heavenly harmony that moves above him and around him and his planet.

In this manner one can look at the cycles of a woman and thereby understand the labour of the Earth to bring the entire race forth from its womb. Our times are indeed the period of labour pains. The Earth Mother is bringing forth her child and is ejecting it into its own independent existence. But the process of birth is not a simple one and there are many different layers, shall we say, different parts of the being, which are born. We shall speak in more detail of this as we proceed in our study of the Gnostic Circle, in what pertains to the individual, but here we are interested mainly in the process affecting the Earth itself and humanity as a whole. We are interested in the future evolution of the human species in general.

Thus as we have studied the circle divided into four parts and seen its profound meaning in the flow of energy, we can also see this division of four as meaningful in the question of the Earth's birth. There are four births, which would correspond to the four different sheaths. We therefore proceed through the Circle of 12 Manifestations four times before the true and full birth is accomplished; nearing the fourth, the child is truly born and delivered to his rightful destiny.

If this is related to time we must allow 311,040 years for the full process (4 × 77,760). Each Great Circle (twelve Manifestations) completed signifies the birth or the fulfilment of one of the four parts of the Body. Therefore, 311,040 would correspond to a full and total manifestation. Within this period, 77,760 years is the time necessary for any one of the 'sheaths' to be matured. Thus in the span of the *Greater Circle* there are four civilisations or empires that come forth, and each one points to a particular sheath, the Physical, the Vital, the Mental and the Spiritual. Remnants of these past achievements always remain on Earth during the full gestation, until the time when the entire work is to be dissolved and drawn back into the womb of the Mother.

Traces of these other 'sacks' are to be found in the legends and fossils and ruins of olden times, of other Great Circles. But essentially what we are interested in here is our period of 77,760 years, related to the evolution of the four quarters. That is, we are interested to know *where we are on the spiral*, with as great a precision as possible, because in this knowing we can assist in the work we have come to accomplish.

For this purpose humanity is left with fragments of past teachings, to assist man in understanding his place on the spiral of evolution. This is the sole and only reason that wise men passed down the Knowledge, as well as constructed monuments that show the race the heights of the achievements of lost civilisations. In our times this would perhaps be Atlantis, and the monument that captures and preserves something of that civilisation's accomplishments absorbed by the present race is the Great Pyramid. From that point we work to bring about another birth or shedding of the sack. We have moved through two such births. The first corresponded to the Physical, the second to the Vital, to which the civilisation of Atlantis belonged, and the third is the Mental. It is supposed that after our period of 77,760 years the birth of the Spirit will fully take place. In this way, 144 signs of the zodiac are traversed to complete the process, the square of 12.

The difficulty in understanding the flow of evolution and the birth of the four parts of the Earth lies in the factor of simultaneous action and perception. While the Physical is being gestated there is present on Earth the fully visible seed of the Vital body. The race, or group of people, that are to develop the Vital are present during the Physical birth, and they then become the link and carry over the fruits of the former work, incorporating it into their own, digesting and assimilating it, until they themselves become the seed for the Mental quarter to absorb, digest and assimilate. It can be said that from the beginning of the Greater Circle all the races that are to arise during its 311,040 years are present simultaneously, until the final birth is accomplished. As in the development of an individual when one part of his being comes up strongly to be worked on during a certain period of his life while the others remain dormant or fade into the background, so the great Earth awakens parts of herself at different times, though the other parts of her being are present but asleep. It can be understood then that when the birth of a particular sheath is completed it does not fall back but becomes an integrated, vibrant and active part of the Great Being reflected in mankind. Thus by the third quarter we are aware of the former two to a much greater extent because their seed is alive and working in us: we represent the fruit of that former work.

In the study of individual horoscopes people are often too concerned with the past. But there is a way of knowing these things without dwelling on the past disconnected from the present. It is possible, and actually better, to penetrate the present fully in order to discover what our past is. If we know how to look at a horoscope in a certain way the details of past incarnations are not seen, but rather what has been carried over from past work and what is alive and active in the present; in such a way we can also look at the evolution's 'horoscope'. By penetrating into the present, by knowing our precise position on the scale, we at once know what lives in us of the past, what is essentially important to know, and then we can discard the useless and cumbersome knowledge, extract the truth from former efforts, thus allowing this truth to be the essence of the future.

However, since we are mental beings we are faced with some problems while

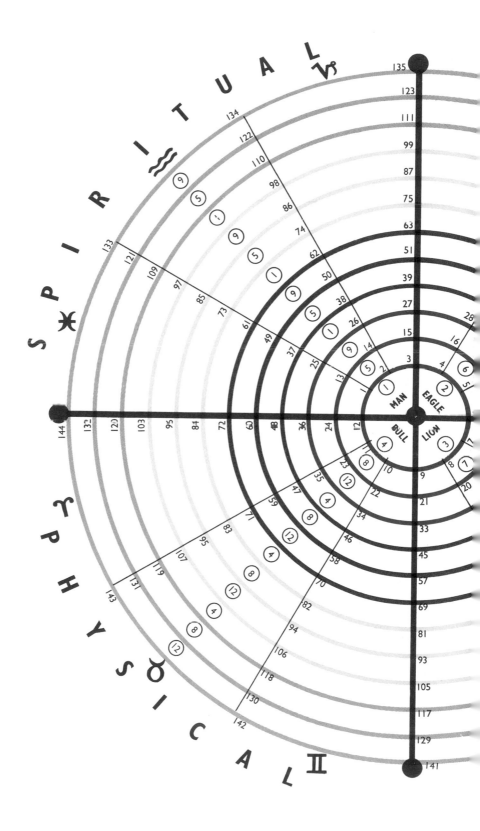

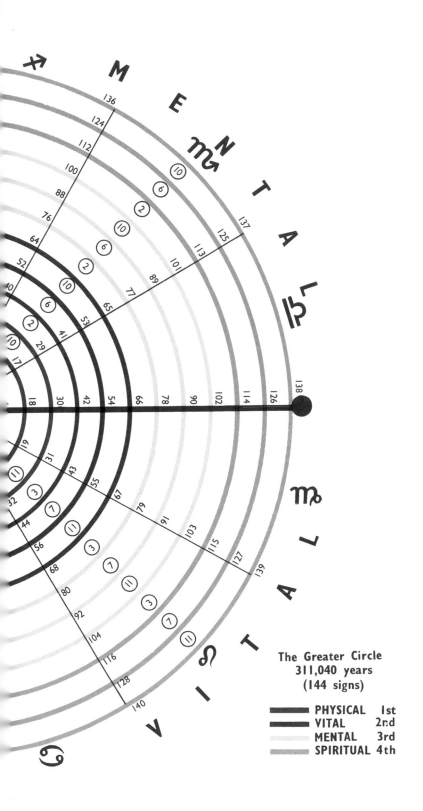

The Greater Circle
311,040 years
(144 signs)

PHYSICAL 1st
VITAL 2nd
MENTAL 3rd
SPIRITUAL 4th

studying ourselves and our evolution: namely, as stated above, the difficulty of simultaneous perception. As we move through a quarter of the Earth's being, reflected in any one of the Great Circles, we must at once realise that proceeding through the 12 Manifestations of that Great Circle we shall also be moving through one of the four quarters of the simple circle, as described on page 16. For example, if we are in the second Great Circle, the Vital Body of the evolution, (corresponding to what we call the Atlantean civilisation), during that period we would also traverse the four parts, which would then be like sub-divisions of this Vital Circle. Thus, approximately 132,000 years ago was the beginning of the Vital Circle, and from that time the first 6,480 years corresponded to the Vital-Spiritual (moving backwards through the Circle together with the precession of the equinoxes); the next 6,480 years would have been Vital-Mental, the third 6,480 full Vital and the final 6,480 years Vital-Physical. This completes the 25,920 years of that first Round. The process is repeated two more times. Therefore during any Great Circle the other parts of the Being are worked on, though they are subjected to the predominant influence of the times. The diagram (page 25) will show this more clearly. Each section, or sign has been numbered, from 1 to 144, and the Great Circles have each been coloured as indicated on the chart.

We are now in the 98th section, in the Mental sheath (coloured in yellow), and the sub-influence would be Spiritual. It is therefore the time of Mental-Spiritual growth. The importance then of the 9th Manifestation of any given Great Circle is very clear: it is the time in which that particular Body is born, never more to recede. At the same time it is the preparation for the new one to come forth. The 97th, 98th and 99th sections on this vast spiral are perhaps the most important in the entire wheel of 144 sections, or 311,040 years. They are the last three months of the 'pregnancy'. The Child is then born. Moreover, of all the 9th Manifestations, the third is especially important, being also the *Ninth Spiral* of the Greater Circle. So, what the 9th Manifestation means in the simple progression of the 12 Manifestations is also reflected in the Twelve Spirals of the full wheel. The culmination and fullness of our times can easily be understood by this double progression which coincides now.

During the 9th Manifestation there is the incarnation of the three aspects, Mother, Father and Child. What takes place in the spiritual body of the Earth is expressed for mankind in this way. These three incarnations represent the three aspects of the Divine: the Transcendent, the Cosmic or Universal, and the Individual. The Child, the Individual, is the product or the fusion of the other two principles. When these Incarnations appear on Earth it is the sign that the birth of the Great Circle—and in our case of the Greater Circle as well—is taking place, and in their lives we can find the details of the Birth, learn of the will of the Transcendent, decipher the cosmic language which this Will makes use of, and then finally witness the culmination in the individual, thereby knowing what the collectivity is to experience and express throughout the remainder of the Round. These beings incarnate each time a 9th Manifestation is reached and in and through themselves carry out the work of the Age. They are the Central Pivot and without them the movement would have no axis, no concentration, no possibility of the diffusion of the descending force, in the same way that the Sun serves as the centre of our system, upon which we depend for our life.

The 9th Manifestation of any Great Circle will always fall in the Spiritual quarter of the wheel, because it is toward this that we move—a spiritualisation of the entire manifestation. As well, the 1st and 5th fall in the Spiritual quarter, and together these three represent the Spirit in manifestation, whether it be expressing itself through the physical, vital or mental perfectioning process. The three Manifestations, or signs, are of the Fire element, they are *the Trinity of Fire*.

Following the Greater Circle through from the beginning shows us that the Physical is the first body that is worked on, the first Great Circle, but the 1st Manifestation falls in the Divine or Spiritual quarter. These two are immediately linked. We see then how the first stirrings in the development of the Physical will not occur, or at least become evident, until the Precession moves through the quarter that pertains to the Physical proper. In Time this would be between 19,440 to 25,920 years after the 0° point of the Greater Circle, or between 203,040 to 209, 520 years ago approximately. As we penetrate in our study it can be seen how the Physical 'seeds' are the slowest to appear, but also how they are the slowest to disappear. Each 4th, 8th and 12th Manifestation then stresses all the more the growth or evolution of the Physical body, for it is during those Manifestations that the Precession is in the Physical quarter of the Circle. For man during those periods perhaps the physical structure underwent noticeable changes—Mother Nature experimenting, in a sense, on the body of man as well as the animal kingdom.

Then, as we move into the next Great Circle, the Second, it is the Vital's turn, the emotional nature, the occult forces in Nature, as well as the first visible signs of the psychic being in evolution. But it is not until the 3rd Manifestation, or 12,960 to 19,440 years after the beginning of the Second Great Circle (112,320 years ago approximately) that the work became evident. Then as the movement passed from the Vital quarter into the Physical, after this period, for the first time there was the commencement of the destruction of the work of the previous Great Circle, and its absorption into the total body. Each time then that civilisation moves through the Physical portion of the Wheel during the Second Great Circle, there is a certain amount of destruction. And though the Physical was the slowest to manifest it is the slowest to be absorbed, for until the last Manifestation of the Second Circle its effects are still felt and are visible, and efforts are needed to break it down and allow the next Body to be developed.

During the Third Great Circle, our own times, it is in the 2nd Manifestation that the Mental development begins, only 6,480 to 12,960 years after the commencement of our Circle, or approximately 47,520 years ago. Then each passage through the Vital quarter would be a time when destruction would be necessary, in order to subdue the development of that part of the Earth's being, so that a balanced and harmonious growth could ensue. If this did not occur, humanity could never reach the pinnacle toward which it moves. Destruction is particularly necessary when dealing with the bodies of the lower half of the Wheel, the Physical and Vital, since in this region Prakriti is particularly strong and the Ignorance can often be dealt with only in this way. When we move into the higher sphere, the realms of Mind and the Spirit, the destructive forces of Nature lessen, though they cannot be entirely eliminated until the full Golden Age, the Satya Yuga or the Reign of Truth, which in the most complete sense is the Fourth and final Great Circle.

Referring to the map of the Greater Circle[1] it can be seen that passage through the 77th, 89th and 101st signs would stress the development of the Mental body. Then passage through the 80th, 92nd and 104th signs would perhaps signify the breaking down and absorption of the Vital formation of the previous Great Circle. If this is referred to events of our times, what we call the Atlantean civilisation would appear then to have undergone certain periods of destruction[2], the first occurring about 40,000 years ago, and the second about 12,000 years ago. The third, which Edgar Cayce has referred to, might have been the destruction that took place during the Second Great Circle itself, not affecting the Atlantean race but rather the remains of the Manifestation of the previous Great Circle, the Physical.

In the Fourth Great Circle to come, as well as in ours, though there may be destruction, it is hardly likely that we shall have to lose the *conscious* link with the past. Working in full consciousness with the harmonies and laws of evolution this evidently will not be necessary. The 'missing link' periods correspond to the great destructions when it is necessary to erase certain evidences of the passage to a higher state, and that only the species perfected up to that point remain. What disappears in the destruction is the negative appendage that served as a transition. No specimens of man's leaps to a higher state remain, the real transitional beings. These are carried away during the periods of great catastrophes, and it is usually at the solstice points of the Circle that this occurs; so this possibility is present while passing through any Cancer or Capricorn Age. The time of destruction in the coming Capricorn Age, some two to three thousand years from now, will most likely leave

---

[1] Page 25
[2] See *Edgar Cayce on Atlantis*, by Edgar Evans Cayce.

only the supramental beings and do away with the transitional race.

If Nature did not cover up her footprints, man would cling to his old form and would be unwilling to move to the next stage, because he always fears the unknown. Thus destruction is a prime part of evolution and is a process that cannot be eliminated. It corresponds to the *guṇa* of *tamas*, Shiva's force, the force of our times. But there is one factor that must be stressed again: if man is conscious enough and understands the coming stage and the work being accomplished, accepts it and willingly discards his old ways, he can avoid destruction. Evidently it has never happened, yet it is possible at this time. It is also possible that instead of sweeping catastrophes being employed, a gradual process of elimination may now occur. Presently the *guṇa* of *tamas*, or destruction, can be realised as an active passivity, an action in non-action, a conscious surrender.

While studying the Greater Circle, as explained previously, we must be aware of the fact that simply because the evolution moves through these four quarters and touches upon one aspect of being at a time does not mean that the others do not exist. Man, throughout the entire Greater Circle of 311,040 years which is unfolding at present and of which we are in around the 209,600th, is essentially a mental being; or to be more exact, he has been evolving with Supermind, as Sri Aurobindo has called it, involved in him and all created things, moving ever closer to its full manifestation. We cannot say that he had no mind 200,000 years ago, but only that this instrument was dormant, compared to what it is today. Moreover, it had to remain in the background in the beginning so as to prepare the other sheaths that would allow for its fullest birth to come about. The early product of our Greater Circle was *homo sapiens*, but heavily engrossed in the physical, very close yet to the animal and operating almost solely on the level of instinct. In the Great Circle after that one Mind was liberated a further degree, the species became more refined, yet its development centered mostly on the evolution of occult forces, the manipulation of universal powers, to which it seems man was then greatly attuned. We have no accurate information regarding these earlier periods, only what clairvoyants have intuited and some brief passages in ancient literature, or else monuments that capture something of past accomplishments. But even these monuments, such as the Great Pyramid and the Sphinx, pertain to our own Circle and were already within the realm of the mental sheath, so a true and vivid reconstruction of anything prior to 50,000 or even 25,000 years ago is beyond our scope and vision. During the Vital part, from the study of the Greater Circle we see that mind was turned almost fully to the accomplishments of the designs of Prakriti, the harnessing of her force —which is perhaps the reason that the legends describe Atlantis as having been destroyed because of the abuse of these powers. Though much was accomplished in the way of knowledge and accumulation of occult powers, the more subtle and refined characteristics of Mind remained hidden. As Mind comes strongly to the fore the race moves away from the intimate contact with Nature it is true, and though this may appear unfortunate and not in harmony with the reason for one's presence on this Earth, it is nonetheless necessary because this separation will allow the spiritual force a wider scope for action and a freer possibility of manifestation. During the present Mental Circle it is supposed that man will move fully through the possibilities of Mind, culminating then in the full advent of the principle of Light above mind, without which it would be impossible to embark on our final journey through the coming 12 Manifestations, that bring to an end these 311,040 years of the Greater Circle of which we are a part.

5

The Twelve Manifestations

THE PERIOD THAT served to leave us the traces of the Atlantean civilisation was between 12,000 to 15,000 years ago. After this, or precisely around 8,640 years before the beginning of the present Aquarian Age, which took place during this 20th Century, there was evidently a minor natural catastrophe,—minor compared to the great destruction that overtook the Atlantean civilisation. It probably occurred during the time that the precession of the equinoxes was moving over the second Cardinal Point, Cancer, or to be more precise, during the last 360 years of the age of Cancer, which being a Water sign we can understand why there exists to this day the legend of the Great Flood. That disaster is said to have covered the globe in water, but perhaps it was only the Mediterranean area that suffered, most of our records of the flood having come from this portion of the civilised Earth. The Great Pyramid survived the disaster and was later restored: it appears that many different hands have passed over this monument, but the essential structure remains the same.

We shall not dwell too lengthily on that civilisation, though if the student is inclined to he can reconstruct the epoch on the basis of the zodiacal wheel, not so much in the details of the material life of the times, but rather with the knowledge of the zodiac and its symbols and time relationships it is possible to understand the spiritual development of the civilisation existing then and what it was to contribute to the movement of evolution. In precisely the same way that we know what the contribution of the actual 9th Manifestation is to be, culminating in the Age of Capricorn, so can we reconstruct the direction of the evolutionary urge during any particular period, based on the zodiac and the harmonies of the spheres. To study ancient history properly the only way possible is on the basis of the cosmic harmonies; there is no other key that can be used in such a precise way. These harmonies do not depend on methods of preservation of knowledge that are fallible and subject to the decaying hand of Time. In the Cosmos the history of the Earth is permanently recorded in a way that is indelible, because the information is ever there in the workings of the cosmos, in the structure of our solar system, and as long as our System prevails, this record is infallible. When the System is dissolved so will the entire manifestation of our universe disappear, or, to be more accurate, the instrument of conscious perception which for this term of manifested divinity is man.

However, man is dependent on one thing for the possibility of deciphering the cosmic scripture: he must receive the light from above, the divine word or revelation must be granted for the task. In no other way can he pretend to know the universal language. The heavens are there, the symbols are preserved, but he is blind to these workings unless the divine will grants him the light whereby to see. This will become rather evident as we penetrate in our studies. However, the Supreme Intelligence periodically sends beings to our planet to reveal certain keys to humanity, beings that live in a particular consciousness, with certain centres attuned or sensitive in a different way than the ordinary Earth being. From time immemorial these entities have been revered in the various civilisations the Earth has known—some called them gods, others divine incarnations or avatars, saints, prophets, messiahs, and so forth. Often these incarnations were grouped all together and considered of the same quality, which is not quite the case. There are, in these more ethereal realms, different degrees of development just as there are different levels or degrees of evolution on Earth, and therefore it is erroneous to suppose that all incarnations are the same, though this may be immaterial in the work that is to be accomplished. Some we call *avatārs* or divine incarnations because they come from a realm that is close to the Source of Light as messengers with a specific task. Nonetheless, we must realise that this is how we view it from our standpoint, and from man's particular position today, because according to his development on a collective scale so will the messenger be that he is to receive from the Divine. He is given the assistance he needs and is in a position to absorb as he goes along. In future times the beings appearing on Earth for this purpose will be of an infinitely more evolved order or, let us say, those incarnations who have already participated in the Earth's evolution will then be able to reveal their light to a much greater degree, perhaps only after their work has in large part been accomplished. Up to the present it has been necessary to clothe this light, revealing only a minute fraction.

Rama, the 7th Avatar and the 7th Manifestation

After the Age of Cancer, or more precisely, as the Earth's ascendant passed over the second Cardinal Point, the evolution moved into a period of darkness. The Indian tradition has preserved certain details in the stories of their divine incarnations which help us to understand these things. In fact, in their mythology and the stories of their gods we find the most accurate description of the movement of spiritual evolution. These stories are most closely linked to the zodiac, for reasons we have already mentioned. If the student refers to the Map of the Manifestations,[1]

[1] Page 19

it can be noticed that the 7th Manifestation is comprised of three signs, Virgo, Leo and Cancer; that epoch corresponded to the incarnation of Rama. We are aware that his incarnation is usually not placed so far in the past, but it must be pointed out that there are no precise records as to the actual time Rama was incarnated. The only accurate information is that he preceded Krishna. Even the actual details of his incarnation, as is the case with them all, we cannot be totally sure of; we do know, however, what his incarnation meant for the evolving race, and this Sri Aurobindo has recorded very accurately in *Letters on Yoga* (p. 415 CE):

... an Avatar is not at all bound to be a spiritual prophet—he is never in fact merely a prophet, he is a realiser, an establisher—not of outward things only, though he does realise something in the outward also, but, as I have said, of something essential and radical needed for the terrestrial evolution which is the evolution of the embodied spirit through successive stages of the Divine. It was not at all Rama's business to establish the spiritual stage of that evolution—so he did not at all concern himself with that. His business was to destroy Ravana and to establish the Rama-Rajya—in other words, to fix for the future the possibility of an order proper to the sattwic civilised human being who governs his life by reason, the finer emotions, morality, or at least moral ideas, such as truth, obedience, co-operation and harmony, the sense of the domestic and public order,—to establish this in the world still occupied by anarchic forces, the Animal mind and the powers of the vital Ego making its own satisfaction the rule of life, in other words, the Vanara and Rakshasa. This is the meaning of Rama and his life-work and it is according as he fulfilled it or not that he must be judged as an Avatar or no Avatar. It was not his business to play the comedy of the chivalrous Kshatriya with the formidable brute beast that was Bali. It was his business to kill him and get the Animal under his control. It was his business to be not necessarily a perfect, but a largely representative sattwic Man, a faithful husband and a lover, a loving and obedient son, a tender and perfect brother, father, friend—he is a friend of all kinds of people, friend of the outcast Guhaka, friend of the Animal leaders, Sugriva, Hanuman, friend of the vulture Jatayu, friend of even Rakshasa Vibhishana. All that he was in a brilliant, striking but above all spontaneous and inevitable way, not with forcing of this note or that like Harischandra or Shivi[1], but with a certain harmonious completeness. But most of all it was his business to typify and establish the things on which the social idea and its stability depend, truth and honour, the sense of Dharma, public spirit and the sense of order .... Finally it was Rama's business to make the world safe for the ideal of the sattwic human being by destroying the sovereignty of Ravana, the Rakshasa menace. All this he did with such a divine afflatus in his personality and action that his figure has been stamped for more than two millenniums on the mind of Indian culture, and what he stood for has dominated the reason and idealising mind of man in all countries, and in spite of the constant revolt of the human vital, is likely to continue to do so until a greater ideal arises. And you say in spite of all these that he was no Avatar? If you like

---

[1] Indian kings of remote history.

—but at any rate he stands among the few great Vibhutis. You may dethrone him now —for man is no longer satisfied with the sattwic ideal and is seeking for something more —but his work and meaning remain stamped on the past of the earth's evolving races. When I spoke of the gap that would be left by his absence, I did not mean a gap among the prophets and intellectuals, but a gap in the scheme of Avatarhood—there was somebody who was the Avatar of the sattwic Human as Krishna was the Avatar of the overmental Superman—I can see no one but Rama who can fill the place. Spiritual teachers and prophets (as also intellectuals, scientists, artists, poets, etc.)—these are at the greatest Vibhutis but they are not Avatars. For at that rate all religious founders would be Avatars —Joseph Smith (I think that is his name) of the Mormons, St. Francis of Assisi, Calvin, Loyola and a host of others as well as Christ, Chaitanya or Ramakrishna.

We have quoted this letter almost in its entirety for several reasons: one is that it beautifully lays clear the role of Rama as an Avatar and thus points out, with very sure and precise vision, how Rama fits into the design which has been captured in the Map of the 12 Manifestations. All the characteristics of Rama's incarnation, as Sri Aurobindo here details, are formed by the association of the signs of the 7th Manifestation, upheld by Aquarius, the Man, in its opposition. Any student of astrology must readily see the exact correspondence. Also to be found in this letter is the clear understanding of the highly evolved being, the saint, the prophet, the holy man and the religious leader. All these are a part of the spiritual evolution, as indeed the whole of creation is, but they are not the direct messengers of the Manifestation and only serve to prepare the way, in a sense, for the coming of the Avatar. One example is the appearance of Christ, which will be discussed later and which Sri Aurobindo here leaves out of the list of the avatars, as we have also found to be the case.

Another important point of this letter is the clear vision that Sri Aurobindo reveals of what he calls the 'scheme of avatarhood', which scheme is captured in the Map of the 12 Manifestations. The only element *en plus* that this Map gives us is the time factor: in it we are able to place these figures in the Ages to which they belong within the proper time cycles. A seer who records the life of Rama and captures the meaning of his incarnation in the light of its importance regarding the spiritual evolution does not necessarily enjoy the capacity of accurate time vision. In fact, it is more often noted that a high degree of intuition or of mediumistic capacities is usually lacking in this ability to pinpoint the event seen within the realm of Time. These sages or seers who in the past recorded and understood the meaning of the appearance of such figures as Rama or Krishna were quite aware of the impact and change these Avatars brought in the spiritual evolution; in their visions they saw all the details of these incarnations, and the legends and tales that have been handed down throughout the Ages were born of such visions. However, the time element was often not accurately given, nor did these seers pretend to resolve this problem. Whatever the case, it is a fact that we have no clear indications of when most of these incarnations appeared, other than the record of the zodiac, based on the movements of the spheres and in particular of the Earth itself. It is to this record, then, that we can turn with total assurance that our vision will not only be true as to the meaning of the spiritual descent, but also to the time factor involved. In fact, it is only now, during this 9th Manifestation, that man is to be allowed to go 'beyond Time,' so to speak, where he will have a true vision of the unfoldment of manifestated divinity within time and space.

It must be remembered that Rama's period corresponds to the seventh sign, Libra, the sign of union and marriage, where Saturn is known to be in exaltation, hence the high tone of morality that his incarnation captured. The appearance of Rama hinges in great part around his union with Sita; this marriage is one of the Principal factors in the advent, in a quasi-moralistic way, in accordance with the work of the Age.

To fully understand the Map of the 12 Manifestations as a record of the appearance of the Avatars, the student must concentrate not only on the three signs of each Manifestation as capturing the meaning of the event, but, as mentioned, these three signs must be seen in connection with the one that upholds them in the opposite quarter, the quincunx, 'Yod', or 'Finger of God' aspect of astrology.

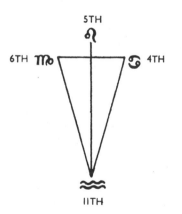

7TH MANIFESTATION

Thus in the case of the 7th Manifestation, the adjacent diagram would give us the full key to the appearance of Rama. His coming would have occurred during the Age of Leo, approximately 12,000 years ago, whose opposite sign is Aquarius, the Man, showing the accuracy of Sri Aurobindo's reference to Rama as 'the Man', and the avatar of the sattwic Human. (We shall see how Sri Krishna fulfils the description of the overmental Superman, as Sri Aurobindo puts it, later in our studies.) Further there is great emphasis in his description of Rama as the *Friend of all*, and he even enumerates these relationships. Aquarius, as all students of astrology know, is precisely the sign of the Friend, as well as high ideals. But perhaps the most important revelation in Sri Aurobindo's account of Rama is the stress on the victory over the Animal, the anarchic forces, and the vital ego. It was, in fact, the time when the Earth's ascendant and hence the movement to be worked out in evolution was passing through the quarter of the Circle which corresponds to the Vital, whereas we are now passing through the quarter which is the spiritual or divine element in creation. Certainly the character of Bali and the Rakshasas of Rama's adventure were of the order which would correspond to that Vital quarter and he had to fight and meet them in their realm and on their terms, these forces taking human or brute-beastial forms.

It is interesting to note that Rama's birthday is celebrated in India on the ninth day of the lunation in an asterism which occurs when the Sun is in Aries, the sign of the Ram. Whether his name has any relation to this *ram* is not known, but we have found that in this realm the element of 'coincidence' is unknown. Each item is guarded and tended to by a greater consciousness than our human one. Aries is known to be the exaltation of the Sun, and the Age of Leo would have been ruled by the Sun. The horoscope of Rama as given in Indian astrology textbooks has been a means of transmitting to man the *exaltation* of each planet, and it does not seem in any way to be the actual horoscope of Rama. Each planet is placed in the sign of its exaltation, Sun in Aries, Moon in Taurus, Jupiter in Cancer, etc. It is hardly likely that Rama was born with such a configuration but rather that astrological wisemen of later times used his birth as a record of the perfect embodiment of harmony and order, and as a means of preserving the knowledge of the Exaltations, which is very necessary for the complete understanding of the spiritual evolution as seen in the zodiac.

It is necessary to point out now that the Incarnations appear on Earth during the times the Earth's ascendant is passing through one of the four Fixed signs, Taurus, Leo, Scorpio or Aquarius. For this reason the Sphinx as a symbol is perhaps one of the most important in esoteric tradition. These signs are captured in the ancient imagery of the Sphinx, and are an indication to mankind of the four important Ages in its progressive development. The Indians have preserved this same knowledge in another way; they call the times of the appearances of the avatars the periods of Vishnu, the *Preserver*. This is analogous to the Sphinx because Vishnu's periods correspond to the Fixed signs of the zodiac, the second part of the Trinity of Creation, Preservation and Dissolution or Destruction, which are the Cardinal, Fixed and Mutable signs.

Krishna, the 8th Avatar and the 8th Manifestation

From Rama's incarnation we must now pass to the Avatar of the 8th Manifestation, Krishna, and once again all the elements are present to accurately place Krishna within the Map of the 12 Manifestations. The same diagram is here reproduced which holds the key of the Advent.

One sees that the Age in prominence is the Age of Taurus, thus many of the chief elements to be introduced in the evolution will be somehow captured in this sign. Krishna himself is very much characterised by Taurus, especially in his early years, the pastoral period of Brindavan when he was cowherd and played his flute for the Gopis. If there is a symbol that can most honestly and accurately be associated with Krishna it is the Bull, or the Cow. One perceives this when visiting places like Mamallapuram, for example, and the bas-reliefs of Krishna which are found there; he is depicted surrounded by many heads of Bulls.

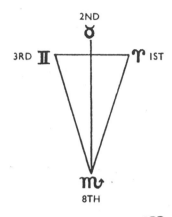

The sign upholding the 8th Manifestation is Scorpio, and the upholding sign is always the sign that contains the 'seed' of the upper Manifestation.
In particular the planet ruling the upholding sign is important, as well as the planet ruling the sign of the entire Manifestation. In the case of the 7th Manifestation of Rama, it was the very strong influence of Saturn, the upholding planet, which gave such a stress on order, justice, truth and morality to the Age, not only because it was the upholding planet, but also by the fact that the seventh sign, Libra, which was the sign of the entire Manifestation, is Saturn's exaltation. Venus is the ruler of Libra, and these two together then give us the right understanding of the times. Venus's rulership is what brought the strong element of harmony, love and balance to the 7th Manifestation.

In the case of the 8th Manifestation, the sign of the entire period is Scorpio, the eighth, and the ruler is Mars. Also the upholding sign is Scorpio, thus Mars is the predominant planet of the Manifestation. Because of the historical closeness of this period we can ascertain the validity of our studies to a much greater degree than we can with Rama's times. The most important document of Krishna's teachings, the *Bhagavad Gita,* which was revealed supposedly during the Battle of Kurukshetra, is our firmest support. The teachings are centred around the factor of War, which belongs to the domain of Mars. Arjuna's dilemma is precisely whether it is right to kill and whether this is a legitimate part of spiritual destiny. It is on the very battlefield that Krishna speaks to him. Certainly we cannot hope for a more accurate correspondence. The times bring forth the glory of the Kshatriya, the Warrior, and the seed sign of the Manifestation falls in the quarter of the Warrior class, the third quarter of the zodiac. A further planet involved in this 8th Manifestation is Venus, the ruler of Taurus, and together with Mars we are given the ingredients that contribute to the strong element of human passions turned into love for the Divine. Krishna's incarnation essentially brought forth the possibility of all man's nature being divinised, his most human drives being a means of realising God. In this 8th Manifestation Mars and Venus combine to call forth the deepest human emotions and prepare the way for the next Manifestation which is to essentially hinge around the advent of a power of Divine Love upon Earth, and one that would precisely signify the divinisation of humankind's even most obscure parts, or the full marriage of heaven and earth.

Krishna's birth is placed around 3,100 B.C., which is certainly more accurate than the time given for the birth of Rama. The various methods of recording time from that period to ours have varied but little and it is possible to approximately calculate certain events on the basis of our actual calendar systems. In this case Krishna's birth would have in fact fallen within the age of Taurus, but it may be that it was somewhat closer to the beginning of the Age than is generally believed. Nonetheless, the difference is minimal.

In *Symbols and the Question of Unity* we have quoted from the Vishnu Purana concerning the birth of Krishna. It is necessary to repeat the passage here so that the student may ascertain for himself how the number 8 was prominent in the records of his advent:

Parasara relates to Maitreya the details of the birth of Krishna as an Incarnation of Vishnu. He tells how Kansa was the charioteer of Vasudeva and Devaki on the night of their wedding, when a voice spoke to him saying that the 8th Child of Devaki would slay him. He promptly wished to kill Devaki but Vasudeva entreated him to let her live and then promised to give up all the children born of her to Kansa.

Parasara goes on to relate how Earth went to Mount Meru and complained of her terrible plight to Brahma and the Gods, how the Asuras were overriding the Earth. Together then they all proceeded, the Gods and Earth, to the Milky Sea to beseech the aid of Vishnu, who incarnates whenever there is need to re-establish order. After listening to their tale of woe, Vishnu plucked two of his hairs out, one white and the other black, and said to the Gods: 'These my hairs shall descend upon Earth and shall relieve her of the burden of her distress' ... and he went on to say how his black hair would be the 8th conception of Devaki and would slay Kansa. He mentioned nothing about the white hair. Commentators believe the white one to be Balarama, Krishna's brother, but I do not find clear enough indication to this effect.

When the time comes for Devaki to conceive, Vishnu gives instructions to Yoganidra, his consort who is known as Durga in the Markandeya Purana, bride of Shiva. He tells her of the details of the birth of Balarama, Devaki's seventh child, and of the method by which he is to be saved from Kansa. Then he continues: 'I will myself become incarnate in the 8th conception of Devaki; and you shall immediately take a similar character as the embryo offspring of Yashoda. In the night of the 8th lunation of the dark half of the month of Nabhas, in the season of the rains, I shall be born. You shall receive birth in the 9th.

Impelled and aided by my power, Vasudeva shall bear me to the bed of Yashoda, and you to that of Devaki. Kansa shall take you, and hold you up to dash you against a stone; but you shall escape from his grasp into the sky, where the hundred-eyed Indra shall meet and do homage to you, through reverence for me, and shall bow before you, and acknowledge you as his sister. Having slain Sumbha, Nisumbha, and numerous other demons, you shall sanctify the Earth in many places....

In this passage it is also evident that Balarama, who came to be known as Krishna's brother, may well be Rama, the 7th Manifestation Avatar. As we have seen in our studies over the years, there has often been a confusion of stories, perhaps because of the devotion to Rama prevailing during the times, and the priests may have been reluctant to extoll the glories of Krishna and exclude those of his predecessor. In this way, perhaps, they incorporated the tale of Rama into that of Krishna. It is also possible that this was a means for the initiated to pass on the knowledge of the Incarnations, to preserve the record for future Ages. As can be seen, the Vishnu Purana not only speaks of Krishna's Incarnation but makes mention of the 7th Manifestation Avatar and the 9th as well. These Incarnations have again been dealt with in the scale of creation in the Puranas, which covers nine stages. The Seventh is Man, which would correspond to the 7th Manifestation and the Incarnation of Rama; the Eighth is the link between the preceding creation and the following, and this is the overmental Superman that Sri Aurobindo speaks of regarding Krishna. In the Puranas this Eighth stage is really not clear; that is, one is not quite certain what sort of creation is indicated therein, obviously because it was a preparatory phase and was concerned more with an in-going movement, a spiritual evolution which was not to be so apparent on the exterior plane. This is also indicated in the zodiac by that Manifestation corresponding to a feminine sign, or a passive element, whereas the 7th, as well as the 9th are of the masculine force, the exteriorising faculty, the light part of the energy as opposed to the dark. Krishna means 'black' in fact, and here again we have the clue to his advent. The other 'hair' of Vishnu which is to incarnate is said to be 'white', and this would correspond to the period of dynamic force in contrast to the in-drawn force of Krishna's time.

The Ninth creation of the Puranic scale is that of the divine man, what Sri Aurobindo has called the Superman, the gnostic being. The Puranic scale ends there, and as far as our studies have revealed, so does the appearance of the Avatars, for from that time on there will apparently be no need to re-establish the order, the task of the avatar. It is a time when each man will reveal the divinity that is the guiding light of any Age. The appearance of the Avatars will not be needed to nourish the creation and guide it to the goal. They are necessary until the Birth takes place, therefore only nine are spoken of as essential and are seen clearly as parts of the cosmic design, indispensable figures without which the Birth would be impossible. The Ninth Spiral and the 9th Manifestation present the Earth with the appearance of not only the Father but the Mother and Child as well. The full birth is lived through, and it is probably the only time that the Divine Mother becomes actually singularly embodied, because it is then that she descends and literally brings forth her Child.

6

The Ninth Manifestation

WE ARE BROUGHT now to the study of our times, the 9th Manifestation. It is possible to be more precise in this portion of the work, because unlike the previous periods, we are in possession of the exact dates and details of the Age's messenger; as well, we can refer to the events of recorded history and the present stage of the evolution in the light of the Map of the 12 Manifestations, verifying in this way the accuracy of our document. But the full story can only be understood as we progress in our study, in particular when we begin speaking of the Gnostic Circle in detail. Here we will mention, therefore, only what is to be seen in the Map of the 12 Manifestations, and how the movement of our times is recorded therein, as well as the details in part of the Avatar of the time.

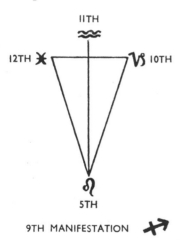

11TH

12TH ♓ ♑ 10TH

♌
5TH

9TH MANIFESTATION ♐

Here is the diagram corresponding to the 9th Manifestation; we see that Aquarius is the sign of our present period, and that being the 9th Manifestation, Sagittarius, the ninth sign, is that of the whole Manifestation. The upholding sign is Leo, which is ruled by the Sun. Thus two bodies are prominent in the Manifestation, Jupiter, ruler of Sagittarius, and Sun, ruler of Leo. These two then are the key to our times, and to the advent of Supermind as Sri Aurobindo has extensively described in his works. The Sun is the orb of Truth, our physical representation of the Divine, and Jupiter is the planet of consciousness, or the expansion of consciousness beyond the known confinements and limitations. Thus they can be combined as 'Truth-Consciousness'. The two are the orbs that indicate the advent of Supermind.

There are many elements which we must deal with here because unlike the other Manifestations where we have but scanty information and must often rely on our inner vision alone to piece together the happenings, it is now possible to speak with greater accuracy. Therefore we can go into the very minute details of our Manifestation, beginning with the Age of Pisces, moving backward through the zodiac until we reach our present period, the Age of Aquarius.

The 9th Manifestation began in the century preceding the year 200 B.C. Approximately at that time humanity was moving over the first Cardinal Point, Aries. This was a momentous time not only because it marked the entry into a new Manifestation and the beginning of a whole new cycle, but it was also the time when a much greater expansion was to occur, because the 9th Manifestation is the first portion of the last Round, the initiation into the final passage through the signs of this Great Circle. Therefore the work to be accomplished is far more intense and important during this Manifestation, and the passage over the 0° Aries point, the first Cardinal point, was vital for the entire Manifestation. We need only go over the known history of that period to understand this, and then to realise what a change was being prepared for mankind. It was, in fact, the actual beginning of the period which would mark the split between Spirit and Matter, or philosophy and science, only so that these would be able to explore themselves fully and then meet once again on the basis of an integral understanding. We see therefore that the Greeks, and their highly scholastic and 'scientific' approach to higher knowledge, present us with the foundations of a split that would become more accentuated during the Renaissance.

In essence though the present 9th Manifestation is momentous for another reason. It was shown previously that we are now on the Ninth Spiral of the Greater Circle as well as in the actual 9th Manifestation of the smaller Circle. Therefore, the birth we spoke of as taking place in this Manifestation also corresponds to the birth period of the entire 311,040 year cycle. These two culminations are simultaneous now, which points out to us the tremendous importance of our times. What is indicated is seen on a smaller scale as well as a larger one, and always in astrology, even when dealing with individual horoscopes, when one sees several aspects or influences coinciding—each indicating the same thing—one knows that there is a major event in preparation and one that will radically change the life of an individual. In larger proportions then, the entire evolution is feeling the impact of these two coincidental births.

In terms of the Greater Circle we are in the Mental sheath, the third Body or quarter, for Sagittarius is the last sign of that group. It is clearly shown therefore that the work is now proceeding in the realm of Mind. This may appear to be in contradiction to what was said about the Spiritual sub-influence we are now under, but, in fact, as we penetrate into the mysteries of the Circle, we see that at any given moment in evolution *all* the possibilities are present. If we care to plunge even deeper into the movement of Time, moving back even farther and discovering our place within a period of perhaps three to four million years, by means of the Gnostic Circle, we would then see that all four Bodies are always there and in one way or another are interrelating constantly, that if there is indication that work is being done on one, we can penetrate deep enough into the movement and find that also present are the other three, though their degree of prominence varies. The work is being carried out on all levels of the Earth's being at any time in the spiral of evolution. What is steady however are the culminations we have spoken of—the births, so to speak—as well as the predominant influence, which in this case would be Mind and the sign Sagittarius, showing us that we are pushing through to the realm of Higher Mind and beyond, that this great birth is nothing more than a preparation for the true spiritual transformation of the species. And through the sign Sagittarius and the birth cycles we have indicated, it is evident that the number 9 is a predominating factor and through it much can be understood in the harmonies of the spheres.

If we simply study the signs by elements, the four elements correspond to the four Bodies—the Fire element is the Spiritual body, Air is the Mental, Water is the Vital-Emotional, and Earth is the Physical. The 9th Manifestation belongs to the Fire element through the sign Sagittarius, and would correspond in this way to the Spiritual body; it is this aspect of creation that, from the existing mental condition of man, must now come forth and experience an awakening.

We can see that any 'birth' of evolution would always correspond to Sagittarius, the sign of the Spirit, the ninth sign of the zodiac. In this sense we see that it is through the mechanics of the spiritual force in evolution that man will see himself evolve into a higher quality of being. In this Manifestation we are still within the realm of the third quarter, the 'Mental Body', but it corresponds to the last of the three signs of the mental trinity, the *guna* of dissolution, which opens the way for the new birth. The death that is connected with the Mutable signs is a death which prepares the way for the new manifestation. In the scheme of the zodiac the factor of death is stressed above all in the third quarter, because there we encounter the eighth sign, Scorpio, which is the death to the lower half of the wheel. Thus the ninth sign is not only a period of the *guna* of Dissolution, but it follows the sign Scorpio, hence the quality of death is experienced in a more intense manner during this Manifestation. Here we can fully understand that the factor of birth is as well an aspect of death, or can be considered in the same light. It is evident that to be born on a certain plane means to die on another. The 9th Manifestation and the Ninth Spiral of the Greater Circle are equivalent to the ninth month of gestation; as for the child the birth process signifies death to another experience, so too must the whole of our civilisation experience this same death and birth and birth and death.

The number 9 plays the same role: it absorbs all the other numbers, draws the previous ones into itself and gives birth to the new cycle: the 10, in actual fact, is nothing more than 1 again.

The point that is necessary to clearly bring forth is the aspect of Dissolution in our times. It is an inevitable process and we can in no way avoid it: in order to be born into a higher world and a deeper, wider, vaster manifestation of the Divine Consciousness, it is imperative that we pass through the experience of Death. Sri Aurobindo has beautifully expressed this in his epic poem *Savitri*. The theme of the epic is the struggle with death and the final victory of the forces of regeneration over those of disintegration. It is a precise representation of what is to be accomplished during this, the 9th Manifestation. In the Eighth Book there is the 'death' of Satyavan; in the Ninth Book Savitri, the redeeming divine power, goes into the realm of Death pursuing the Dark Lord, seeking to bring her lover back to life. She is warned not to follow into his kingdom, where no mortal is allowed to enter and from where one is not permitted to emerge. Conscious of her immortality, the Goddess continues her pursuit fearlessly, and in the Tenth Book, corresponding to the tenth sign, Capricorn, she is victorious: the Dark God is absorbed into the Light.

We are now in these very realms of Death; we are experiencing this passage fully, and we need only look about us to see the forces of disintegration that appear to be rampant and on the way to absorbing the entire civilisation into the realm of darkness. But the zodiac is an infallible record of the process of evolution, and in this most ancient and sacred scripture we are given the knowledge that the forces of light will be victorious, are in essence *already* victorious, because in fact the zodiac is a map of *progression within the Eternal*, where we see that what is to be *is* already, and this design only affords us the possibility of following the movement of the eternal in its aspect of motion. We are therein able to see the Timeless as well as that which is bound by time, the Infinite as well as that which is finite.

The sign of Sagittarius can never be understood unless one passes through the experience of Death; the Knowledge that is acquired in the ninth stage of one's development, as expressed in the sign of Sagittarius, is precisely a Knowledge which 'comes from the other side'—what is to us *the other side*, to move into the realm of the Immortals and from there receive the higher light. The eighth sign is the Abyss, the plunge into the darkness, the death. From this state there is the opposite movement that is experienced, the soaring into the light of the spirit, the ninth stage. In the tenth both these states are experienced simultaneously. The tenth is the abyss and the heights, the Dark Lord and the Bright God which are seen and experienced as One. The key to understanding the zodiac rests in this factor of a reversal of consciousness which shows one that in fact there is no full knowledge without the knowledge of the depths as well as the heights, there is no total manifestation of the divine in creation unless the dark part as well is grasped in its true sense and made a part of the experience of God. It is this factor that has most discouraged the religious seeker for aeons. How to reconcile these aspects of God? His goodness and His downright perversity? What is the truth in the suffering of the world? How can the new world come forth from the state of chaos, confusion, disintegration of our times? Above all, how can evil at all exist, if all is indeed the Divine? For it is a fact that evil as well as good is a part of the Absolute, and no matter how we try to philosophise the matter and construct a theory which presumes to show that evil can be excluded from the scheme of things by relegating it to the abode of the devil and his inferno, within us we are ever faced with the reality of the matter: all things that exist, no matter how revolting and degenerate, are a part of the creation, and the creation in its entirety is the body of the Lord. If Hell does indeed exist, no matter to what this corresponds, there is no possibility of its existence apart from God.

The Indian tradition has come closest to answering the question. In the experience of the Divine Mother one is made to see both Her dark and Her bright side, and ultimately one is made to realise the Oneness of all things. The accomplishment of Western religion, as well as some branches of Indian thought and yoga schools, has been to label the feminine aspect of the Divine as 'evil', in one way or another. And this corresponds to the current state of man's being, whereby Mind has obliged him to perceive in terms of differentiation, of separation; the development of a moralistic outlook—the fruit of the religion of the Occident—has resulted in a split between the so-called Good and Evil, God and the Devil, Adam and Eve, and so forth. Ultimately those who love the creation, the manifest Divine or Matter, have had to take refuge in Science, the apparent enemy number one of Spirituality, which has been necessary to prepare for the experience of our times, the more complete experience of God.

There is no sentimentality in the Divine, rather it is our own sentimentality that makes this distinction between good and bad, right and wrong; there is only the timeliness of action. All these questions resolve themselves when we have understood the factor of Time. In India, the power of the Time-Spirit, Kala, is Kali—the Mother who dissolves and creates, who devours and brings forth. The understanding of her actions comes only when one sees that the rightness of anything depends almost exclusively on its just relationship to the force of Time. During the Dark Ages we can see, therefore, why Saturn, the Time-Spirit, was thought to be a malefic planet. With ignorance of the true correspondence of the planet to the realm of Time, naturally its effects would be seen as negative. Saturn has been equated to the devil, as has the sign Capricorn which it rules. And by this we can see why the sign is the least understood of the zodiac. Capricorn speaks of the *simultaneous experience of all aspects of the divine, as well as the simultaneous experience of the 'three times', past-present-future.* If we break through these three times we can come to know the rightness of all things and the two, or the many, faces of God.

Humanity is at the point of breaking through the actual limited vision it bears of Time; some day it will be a common experience to live in the state of simultaneous time. At first this will take place in flashes only, it will remain for a while in the realm of *experience*, and slowly as we progress into the Age we will develop the capacity to crystallise the experience and make of it a *realisation*. The brief glimpses will grow into longer spans and finally the vision will be permanent.

In the zodiac, the possibility of a greater time-vision corresponds to Uranus, the co-ruler of Aquarius. Because Saturn is no longer the sole ruler of Aquarius or of Capricorn, the higher and most profound significances of these signs can now be experienced. The co-rulers signify the expansion into wider realms and greater vistas, in this time of the ninth sign, the sign of Expansion. Breaking through the barriers of Time does not mean dissolution of Time but rather the experience of the unity of Time; it is not a question of living in a timeless state which would then indicate that one is beyond manifestation, but it is rather that within Manifestation, within the rule of Time, one is to have the experience of unity, one is to make of the multiplicity an integral part of the One. It is only our fragmentary vision that has created all the problems, our perverse capacity to break things down, to divide and separate—which is the process of Mind. In order therefore to move into the sphere of total vision and all-embracing time, man must move out of the sphere of Mind. This is the plane of Supermind that Sri Aurobindo has revealed. The 9th Manifestation is the period of transition into the realm of Supermind. Therefore we say that Sagittarius is the sign of Supermind. To be more accurate we must say that in relation to our times this sign indicates the state where the evolution moves out of the realm of Mind and into the sphere of Supermind. And this then precedes passage into the final three signs which are Sat-Chit-Ananda, Capricorn, Aquarius, Pisces, precisely the signs that make up the 9th Manifestation. We can easily say, therefore, that of all the periods of evolution, this is one of the most momentous, where man is offered the greatest possibilities and the fullest experience. For our civilisation, what we are experiencing at present is preparing the way for the maximum we can aspire to in this Great Circle of 77,760 years, approximately 17,000 of which remain, and of the Greater Circle of 311,040 years.

Indian tradition has given us numerous revelations of this process of expansion. In all the stories of the Avatars the knowledge is passed on, sometimes in most clear terms. For example, it is said that Sri Krishna was slain by an arrow which pierced the sole of his foot. The arrow is the symbol of Sagittarius, and the feet are ruled by Pisces. It is clear that the image used for Sri Krishna's passing was such as to indicate that the end of the 8th Avatar would introduce the next phase which would pertain to Sagittarius, the ninth sign, as well as the entry into the age of Pisces. In the full study of the Gnostic Circle more facts will be shown regarding this sign and the events connected with it in the life and passing of Sri Aurobindo. For now we can point out that Sri Aurobindo's Siddhi Day, 24 November, 1926, when the Sun was in Sagittarius, was a numerological 8 day. What occurred around that time for Sri Aurobindo was precisely related to the eighth sign and Manifestation, for it was then that the Krishna Consciousness descended into him. It can be said that this was the real beginning of his work; the Ashram in fact was officially begun at that time.

After Sri Krishna's death, for the remainder of the 8th Manifestation, and well into the 9th, there is, of course, the degeneration of the dharma, as the scriptures state; but the decline is only a preparation for a greater and more powerful, solid and lasting rise.

Krishna lived for 36 years after the battle of Kurukshetra. In the history of his life we find constantly repeated the two numbers 18 and 36. The sages who recorded the events in his life must have been well aware that these multiples of nine held the key to the mysteries of the manifest Divine and the future of the races of the Earth. And finally Krishna succumbs by the arrow which pierces his foot, opening the way for the work of the next Evolutionary Avatar, as we have called them, precisely the one who is to embody the meaning of the sign Sagittarius and would be born in the age of Pisces and live during the shift to Aquarius, as the story of the passing of Sri Krishna reveals.

After Sri Krishna there seems to be some confusion in spiritual circles regarding the next Avatar and the subsequent stage of development for the Earth. One factor which contributes most to this reigning confusion is that it seems to have been forgotten that the Evolutionary Avatar, when appearing for that particular work, can only come during the Ages which pertain to Vishnu, the force of Preservation, the four faces of the Sphinx, or the four Fixed signs of the zodiac. But it seems that man is in a hurry to fill in the blanks before the time periods are completed, and before even entering the 9th Manifestation he has already proclaimed the next Avatar, before actually understanding in full what it is that the advent is to truly mean. Therefore to include the Buddha in the list of Avatars as the 9th, which in the deeper meaning would signify that he was the Avatar of the 9th Manifestation, is impossible. The Buddha's birth and the span of his life formed a part of the 8th Manifestation, opening the way to the 9th, and his function was precisely to bring about a greater cleavage between the seekers after the 'Void' and those seeking fulfilment in the full manifestation of the Divine. It may appear odd to speak here in these terms of the Buddha and the student may consider that one is attempting to minimise his role, or in some way to place him in a negative light. In actual fact we seek to do the contrary. This great spiritual figure was an element that served to bring about a certain depletion in the spiritual effectiveness of India as a nation, and thus contributed to the full entrance of humanity into the age of darkness, a preparation for the coming light. This was a necessary step, though one which nonetheless requires a subsequent corrective measure, the work of Kalki, as Sri Aurobindo and the Indian scriptures have pointed out. Kalki, the last Avatar of the Hindu tradition, has as his mission to bring the movement back to its rightful destiny, to join the two poles and then erase the separation that exists in the reservoir of spiritual energy on the planet. All paths, all realisations can give us the experience of God, but the plan of evolution is only one, though this is all-embracing and makes use of different means to arrive at the Goal.

All forms of spiritual thought and practice that have served to heighten the rift between the two poles of spirit and matter must, at this time, give way to the new creation. If the student is truly perceptive he can see that even within the provinces of the Spirit there can be a materialism opposed to spirituality—but neither one nor the other is the way leading to the establishment of the Era of Truth. There must be a unity of the two; only in this realisation can the Earth know its rightful destiny in full.

Kalki comes precisely for this purpose: to establish the reign of Truth. In order to do this he wields the sword of Fire, the power of Truth, and thus eradicates the falsehood prevailing, first and foremost in the spiritual realm on Earth. This does not at all mean that religions, for example, do not contain the seed of Truth. What is meant is simply that each movement is correct according to the Time-Spirit. The advocates of the theory of the 'illusion' of creation, or those who would escape into the unmoving heights of Nirvana, propounded the truth of the times in which these teachings were revealed and prevailed. Once out of that period they no longer have the Power, the Shakti, working through them, so what then develops is a religion, the fossilisation of the truth which, because of its dogmatic and unfluid form, is carried over into an epoch where it does not belong. This is the error of all religions. Because of the formidable body or structure of their organisations, they are able to survive through periods of decline, when in actual fact they should give way to the plastic and dynamic action of the truth of the Time-Spirit. They modify themselves during those periods just enough to accommodate their organisations so that they do not collapse entirely, and then usually come to rely upon material power in the place of the power of realisation, the Power of Truth. The extent of degeneration of any religion can always be measured by its reliance on material power; the greater this is, the more acutely will the force of degeneration manifest.

When a religion forms around a seed of truth it is a sure sign that the Shakti has retired from it and is placing her energies elsewhere. The true Evolutionary Avatars have never formed religions, nor have religions sprung from their teachings. Neither

Rama nor Krishna is responsible for a new religion. They capture the hearts of people and become the centre of worship, because this has been the way of mankind, but they do not have a formal structure attached to this worship, which would only serve to fossilise the Truth they have come to establish and go against the movement of evolution. Hinduism absorbed these figures into its body, because this is its wide way. Of all religions one can truly say that this one is the most plastic, the broadest and hence the most likely to survive all the movements of decline, still capable of maintaining its inner Fire precisely because it does not reject the message of the Avatar but embraces it and leaves the spiritual experience the liberty to explore itself and manifest through a wide and varied system of yogic disciplines. The individual is allowed the fullest freedom, and the actual *experience* of God is demanded of him instead of a mere acceptance on faith and adherence to dogma. Even if rituals of some sort are performed they are geared exclusively to accelerating the disciple's approach toward the experience of the Divine. Religions exist and survive on the basis of dogma and faith. Yogic disciplines depend for their life solely on the realisation of God in each who follows these paths.

The Avatar of the 9th Manifestation does not lay the foundations for a new religion, which would defeat the purpose of his advent. It is only the revelation of the next phase of spiritual experience and expression, and the discipline and yogic sadhana that accompanies it, that is his purpose, because each coming must lay before mankind a fuller experience of God. Each Manifestation signifies for humanity a greater possible expression and realisation of the Divine, and it is this that he comes to reveal. The Avatar cannot follow the traditional way, except insofar as he shows how that way prepares for the next step, the next piece in the divine Mosaic. He must explore the past, digest it and assimilate it into his own experience, and then he begins to reveal the actual thrust of the Age. He is the seed of the movement, as we have shown in our diagram of the Manifestations based on the quincunx (inconjunct) aspect.

Sri Aurobindo is this seed. He was born with the Sun in Leo, the upholder of the three signs of the 9th Manifestation. However, he does not come alone in this work, because the work of Kalki is to embrace the several aspects of the Divine and render the whole of creation the image of the Lord. In the scriptures, though we cannot rely on them fully because many irrelevant pieces have been added along the way, it is said that Kalki comes with two other persons. Sri Aurobindo's advent is intimately bound with the Mother's birth, and in the diagram she fills the position of Pisces, being born, in fact, with the Sun in that sign. The third position falls in Capricorn, and the Age of Aquarius, cupped in between the two, is the entire humanity, the collectivity as a whole, standing directly in opposition to Leo, the seed, the *puruṣa*. In fact, the meaning of Leo in the zodiac *is* the Purusha, and the spiritual quarter of the Circle, unlike any of the other quarters, is upheld by the Sun, which is also the Purusha of the entire system. Here, in the Spiritual Quarter, the Sun is a *direct* influence. What it signifies for the structure of the whole solar system—the central and sustaining Light—shows itself to be true also for the spiritual quarter of the evolution of the divine body. It is the Sun, the light of Truth, that feeds the trinity of the body of the Spirit in manifestation.

The Fire Trinity and the Evolution

The movement of the Precession through the signs, the basis of our present studies, is 50 seconds of celestial longitude per year. It requires therefore 2,160 years to pass through each sign, and as we break this rhythm down to a smaller and smaller measure, we arrive at a pattern of 72 years for the Precession to pass through each individual degree (trimshamsha) of the zodiac, and finally 6 years and 6 months are the time spans for ascertaining the prevailing influence and direction of the evolution based on this movement. In the lives of Sri Aurobindo and the Mother we find the same rhythm prevailing: the Mother was born 6 years, 6 months and 6 days apart from Sri Aurobindo, in terms of numbers. This very precise pattern in their births is in part a revelation of how the cosmic harmonies are to be deciphered. (When the Mother left her body in 1973, she expired exactly 6 hours before the hour and 18 (3×6) days before the day of Sri Aurobindo's passing.[1])

Both their births took place during the Piscean Age and they then ushered in the Age of Aquarius. The third element in this rhythm does not figure in the scheme until their ages were 66 and 60. This element representing the *Individual* was fully a part of the new creation, the New Age, and its appearance meant that the movement had taken firm roots in the individual and had become a concrete solid part of the Earth consciousness as a whole. These three terms, as represented by the three periods we have spoken of, capture all the aspects of man's quest for Truth. The first period is the *Transcendent's*, represented by the number 9, the apex of the triangle: this is Sri Aurobindo. The Mother is the *Cosmic* aspect of creation, the Shakti: she is the 6 point. The *Individual* is the third term and its number is 3. This triad is the structure on which all quests and teachings have been based—God, Nature or Cosmos, and Man. When affirming one, the old schools have invariably denied the others, but the way of integral knowledge shows us that each part of the Trinity is inseparable from the other two, each *contains* the others. Thus, in the individual, in man, all the different modes of the One Principle can be experienced and expressed. The Trinity is the basis of every created thing and is a reflection of that which supports the creation, the

[1] Vide: *Symbols and the Question of Unity*, 'Transformation of the Body and the Cosmic Rhythm.'

4

Unmanifest; it is the balance of the three energies, Creation, Preservation and Destruction, or Capricorn, Cardinal, is Creation, Leo-Aquarius, Fixed, is Preservation, and Pisces, Mutable, is Destruction.

The work of this Aquarian Age is to establish the foundations of the reign of Truth, and for this there are three phases of the work, three periods which we must understand. The first two are closely allied in spirit as well as in time; their combined actions settled the work on occult planes, conquered the forces that would interfere with the new creation, and therefore in order to understand fully the work that was accomplished it is necessary to have an occult vision, or some means to *see* which are not available to the ordinary individual. Their work was largely on the subtle planes, and found its culmination in the Second World War, the most critical point in the movement of spiritual evolution. The two World Wars were both turning points: the First closed the old and opened the way to the new; the Second was the full and terrific battle with the Asura, as prophesied in the legend of Durga. She slays the Bull, her *vāhana*[1] is the Lion, and her main weapon is the Trident, which finally accomplishes the work of destruction of the Asuric forces. This legend holds the key to our times and it took shape in world history in the Second World War, the 'Mother's War', as it was termed in the Sri Aurobindo Ashram while it was taking place. Sri Aurobindo and the Mother were then engaged in the full struggle; it was then that the forces of Darkness arose in their greatest might to try to impede the full light that had descended from conquering and establishing itself for good. At that time all the pieces were joined, the design was complete. Sri Aurobindo and the Mother knew of something important that was to have happened at that time. The full manifestation had taken place on Earth, which was a terrible blow for the Asura. It arose at once, first by an attack on Sri Aurobindo the very morning of the Siddhi Day celebration, 24 November, 1938, which left him confined to his bed for a long period. The attack was precisely on the portion of his body, the thigh, *which is ruled by the sign of the entire manifestation, Sagittarius*.[2] It was an attempt to destroy the Light, or enfeeble it to such an extent that it would be rendered ineffectual and be unable to accomplish what had been divinely ordained. But the Power was too strong, Durga's aspect of protection too overwhelming, and that attempt failed. Thus that year the full Power of the Age had become a consolidated fact.

The Asuric forces organised the next attack, this time directed at the world at large where perhaps it was thought that an easier opening would be found to its influence of darkness. Immediately after the above incident the world entered

---

[1] Vehicle, carrier.

[2] In this we can see the correspondence with Sri Krishna, the Avatar of the 8th Manifestation, who succumbed according to legend by 'an arrow in the sole of his foot.'

into its darkest period, occultly speaking: the full war of Durga was waged. In 1939 the Second World War began which was the most powerful attempt of the Asura to gain complete control over the Earth. Sri Aurobindo and the Mother were aware that this was indeed the 'Mother's War'.

The myth of the Battle of Durga is captured in the 'Chandi' from the *Markandeya Purana*. It is recited throughout India every day by thousands of worshippers of the Goddess. Durga, whose aspects are protection and victory over the forces of falsehood, is the incarnated force of the 9th Manifestation[1]. Durga's *vāhana* is Leo (Sri Aurobindo) and the Trident is Pisces (the Mother). The Bull she slays is Taurus (Hitler). All three were born with the Sun in the signs we have indicated, as was predicted in the legend so long ago.

Hitler was the instrument used by the forces of Darkness, a very receptive one, in fact. One need only go over the events of those times, study the prevailing psychology of Germany and the Nazi movement to realise that it was a war of the Asuric forces, as no other war has ever been. We can say that all wars are the work of the dark forces, but in this one they put forth their full strength, expecting to be victorious, taking up the guise of Truth, even to the use of the Swastika, a sacred symbol, and the ideal of the 'pure race'.

All the horrors and atrocities of that war took place essentially to protect the new creation, which marked the third period of the work. There was a concentration of Karma, so to speak, which was worked out then in an accelerated fashion to make the creation ready for the important and momentous events of the near future. Only at this point could the work come down to the level of the Individual: the Work is now made visible to a greater degree—the triune manifestation of Transcendent, Cosmic and Individual. The Father and Mother worked essentially on occult planes to prepare the way and conquer that which would have impeded the new creation. All that remains to be done now is the working out of the Divine Mother's force in the material world, the bringing down of the Light that is well established on the other planes. For this reason, if there is sincerity there appears to be no limit to what now can be accomplished.

The ages of Sri Aurobindo and the Mother became 66 and 60 in 1938, or 66

---

[1] In the 'Chandi' Durga is made up of three forces—Mahakali, Mahalakshmi and Mahasaraswati. The images are arranged in this way: first stands Mahakali with 10 arms, behind her is the couple Shiva and Parvati; then there is Mahalakshmi with 18 arms, the principal figure, and behind her stands Vishnu and Lakshmi; finally there is Mahasaraswati with 8 arms, behind whom stands Brahma with his consort Saraswati. In all therefore there are 9 figures (the 'Nine Durgas' are the basis of the worship). The arms are 36 in number and the fingers would be 180. This is the number of degrees of the triangle. This Trinity is said to be upheld by the fourth, Maheshwari, who in fact, corresponds to the sign Leo. It is said in the *Chandi*: 'worshipping the 18, 8, 10, Kala (Time) and Death are mitigated'.

years plus 6 years. We are well aware that the 'Book of Revelation' speaks of this as the number of the Beast. The evil significance attached to it is however a distortion by the Christian Fathers. 666, or 18 (9) is a sacred number. It was when the ages of Sri Aurobindo and the Mother had completed this number that the full Light was established. In one sense we could say that 666 is the number of the Beast, the Asura, because when they were '666' the Beast (Hitler) arose and through him the Asuric forces tried to gain supremacy over the Earth. 18 years (6+6+6) after 1938, in 1956, the Supramental Manifestation occurred, which was made possible only because of Durga's War and Victory. It is now 1974, again a period of 18 years after these two victories, 1938 and 1956. This is therefore the year of the third Victory and many things hidden until now are revealed because we are in the third phase of the Work, when all things shall now become manifest; if the previous two victories had not taken place we should not be able to write these words.[1]

The Gunas

The diagram taken from the Map of the 12 Manifestations that is being studied now[2] is unique in that it incorporates signs of all the Elements and all the energy flows or Qualities as well. For this reason it is a powerful indication of the spiritual progress of humanity during any given Manifestation. The three Qualities correspond to the *gunas* of Indian tradition: Cardinal is *rajas*, Fixed is *sattva*, and Mutable is *tamas*. This is also the trinity of Creation, Preservation and Destruction. The interpretations of the *gunas* have undergone considerable change over the centuries and it has become difficult for students of cosmic harmonies to allocate them with certainty to the astrological sections. We can be sure of the correspondence of *sattva* to the Fixed signs, those of the force of Preservation, but the other two become confused and the student often mistakes one for the other. This is a reasonable error because the Cardinal and Mutable signs are themselves intimately connected. In essence they have a certain aspect which is very similar. Both are closely related to Death and Birth. Mutable, or the guna of *destruction* is more closely con-

---

[1] 18, the Saros Cycle, or the cycle of the Dragon's head and tail, is the prime figure for the Earth, and based on its composition of *3 levels of 6*, 0 to 6, 6 to 12, 12 to 18, one can perceive the order of appearance of the Avatars, or the order of the accomplishment of the Work for the Earth. 0 to 6 is the first level, or, according to the diagram on page 13, the level from the 0 (Transcendent) point to the 6 (Cosmic) point; then 6 to 12, or 3 by theosophical addition, brings the movement to the 3 point (Individual); and from there the last level is 12 (3) to 18 (9), or from the 3 point once more back to the 9. By means of theosophical addition and the all-important number 18, we are given this essential information. At present therefore the movement is on the last level, from the numbers 12 10 18, the third of the sixes to manifest.

[2] Page 42.

nected with death, and Cardinal, or *creation* is more intimately involved with birth; yet in themselves Birth and Death are inseparable.

In the case of the Mutable signs the activity of *tamas* and the force of Shiva are the key, the plunge into the Void. Tamas can be spoken of in its highest sense, with regard to the zodiac, as an 'action in non-action', this being the true key to the Mutable signs. The quality of inertia that is most often attributed to the guna of Tamas is, in actual fact, a deformation of the true movement of *action-in-non-action*. When this state is reached the essence of Tamas is experienced. The false characteristic of Tamas, inertia, is what makes one feel that the guna should correspond to the Fixed signs of the zodiac, because these present the picture of that which is blocked. But the quality of the Fixed signs is the state wherein the dual aspect of Birth and Death is absent, a steady pace and prevailing peace, involved in the Play yet at the same time removed. The Fixed signs are then the 'seeds' of our Manifestations: they become the Purusha who sustains and upholds the play of Prakriti. These signs correspond to the guna of Sattwa, they are free from involvement in the action of Birth and Death and Death and Birth, which correspond to the Cardinal and Mutable signs of Creation and Destruction that encircle them. From this the student can understand why the Sattwic quality has been glorified in the spiritual world, especially after the appearance of schools which extolled the quality that was removed from the Play and apparently uninvolved in the conquest of life and death on this plane of manifestation. They occupied themselves solely with the work of the Fixed signs, the Sattwic quality, and the work then became fragmented, losing much of its power and force. One can clearly perceive this in India, where the separation caused a depletion of the power, the Shakti, and soon the quality of our times, Tamas, degenerated into the lesser aspects of inertia and ignorance in the race as a whole. In the spiritual life of the Indian race, an exclusive concentration on the Sattwic guna merely served to deplete it of its power and plunge the race into a period of darkness, incapable of dealing with the evident pressing and growing problems of life. Essentially it created a split in the *spiritual force* of the nation, the core of India's destiny, the reservoir from where she is to feed the consciousness of the planet in order to resolve for it the only true and urgent question of the evolution, the question of the conquest of life and death.

The Sattwic quality is not the full manifestation, and cultivation of it alone can only end in a depletion of energies and an ultimate decadence, even more accelerated than we know at present, in the races of Earth. The factor of a balanced and unified growth of man into a gnostic being, fully capable of action on all levels, employing all the centres and giving expression to the largest possible vision of divinity for this present stage in the evolution, has not been the apparent aim of previous spiritual societies. Nonetheless evolution moves toward this realisation, and only this: there must be a balancing of forces. In the Gnostic Circle we see that the Sattwic guna is the 'upholder' only insofar as it is an indispensable support for the play of Shakti: disengaging the two, the unity of the Divine disintegrates. When these dual powers become joined the possibilities open to the race are tremendous—then we can begin to speak of a race of Immortals and of a Reign of Truth.

The Age of Truth implies a balanced state in which each element expresses itself in its truest and fullest way. It is a condition of *unity of being*, the true Pure Existence, *Sat* of the Trinity, and therefore the period of Capricorn is spoken of as the Age of Truth, for Capricorn is this, it is *Sat*. Its guna is Rajas, which is the Birth emerging from Death, the Void; it is also the time of the victory of the Shakti.

The Sattwic guna that upholds the 9th Manifestation is the Fixed sign Leo. As

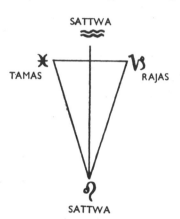

we have explained previously, this sign is precisely the Purusha of the zodiac. We can see, therefore, how powerful the upholding Purusha force is during our times. In the adjacent diagram the triangle is formed of Leo, Pisces and Capricorn. The latter two are Tamas and Rajas, respectively; Tamas—which is birth and death, and Rajas which is death leading to birth. The rajasic element, or Capricorn, is the last to be manifested. This subtle nuance shows us much. The guna of the entire period, 6480 years, is Tamas, and it is a time when the Divine Mother incarnates to bring forth the Child. She incarnates under Pisces, also a mutable sign of the guna of Tamas.

Pisces is the sign of the sacrifice. Her birth is the sacrifice because in her death she brings forth the child, and through death the Child lives. We have had an extraordinary confirmation of this event in the coming of the Comet of 1973-1974, the Mother's Comet, which reached the Sun during the period of the Mother's passing. The subject has been amply treated in the work, *Symbols and the Question of Unity*.

The essential oneness of Pisces and Capricorn, Tamas and Rajas, can also be understood by the very symbol of the sign Capricorn, which is the Goat *with the tail of a Fish*; Pisces is captured in its symbology in this way.

The action of which we are speaking and which has its physical counterpart, is a very delicate one, perhaps difficult for the student to understand, but it is essential to the true comprehension of the Gnostic Circle. The important point is the re-discovery of the real character of Tamas, which is the force of *destruction* of the Trinity Brahma, Vishnu and Shiva. In this guna we have the total and veritable surrender, so intimately a part of the sign Pisces, and so perfectly embodied in the Mother, Sri Aurobindo's co-worker. Her whole life revealed to us the highest characteristic of the sign, the embodiment of Divine Love, the supreme surrender and most noble sacrifice.

In this light we reproduce here words the Mother spoke after she had passed through the portals of Death....

The Mother's Experience on the Night of April 12, 1962[1]

After a month of grave illness which had threatened her life, the Mother spoke for the first time on April 13, 1962. She lay stretched on her bed, in her room, very thin.

'Suddenly in the night I woke with the full awareness of what we could call the Yoga of the World. The Supreme Love was manifesting through big pulsations, and each pulsation was bringing the world further in its manifestation. It was the formidable pulsations of the eternal stupendous Love, only Love: each pulsation of the Love was carrying the universe further in its manifestation.

'And the certitude that what is to be done is done and the Supramental Manifestation is realised.

'Everything was personal, nothing was individual.

'This was going on, and on, and on, and on.

'The certitude that what is to be done is *done*.

'All the results of the falsehood had disappeared: Death was an illusion, Sickness was an illusion, Ignorance was an illusion—something that had no reality, no existence.... Only Love, and Love, and Love, and Love,—immense, formidable, stupendous, carrying everything.

'And how to express in the world? It was like an impossibility, because of the contradiction.... But then it came: "You have accepted that the world should know the Supramental Truth ... and it will be expressed totally, integrally." Yes, yes ...

'And the thing is *done*.'

(Long silence)

---

[1] From *Mother India*, February 21, 1974, pp. 108-109.

'The individual consciousness came back, just the sense of a limitation, limitation of pain, without that no individual.

'And we set out again on the way, sure of Victory.

'The skies are full of the songs of Victory.

'The Truth alone exists; it alone shall be manifested, Forward ! ...

'Glory to Thee, Lord, supreme Triumpher!'

(Silence)

'Now, to the work.

'Patience, endurance, perfect equality, and an absolute faith.'

(Silence)

'What I am saying is nothing, nothing, nothing, nothing but words, if I compare to the experience.

'And our consciousness is the same, absolutely the same as that of the Lord. There was no difference, no difference ....

'We are That, we are That, we are That.'

(Silence)

'Later I shall explain better. The instrument is not yet ready.'

(Afterwards the Mother added:)

'The experience lasted at least four hours.

There are many things which I shall say later.'

*
* *

Tamas is now considered to be unconsciousness, the Ignorance. For example, in sleep states it would be unconscious sleep; but in fact, it can mean the capacity to go into these very deep states with full consciousness, not losing the link with the waking state. It is the ability to 'let go' of one's waking consciousness and plunge into the Void. In the physical sense the true realisation of Tamas would be the entry into Death without the loss of consciousness. That is, a *conscious death* in which one does not need to go through the stages where one forgets oneself and severs the link with the present life. The transitional stage of our times will manifest in the capacity of gnostic beings to pass through death, change the physical sheath if necessary, without breaking the conscious link with their actual life, which would interrupt the line of growth and progress and necessitate a great effort to re-awaken that which was accomplished in past lives—a long and tedious struggle, groping in the dark, blinded by the ignorance. The Personality would not be lost, because that Personality is then one with Essence, the Individuality, no longer a product of the Ignorance. It becomes an indivisible link and the condition of Immortality is achieved. Immortality cannot come about unless man becomes fully conscious of all the planes and is able to retain that consciousness when moving from plane to plane, from state to state. If we have spoken of a New Birth in this treatment, we must also speak of a New Death. Essentially we must now learn to die. We must now come on this Earth to learn how to die the New Death.

It is not the creation, or life in Manifestation, that is the illusion. The only illusion that exists is the illusion of Death and the illusion of the ego which creates in us the fear of death, because it is precisely the ego that dies at death, and nothing more. For this reason man as he is presently constituted fears death, because he lives in his ego. Rid of ego, he is rid as well of the fear of Death. The dissolution of one illusion brings about the dissolution of the other. In the present circumstances man fears dying because it signifies for him the loss of the conscious link with the Self. In consequence he fears Time, because the passage of Time draws him ever nearer to his ego dissolution. If by the dawn of a Truth-Consciousness he acquires the ability to retain full self-consciousness even in the passage through the portals of Death, there will no longer be the fear of Time. For that man Time shall exist no longer.

Fear is precisely the major obstacle in this realisation, so now is a time to become Warriors, for which reason a principal part of the process of Initiation, which takes one through the dissolution of the ego, is fear. One literally lives the same experience of death, burdened by the same limitations,—and only when the fear is conquered and one has plunged into the void, the Unknown, does true liberation come. In sleep and the dream state the same circumstances arise: one must 'die' consciously in order to move through the more subtle planes consciously. It is a process of 'letting go', and at first one may be gripped by a grave fear during these nighttime experiences.

From whatever position we view our condition on Earth we see that the key to life lies in death, and the key to death lies in life. The two are faces of one coin: conquering one we conquer the other, experiencing one in its totality we must necessarily touch upon the other. If we plunge totally into the abyss we shall find ourselves on the heights. This is the meaning of Capricorn; and in truth the zodiac and the secret of evolution, as ancient tradition tells us, is only understood when that sign is understood, or, better said, when the sign is experienced and realised.

It has been necessary to dwell at length in the study of the Manifestations on the advent and work of the Avatars, because these beings hold the key to the direction of the evolution for any given Age. For this reason, if the seeker truly cares to perceive the work as it is being executed, it is evident that there must be some knowledge of the Avatar. Usually the knowledge comes well after these Incarnations have left the Earth scene: it is a discovery of future ages which are in a position to view the totality of the Work and its significance. But if we can perceive the work as it is being executed, it is evident that the vision and perceptive capacity of man have indeed greatly widened and he is moving closer to the full reign of Truth. In that Age the knowledge is immediate; things are seen for what they are, in their actual condition.

Man's perverse rejection of the light of the Age only reveals the hopeless halflight in which the evolution is immersed. In truth we can say that for the Divine to manifest fully on Earth it is necessary that man first evolves to the point of being able to see and recognise the Light. It is a fact that when he is closer to the animal nature than to the divine, he is incapable of perception of the Truth, for the Avatar and the Divine Manifestation move into the Earth sphere silently and gradually, almost imperceptibly taking possession of the Earth consciousness. If this were not so, if he were to come with the roar of a lion and announce the work before it was accomplished, the human races would reject or crucify him. (It is for this reason that he is held back in his advance by a conscious plunge into the Ignorance at birth, when he forgets himself only to discover himself again as the work develops.) It is only after his task has been accomplished and the Child of Truth is developed to a sufficient degree, that one is able to speak of what has been. Evidently there is a great acceleration in process now, because so much has been revealed and continues to be revealed.

On Indian soil the Avatars have come,—India, whose national bird is the Peacock, the bird of victory, whose very land is Durga, the Mother of Victory, whose sign is Capricorn, the Tenth Day of her Victory.

The Indian Yugas

Indian scriptures state that the Kaliyuga began with the death of Sri Krishna. This is true to an extent, but first of all it is necessary to understand that the figures of the Yugas (Ages) are not in actual fact *years*, as is commonly believed, but refer rather to *seconds of degrees* of celestial longitude.

They are as follows:

SATYA YUGA	—	1,728,000
TRETA YUGA	—	1,296,000
DWAPARA YUGA	—	864,000
KALI YUGA	—	432,000

432,000 would be four zodiacal signs converted into seconds of degrees. The seconds of one sign are 108,000, and 4 times this is 432,000. If then the Kaliyuga is to last 432,000 seconds of longitude after Sri Krishna's death, this would take us through four signs or, presuming that he was born in the age of Taurus, up to the Age of Capricorn, the traditional sign of the Golden Age, the Satyayuga of the Hindus. In this case we can agree with the scriptures regarding the period of the Kaliyuga. It is by no means 432,000 years that the age of Darkness is to last, but simply four signs in the precession of the equinoxes. The so-called Kaliyuga is a time when a powerful churning takes place, when all forces come together and strongly vie with one another, seeking to establish their individual supremacy over the whole of the evolution, which is nevertheless destined to progress toward a unity of being and a harmonisation of forces. The work of the times is particularly characterised by the rift between science and spirituality. Science might appear to be the major obstacle in the development of the Spirit and the obvious cause (or effect) of the dawn of a Kaliyuga, when mankind turns toward all the aspects of material life and concentrates its energies on them, to the exclusion of a refinement of its finer substances. But, as we have stated elsewhere, this is only the first and necessary step, leading to a final fusion which will be the foundation of the Age of Truth, the Satyayuga.

There are many interesting facts to be noted regarding the so-called Kaliyuga. In the first place, the word *kali* is derived from the Sanskrit root *kāla*, to *measure*, the stem of our English word *calculate*. It is connected to the Goddess Kali in that she is the power of the Time-Spirit, Kala. So we can say that Kaliyuga means both time-measure and the goddess Kali, both in essence being the same. 'Black', which is another meaning attributed to *kāli*, is also appropriate, for truly the times are a darkening of the Light.

However, let us go more deeply into the study of the Yugas and try to unravel the real meaning, which will then show the student how in fact the Yugas are equal to our Map of the 12 Manifestations, how they are connected with Greek and other ancient traditions, and how they are the same revelation and prophecy as of the Giza Sphinx. In this manner we shall see that the Knowledge is truly One.

We have stated that Kaliyuga is only the measurement of Time. For this reason, therefore, the count does not actually begin with Kaliyuga, 432,000 seconds of degrees of longitude—equivalent to four signs of the zodiac; Kaliyuga is simply our key of measurement. It can be understood how this figure would be the key to the measure of Time since it is also *the radius of the Sun*. The Sun's radius is the key of Truth in that it unites the outer circle of the disk (the Multiple) with the inner central core (the One). We could call this: 'The Measure of Unity.' It is precisely the Sun's symbol, the point within the circle, that contains the Knowledge, as has been explained elsewhere in the text, and this corresponds as well to the orb's physical characteristics, thus showing the harmony between space and time and the evolutionary cycles of man on Earth which are determined by the unfolding and perfectioning of consciousness.

The *Rig-veda* also appears to contain the same key to the measurement of Time based on the Sun of Truth because it is said to have 432,000 syllables.

In the December 1972 issue of *Mother India*,[1] the article entitled 'The Mysterious Yugas' marked the beginning of our attempt to decipher the secret of the Yugas. In that article certain essentials were brought forth which are still valid, but the fuller understanding had not yet come. It had been seen that the figures for the Yugas were seconds of degrees of longitude which were then to be converted into years by means of the precession of the equinoxes, and that at present we are, in fact, in the Satyayuga. But at that time there was too great a timidity to follow the movement through to its conclusion and be audacious enough to entirely re-arrange the count, based on the development of the numbers from 2 to 3 to 4, in this way moving from Dwapara to Treta to Satya. It was stated in the article that all the four Yugas would give us three rounds of the zodiac plus one third, and the one third made the design imperfect. Kaliyuga is only the key. In effect it does not exist, or, as was stated in the article: 'We are always in a Kaliyuga.' The very fact that the word is also taken to mean *black* is another important key, because men have been under the yoke of illusion for thousands of years, since the death of Sri

Krishna, whose name also means *black*, believing that they were in the Dark Age. In truth, mankind is in the 'dark' simply by not realising that there is no such thing as a Kaliyuga, and that in effect the Age of Darkness is only determined by an ignorance of Truth, which can come about in any Age. Man has believed himself to be in an age of darkness, which is only the illusion of Time, and consequently Time is illusion only in so far as vision is fragmentary. When one breaks through to a full vision of Truth, Time then is the key and saviour, not the bondage.

The Kaliyuga exists whenever man has lost the Knowledge; then he becomes lost within the measure of Time, Kali, and cannot see beyond. He has divided time—past, present and future—and lost the vision of Unity whereby he is able to follow the real movement of the Ages. The man of ignorance is always bound by Kali to the wheel of life and death, and can never realise himself within the Age of Truth, while the gnostic being has the key of knowledge, the light of Immortality.

In a rather precise manner we can examine certain interesting facts of the Yugas, and show very accurately how we are in the Satyayuga, the Age of Truth, and have been for over 10,000 years.

Since Kaliyuga is only the measurement, we begin the count of the Yugas with Dwapara, two times Kali, 864,000; after this we pass into Treta, three measures of Time; then Satya, four measures. There are then the numbers 4, 3 and 2, which are the very digits of the *kali* measurement: 432,000. They are, as well, the most important numbers in the structure of symbols: 2 equals the Line, 3 equals the Triangle, and 4 equals the Square. With these it is possible to construct the zodiac because 2, or the Line, is the division of feminine and masculine signs, 3, the Triangle, represents the energy flows of Creation, Preservation and Destruction (Cardinal, Fixed and Mutable), and 4, or the Square, is the division of the elements, Fire, Earth, Air and Water. Therefore these numbers, 4-3-2, are the basic numbers of the zodiac, as well as the measure of Time, and the zodiac is in effect the Great Timepiece; 4+3+2 equal 9, the number that absorbs all the others.

This discovery brings to mind the Sphinx of Thebes, the Maiden with the body of a Lion, and the riddle she gave Oedipus to solve, based on these very numbers, 4, 3, 2. The symbol of the Sphinx has long contained for man the key to the mystery of his evolution on Earth.

Following the precession of the equinoxes in the manner of the Indian Yugas, the count begins at 0° Aries, the perpetual starting-point in the zodiac, with the Dwaparayuga, and moves through 8 signs (864,000 seconds of celestial longitude); by proceeding backwards, as the precession of the Ages moves, this brings us to 0° Leo. It must be pointed out that Leo is ruled by the Sun and that the figure for the Dwaparayuga, 864,000, is in terms of miles precisely *the diameter of the Sun*. 2,160 miles is the diameter of the Moon, and it takes 2,160 years to move through one sign of the zodiac. The student can understand therefore that with regard to the Earth the Sun's diameter is translated into *seconds*, while the Moon's diameter is *years*, which is the proportional difference in the experience of time between one body and the other, due to the difference in density of the two bodies: the finer the substance, the greater is the acceleration of Time.[1]

Dwaparayuga brings us through 864,000 seconds or 8 zodiacal signs, up to 0° Leo. The next Yuga is Treta, 1,296,000 seconds, or 12 signs which, from where we find ourselves at the end of the Dwaparayuga, 0° Leo, would simply take us through one complete round of the zodiac, back once again to 0° Leo. Here then begins the last of the Yugas, Satyayuga, 1,728,000 seconds of longitude, or passage through 16 signs of the zodiac; from 0° Leo this would be one complete round plus 4 more signs, ending up at the starting-point, 0° Aries,—a perfect design of the unfoldment of Time. In this manner *36 signs* are traversed, the very same as in the Map of the 12 Manifestations, or passage through three complete Rounds of the zodiac. To render the process clear, here is a list of the Ages and their equivalents in signs and time:

Dwaparayuga	864,000″	=	8 signs	=	17,280 years
Tretayuga	1,296,000″	=	12 signs	=	25,920 years
Satyayuga	1,728,000″	=	16 signs	=	34,560 years
			36		77,760

In this revelation the most important discovery is that it clarifies the riddle of the Giza Sphinx. As can be seen, the count of the Yugas hinges on the 0° Leo point, and consequently on 0° Aquarius as well, since the equinoctial axis cuts through the zodiac from one sign to its opposite. This is precisely the Giza Sphinx: a Man (Aquarius) with the body of a Lion (Leo). And this marvellous monument has silently been revealing to mankind throughout the millennia the precious know-

[1] One Age (one sign) of the Sun, based on its diameter, is equivalent to 8 Ages (8 signs) of the Moon, based on its diameter, together equalling 9. Drawing another diameter on the faces of these bodies so as to form a cross produces the most important symbol employed in deciphering time by means of the circle. In this way the Sun yields 16 Ages (the Satyayuga), 34,560 years, and the Moon 2 Ages, 4,320 years; in all 18 Ages. 18 years is the *Saros Cycle*: the amount of time it takes for the Sun, Moon and Earth to return to approximately the same position with respect to one another. Rahu and Ketu are significantly involved with the number 18 since it takes 18 years for these Lunar Nodes to make one complete revolution of the zodiac. The Nodes represent the soul of the Earth. For this reason the number 18 has played such an important role in Indian mythology, particularly in the life of Sri Krishna; *vide* the *Mahabharata* and in particular the *Bhagavad Gita*.

ledge of the Satyayuga, the Age of Truth which would begin when the precession of the equinoxes had passed for the last time over the 0° Leo point in our Great Circle of 77,760 years. This occurred 8,640 years before the beginning of our 9th Manifestation, the time *in years* of the seconds of the Kaliyuga, numbers that once again recall the diameter of the Sun, ruler of Leo. Thus, from that point to our times, the era of Kalki, there is one measure of time, or a 'kaliyuga'. Our 9th Manifestation is the epoch of the unveiling of truth.

In this way an accurate connection has been made between the knowledge of pre-historic Egypt, historic Greece, and India of our 9th Manifestation. Above all, the student can reflect on the magnificence of the Sphinx and the Great Pyramid, monuments which the sages of old left for the coming races, wherein the knowledge of humanity's destiny would be contained and preserved, and whereby man would be able to follow the course of his progress and understand that the Cosmos of which he is a part *is* a perfection, and that he is destined to become a vivid embodiment of that Perfection. The manner in which they have preserved the knowledge is the simplest of all, a mere triangular form which would reveal the way the circle is divided in order to understand Space and Time—four sections of three —and the sublime symbol of the Sphinx which is the message of the Age of Truth. The Sphinx was built precisely at the time the precession was passing over or within the vicinity of 0° Leo, carrying humanity into the Satyayuga, some 10,800 years ago.[1]

It is perhaps difficult for us to accept this, because man cannot believe that the Satyayuga can bring with it such darkness, for the times appear to be darker than ever before and humanity seems to be sinking ever lower into the black hole of materialism. But the Truth has first to be lost, so that the depths of Matter can be explored and redeemed, so that the light of Spirit can truly render the very cells of the human body a luminous tabernacle of light. The plunge into darkness is only so that the depths may receive the light of Truth. For such an accomplishment to take place a great many years are needed. Observation of the list of the Yugas shows that the development augments, so that the Satyayuga is double the years of the Dwapara. Of all the Ages it is the longest, because of all the Ages its task is the most intricate and laborious. Man has a rather sentimental notion of what the Satyayuga is. In his reveries he imagines, perhaps, an idyllic pastoral Elysium on Earth. This may be, but first a very long, difficult and seemingly dark period must ensue.

In order for humanity to know and understand this process and not be lost

---

[1] 10,800, the number of stanzas of the *Rig-veda*, which, by its 432,000 syllables and these 10,800 stanzas, can be seen to be an accurate time-piece in itself, indicating when the Age of Truth would begin to reveal itself.

in despair, when the moment is blackest, the Supreme has left us the Sphinx, the Pyramid, the Zodiac, and all the other keys of knowledge, at the dawn of the Satya-yuga, the time of the incarnation of Rama. The 9th Manifestation is the period of Kalki, the unmasking of the illusion in which man has been living since the death of Sri Krishna, the 8th Avatar, the Incarnation of the 8th Manifestation which was the reign of Scorpio, the sign of Death. This order Kalki comes to re-establish, to awaken man from his slumber in illusion to the reality of the Satyayuga.

It is true that the Dark Age began with the death of Sri Krishna, because it was just at that time that the knowledge of the zodiac was lost and man could not insert himself into the pattern of evolution in the correct manner. He could not make sense out of the cosmic harmonies and thus they appeared to him imperfect, a part of the Ignorance; and the way was then prepared for the spiritual movement which was to pull him away from the Cosmos and make him seek to satisfy his quest for Truth in an isolated experience and realisation of the Transcendent Divine, calling the Cosmos 'Ignorance' and 'Illusion'. The illusion was certainly there, but it has not much to do with the Cosmos: it was man's illusion regarding Time, the loss of the key of Truth. *Kaliyuga* has since then become synonymous with dark-ness, ignorance and illusion, and the difficult part in the matter is that we are *for-ever* in a Kaliyuga, because we are forever in the measurement of Time. If we are in manifestation we are immediately thrust into the Wheel of Time; from this Wheel we can never escape, though we may believe ourselves to have become free of its bondage through various spiritual disciplines and realisations. The freedom we seek is an illusory freedom, if we intend it to carry us beyond the Wheel. We can in no way disengage ourselves from Manifestation, and even our experience of the static Brahman is from and within this realm of Time. Back into the body we must come, no matter to what planes we soar in meditation and trance; or even if we are absorbed into a subtler plane, our being in time does not change, only our per-ception and experience of it changes. If we merge into the so-called Void without taking birth and a body on this planet, can we truly say that we are out of the Mani-festation? Or is it not that we have simply dissolved the instrument of perception of individuality and have moved into the Consciousness of the Great Being,—to us, at this point on Earth, 'unmanifest'? Can we not say, in truth, that there is really no difference between the Manifest and the Unmanifest, and that it is simply our faculty of perception that makes the division?—that, in fact, Brahman and Shakti are One?

Our problem arises with *language*, with the expression of *That*. But it is not by the spoken word that the division truly begins: it is the moment the *faculty* appears which is capable of the perception of division, of isolation, through the word. Speech leading to the word which divides and gives independent existence to a

phenomenon, is very closely allied to Matter—or let us say, its process and finality are the same. Consequently in the zodiac the sign of Matter, Taurus, is also the sign governing the organs of speech. It rules the throat, the larynx, and is the sign of 'the Voice'. This can be understood through the drawing here reproduced of the human larynx and the astrological symbol of Venus, which rules Taurus.

Taurus is then followed by Gemini, the sign of Mind, and so the process is completed by the introduction of the instrument of perception and the word or language itself. The very structure of language gives us an understanding of the process of creation and manifestation. Speech may limit and divide, but at the same time it renders a phenomenon *solid*, fully in existence, equipped with its 'body'. In the same way Matter is the solid body of Spirit. The first three signs of the zodiac, Aries, Taurus and Gemini, are the Trinity: *Speaker*, *Voice* and the *Word*, the creative process of all manifested things.

In our limited earth-consciousness we can say that something does not exist until it is named, though we name it 'the Nameless'. It is Mind which labels, and which therefore divides, and because we are in the sphere of Mind as yet, we cannot know that Brahman and Shakti are One and simultaneously exist within the Eternal; nor can we perceive that what we call the Absolute or the Unmanifest is only that which is not perceivable by Mind and which we must therefore call 'the Nameless'.

Our whole understanding of the Void, the Manifest, the Unmanifest, and so forth, will be radically changed with the dawn of the truth-consciousness in this Satyayuga: we shall come to say paradoxically, 'All is only Matter, yet all is only Spirit—there is nothing but the unmanifested Manifest, and the manifested Unmanifest.'

If we do not see this truth, we are ever bound by Time and live in the Age of Darkness, for since we are always in a Kaliyuga, it is only by having the true key of Time that we can fully escape from the Ignorance. The Satyayuga can only take shape once the gnostic being has revealed man's right relation to time and the Cosmos. The Cosmos is a perfection. Through this brief study of the Yugas the student has been able to share in the experience of this perfection. We must only lift our heads and break through the veils of Maya. Time (Kala) is at once the bondage and the liberation. Therefore it is said in the 'Chandi': 'Worshipping the 18, 8 and 10, Kala (Time) and Death are mitigated.' 18, 8 and 10 are the numbers of arms of the goddesses that are worshipped, and 18+8+10=36, the signs of the true count of the Yugas, the signs of the 12 *Manifestations*.

Throughout we have spoken of Capricorn as the Divine Mother's Victory, the victory over death, the divinisation of matter, as well as the symbolic sign of the Satyayuga. It rules India. It is India's land itself, precisely *Mother India*. There is no better way to show this than by its symbol; for the shape of India is the very shape of the symbol of Capricorn. But the vision is incomplete if one does not take the true map of India, as Sri Aurobindo and the Mother have stressed, the map of a united India, its spiritual integrated power.

With the symbol of Capricorn superimposed, the map stands as here reproduced. This is deeply significant because the symbol of Capricorn, which in

occult circles has always been called the 'Name of God' and which when deciphered would mean the beginning of the Golden Age, represents the triune manifestation, the Divine Trinity incarnate and the completion of the three energies, the three gunas; because of this it governs the Age of Truth. In the zodiac the three energies fall in the order—Rajas, Sattwa, Tamas corresponding to the progression of the energy flows of Cardinal, Fixed and Mutable qualities. Thus Rajas is Cardinal or Creation (Brahma), Sattwa is Fixed or Preservation (Vishnu), and Tamas is Mutable or Destruction (Shiva). In the symbol of Capricorn these three forces are seen as well. The first guna, Rajas, would correspond to the first ascending line, the peak. It is in fact representative of the top of the mountain and as we can see on the map it dominates the region of the Himalayas. The middle portion is Sattwa, the apex of the descending triangle, the plunge into the abyss, the light that illumines the depths of matter. For this reason the Avatars appear under this guna. In the map it is the descent from the lofty Himalayas onto the even plains. The last, Tamas, is the portion which is captured in the symbol by the tail that swings back upon itself. It represents the Transformation, the dissolution which brings about a new birth. In the ideal sense it is the perfect surrender, the *action-in-non-action*. The three phases of the symbol then represent Heaven and Earth and their Union.

India as she is now is formed only of one portion, the central Sattwic; on cither side of her there is a cutting away of her original components: thus two portions of her are lacking. The addition of these two can alone bring about the full and complete manifestation. Their lack is the result or outcome of the nation's years of depleted spiritual energy. The full nation, or the full symbol, is truncated. The Sattwic heart is left intact but without the power to bring forth the central Fire and stamp it upon the outer creation. It is as if the arms of Durga were cut off, for she is Capricorn, she is Mother India.

So the Satyayuga comes forth when India—however that may happen—is really united in this symbol which the Supreme disclosed thousands of years ago. The nation shall not fully rise, Truth shall not reveal its face, the Earth shall not be divinised until this symbol is made complete.

The occult meaning of the sign, the divinisation of Matter, is reflected in the symbol by the V. From the heights Durga plunges into the depths of matter to bring there the light of Truth. It is there that her Victory is achieved and the transformation takes place. On the map the location of this critical activity is the South, where the transformation of matter in its most profound and complete sense has begun and the message of the Satyayuga has been revealed—where the Dark and the Light shall be seen as One.

The Satyayuga is made up of four measures of time: 4 is the number of the Square, the Square is the symbol Sri Aurobindo has given to Supermind, the Truth-Consciousness and, as we have shown in this brief study, the figures of the Yugas are taken directly from the Sun, which is also Sri Aurobindo's symbol of Supermind. It will take 4 Kaliyugas to firmly establish the 4 'feet of the Cow' in the Earth, to render Matter perfect and an image of the Lord. It is time that a more accurate understanding of the Yugas should come to the Indian nation, for the good of the nation itself, and for the destiny of the Earth.

In conclusion, it can be said that *we are in the Kaliyuga within the Satyayuga*— for we have not yet become living embodiments of Truth.

7

Sagittarius and Aquarius

The Body Transformation and the Earth's Atmosphere

THE EARTH, TOGETHER with man, must undergo a transformation,—its atmosphere must change if on its body it is to house a species of a finer substance.

Transformation of the Earth's atmosphere is a near reality, we are witnesses to this fact and no doubt within our lifetimes we shall come to know the extent and meaning of this transformation. The atmosphere of the Earth is like the aura of a person which is a protective sheath he carries with him permanently. This sheath is a reflection of what he is in his inner being as well as the condition of the cells which constitute his physical form. What 'soils' this aura, as it were, is his ego, the element of falsehood and the Illusion.

In the same way the Earth has a 'soiled' aura, polluted due to the unconsciousness of the races who inhabit her. And the time approaches for her to shed this sack, which will then signify a total transformation, the extent of which we ignore.

There are many signs to indicate that we are moving toward this liberation, the principal one being the excursions into outer space by Earthmen. The whole of our present 9th Manifestation hinges precisely on the factor of *travel*, and expansion and penetration into realms unknown and unexplored. This is the main attribute of Sagittarius, the sign of our Manifestation. In a host of ways we can see how this element of travel is a key to our times.

For the first time in recorded history the body of the Earth has been fully known; this has occurred during our Manifestation. There may as yet be portions which remain virgin to the tread of the scientific explorer, but the entire body is at least fully photographed, particularly since the introduction of artificial satellites in the field of communications. During the Age of Pisces, a Water sign, it was conquest by sea that absorbed much of the Sagittarian impulse to travel and expand. It was as well a time when the major political powers expanded through the conquest by sea of a new continent, which served not only to reveal the full body of the Earth but to enhance the power of the nations involved. The discovery of the American continent occurred when the precession of the equinoxes was moving through the first decanate of Pisces, therefore under the full influence of the sign. We cannot explain the phenomenon of this intense involvement with travel and new modes of exploring the Earth and space simply by studying the signs Pisces and Aquarius as indicators of the Earth's evolution. It is only through the Map of the 12 Manifestations that we are given the knowledge that *the prominent influence of our times is Sagittarius, consequently there is the stress and concentration on travel.* Speed as well is an attribute of Sagittarius, and man has now come to the point of manufacturing vehicles which move faster than any hitherto constructed of which we have record. In fact, when the first satellite that was sent to photograph Jupiter, ruler of Sagittarius, reached the planet in December, 1973, and sent back its first pictures, it attained the highest speed of any man-made object up to that time, and this occurred when the Sun in the actual sky had moved into the zodiacal sign of Sagittarius.[1]

In this same Manifestation during the Age of Aquarius, belonging to the Air element, we are occupied with the exploration of Space, and in the same way that the Pisces era brought the full investigation of the Earth through water, so will this Age bring the fullest possible exploration of not only the Earth but the entire solar system as well, through air-space travel, since Sagittarius's tendency is precisely to expand beyond borders, whatever these may be.

This, however, is only one characteristic of Sagittarius. The sign is also an indication of expansion of consciousness, and even the physical expansion through exploration on water and in the air tends to effect a change of consciousness in the people, or, rather, the two modes of expression are inextricably linked. Particularly significant is the fact that in 1961 a human being left the gravitational field of the Earth in the physical body for the first time, thereby putting the body through a very important experience for its subsequent transformation. Such an experience has had a decisive effect on the body's capacity of perception, a radical effect on the body-consciousness which is sorely in need of transformation in order to keep abreast with the newly-manifested forces.

In this experience too we find the factor of Time involved, for if it is true that as proven in physics time *lengthens* as the gravitational pull increases, it is equally true then that where this pull lessens there is an *acceleration* of time. Once out of the gravitational pull of the Earth there must be a *new experience of time*, and as the body becomes more subtle, as its present gross substance becomes modified, there is at the same time a modification of temporal experience. The fullest extension of this experience would be to arrive at the point of living in simultaneous time. Following the experience through in either direction should, however, lead to the same point. That is, whether we move through intense densification until the point of 'no time', or if we move in the other direction into the subtlest and least dense stratum, we

[1] The second satellite to Jupiter, Pioneer 11, also reached the planet during the month of Sagittarius in 1974.

would ultimately arrive at a point of 'no time'. As a symbol in the physical that man is moving toward a new experience of time there is the fact that for the first time scientists have actually photographed the Earth in toto. This is a symbol of the vision of unity that is soon to be achieved, as well as a detachment from the lower planes—a positioning in the Witness Consciousness, while as yet functioning within the sphere of Nature, that is, while as yet in the domain of the body-consciousness. The whole process of expansion and transformation of consciousness cannot be fully understood or experienced unless into its field we bring the modification of the substance of the body. The revolution that is taking place in the Earth's body today is revealing this relation, that neither spirit nor matter shall be able to continue on its disconnected journey; in fact, it is becoming ever more apparent that these two have never really pursued different paths, nor have they moved in radically opposing directions. It is simply that man's capacity of perception is disconnected and he is incapable of observing the movement of the Whole. Enjoying this capacity he can fully appreciate the work done in both the scientific and the spiritual realms and recognise the oneness of their action. For this to take place it becomes imperative that a transformation of the consciousness occur, which is the field of Sagittarius,—to open man to the planes above Mind which will put him into contact with the power of Truth-Consciousness that will ultimately determine the new condition of the races. Therefore the mind of man is in the throes of a radical transformation or perfectioning; this has been one of the principal reasons that the split between science and spirituality had to come about.

The refinement of Mind into a more perfect instrument will signify radical changes in the behaviour patterns for the Earth species; yet the most radical will be noticed in the field of spiritual evolution. This change is perceivable to us during our times,—discernible, that is, from the study of the first scriptures that have come down to us. If we look to the movement of spirituality as recorded in the old scriptures we see the difference—namely that though the being was spiritualised and on the road to perfection, it was nonetheless a mental approach or, shall we say, an exaltation of the human capacities, an inherent belief that man could *do*, could acquire power, and sustain a will that would prevail over the myriad circumstances of life. As we move closer to a spiritualisation of the entire being we perceive that this attitude is replaced by one of *surrender*, where man recognises his ultimate limitations in front of the vast, absolute Being. He understands that the way which is closer to truth is to allow this Power to act through him, to prepare the instrument that he is, to recognise that he cannot *do* unless the Power wills that it be so; and to understand that the power he believes himself to possess and to be the originator of is only the Great Mother, who allows him to believe himself the creator for as long as it is necessary to do so.

The scriptures of old, particularly those pertaining to cosmic harmonies, were for the most part directed toward the acquisition of the power to control or change events; to know these harmonies in order that one might alter one's destiny or use the knowledge perhaps to harness a force that would bring the realisation of God closer. All this is in the process of being changed. The more deeply one penetrates the secrets of the Cosmos, the more fully one perceives the fallacy in such seekings. As Mind prepares to receive the higher Light it becomes more evident that the purpose of these studies is another.

The Split that we have mentioned has to do precisely with this change, though initially it appeared to be a reversal of the process. In the beginning of the Manifestation there was a powerful movement that actually seemed to carry the Work in an opposite direction. It served to pave the way for the development of the physical sciences, but its effect on spirituality was to bring about a dark period that would one day need to be surpassed and corrected if the real goal was to be reached. The emphasis on the realisation of the static Divine, wherein the Ignorance is left to reign over the lower planes, is essentially the reason for the lamentable condition in which man finds himself and his planet today; it brought him to detach from an active involvement in the universe and left science free to occupy itself with certain essentials that were better left in the hands of the spiritually enlightened. The threat of nuclear warfare is one outcome of the Spirit-Matter split, where unenlightened beings appear to control, in a certain way, the destiny of the Earth. Most religions we know today are responsible for the same fault. Christianity, though carrying the message of the divinisation of Matter, which is the deeper meaning of the Christ's teachings, fell back into the inevitable and comfortable belief in a divine life beyond this universal existence. Faced with an overwhelming movement of the Ignorance, the apparently unredeemable condition and impositions of the flesh, and the stubborn behaviour patterns in humankind which constitute the lower nature of man, the spiritual leaders and their followers believed that the only way to keep the fire of God alive in the hearts of men was to convince them that in spite of this impossible creation, with all its pain and agony, God *is* and is waiting to carry their souls to Him upon their death or in their deeper states of meditation. Though God may not be apparent in Creation, in the Beyond He is sure to be fully known...and so the unity of Creation was lost to the perceptive faculties of mankind.

For thousands of years then we see that this has served to isolate man more and more from his brethren and his surroundings, from the experience of the Divine Mother who alone can open in him the full understanding of the unity of creation. Such isolation, even and in particular in the spiritual world, brought the difficulty of indifference and irreverence toward the Cosmos, and the very planet we inhabit. The planet itself lost its pulsating life. Nature became man's enemy and toward her man assumed an egotistical and wicked air. Today the consciousness of the 'being' of the Earth is perhaps lower than at any point in the evolution of the planet.

But the truth is nonetheless preserved in almost every major teaching and religion today, for each religious body awaits the 'return' of the Messiah, the Christ, the Buddhist Lord Maitreya, the last Imam (the Mahdi) of the Muslims, and so on. The universal waiting for the return of the Teachers, so intrinsic a part of the signs Sagittarius (the Teacher or the coming Saviour) and Aquarius (the universal scope), is merely humanity's unconscious inherent understanding that as yet the full reign of Truth has not come, that no leader, no matter how enlightened, no matter how high his or her message, no matter how sublime the plane from where he or she has descended, has completed the task; their missions as yet remain apparently unfulfilled and the heaven of man's intimate vision has not yet been fully established upon this Earth. The awaited Returns have no other reality than to announce to mankind through the media of religious doctrine, prophetic vision and inspired writings of the sages that the process of divinisation of the Earth has not been abandoned and is still being effected and is, moreover, drawing nearer to completion each day, in an ever more accelerated fashion. The 'second coming' of whatever order is the advent of the power for universal uplifting.

The time is upon us in this Aquarian Age to bring about a *universal transformation of consciousness* and to open man up to the consciousness of the universe, to expand in the Sagittarian way beyond the present limits of his mental instrument and prepare for the descent of a power and light that will allow him to live in the consciousness and being of the Whole. This is the Aquarian universality, the vision of Unity, and the Sagittarian impulse to reach the planes of the consciousness of Truth.

The Age of Pisces

WE HAVE GIVEN some significances of Sagittarius as an influence in this Manifestation, lasting for 6,480 years, and also a view of Aquarius, which specifically governs our times. It is possible to be even more detailed in our study, mainly by breaking down each sign of the Manifestation into the smaller divisions which contribute to giving us the full Gnostic Circle. Thus, we can first observe the division of the sign of Pisces in *decanates*:

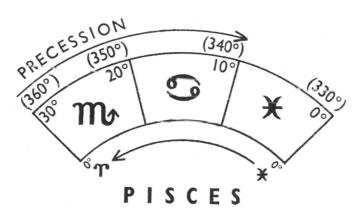

PISCES

    The decanates of a sign are most interesting because this division produces a sub-influence of all the signs in the zodiac of the *same element* to which the sign belongs. Thus in this case it can be seen that the first 10° are the full Pisces degrees, the next 10° (from 10 to 20) receive the sub-influence of the following sign of the Water element, Cancer. After that, from the 20th to the 30th degree, there is the sub-influence of the third sign of the same element, Scorpio. In this manner the three signs of the same element are captured in the single sign.

    The deeper significance of this division is very important because it shows us that within one sign three stages of development pertaining to that element (in this case Water) are experienced. Moreover, not only are the full effects and qualities of the element felt but in this way we experience in one sign the three energy flows, Creation, Preservation and Destruction. The manner in which these energy flows are arranged in the sign is what shows us the true progression in its more profound meaning.

Taking the sign we are studying, the first decanate met in the retrograde motion of the Ages is Scorpio, a sign of Preservation (Fixed energy), the first sub-influence of importance that is encountered. In fact, each complete Manifestation of 6,480 years will begin with the Sattwa guna, the aspect of Preservation. Consequently, the first 720 years of the Piscean Age (2,160 divided by 3 = 720 years) will be marked by the Fixed influence of Scorpio. Thus we are able to see that *death* plays a key role in the entire Age due to this initial influence of Scorpio.

The prominence of Death in the spiritual experience of humanity during those early years of the 9th Manifestation is evident. Christianity is constructed almost entirely around the death and subsequent resurrection of the Christ; not only is this factor present in the inner core of the teachings through his death, but it is also there in the lives of the early Christians, the trials of martyrdom, for example, which are such a firm pillar of the Christian faith. In fact, there appears to be a glorification of Death. But the breakthrough into the full experience of the Resurrection was not a part to be experienced by the Christians, and as such they still await the return of the Christ in a glorified body. The following words of St. Paul show us the deeper and occult teachings of Christianity:

All flesh is not the same flesh: but there is one kind of flesh of men, another flesh of beasts, and another of fishes, and another of birds.

There are also celestial bodies, and bodies terrestrial: But the glory of the celestial is one, and the glory of the terrestrial is another.

There is one glory of the sun, and another glory of the moon, and another glory of the stars: for one star differeth from another star in glory.

So also is the resurrection of the dead. It is sown in corruption; it is raised in incorruption.

It is sown in dishonour; it is raised in glory: it is sown in weakness; it is raised in power.

It is sown a natural body; it is raised a spiritual body. There is a natural body and there is a spiritual body.

And so it is written, The first man Adam was made a living soul; the last man Adam was made a quickening spirit.[1]

Howbeit that was not first which is spiritual, but that which is natural; and afterward that which is spiritual.

[1] Adam, the first Man, is the 0° Aries point, the beginning. In the retrograde motion of the Ages and the evolution of man, the progression moves immediately into Pisces, a Water sign, which is the soul. The Precession ends the Round again at the 0° Aries point, but this time the last sign it moves through is Aries, a Fire element, which is the Spirit, thus Paul says: 'The first man Adam was made a living soul; the last man Adam was made a quickening spirit.'

The first man is of the earth, earthy: the second man is the Lord from heaven.

As is the earthy, such are they also that are earthy: and as is the heavenly, such are they also that are heavenly.

And as we have borne the image of the earthy, we shall also bear the image of the heavenly.

Now this I say, brethren, that flesh and blood cannot inherit the kingdom of God; neither doth corruption inherit incorruption.

Behold, I shew you a mystery; We shall not all sleep, but we shall all be changed.

For this corruptible must put on incorruption, and this mortal must put on immortality.

So when this corruptible shall have put on incorruption, and this mortal shall have put on immortality, then shall be brought to pass the saying that is written, Death is swallowed up in victory.

O death, where is thy sting? O grave, where is thy victory?[1]

Christianity is a religion of Scorpio; in the passage quoted here St. Paul speaks of the *sting of death*, the image of the Scorpion; and the victory that is awaited is the victory of Capricorn, the sign of the birth of the Light and the traditional birth sign of the Saviour. But the Christian religion has not yet seen the light of the Sun, the resurrection. It has crystallised the Faith at the point of Death, constructed dogmas and doctrines around it, impeding the way to the full experience and passage into the further steps of spiritual growth. In 1957, the Mother of the Sri Aurobindo Ashram gave this New Year's message: 'A Power greater than that of Evil can alone win the victory. It is not a crucified but a glorified body that will save the world.'

The followers of Christ glorified Death, and as with every religion a fossilisation then set in which tends to impede the expansion that awaits the spiritual evolution. The early Christians were not able to live the resurrection process and yet the dogmas that evolved closed for others the future possibility of the living experience, for it is a fact that the modes of expression of the Supreme are plastic and in the details of their workings are in large part unpredictable. Therefore further growth within the walls of Christianity, following the Christ through to the next stage of his spiritual experience, might well be impossible within the body of the Church. In fact, when such free seekers have come along the Church itself has rejected them, thus crippling and suffocating the Body's finest energies. Teilhard de Chardin is one example of recent times. Throughout the history of the Church there have been many such cases, often tragic ones, where the courageous mystic has had to forego even his very life in order to remain true to the truth of his own experience which seemed to contradict the dogmas of the Faith.

[1] I *Corinthians*, 15.

Such a narrow and deplorable view was in force during the second portion of Pisces, under the influence of Cancer by decanate, the second period of 720 years, which began in the 5th Century A.D. and lasted until the 13th Century. It is the middle portion of the Age of Pisces, embracing precisely the period of history that is referred to as 'the Middle Ages'. It covers as well the time known as the 'Dark Ages', and it must be remembered that in the development of the zodiac Cancer especially characterises the *Fall* and the reign of Ignorance, *Cosmic Midnight*, the dark Night of mankind. This second decanate brought as well the dawn of Islam to the world.

The energy flow of the times, according to decanate division, is Cardinal: a powerful direction is felt, even if this be in support of Ignorance. It was during this period, however, that the full seed of the Science/Spirit division bore fruit, and though the spirit and soul of man was made to suffer, the Dark Ages brought the first glimpses of the foundation of the material sciences which ultimately aimed at showing mankind a much fuller picture and experience of God than was known to it before the Split, at least during our period of recorded history. The note of Death still rang through the Piscean Age, however, and the pioneers in the work of the time, particularly during the Renaissance, once again became martyrs. The breath of the Spirit became very much crippled from this point onward; intolerance was the keyword and each religious body, Christianity, Islam, etc., attempted to establish its vision of Truth as the sole means for the attainment of a diviner life for man. Each religious body—and even different sects within the different faiths, in particular the Christian—sought to take full possession of and cramp into a meagre house this Breath of the Spirit that all the religions in the world together cannot contain, because it is the very Centre of all these and much more, not to be confined and limited to any one sect or experience or system or belief. The Crusades are a symbol of the bigotry and limited vision of these times, the culmination of the Middle Ages of Pisces, the so-called 'Holy Wars'. The thirst for power of the two religious bodies, Islam and Judeo-Christianity, knew no bounds and in the name of the Lord they sought to expand their kingdom and establish their ways as The Way.

The last 720 years of the Age, from the 13th to the 20th Century, were the outcome of the Cancer gestation. As Cancer is the sign of gestation and maternity, it once more gave forth the Light that it had been nurturing in its womb in the form of the Renaissance, the Re-birth. The fossilisation of the religious experience reached its peak during this latter portion of Pisces when the evolution fell under the full influence of the sign and therefore the Mutable quality of Destruction intensely prevailed. In the Inquisition we see the power of destruction or dissolution at work, not so much in the elimination of the 'heretics' by arbitrary and bigoted proceedings, but simply by the very fact of its existence which served to liberate the spiritual seekers from the confines of the Church. The atrocious phenomenon of Inquisition helped to cause the downfall of the Church itself; if not in exterior appearances, the intimate foundations of the Faith at least had to bear the shakings of this black Scourge, and this caused irreparable damage to the Church's structure. No doubt this darkness is what served to plunge the seekers of the time even more dramatically and fully into the bosom of Truth, with a greater intensity than otherwise would have been the case.

For the major portion of the Piscean era the planet Neptune, the co-ruler of Pisces, was not known. The Age passed almost entirely under the influence of Jupiter as ruler of the sign. But this is what characterised the movement of the 'dark ages', for Jupiter was then no longer sufficient to express the sign Pisces, hence humanity was in a sense 'crippled', walking on one limb, so to speak. Thus the qualities of Pisces were very restricted and it was during the first 1440 years of the Age that the spiritual experience became dogmatised and subject to the rigid demands of *ritual*. We find this not only in the religions of the West but the East as well contributed its part to the mosaic. In India a wealth of ritual was born, flourished, and took a solid form during this early period, the major reason for the fossilisation of the Hindu Faith that has only survived because of the living power of its yogic systems which somehow or other have managed to remain within the embrace of Hinduism.

It is a fact that when the newer planets were first *seen*, their effects on the spiritual movement were only then beginning to be felt. For the major portion of the Piscean Age it is Jupiter we are to consider as the influence of the times, which is all the more emphasised because Jupiter is also the ruler of Sagittarius, the sign of the entire Manifestation. Therefore during the era of Pisces the characteristics of this, the largest planetary body in the System, came strongly forth.

Some basic Jupiterean attributes are connected with ritual, and it is possible to see through this that religion, or the experience of orthodox religion, reached its culmination during that time, and was then exhausted, leaving only the truth of the experience for the next Age. The focal point here is Judeo-Christianity. It is possible to see the power of this faith and the force that was supporting the movement simply by studying the way in which Christianity has overtaken the structure of man's civilisation, influencing it to the depths of its core. Together with Judaism, for we cannot disengage the two, perhaps no other religion has so readily and thoroughly captured the consciousness of mankind and influenced the entire body of its societies, even though this be in an indirect way. Jupiter is *expansion*, mainly through the spiritual-religious experience; it is also power, kingly or divine. In its lesser attributes it is a power of material standing, material wealth or the class of nobility which controls the wealth and growth of a society. During the Piscean Age the power came forth and culminated in colonial expansionism, which prevailed into the actual Aquarian Age. Empires, monarchies, the so-called theocratic and the plutocratic rules are fully Jupiterean in essence, when the planet steps down from its divine plane and dons the robes of temporal power. On the other hand, the rise of democracy is connected with Neptune, and this only because of Neptune's role as *higher octave* of Venus, which we shall discuss further on.

Jupiter is also philosophy, and the student can observe that during the Piscean Age the fullest expression of the philosophic mind came forth, beginning with the Greeks and culminating in the last decanate, the full Piscean period.

During the last years of the Piscean Age, Neptune was discovered and this brought forth a different aspect of the Jupiter 9th Manifestation; spiritism began, almost as a reaction to the gross imposition of the material sciences and pragmatic philosophies. Neptune awakened in man the thirst to experience the more subtle regions which Science had so blatantly condemned to the prison of superstition. Up until the 19th century the presence of Neptune in the evolution of Man was veiled though active; since its actual 'discovery' its power is a conscious one and very great strides have been made in the direction in which the planet is to carry us. This is significant of all the three latest planets discovered, of which much more will be said when we begin discussion of the Circle divided into 9, in a later portion of this synthesis.

Neptune is a planet most intimately connected with the experience of Death, being as it is the planet of trance states, of which death is one aspect. It contributes as well then to the Piscean Age's involvement with Death. But Neptune is also the planet of Illusion, the veils that must be drawn back in order that man perceive the Harmony and Perfection that is, and above all the condition of immortality which is man's right. We can therefore say that Neptune is connected to death in that death, or at least the way death is experienced by man, is Illusion.

The central figure in the manifestation of the spirit in the Piscean Age is Jesus Christ, or what the Christ symbolises as a focal point, an incarnation onto whom the symbols of the Age were projected. Whatever great spiritual figures may have existed during the same period, the Christ nonetheless stands out as the principal personage of the times and the one who has most influenced the turn of events for the races of Earth, because the world entered a materialistic phase of expression to which Judeo-Christianity bore a great affinity. His connection with the Essenes, the third power of Judaism, is very interesting to study as a part of the Aquarian Age, since this discovery is another essential feature of our present times with its attribute of the unveiling of the Truth.

Hinduism during the Piscean Age cannot be said to have competed with and gained any ground over the religion that sprang from the Christ's teachings. In fact, we can safely say that it was Hinduism's 'dark age'. We can go even further by stating that its full birth has not yet fully taken place; but this will happen only when it dissolves certain of its constricting religious structures and re-establishes itself as a body organised primarily to give shelter to the Light of any given Age and to harbour the schools of yoga that come forth from the teachings of the Evolutionary Avatars. The more rigid it becomes in its structure, the more it becomes dogmatic in its adherence to scriptures, the farther away does it place this re-Birth.

Particularly debilitating is the great regard for the *śāstras*, and all the voluminous quantities of scriptures to which each sect of Hinduism feels itself obliged to adhere. In all religions this is the most crippling factor. There is no way in which a spiritual experience can be free and spontaneous if one is obliged to seek for its confirmation and validity by means of the scriptures. The spiritual experience is in continuous flux and flow, accompanying, and growing according to, the evolution of Man; it is, in fact, that which is the substance and core of this human evolution. It can never be confined therefore to a strict and rigid process or be dependent upon what has been laid down as Law in the scriptures. The surest way to stifle a movement of Truth is to give the character of 'scripture' to a work that contains the essence of the movement. There are always these works which are written to accompany and clarify the seed of the times, but the possibility is there that they may become dogma. Yet no matter how much humanity sees this and determines *not* to fall into the same patterns of the past which have proven disastrous for the growth of the spirit, nonetheless the very same errors are repeated over and over again. In this Age we are faced with the same problem, and we can only pray that the force of the times is stronger than the understanding capacity of man and that it will oppose this tendency and leave the spiritual seeker the liberty to accompany the movement of Truth in total freedom—no authorities, no sanctions, no high and mighty proclamations. It would seem that this force is working, for it has been experienced within the Christian faith regarding Teilhard de Chardin. No matter how much the Catholic Church tried to suffocate his spirit, in the end this attempt was not successful. One feels in his case that were he not bound to the structure of the Church, there were no limits to the heights his spiritual genius would have attained.

The Avatar, the Messenger, the Teacher never needs or demands that his teaching become dogma. This is always the work of the disciples, the devotees, the 'followers'. The problem lies with the 'faithful'. This is in fact a very good word to describe the body that survives an Avatar, because it generally clings in sincere faithfulness to the teachings of the Messenger, even in cases when the Teacher himself would have obviously progressed to another stage.

Returning to Hinduism, whatever its future stage with regard to the past, the Piscean Age was for it a dim period. Hinduism has little hope for survival in a civilisation that separates Shakti and Brahman, because its very core is the understanding of the unity of the two and the equality of one in face of the other, their Eternal Identity. So-called 'non-dualistic' philosophy, though harbouring itself in Hinduism, only served to weaken it and render it impotent. The work of Kalki is to re-establish order, to reveal the Eternal Word once more, and bring the experience of God in this religion back to the light of its eternal Truth.

The energy tide of the Piscean Age surged through Christianity, which is a religion based on the suffering of man, one aspect of Pisces, as mirrored in the Christ and his crucifixion. Hinduism could not follow this movement because it tends to uplift and free man from his sorrows, rather than to indulge them hoping in this way to appease an All-Mighty Creator, or else to content man with the acceptance of pain as a means of reaching the heaven beyond death, beyond the earthly existence. Hinduism is far too enamoured of either Krishna's *Līlā*, the divine Ecstasy and the emphasis on seeking this union with the Supreme, or else of extinction in the Void, where pain and suffering, instead of becoming exalted and a means to touch the Creator, dissolve entirely from the experience of the seeker, and are simply extinguished and ignored, experienced as a part of the illusion of Earthly existence.

The most recent and complete contribution to the Hindu-oriented quest was Ramakrishna, who lived from 1836 to 1886. He was perhaps the most sublime representation of the Piscean Era, or let us say, the culmination of what the Piscean Era could bring, its most perfect specimen, for in Christ we have not as yet the full accomplishment, as his awaited return indicates. Ramakrishna is the most complete product of the realising possibilities of the time. This God-man in his life and spiritual realisation, presented mankind with the purest example of the utmost the sign Pisces can give: the total and most perfect surrender to the power of the Divine Mother, the complete abandon in her arms as a child, the realisation that no matter how high one goes in one's spiritual states, no matter to what planes one soars—even believing oneself to have perhaps passed *out* of the Manifestation and hence out of the realm of the Mother—Ramakrishna always knew these states and planes to be *within* the Manifestation and given to him as a grace of the Divine Mother. Always she was the *doer*, and he the perfect instrument in her hands.

The purest note of Pisces is *surrender*, abandon into the ocean of Bliss, *ānanda*, and the essence of Divine Love. This was Ramakrishna's realisation, though he pursued many different paths to attain it; he trod all the known ways, explored all the possibilities at the seeker's disposal, yet each one brought him ever and always to the same point and was for him a further means of proving that the multiple forms of the Mother and her myriad paths were in essence One, that through them one would, if one plunged deeply and sincerely enough, come to her Heart.

This was Ramakrishna, the Child of the Divine Mother, who then used Vivekananda as his Sword of Truth, to transmit the power to the four corners of the globe. The Piscean Age has given us no greater product of spiritual realisation. It was he who paved the way in the fullest sense for the spirit of the Aquarian Age, and he was in fact born with the Sun in Aquarius. His birth coincided nearly with the discovery of the planet Neptune, so by the time he began his life of experiences, the planet's power was fully manifesting. Ramakrishna showed the way to universality, a condition of our Aquarian times. He acquainted the world with the Divine Mother and, through Vivekananda, with the truths of the Hindu faith, and paved the way for the advent of Durga.

It is possible to go into much greater detail regarding each Age by means of the Gnostic Circle and the zodiac. As mentioned elsewhere we can break the Age

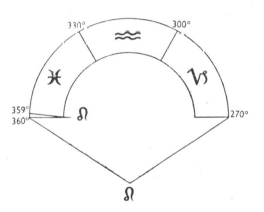

down into periods of 720 years, 240, 180, 72, and finally 6 years, in this way coming to the very minute influences prevailing and combining all these to arrive at the fullest understanding of the process. This is left for the student to undertake, if he so wishes. Only one further piece can be added here and this is that in the diagrams we have been studying which indicate the Avatar of each Manifestation, the first degrees of each Manifestation met in the retrograde motion of the Ages will always be that of the sign *upholding* the Manifestation—the Seed, as shown in the diagram.

The very first degree one meets in the retrograde motion of the Ages is thus the 'seed' note that is played, the essence of the entire Manifestation. Each one, it can be seen, will begin on a note of Fixed Quality, either Leo, Scorpio, Aquarius or Taurus, which are the four figures of the Sphinx symbol, the 'faces of God' or the four aspects of Vishnu which become the Avatars on Earth. The Manifestation in its very beginning carries the seed of *Preservation* in this way, in its depths, and it springs from that source.

In the chapter on the *Indian Yugas* it was pointed out that 0° Leo was the beginning of what the Hindus termed the *Satya Yuga*. This point, ruled by the Sun, is then recaptured in the essence of the 9th Manifestation, for which reason *the knowledge of the Satya Yuga is revealed during that time*, because the essence of the Satya Yuga is Truth, which is the Sun. In the number scale the Sun is Zero, the Nought that contains the All. It is the sustainer of the entire System, hence the sign in the zodiac which it rules must occupy a prominent and essential place. It is only natural then that the Incarnation who reveals the message of the Age of Truth would be born with the Sun in that sign and also have the luminary, together with Jupiter, rising in Leo at the time of birth; for this latter planet and the Sun give us the planetary image of the truth-consciousness. In the chart Uranus as well is found on the Ascendant, hence Sun, Jupiter and Uranus are all rising in Leo: the Sun is the *seed* of the 9th Manifestation, Jupiter is the planet ruler of the 9th Manifestation, and Uranus is the co-ruler of Aquarius, the Age of Preservation, the Age of the appearance of the Avatars of the 9th Manifestation.

If we have spoken so extensively of the Avatar of the Age and laid such stress on clearly establishing who this is, the student must understand that the reasons which prompt us to do this are not at all connected to aspects of devotion, or faithfulness to a doctrine or school, or any such consideration. It is only for the sake of truth, and mainly for the truth which is contained in the zodiac. The purpose of this work is to show how the zodiac is a map of the evolution, and the only way to do this effectively is to pinpoint the Evolutionay Avatars, as we have called them, within this map, and through them to reveal the truth of the zodiac for mankind. There is no other way, because it is only in their lives that this truth is revealed to man. Any sincere student of cosmic harmonies must look at this fact, rid himself of any resistance, and then he can be carried to the essence of astrology, and if this study is to descend from the realm of *theory*, the concrete facts must be given. It is not our intention to become a mouthpiece of any sect in formation, of any new religion. Our task is to be at the service of Truth, exclusively, and to show some hidden aspects in the study of the harmonies of the Cosmos.

There is, as well, no intention of setting up comparisons between one spiritual figure and another, seeking to establish which is the greater. We strive only to show the role they are playing and to bring clarity into the field of knowledge which has been all too much abused and obscured. If, for example, we have spoken about the mistake of placing Gautama, the Buddha, on the list of the Hindu Avatars, it is simply because he does not belong on that list, not that he is unqualified as a spiritual and religious leader. In this study we are dealing with the evolution, which is the essence of astrology; in dealing with the evolution we are dealing with man and his spiritual destiny and experience as well, for none of these can be separated from the other, nor can man in any way extract himself from the evolution of the races of

Earth. If he is a part of this Earth life and has taken birth on this planet, there is no way he can escape participating in the destiny of its evolution. Perhaps on other planets this is not so, perhaps in other worlds, other planes, other universes even, there is no evolution. But this is of no concern to us at this point. We are here, and we must be here fully, and be conscious of what we are doing. Consequently we must understand our evolution in its deepest and most profound sense which is the spiritual sense of the progression. If it seems that we have exalted the two evolutionary Avatars Rama and Krishna and made a definite statement about the third, the Kalki of our times, it is purely to bring to mankind the true understanding of the zodiac, which is the Earth's map of evolution.

Man perhaps does not realise what a sublime revelation the zodiac is, that in effect he can know the destiny of the planet therein. It is time he awakens to this fact, for we have moved into the most important period of our Greater Circle of 311,040, years—this Aquarian Age we are living in at present—because it is now that the birth of the Child of Truth in this Age of Truth can be termed 'successful' or 'unsuccessful'. In order to move ahead in full consciousness with the times, as they demand, man must know and have implicit faith not only in his destiny, but in the destiny of the Earth and its entire evolution.

9

The Aquarian Age

OUT OF THE darkness and into the light: this is the Earth's present destiny. From the waters of Pisces, where the soul of the Earth experienced the intimate communion with the Supreme and took the essential steps in the attitude of *surrender*, the evolution now proceeds toward the victory through Knowledge, through identity with the universal consciousness, and into a phase of mass transformation, a breath vast, extensive and universal in its scope, which will not leave any hidden recesses or dark corners in the fight for a total victory of Truth.

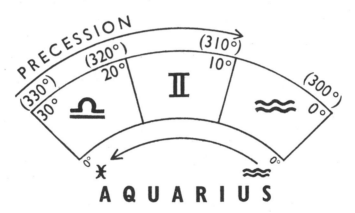

It is only now that we can truly say 'the Sun of Knowledge illumines the horizon', for the Sun itself, the Divine in the physical manifestation, is the upholder of our times, and for the next 2,100 years, we will proceed toward the condition of full identity with the truth-consciousness that is symbolised by the Sun. We move into the Age fully equipped with the necessary powers to accomplish the task. Unlike the Piscean Age where the higher range of possibilities—as epitomised by Neptune—were not active until the very last century of the Age, in this present era we are already working with the full power of Uranus, the force of the higher expression of Aquarius. In fact, this power, which is the power of transformation, was the first to appear in the higher gamut. Afterwards came Neptune, and then finally Pluto.

The specific characteristic of our present Aquarian Age, the 98th section of the

Greater Circle, is that the usual methods of doing things that have been considered adequate for thousands of years are now being upturned. In the simplest manner mankind will be brought to live in a consciousness of Truth whereby very shortly it will fully understand that all its suffering is self-inflicted, not an inherent part of the evolution, nor does this represent the goal toward which we move. This goal is *Perfection*,—but perfection itself is not a static condition. We can say, *Perfection is not static; it is an eternal Becoming, being at each moment what the Lord wills and therefore always what should be. It is the celestial harmony unfolding itself into Eternity, and as such each moment is in itself a perfection.* We shall come to understand during this Age that 'each moment is in itself a Perfection.' Illness, suffering, anguish, and Ignorance—the source whereupon all the others feed—are not a permanent part of the plan. These are only temporary manifestations, part of the illusion of Prakriti. This seems impossible to believe because we are so habituated to our suffering. To conceive of a life without pain seems almost impossible for Earth beings, let alone to speak of life without death. Yet this too shall come. The very things we find most impossible, most incomprehensible, most threatening to the comfortable and crushing rut the evolution presently knows, shall come to pass. This is the Age of the Universal Transformation, the very time that our pain shall change to its opposite, when we shall be made to see that all pain and suffering is only a distortion of the Divine Bliss. And this will not be accomplished merely by a withdrawal into a nirvanic paradise, a detachment from the flesh and its experiences in such a manner that the consciousness alone will be liberated, leaving Matter in its disintegrating condition, or else an acceptance of pain and the Ignorance by seeing 'the Divine in All'. The physical itself is now to know the divine ananda.

It is a fact that the present condition of man's being, and in particular his body, creates within him a greater affinity with *pain*. In certain yogic experiences it is possible to perceive pain as 'vibration' and then to experience this vibration which we feel as pain as its opposite, that of bliss. One can know through such an experience very concretely that pain is only the distortion of the divine *ānanda* or bliss, and that because of the density of our manifestation this characteristic distortion takes place. The body as it is now formed cannot withstand the equivalent vibration of pain transmuted to bliss, returned to its natural and pristine potency, and not dulled by the grossness of form of the more dense planes—for it is a fact that the experience of pain in the body, or suffering in the emotional nature, is merely due to the type of existence, or the level of evolution of the planet, its position within the solar system, which renders the experience deformed in the way we know. Yet this is an interesting fact of Earth life. Because of the density, because of the actual condition of organic matter on this planet, which differs from the particles of matter on other planets in the System, a greater acceleration in evolution is experienced on Earth, and therefore progress is heightened, the possibility to make quicker and greater strides forward toward the total consummation is more easily available to beings incarnated upon Earth. It is a fact that existence in a more static dimension, formed of a more subtle matter, is not 'painful', but this very fact is what arrests the possibility of more rapid evolution. The decay and degeneration of the Earth cell, rapid as it is compared to matter of other dimensions, is what grants the soul incarnated the possibility of accelerated growth. For this reason we may say that evolution is an intrinsic part of Earth existence and is not to be found on other planets in our System. Actually we must be more precise and say that it is really the *accelerated* pace that is evident; other life, on other planets, and in particular within other dimensions moves, varies, progresses as all manifest things do, but at such a slow pace as to render it almost imperceptible. Thus *it is the condition of Matter that imposes the pace of evolution on Earth*, and that consequently grants the soul the possibility of a much deeper and wider experience of the manifest Divine. Man's body is at once his prison and his promise, just as Time is the limitation yet at the same time holds the key to liberation. The key would be to transform the cell, or to come to a new experience of Time, which would not alter the evolutionary capacity of Earth life but rather render the experience free from the impositions of the Ignorance while still retaining the possibility of fully accelerated growth.

In this sense the Earth is a privileged place in the System, and pain and suffering are merely the outcome of Matter's inability to withstand in the physical, as it is presently constituted, the one unique Vibration which is the essence of life.

The first degree of Aquarius in the retrograde motion of the Precession falls in Cancer, and is ruled by the Moon. Therefore we know that for 72 years of the Aquarian Age it is Cancer and all that it signifies that will be particularly prominent, that will especially feel the transforming energy of Uranus. The principal aspects of Cancer, maternity and gestation, are undergoing radical changes. In this light we can show one aspect of the painless condition that awaits humanity, which is its natural right. We are already witnesses to the fact that a woman is now able to give birth to a child in a painless state, a natural one, not induced or maintained by drugs. Particularly important is that this condition is brought about largely by breath control. A mother comes to know in fact that it is the natural way to give birth, and that the scriptures stating that a child must be born in pain are perhaps not accurate; they are scriptures of the Age of Darkness, pertaining to a process that is only valid for the period of darkness. In the Aquarian Age all these 'old-consciousness truths' will simply dissolve in the light of a higher Truth and Knowledge.

Not only has the question of pain for the mother been dispensed with, but as of 1974, through the enlightening work of Frederick Leboyer in the field of *childbirth without violence*, as he calls it, the infant himself can now come into the world in a state of peace and harmony, rid of pain and fear. This is a unique and important contribution. Both new systems, for the mother and the child, are the first steps along the way to the full truth consciousness regarding this essential aspect of life on our planet.

Apart from governing birth and maternity, Cancer is also related to the *cells*. In this sense the same transforming element is felt and will last for the first 72 years of the Age. Though the human races are not yet aware of what is taking place, the very cells of the bodies of men are being acutely pressured to evolve into a finer and more illumined substance, to be able to withstand a more intense vibration, closer to the essence of Life. This is not immediately evident because the process is yet restricted to the subtle planes, but before the end of the millennium it will in some way reveal itself in a manner which will be evident to all. We can say that the process has been carried out on a *cosmic level*, and as of 1974 it descends a triad further and begins work in the Individual. What was accomplished on the cosmic scale is now destined to take root in the individual for the Earth's evolution. This is the third phase of the Work we spoke of earlier in the text.

Cancer is the ego, the Ignorance, Prakriti. It was during the Age of Cancer, and in particular when the Precession was passing over the Cardinal point of Cancer, that the Ignorance came fully forth and began to overtake the races of the Earth. The Age of Truth had begun after the passage of the Precession through Leo—some 12,000 years ago—and that was indeed a glorious time for the Earth, when the Knowledge was given out for the benefit of mankind. The condition on Earth in certain centres of civilisation must have been truly magnificent, for the races were governed by men of gnosis, arranged so that the Truth, through them and their work, would remain on Earth. It was the time of Rama, the time of the Pyramids and the Sphinx in Egypt, the priesthood of On who were worshippers of the Sun and enlightened by the knowledge of the zodiac.

The passage into Cancer brought the plunge into the Ignorance, but only as a temporary condition. In any case, it was the period of the legendary Flood; whatever that was in actuality it was nonetheless symbolic of the destructive power of Mother Nature and the dissolution of the civilisations that were so formidable in knowledge, as we have spoken of elsewhere in the text.

Consequently it can be seen that Cancer is intimately associated with the Ignorance and the Falsehood in the cells, and thus the illness which is precisely the *falsehood of the cells* is named after the sign. During this Age of Transformation this too shall be conquered, but mankind in its conquest will learn that all illness is due to ignorance, and that all illness will disappear the very day the Falsehood is completely abolished. The cure for cancer will bring this understanding. As an illness it becomes the symbol of the transformation of physical ailments which are a rejection of the Light, to the state of peace and harmony of the cells. It is the process of 'death' in the cells, because they have broken away from the central Light and have set up their own autonomous rule, so to speak. In the very same manner the whole of the human organism must now learn to arrange itself around a centre of Light, contained in each cellular nucleus, which is in tune with the Unique Centre, the Divine Light.

During passage through the first degree of the Age man will not only find the cure for cancer, but through it the basic victory over physical ailments will have been achieved. As in the case of childbirth, the solution will be quite simple and will depend almost exclusively on enlightened consciousness. The key to the cure of man's illnesses, those mental as well as physical, lies in this realm.

The sign Cancer is the end of life period called *the Tomb* of the zodiac. In this way it is connected with death but only insofar as the entry into the tomb is symbolic of the return to the state of a foetus, this time not a return within the womb of the physical mother, but rather within the womb of Mother Earth herself.

The first *decanate* met in the retrograde movement of the Precession falls in Libra. We know that this is the sign of *Cosmic Sunset*, which represents the light of a higher consciousness beginning to illumine the Creation. In the individual progression this is the point of Yoga where the two poles which became divided are joined once more and the consciousness widens. Libra is a harmonisation of energies, an equilibrium of the manifestation of forces, though it may not signify the total union. Because of its meaning of unification and harmony we can say that this period of 720 years of the Aquarian Age will be understood as the *Age of Unity*.

Libra is the Power of Truth which begins to make itself felt. *Harmony* is a keyword of the sign, and in this sense the studies of cosmic harmonies as well as the development of a new process of Yoga will be very much favoured during the time the Precession passes through the first 720 years of the Age. The cosmos will reveal its magnificent harmonic structure to man, but this will not necessarily correspond to the scientific approach, nor for that matter to the purely spiritual. In fact, it is not through science that the cosmic harmonies will unfold themselves, because in order to understand them one must be aware of, and in tune with, the subtle planes. One must be able to perceive the celestial sphere and the myriad occult circles which weave through the subtle atmosphere, and see that in their interrelationship the evolution of the planet as we know it is revealed. Man must have eyes to see in a new way, not directly related to science yet having received from science the eye of precision and the demand for a concrete experience in which matter and the physical are the chief participants. The more accustomed man becomes to viewing the expression of the Divine in this manner, the more readily shall the harmonies reveal themselves with greater precision.

Subsequent to her experience related on page 57, when she had actually moved into the realm of death, with the complete cessation of pulse and heart-beats for a considerably long time, on May 24 of the same year the Mother spoke to a group of disciples about a *third way* for mankind which would be neither science nor spirituality but something beyond these two:

'It is that something that we are searching for. Perhaps not merely searching for, but *building*.

'We are being used so that we may participate in the manifestation of that which is as yet inconceivable for everyone, because it is not yet there. It is an expression that is yet to come.

'...these positions, the spiritual and the 'materialist', if one may call it so, that are believed to be exclusive (exclusive and unique, so that one denies the value of the other, from the viewpoint of Truth), are insufficient, not only because they do not admit each other, but because even admitting the two and uniting the two does not suffice to solve the problem. There is something else—a third thing which is not the result of these two, but something that is to be discovered, which will probably open the door to the total Knowledge.

'...I do not think that a single individual (on the earth as it is now), however great he is, however eternal his consciousness and origin, can alone by himself change and realise,—change the world, change the creation as it is and realise the Higher Truth that will be a new world, a world more true, if not absolutely true. It seems a certain number of individuals (till now it appears to be rather in time, as a succession, but it may be also in space, a collectivity) is indispensable so that this Truth may concretise and realise itself.

'I am practically sure of it.

'That is to say, however great, however conscious, however powerful an Avatar may be, he cannot, all alone realise the supramental life on earth. It is either a group in time, arranged in a file in time or a group spread over a space—perhaps both—that are indispensable for this realisation. I am convinced of it.

'For a long time it seemed to me that if one made a perfect union between the scientific approach carried to its extreme and the spiritual approach carried to its extreme—its realisation—, if one joined these two, one would find, one would obtain naturally the Truth one seeks, the total Truth. But with the two experiences that I had, the experience of the external life (with universalisation, impersonalisation, with all the yogic experiences that one can have in the material body) and then the experience of the total and perfect union with the Origin, now that I have had these two experiences and there has occurred something—which I cannot describe now—I know that the knowledge of the two and the union of the two are not sufficient; that there is a third thing in which these two terminate and it is this third thing which is in the making, in the process of working itself out. It is this third thing that can lead to the Realisation, the Truth that we seek.

'I arrived, by yoga, at a certain kind of relation with the material world based on the notion of the fourth dimension (inner dimensions that become innumerable in yoga) and I made use of this attitude and this state of consciousness. I studied the relation between the material world and the spiritual world with the sense of inner dimensions and by perfecting the consciousness of these inner dimensions—that had been my experience before the last one.[1]

'Naturally, for a long time, there was no longer any question of three dimensions—that belonged *absolutely* to the world of illusion and falsehood. But now it is the use of the sense of the fourth dimension with all that it entails which appears to me as superficial! I do not find it any more, the thing is so strong. The other, the three dimensional world is absolutely unreal; and the other one appears, how to say, conventional. It is as it were a conventional translation to give you a certain kind of approach.

'And as for saying what it is, the other one, the true position?... It is so much beyond all intellectual states that I am unable to formulate it.

'But the formula will come, I know. But it will come in a series of lived experiences, that I have not had yet.'[2]

The formula did come to the Mother in a series of lived experiences which she began recording in 1965, appearing in the *Bulletin* for a period of nine years under the title *Notes on the Way*, until the time of her final withdrawal.

When the 0 and the 9 are pushed to their extremes in a simultaneous process, then the third arises which is the unpredictable because it is as yet beyond our capacity of perception and translatable experience. We can only think of it as either

---

[1] The Mother's experience of 13 April, 1962, recorded on page 57.

[2] Extracted from the *Bulletin of the Sri Aurobindo International Centre of Education*, August, 1962, pages 69-76.

a spiritualised science or a scientific spirituality; but perhaps it is something else, which neither of these ways yet knows. It is a true *new consciousness*.

The problem does not lie in Science or in Spirituality; the problem lies in the division of the two and the separation of the experiences. If there were no division, if one would—from the very beginning—approach the goal in the unified consciousness, there would be no difficulty, we would freely speak now from the 'new consciousness'. It is the duality of Mind and its method of approach to the Eternal Truth that has rendered the experience unexplainable and inexpressible to our actual perception and through our subsequent language.

In the cosmic scheme of things it would appear that this third possibility, the 'neutral force', leaving aside the question of individualised avataric descent here, is simply the really integrated or unified consciousness, making use of a faculty which is as yet unknown to man because he is still in the realm of Mind. No matter how far we have progressed in our spiritual realisation, we have still made use of Mind, as we know it, to express the experience and perception, to explain that which lies in fact beyond it. Herein lies the problem. It is the emergence of a *new faculty*, which then appears to us as the New Consciousness, that will cast the new light onto that which hitherto had been approached in a fragmentary fashion. In truth, neither Science nor Spirituality can alone answer to our needs at this moment, because both are subject to Mind. Therefore it is only by going truly *beyond* this instrument, reaching a higher light and bringing that light into the Mind of Man, that we can begin to express our experiences of God in a manner more compatible with the Divine Reality and with the times.

We have stated elsewhere in the text that no matter how high a Master has proceeded in the past he has been subjected to the instrument of Mind for the translation of his perception. This has immediately introduced the element of *division* into his experience, either during the experience, or else as a way in which he translated his experience into the language of the waking consciousness. Consequently all the problems of conflicting doctrines—the One without the Second, the unity of Brahman and Shakti, the monotheistic or polytheistic worships, —have arisen. These conflicts in the existing religious thought are inevitable while man is wholly a mental being. When he proceeds but one step beyond that his perception widens and his experience tells him that all these are not the way, because the Way is beyond any form of division in perception. Multiplicity there is and must be for the existence of Unity, but a Multiplicity which is perceived from the position of a unified Consciousness. When this comes about one begins to issue forth from the womb of Mind and to emerge into a higher consciousness, to us considered 'new' on this planet. The third possibility is in a sense so distinct that it appears to us unrelated to the two old ways.

In this light we can see that all division is born of Mind, and the violence that the Earth knows, an outcome of the disunity of its people, shall not change until at least a group of individuals attains the New Consciousness. As long as the world is governed by Mind, as it has been for these thousands of years, we can know no peace. Peace—true and lasting—can come only when a unified consciousness determines the affairs of man, on a collective as well as individual scale. In that consciousness there is no difference between Science and Spirituality, between Brahman and Shakti; the very use of the terms is foreign to it. There is only TRUTH, and this is BEING.

In this process one is constantly faced with the problem: How to express it in words? In the Mother's *Notes on the Way* one encounters this phrase continually. But there is an essential point to be understood, and for which reason perhaps the Mother herself sought to put the process into words: we *must* find the words, we *must* be able to express our experience of the Inexpressible. That is, it must not remain in the realm of the Inexpressible or Un-Nameable, because if it does this reveals that the Goal is yet far. This reveals that the Truth has only partially come forth, that Spirit has not acquired its 'body', that the Supreme Truth-Consciousness has not revealed itself in Matter. There must be a language of Unity to express the Unity. And this does not mean a universal language, an Esperanto, or some such attempt at communication. It means simply a faculty which is able to put into words the new and fuller experience of God without the need of calling it the Unnameable, or the Inexpressible, or the Unmanifest, for that matter, simply because this is the only way we can face the Paradox; otherwise Truth shall yet reveal itself to be far from having taken possession of Matter.

We explained previously that language is closely allied to the process of material evolution. To move toward a divinisation of the evolution means a language which springs from a consciousness of unity,—as yet new to us. Our whole understanding of the actual phase of evolution hinges, as has been repeatedly pointed out in the text, on the number 9, due to our location within the 9th Manifestation and in the 9th Spiral of the Greater Circle. In all the root languages 'new' and 'nine' have the same meaning, the same stem. They relate, of course, to the process of birth. So this 'newness', in all its aspects, is the great key to our times. In all ways everything will appear to us as *new*, even, and in particular, the Absolute that we adore.

All of these processes are closely a part of the Aquarian Age transition and birth. It is precisely in the field of language and expression of the Reality that the transitional movement is being felt strongest for the present: man must be taught to *see* in a new way, and then to speak a new language which expresses that which he is now newly capable of perceiving. And this will take the shape of a continuous pro-

cess of *synthesis*. Whatever aspect of the Divine he wishes to explain he will ultimately end by speaking in terms of synthesis. This Age of Unity that we are in
could very well be called the *Age of Synthesis*.

Because Saturn, the ruler of Capricorn, is said to be 'exalted' in Libra, we know
that the sole power to be used for the spiritual conquest is the Power of Truth. This
is the contribution of Libra to the Aquarian Age. In this work, therefore, one must
proceed with the accuracy of a scientist and the vision and perceptive faculties of a
spiritualist.

As was stated, Libra is the first manifestation of the higher consciousness. It is
the first sign of the upper half of the wheel; thus, the initial awakenings of the Origin come into the play, and the path which can lead to the unity of man becomes
visible. It is enclosed between the two signs which show the play of the vital energy,
Virgo and Scorpio; it is precisely an inner union which brings about the conditions
needed for the unawakened Kundalini of Virgo, as shown in the sign's symbol ♍,
to raise its head and follow the movement upward which leads to the full birth of the
psychic being. We shall go through the signs in greater detail in the next portion of
this work. However, what should be stressed here is that by the influence of Libra
humanity is awakened to a higher consciousness, and since this Libra influence is
being subjected to the Aquarian force, now in its Uranian phase of expression, the
sign will not only indicate the development of a higher consciousness, but of an entire *newly-manifested* higher consciousness. It is the third possibility the Mother
speaks of. The yogic experience of old which brought man to the vision and realisation of the higher reality is no longer sufficient to satisfy humanity's thirst for Truth.
Since the Split man can only be satisfied by an experience of God which embraces all aspects of His creation. He can no longer confine his search to the realm
of the invisible, nor can he remain content with exploring the profundities of
Matter without considering the secret Reality which upholds the display of material
creation through the succession in time and space. If God-realisation is to live and
not to die in this Aquarian Age, it must be found in a more total way. But for this
new faculties of perception must be placed at man's disposal; new lights, new experiences,—until eventually the body of a new language will be shaped.

*
* *

The symbol of Aquarius is the force of consciousness manifesting in the Cosmos, which the Earth can experience as cosmic waves that reach it from other
dimensions and more subtle planes. During this Age it is known that man shall
become fully conscious of these subtle waves and subtle planes, but not in the
way which seeks to uncover a phenomenon for the sole sake of the study of pheno-

mena. While the forces of the Cosmos are studied with respect to Earth, their transforming power will also be learned, and an accurate knowledge of the subtle planes or occult dimensions from whence these forces proceed shall be attained. In this way we approach occult studies, the field which alone can provide a complete understanding of the body of the Manifest Divine.

A particularly interesting and as yet virgin field of study in this respect is dream and sleep experience where man can now come to know the difference between a subjective dream and the entry in a subtle body into an objective plane. He shall be able to follow his passage into these subtle planes consciously, and then to discover what his mind contributes to that which he perceives, and how he translates this objective experience to his consciousness by use of this instrument. In fact, the images he forms of reality belong to the instrument of individualised mind, yet the reality of the plane is not obscured by this translation, so long as the mind is operating from its true position, from the poise of silence, peace and light. By the right approach to dreams man can now come to know that most if not all of his dreams are the outcome, in fact, of the *images* that he forms of that which he perceives in his wakeful states; that is, he can in this way begin to understand the illusion in which he lives, how he weaves certain images for himself, which have little or nothing to do with the Reality, and based on this ephemeral and illusory stuff with which he fills his mind, he feels and acts. His contact with reality is solely through mental images which he arbitrarily concocts in ignorance of the process, and therefore, bound by mind, man relates to his neighbour constantly from this divided state. In his actual condition there is little hope for him to function in unity and harmony with his fellow man because Mind is the instrument of Ignorance and is at the service of ego. This is the veil that stands ever between him and his brethren, between him and the cosmos, between him and his God: if an individual retains full consciousness in sleep he can easily come to know of these processes and become aware of the manner in which he translates everything he perceives in the waking state into that which his ego determines, with all its preferences, desires, lusts, greed and so forth, and which constantly distorts the divine reality. And in this way he shall come to see the imperative need to achieve the Silent Mind, so that this distorting process begins to wane.

Also to be discovered during this Age is the full extent of the functioning of the subtle sensation body, the vital body, which depends on the physical mind, the brain, for enjoyment of the sensation. The brain is the mechanism used to complete the experience of the vital body, even when liberated from the physical, bringing the sensation back to the faculty of perception of the individual.

The experience of the conscious release of one of the subtle bodies from the physical at the time of sleep will become a more universal occurrence during this Age, as the instruments of perception become illumined by a higher light and power and knowledge. This will serve to liberate man from the false impression he has of the needs of the physical, and is ultimately the first step for the masses to approach the New Death. The effect this will have on the actual functioning of the senses is the important point. It will ultimately result in the outcome of a more sensitised body, wherein the physical itself shall be able to enjoy the Divine Ananda, the cells themselves shall have their full experience of God.

The Aquarian symbol signifies a communion with other planes, wherefrom 'transforming currents' are sent on Earth, in order to facilitate the evolution of the races. It is also a symbol of man becoming aware of the subtle plane of Ignorance, the detrimental factor of present human existence. He must be aware of the envelope of falsehood in order to transcend it and allow the processes of higher and purer planes to act unobstructed in the movements of Earth evolution. To combat the forces of Ignorance one must be conscious of them. One must see that most of one's impulses and actions are determined not 'by oneself' but that one is simply a receiving instrument: whatever man is in tune with, that transmission shall he receive. If he is not rid of ego he will only be able to receive impulses from the plane of the Ignorance, or at least ones strongly coloured by the Falsehood. When holes are pierced in the 'sack' that constitutes the region of his lower nature, he can then begin to receive from higher levels. And this is accomplished by Yoga, or any discipline which brings him to the experience of the egoless state.

However, the times call for a unity of being; this too is the meaning of Aquarius. We must consider the sign as a part of the entire 9th Manifestation, which is the zone of unified man. Hence, the Yoga needed to bring about an opening to other planes must be one that we can call 'integral'; that is, one which does not ignore any part of the being, particularly not the physical. It is only a *synthesis of yogas* which can now carry man to his destined experience of God. The three signs of the 9th Manifestation are in fact the three major yogas—*Bhakti*, *Jñāna* and *Karma*, Pisces, Aquarius, Capricorn, the soul, spirit and body of man. Therefore it is understood that in the area of unity of the zodiac the process for synthesis will make itself most felt in this unification of the three Ways which only the gnostic being can achieve. His life then consists of *Bhakti* Yoga, or surrender and love as his attitude, *Jñāna*, or Knowledge, as his tool, and *Karma* Yoga, or work and action, as his field of expression.

Once the ego has been eliminated,—the mind's ego, the vital's ego, the body's ego—then we can begin to speak of a 'New Aquarian Age Consciousness'. We have not as yet touched upon this, though today our talk and our publications are full of 'New Age' this, 'New Age' that. The Age has just begun and its complete power cannot manifest until there are a number of men rid of ego and able to become embodiments of the Truth-Consciousness. These individuals will naturally be in tune with higher planes and without any major effort they shall live and reveal the new consciousness for the Earth. Through them, the race of gnostic beings, mankind shall be lifted to a new level of being.

To experience this it is necessary to experience Death. From what we have reproduced of the Mother's experience of 13 April, 1962, when she lay seemingly dead for some time, and her talk of 24 May, following that experience, it becomes evident that a race of people living in the consciousness of Immortality must evolve for the sake of the evolution. For this it is necessary to move into the realm of Death and to 'move about' therein, without severing the contact with the physical, without the life force of the body being withdrawn, but at the same time carrying the body as well through the initiation of Death, which, for the race of gnostic beings, would be simply the Initiation of the 'degeneration and regeneration of the cells.' In the past, initiations were limited to the realm of spiritual consciousness; Matter, or the physical, played little if any part in the experience. Today's Initiation, this Aquarian Age phenomenon, is one wherein the body as well is made to undergo the same process, therefore it is one that must be experienced in full waking consciousness. To begin with, all the subtle planes must be traversed or, shall we say, must manifest by a lived and totally conscious experience in the waking state, and the body in full consciousness must know the experience of Death. This can come about in different ways, depending much upon the individual preparation, temperament and inclination. But however it may take shape, the Initiation of today is the illumination of Matter and the death of the physical ego. In this lies the key to the Gnostic teaching of the death and resurrection of the Christus.

The realiser of today therefore must be not only a yogi, as the term is commonly understood, but he must as well be an occultist, a mystic, an astrologer and a scientist, among other things; he must be capable in all directions,—what to the Earth will surely appear to be the *Superman*. The gnostic being is one who lives in, or is rapidly approaching, an identification with the Truth-Consciousness, therefore he knows no moments of a loss of light. He cannot, for example, truly consider himself an integrally realised being if part of his existence is passed in a totally unconscious state, unless this is by his express will. Thus the gnostic being must be fully aware in his sleep as he is in his waking states. We cannot in truth speak of Gnosis until there is the perfecting of conscious sleep and trance states. A meditation which transports us into a realm wherein we lose consciousness and then return to the body without full recollection and knowledge of the planes experienced, is similar to unconscious sleep.

But to have these experiences one must nonetheless have crossed the threshold of a unified vision and total surrender to the Divine Mother. It is she who is to carry the being through the different phases of sadhana, because only in this way do the experiences form a part of a unified movement which ultimately makes sense out of the Chaos. To induce these experiences as determined by a human consciousness is to remain in the realm of mediocre realisation. This too is a part of the Aquarian Age manifestation: a surrender to the Divine who alone can evoke in us the experiences which will not confuse us all the more in our quest, but by the orderly manner in which they appear in our sadhana will reveal the unity of being. From below, immersed as yet in the Ignorance, we cannot understand the process as it should be carried out in this transitional stage, in order to have the vision of unity which will then create a gnostic centre. We must give ourselves over to a higher power, the Inner Guide, the Divine Mother in our hearts, in total sincerity, not as a blind for our egos. And then we can begin to experience the Power of the Divine, the Shakti in action. Piece by piece she will build the inner mosaic that will reflect a new consciousness, a new being, a new race.

Universality of Aquarius is to be understood not in the limited sense sometimes attributed to the word today. It is considered to mean there is one Truth in all religions and therefore this is a time of the flowering of the true religious spirit, when man will see that all religions have the same message and can lead to the same goal. Yet this is only partially true for the universal Aquarian breath means that the truth of the times *is* to flourish universally, but this does not imply that the means will be orthodox religions. In fact, each of the known religions leads in a slightly different direction, all do not take us to the accomplishment of the Ideal of today, for the pressure over the world at this time is to eliminate religion as we know it from the consciousness of mankind. We move toward a liberation from the limitations that dogmas and doctrines impose, and not a strengthening of these bondages,—though these may hide under the guise of a universal reformation of the religious spirit, to uncover their one truth and common origin. Religions belong to the Overmental creation, the 8th stage of the Indian Puranic scale, and they flowered during the 8th Manifestation which belonged to the Overmind, and have endured up to the beginning of this present Aquarian Age. But the forces that are behind the manifestation of the Earth's religions are not content with the fact that their hold is to be lessened, and so today they hide behind various masks and try to take possession of the hearts of men in a different way, without labelling themselves as religions. Yet the old consciousness to which they owe their being is still there and no essential transformation therein has taken place. This is particularly noticeable in 'New Age' groups, societies and communities of many types, many of which propose to reveal the occult sciences, astrology, or claim to be in contact with the Higher Power, God, etc. The consciousness prevailing in these groups is religious in its essence, and though using different means and words, their movements are impregnated with the spirit of the past. Astrology and Yoga are two fields which have especially suffered under this pseudo-New Age scourge.

Moreover, there is no religion existing today that fully understands where the Time-Spirit is moving in the light of a true higher knowledge. In one way or another, all of their goals are seeking for the liberation beyond this Earth. There is not one which has as its active and living aim the divinisation of the Earth itself and the very body of the planet's prime species; nor does the religious doctrine admit of a new and finer and more divine race of men to enjoy the kingdom of the Lord in this very place where He has put us. Where any such advanced goals are to be found is always in the teachings of secret societies, initiatic schools and esoteric groups which may outwardly form a part of a religious body for convenience, but inwardly they correspond to a law higher than the religious.

Religions are temporal manifestations. They came and will go according to the spirit of the Ages to which they belong. Though their goal is God, whatever be the name they have given to Him, the ways they lead their followers upon are limited and encompass a very small band of time. Their scope is not eternal and must therefore form a part of that which comes and goes and is constantly under the pressure of a higher Truth. When Truth—in its living and pulsating form—is to be established firmly then aids along the way will be clearly seen as a moment in the history of the process of affirmation.

The Descent and the Ascent

Regarding the movement of the Precession within the zodiac, the first sign of any one of the 12 Manifestations will always be of Mutable Quality, or the energy flow of Destruction or Dissolution. This is so that the evolution may never become a static reality; what was established during one Manifestation is then broken down in the beginning of the next, and thus the first Mutable Age of any Manifestation will invariably present humanity with the experience of *disintegration*, and towards the end of that Age and nearing the next, a building up or a laying of the foundations for the new teachings of the times. Thus the Age of Pisces served to 'undo' the structured teachings and accomplishments of the previous Manifestation, the 8th, and slowly as the Age of Pisces moved on, the seeds were planted for the actual Aquarian Age, the time of Preservation, when the Avatar once more appears to spread the seed of Truth.

After this the Manifestation always culminates in a Cardinal sign, the flow of Creation, the period of the real glory of the Manifestation; after which another Mutable (Dissolution) sign is encountered and the same process of seeming disintegration takes place in order that the Truth renew itself and reveal a greater face of the Almighty Mother.

The movement in Cosmic terms is from Cardinal to Mutable, Creation to Destruction. For the individual it is Destruction to Creation, Mutable to Cardinal; but always between the two, no matter what the order, ascent or descent, there is the flow of Preservation and the guna of Sattwa, the mighty and indestructible Sphinx.

The Divine Incarnation begins the journey in a way opposite to the human's: he *descends*; the human being *ascends*. In the Circle divided into four we see that the Avatar follows the movement of evolution beginning with the spiritual quarter; in this way he reveals the true course of evolution which begins in the Spirit and is to return to the Spirit once more. Whereas the human being, after entering into the wheel, meets in his progression first the Physical, then the Vital, and only after being fully immersed in the lower hemisphere does he begin to rise to a higher light, carrying with him the ignorance of the lower nature of which he must eventually rid himself. On the other hand, the Divine Incarnation carries the higher light well established into the lower regions, illumines and transforms them and thereby assists the creation in its return to the original state of oneness and purity. The Tantric tradition explains these four stages in terms of the manner in which procreation is carried out during those four levels of creation. In the first, which would correspond to the spirit, it was carried out by the mere *will* of the Supreme. In the second, already one step removed from the total Identity, the *glance* was the method—this would correspond to the Mental Quarter. Then in the third, the Vital, there was the *touch*, and the fourth, the Physical, is procreation as we now know it. The tradition goes on to state that the goal of spirituality is to bring the creation back to its original state of purity. This is the task of the Divine Incarnation and the gnostic being.

It is the faculty of total awareness and total identity with the Divine that will change for the evolution the known pattern of procreation, as well as the rhythm of Creation followed by Destruction, and the occurrence of Pralaya—total dissolution or absorption. By our acquiring the possibility of consciously moving into realms which we now experience in ignorance and half-light, these periods of destruction which are an inevitable part of the evolutionary scheme will not signify the end of our civilisations but only the movement of *conscious* withdrawal of the faculty of perception. This is the condition of immortality. Subject to the light of such a consciousness, Matter itself will be made to do the commands of the Truth-Consciousness, because it will be a part of the integral experience of being, centered in its expression around a divine light, the unifying element of gnosis; and therefore the experience of the cells in themselves will follow a scheme which until now has not been known to evolving humanity. If the consciousness of man becomes truly immortalised,—that is, if that which is already immortal becomes perceived and experienced as such—without the need of withdrawal from the body, then this same experience will ultimately be the conquest of Matter. The disintegration of the cells in the present manner will reveal itself to have been a part of the 'old consciousness', the consciousness wherein Death reigned and imposed its darkness on the body's expression. The cells as yet have not manifested the full power because the divine light which is their core has not yet been allowed to come forth. Following the path of the gnostically illumined consciousness, their experience will also be one of immortality. But still Matter will retain its characteristic of *eternal motion*, of *perpetual change*. This is the true victory of the Divine Mother: the divinisation of Matter, its immortalisation, for the immortality of the spirit is an old and known experience and needs no newly manifested force (the Supermind, as Sri Aurobindo calls it) to make us aware of its immortality. If there is to be a victory during the 9th Manifestation, it is in the realm of Matter, where Death is Lord and Sovereign. This is the field of the Supreme Shakti, perpetual motion, the conquest of the Golden Age, 2,000 years hence.

To reach this point there must be a transformation of the consciousness, into a consciousness that has unmasked Death, has seen its illusion and in this state is able to work upon the structure of the cells in their own field—that is, the field of Eternal Motion.

This brings us to the next portion of the study of the Circle, its division into 9, which can reveal to us the patterns and harmonies of the Shakti in *perpetual motion.*

the Mother
the body
the play

6

The Cosmic

"...*We shall take up the mind not as a separate mentality imprisoned in a petty motion, but as a large movement of the universal mind, the life not as an egoistic activity of vitality and sensation and desire, but as a free movement of the universal life, the body not as a physical prison of the soul but as a subordinate instrument and detachable robe, realising that also as a movement of universal Matter, a cell of the cosmic Body....*"

10

The Circle Divided into Nine

THIS IS PERHAPS the most meaningful division of the Circle for us on this planet, at this time. First because we are in the 9th Manifestation, the 9th spiral of the Greater Circle, in the 98th sign of that Circle, and because our present Age of Aquarius began exactly in the 54,000th (9) year of this cycle of 77,760 years. In all these figures the 9 is an outstanding factor, and certainly if we want to delve deeply into the meaning of our times we must understand and make use of this key.

The second reason is that this number is the last digit of our numerical system; our numbers actually go from 0 to 9, as we have often stressed in this work, the 10 being merely the 1 again. In this way, the circle divided into 9 is what joins the heavens to the Earth's time cycles through the calendar, no matter what method is adopted of recording time and no matter what calendar is used.

Third is the fact that 9 is a most meaningful cycle for any human being because the gestation process at present requires a period of 9 months; though there are some cases which break this pattern, for the majority a cycle of 9 months is required for the cells to evolve and for the foetus to fully develop into the infant. Thus, in the Circle divided into 9 we can see the cycle of a *cell* and its complete process of creation, preservation and destruction or dissolution, or its birth, generation and degeneration, the period of the cell's fullest experience.

Finally the importance of this division of the Circle is to be understood with regard to our solar system, which consists of nine planets and the Sun, the zero. In this way it becomes evident that the 9 Circle is for us at present the most perfect representation of the microcosmos and macrocosmos, and tells us the way in which we can link these together. It tells us in its harmonics that in fact the vast and the small are one.

To begin the study, let us look at the details of the division and see how by simply observing the play of the numbers it embraces the fine patterns of its harmonies come forth. As well, we can observe in this phase of the study how the method of theosophical addition is the indispensable formula in order to approach and understand cosmic harmonies, that it is in no way an arbitrary measure and that the justification of its usage is to be found in the numerical system itself, through geometry and plain arithmetic, and thus in no abstract way we must understand that form and number are one. Essentially we can see that no matter how high we count, how extensive our figures, these can and must always be reduced to one digit if we are to learn the secret of any process in creation, and that no matter what the process, the phases of its development are always nine. In this light we can observe, for example that any of the figures obtained so far in the other divisions of the Circle, for the purpose of following the map of evolution, invariably yield 9. The 311,040 years of the Greater Circle equal 9, the 77,760 years of the Great Circle equal 9, the 6,840 years of any Manifestation equal 9, the 2,160 years of any Age equal 9. All the figures of the

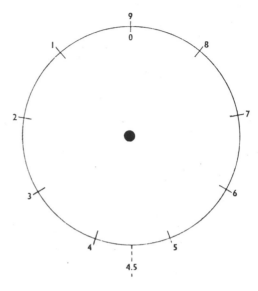

Diagram A

Indian Yugas equal 9, and the radii of the Sun, Moon and Earth as well equal 9.

In the Map of the Greater Circle on page 25, it can be seen that if each line of numbers is added in any of the signs from the first spiral to the last, the follow-

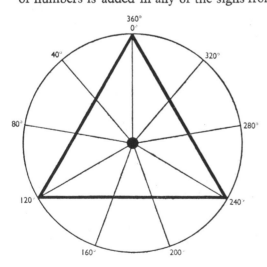

Diagram B

ing figures are obtained: beginning with the Pisces line and moving backwards along with the Precession, the development goes from Pisces 804 to Aquarius 816 to Capricorn 828 to Sagittarus 840, etc., ending at the 0° Aries point with 936 (9), the key numbers in fact in our entire study. The numbers of the signs are themselves interesting because the total count in the Greater Circle is 144 (9), the square of 12, while in the Great Circle it is 36 (9), the square of 6.

Returning to the simple 9 Circle, the first step in the study is to see the numbers placed around the circle and the pattern this forms. It is imme-

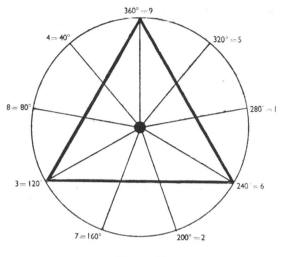

Diagram C

diately evident that if we start at the top and move down either side of the circle we can progress through all the multiples of 9 in this way, reversing the process at the bottom (which we have called *the 4.5 point*). There is then 18, 27, 36, 45, 54, 63, etc. We shall see further on in the study how important the reversal point is, that it is as it appears: the revolutionary axis. (Diagram A)

The next phase in the study is the geometrical circle and we see that in dividing the circle by 9 we come to fragments of 40° each, as in diagram B. If by the process of theosophical addition these digits are reduced to one, all the numbers from 0 to 9 are obtained (Diagram C). Going up or down either side of the Circle as has been done with the simple circle of diagram A, there will always be 9 achieved and its multiples: $4+5=45=9$, $8+1=81=9$, and so forth. In this way we are shown that the geometrical circle of 360° is in fact a most harmonious arrangement, for pushing our investigation further shows that this geometrical circle is in truth the revelation of Perpetual Motion: starting with the 0-9, we skip one number and go clockwise through the wheel, 1 to 2 to 3 to 4 to 5 to 6 to 7 to 8 to 9, then by continued use of theosophical addition, 10 becomes 1, 11 becomes 2, etc. It is seen that 9 holds the key to perpetual motion, it is seen to

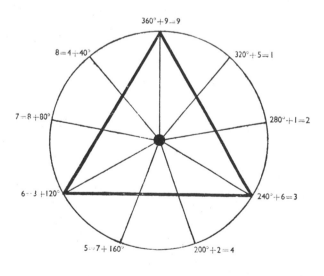

Diagram D

be equal to the o, and this perpetual motion is the Eternal Movement of the Divine Mother, Shakti, the power of Brahman. This division of the Circle gives us the most revealing vision of the action of the power of Brahman.

Continuing the 'game' the marvels of the geometric circle can be even more evident, for it is necessary that the student obtain a firm and fundamental understanding of the harmonious attributes of this wheel. By adding the numbers we have so far, based on the 40° segments, we come to this stage, the full progression of numbers from o to 9 once more (Diagram D) and then by numbering the wheel in counterclockwise fashion, from o to 9 as the zodiac goes, all the numbers of each segment together will dissolve into 9:

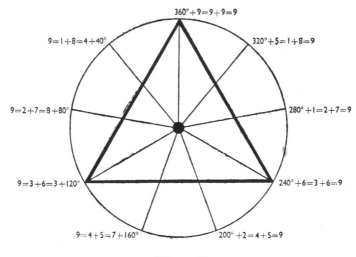

Diagram E

Being fully acquainted with the numerical structure of the 9 Circle, the student is given the first lesson that will facilitate his understanding of the subsequent aspects of creation that are to be unravelled based primarily on this Circle, when we bring it into play in our own lives on this planet.

In the wheel we are studying, there is one point that must be mentioned before continuing any further. In spite of all the various combinations of numbers that have resulted from the 'game', there is something that remains ever stable and does not essentially change: the triangle of 9-6-3. It is clear from all the reductions we have gone through based on theosophical addition that no matter what process we undertake, this triangle never varies. At most the 6 angle becomes 3 and the 3 becomes 6, but never are any other numbers incorporated at these two points. And as for the 9, the only exchange is with the 0. We can see that the 9 and 0 are one, and the 6 and 3 are interchangeable and together simply equal 9. Hence the base of the Sacred Triangle is equal to the apex. The Apex is the 'seed' of the arrangement, and the 6 and 3 are equal to each other, and then together are equal to the 0-9. But however we care to study the wheel of 9, it is evident that this triad is the support of the entire play, and it is unchanging and the sole basis of stability of the creation. Without it the Manifestation would have been absorbed back into the Point, or would never have known the possibility of expression. This Sacred Triangle represents the divine spark in creation, the soul; it is the Triangle of the Avatars; or, shall we say, the Incarnations who appear on this planet to assist the evolution automatically step into the cycles and rhythms which are formed by the play of these three numbers, the 9, the 6 and the 3. It is this, the *Law of Three* as it is called in certain schools, that is the foundation of the Work as well as the essence of the structure of our solar system, from the infinitesimal atom to the formation of the galaxies. Indeed, the Sacred Triangle is the inherent spark of the Divine of each human being, because his very life and development are arranged so as to fit into the flow of this rhythm and Law of Three, and of it he is to become an ever more perfect expression. The growth of the foetus should be divided into three stages, each one culminating at one of the three angles until, from the 0 (conception), birth takes place at the 9. From conception (0) the embryo passes through the first stage of growth and reaches 3, in the third month; it moves through the second phase which culminates at the 6 point, the sixth month and growth of the foetus is essentially completed; and then the final stage culminates with the birth at nine months, falling at the 9 apex of the Triangle. The entire process incorporates four numbers: 0-3-6-9, and four, or the Square, is the number of manifestation of life on this planet. The degrees in each segment of this Circle are 40, which in theosophical addition is 4. The number of the Ages of the Great Circle is 36 or the fourth multiple of 9, the number of *kaliyugas* in the Satyayuga is 4. This is the necessary element for the construction of a solid form, for three sides are simply one plane; it is only by adding a fourth that a solid form can be obtained. This would be 'that certain fourth poise', (*turīyam svid*) of Upanishadic tradition, the silent upholder, the 0 or the Sun. In this we have an explanation of the Sacred Triangle and the appearance of the Avatars: for this planet true perfection can only be finally expressed in Matter. However sublime the properties of the Trinity may be it can only be rendered solid, lasting and crystallised when it incarnates on Earth, and takes on the density of form. For this reason in the progression of the symbols of form the triangle appears *after* the square in the descent from 9, or the Divine Mother. She is only made fully manifest when the essential part of her has accepted the limitation of Matter, the Square, and determines then to awaken this element to the inherent divine Light. This is the key to the process of evolution which the Avatars hold in their palms, because their sole reason for coming is the divinisation of the Earth, which is the revelation of the zodiac. We can actually say that the Trinity has no meaning beyond our Earth life, that its sole purpose is to divinise the Earth. The Trinity represents the psychic being of the planet itself; just as each individual has a psychic being, so also does the planet, and this Trinity, which sometimes incarnates, sometimes remains behind the play as a silent participant, is the manifestation of the Earth's soul and is therefore a constant and intimate and essential part in the entire evolution of the Earth, from the very first of its embryonic manifestations to the last of its vital pulsations. The span of action of the Evolutionary Avatars is therefore as long or as short as the planet's existence. The Lunar Nodes are the orbital indications of this psychic being and are a prime factor in the appearance of the Trinity on Earth.

In the structure of symbols we move from 9, the Circle, to 4, the Square, to 3, the Triangle, to 2, the line, which then is absorbed into Zero, the Point. The Circle is the Manifest Divine, the Mother, the Point is the Unmanifest, or Brahman. This understanding can never be stressed too often, because without the realisation of the Circle being the number 9, the student is hindered in his advance in the study of cosmic harmonies. More than simply reading and accepting, the true knowledge can only evolve when one has *realised* this truth; it must be the outcome of spiritual realisation, when one *lives* the 9 and the 0 and finally when one is granted the living experience of the equality of the Point and the Circle. In this way only is it possible to understand that number and form are one, which are then known to be vibrations of energy, the one unique Energy, manifesting itself in an infinite variety. One comes to see that Shakti is merely the *form* and *movement* of that which, deprived of her play, would never perceive the state of its own perfection. The Shakti is ever carrying the Golden Brahman within her womb, displaying before him the wonders of himself. And when this Golden Brahman comes forth then is the creation able to know its own perfection, then can Brahman and Shakti stand face to face and realise their sameness, their identical perfection. When this takes place, the evolution experiences the Age of Truth, and the sign of Capricorn, *Sat* of the Trinity, is fulfilled. It is then that the consciousness of man has evolved to the point where it can perceive each moment as a perfection, and the eternal perfection of the movement of Becoming within Being. This is the Great Birth of our times, which requires the consciousness of Unity.

In the Circle of 9 we are describing the most essential part is the 0 which unites itself with the 9, becoming the Serpent biting its Tail. Herein we see that Spirit and Matter are but different densifications or rates of vibration of the one all-pervading Energy, which to us is the Absolute, God, Brahman. And by means of this diagram we are going to see how this apparently abstract concept is related to us in the most intimate way and reveals this relationship in the experience of Time on our planet, using the mechanics of evolution. It can be perceived by this diagram that the Divine we seek is not only beyond us but is the most intimate part of us, is not only Impersonal but is as well and simultaneously Personal, that we are THAT, in a most concrete way, that without That we could not have our being in Time, nor beyond it—whatever that may mean—for It is the All of which we are parts.   We can see from this simple diagram that as long as we view the question of Spirit and Matter linearly, we cannot come to the true Knowledge: to understand that they meet at a certain point in the development, simply because they had never really been separate, a truth which we ignore in the normal consciousness. It is only because we cognise as yet with the instrument of Mind that we are obliged to consider Shakti and Brahman as separate, and to experience unity only sporadically. Shakti moves away from Brahman yet always within him, only to gather a fuller scope and reveal a deeper and wider range of her Lord.

This becomes evident even in the question of the Earth's population. We know it is becoming excessive, yet at the same time we are brought to wonder at the fact that in almost every inhabitant on this planet there is a spark of the Divine consciously evolving and knowing itself and its perfection. Thus, the power of the Spirit is greatly intensified at this time, if only man would awaken. The over-population of the Earth is a factor that could signify imminent destruction, yet at the same time it could also be the even greater capacity of the Spirit to overpower the Ignorance which is in possession of our planet. Man will become a true instrument of the Light only when he recognises that the war being fought for the planet on the subtle planes is precisely to liberate it from the clutches of Darkness. For this, both the Dark and the Light have sent their armies to Earth. It is up to us to bring about the Victory or the Defeat, the miscarriage or the successful birth of the Golden Child.

Saturn (Kāla), the Time-Spirit

When it is time for the appearance on Earth of the Supreme Mother's emanations, when a decisive and not a meek step is to be taken forward in the evolution of the manifesting Spirit, we find ourselves speaking of the War between the Dark and the Light, the Devas and the Asuras of Indian tradition, or the Gods and the Titans of Greek mythology, the hostile forces versus the forces of Truth. This is an ever-recurring contest, and the values are continually changing. What were considered the forces of Light during the 8th Manifestation become the powers of Darkness in this, the 9th, simply because they are not in harmony with the Time-Spirit. In fact, we can say that there is really no question of absolute darkness and that all is only Light, with the sole problem that when the right harmony is not found that which is inherently bright moves out of step with the march of the Time-Spirit and no longer receives his illumination, therefore it becomes the Shadow of his figure and this then is the power of darkness, the Asura. In Medieval etchings of Cronus (Saturn or Kala), the Time-Spirit is often seen carrying a lantern and illuminating the path in front of himself. In this image we are given the understanding of the process: the Time-Spirit is the Light, in Time light is inherent, and this in fact is the key to the Earth's evolution.[1] It is Time, and in particular the Power of Time, Kali, that bears the entire evolution forward, She is the *motor* and light of the Manifestation, we can say, and it is she who determines whither the light is to fall. If we have the correct understanding of this process and the true knowledge of the Spirit of the Age, we can then know with precision what is Light and therefore what is Darkness, being no longer in harmony with the Time-Spirit. The asuric forces are only those elements which have become the wayward children and the opponents of Truth, for this light is Truth. Often though, these forces work with a partial truth, they cleverly hide behind the guise of spirituality: the truth of yesterday can be the falsehood of today.

The phenomenon is evident in our times. The forces from the Overmental plane, the 8th stage in the Puranic scale of creation, are trying to maintain their hold over the Earth: the *devas* (gods) which belong to this plane are becoming, for all practical purposes, the asuras (titans). The experiences and the words they communicate to their instruments on Earth are very beautiful, words of 'truth', 'love', 'the brotherhood of man', etc. The powers these instruments enjoy are often remarkable, their communities appear to flourish, there is always a tinge of the miraculous about everything they influence. But the real Knowledge is lacking, the real new consciousness is not theirs and the movement is 'old' and smells of death though it speaks continuously of newness: it merely is a masked religious consciousness. Most of us are not able to distinguish these subtleties because we have not a clear vision of the Time-Spirit's march, and this makes the work more difficult because vast numbers of people who turn toward spirituality are deviated by these forces into ways of half-truth, half-light.

Thus the very devas and elementals can become the asuras of today because they strive to maintain the consciousness of the 8th Overmental plane on the planet. Today the Time-Spirit moves on, and these forces must relinquish their hold.

We find that such forces easily establish themselves in Western society because of its lack of knowledge of the occult planes and forces and their influence on Earth,

---

[1] We measure astronomical distances by 'light years'. 186,000 miles per second is the speed of light. Numerologically this figure is 6, the Time-Spirit's point on the 9 circle.

and because of the society's strong affinity with the material consciousness which has difficulty in perceiving behind the appearances. In the East the same problem makes itself felt in spiritual realms, the hold that strong religious traditions of the past maintain over the seekers.

The War between the Dark and the Light is therefore as real today as it was yesterday and at the time the myths were conceived which narrate these subtle conflicts; they will in fact be eternally recurrent episodes until the Truth-Consciousness is well established. The War today has only become more subtle, for which reason Knowledge is essential in this Age. The asuric forces are now using the weapon of an over-exposure to spirituality; they create confusion by flooding the Earth consciousness with the possibility of a myriad paths, claiming that in this lies the Aquarian consciousness of universality, so that they may distract the seekers and dilute the forces that could unite to bring about the Reign of Truth. Whilst man cannot discriminate and understand that he must now move from the Overmental to the Supramental plane, whatever the name he gives it, and while he does not understand the difference between the two and in particular how it is to be recognised in the world's activities, the Earth cannot be brought to its rightful destiny of a birth of a higher level of consciousness.

Because humanity cannot accept the Time-Spirit's arrangement it has had to face destruction in its evolution, and therefore Kali is known as the Mother of Destruction as well as Creation, Death as well as Birth. The meaning of Immortality, the essential realisation of the gnostic being, is to be in a position through Knowledge to ever re-new oneself, to be in such harmony with the Time-Spirit, Saturn, that one consciously dies to whatever moves out of the ray of Kala, even if this be yesterday's sublime experience of God. The gnostic being can detect the face of Falsehood behind the mask of Truth.

We see therefore that in reality there is only Truth, but when the movement is not synchronised, when it is out of rhythm with the light of Time, it is Death, it is the corpse of Light. The task of the gnostic being of today is to conquer Death, the Shadow of Light. But first he must understand what Death is, where he is going, how he is to conquer, and what is his weapon.

The weapon is Truth, and the process is found through Knowledge which reveals to us that only that which is out of Time's rhythm is dead. All that which can find its rightful place within the scheme of Time is Immortal. For this Being, Death exists no longer and is a mere illusion. This is the perfection we seek, whereby we realise that each moment is indeed a perfection, if we can but see it. Without light, without knowledge, each moment is darkness and we are the living dead.

Our first step is *freedom from the Ignorance.*

But there are different phases in our understanding of freedom. In the beginning, before dedication to a yogic sadhana or any kind of work for the object of liberation, there was perhaps the illusion of being free. We say 'perhaps' because having been asleep at that time it is difficult to be certain what ideas we had of ourselves. Then with the first experience of Yoga it becomes evident that before we were not at all free and that we were bound to the lower nature, living in the illusion of freedom, in the illusion of enjoying the capacity to 'do'. Further along the way, however, the very notion of *freedom* undergoes a change because as we become aware that our bondage was an illusion, the veils of the ego, we begin to understand as well that freedom also is an illusion. At the moment of the radical change of consciousness, there is the dissolution of the notion of freedom: one realises one's dependency and the impossibility of escaping from this condition, but this dependency is on the Divine and we know ourselves to exist ever and always within the Divine. In union with this Divine Consciousness all quest for freedom vanishes, for freedom is a notion of the mind, born of the divided consciousness.

The only real liberation we can speak of lies in being free from the lower nature and being in the state of Truth which is being in tune with the Time-Spirit always—Objective Truth, unchanging and not dependent upon circumstances. It is the changeless element within change, the eternal within the temporal, the infinite within the finite. For Truth to be, there must be unity as well as the multiplicity; hence, Truth is not an experience of the Void. Truth is born with the Manifestation; beyond the Manifestation we cannot perceive or conceive of Truth. It is born of *Sat*, the first mode of the Creative Consciousness, pure existence within the Manifestation. Its symbol is the Sun, ☉.

Truth degenerated is Falsehood,—the loss of identification with the consciousness of the eternal. Therefore we can know that the Falsehood is an illusion because it is but the *shadow* which Truth casts when it becomes temporal, finite, identified only with the fragments of the multiple, when the rays of the Sun are no longer directly received. Walking with the Sun overhead no shadows are cast. But as can be seen by the symbol of the Sun ☉, Truth comes into being where there is the realisation of the One and the Many and an equal expression of both. *Sat*, pure existence, and *Satya*, Truth, are aspects of Capricorn, the sign which Saturn, the Time-Spirit, rules, and this is the cardinal point of *Cosmic Midday*, when the Sun is directly overhead and illuminating all and everything, casting no shadows. It is consequently the sign of *simultaneous time*, similar in a way to Pisces. But in Pisces there is an extinction of that which perceives, producing the experience of 'no time'. Pisces is the surrender of the faculty of *doing*, placing this in the hands of the Beloved; it is the abolition of all sense of ego as well as individuality.

The more complete realisation is in Capricorn, the true Victory over Death where the Dark is brought before the face of the Sun and thus *the shadow of Truth which is Death is dissolved,* for which reason Capricorn is the sign of the Golden Age. In Capricorn there is the possibility of extinction yet participation, and consequently there is simultaneous time. When both actions are there, there is the Multiple and the One, that which stands above and that which is engaged in the Play. This is the secret of simultaneous time, the key of which lies in the Sun, and the realisation of which belongs to Saturn, the Time-Spirit of Capricorn.

The minute details we are now studying in the Circle will bring us closer to this understanding and will give us some knowledge whereby we can see the direction we are to take, in relation to time on Earth and the rhythm and cycles of our lives. The purpose of the Avatars is to reveal this knowledge, and it must be in a concrete, not an abstract, way. If the Avatar speaks of the rhythm and the process needed for man to attune himself with the divine consciousness, this process must be found within his own life itself and it must be the manner in which he guides the Earth. The human incarnation is identical to the divine in the possibility of realisation. There would be no point to the appearance of such beings if there were an insuperable chasm between the two, which the human soul could never hope to bridge. As explained previously, the Incarnations represent the Earth's psychic being, the Spirit of the planet in evolution; so the moment of their appearance is the very confirmation that the time has come for humanity to experience that of which they are the messengers. We can even say: there is no question as to whether or not they are so-called 'divine' and that they are more 'of the Earth' than any human being, but it is only that they represent the phase which lies before man and of which he is ignorant. For this reason it is only rarely that an Avatar is recognised by the milieu in which he moves. At least until now this has been the privilege of only a small minority. Even rarer still is that his message be accepted by the spiritual provinces already existing on Earth, for his is the Spirit of the New which finds tremendous resistance in the achievements of spirituality of the past. He is generally crucified by his own people, as the legend of the Christ points out to us. Yet during this Age the spirit of the times can change this habit by the Power of Truth. If the Avatars are to be recognised today while the movement is in its prime, they too must be equipped with a Power which has not yet been in evidence in the past to the degree that would render it undeniable. If the Message is to be accepted, it must be through a power inherent in itself that the task is accomplished. We cannot hide behind the ignorance of humanity, for if the reign of Truth is here, it means that Truth will conquer, for it is invincible once it shows its full face. If this does not happen, the fault lies in the Message and the way in which it has been transmitted—or, ironically, in the Supreme Herself.

All the attainments of the Avatars are laid before the individual in an identical degree and potency. The only difference is that the divine incarnation is always guided in his steps through Earth existence by the strength the knowledge of his origin grants. He plunges into unconsciousness when he takes a body, it is true, because this is the way of birth at present, but this is to allow him to take on the full nature of the existing humanity. He places himself in the same conditions and from within these he must work. Yet he is assisted by the fact that his steps are sure, he moves with the consciousness of the divine power in him after realisation of the plane from whence he has descended and the awakening of the unity of his consciousness with the Divine's. In this way we can say he does not have to make an effort after the initial breakthrough as ordinary humanity does, for his energies are then needed in the pioneering work of the Age; he moves on to other pastures, while the Earth being must continue to cope with the impossible and rebellious condition of his human nature. The Avatar plunges into these conditions, liberates himself from them and then with the knowledge of the state of humanity, he reveals the next phase of evolution which mankind must achieve. His steps are flawless because identity with the Divine Power is so complete. Each individual can acquire this flawless energy and action if he merely carries out the same total identification with the divine Consciousness. The more perfect this is, the more he resembles the Messenger in his action. Yet the ways through which the Messenger proceeds are the same as the human's, his experiences are the same, and his realisations as well. He comes only to show humanity what it can attain if it does but one thing: it must make *the effort at identity of consciousness.* The Divine being is ever in this state though he may appear to be moving unconsciously, for to him reliance on the Divine Power is complete and there can never be a question of ignorance or unconsciousness. What he does not know, the Power in him knows and reveals when it is necessary for that to be revealed, for the benefit of the work he or she has come to do. Man, however, must make a *constant effort to remember,* to wake up and not to sleep.

If we say that the Absolute is light and not darkness, we are saying that this God we speak of is Shakti, for there is no possibility of the experience of light without movement, without vibration; and the instant there is movement there is the manifestation, the realm of the Divine Mother. Therefore, for beings in manifestation any concept or experience they can have of God must always be in the feminine form; all which until now we have known to be the experience of the Absolute is a vision of a part of her. As we are now formed, there is no way of going beyond: an experience of God without 'form' is inconceivable to us, be this only Light, or Darkness for that matter. Consequently the instant there is light, or sound, the Word, Om, there is Shakti, there is movement, and there is then also Time, Kala. In truth, Kala stands above all the gods, as the Indian scriptures state. And, as Ramakrishna has revealed to seekers, no matter what experience one can have it is only the Mother Kali, because we are ever in movement, ever in the Manifestation. This is the universality of Ramakrishna: to show mankind that the sole truth lies in the Divine Mother, and not in religions, as some would have us believe of his mission. His incarnation was a force to revolutionise the concepts of Indian spirituality, not to unify the world's religions. But in the womb of the Mother, in her secret recesses, there is That, which only she knows, to which only she holds the key.

This then is the basis of our study of the Circle divided into 9, which will help us to understand why in India this number is always associated with the worship of the Divine Mother. We are to penetrate the secrets of Time and thus to come to a fuller understanding of the Divine Mother, for if there is a division of the Circle which is able to reveal her in such an intimate way to Earth beings at the present stage of evolution, it is this one, which contains the knowledge of man's time. The gnostic being, the aspirant to immortality and the total transformation of the Earth nature, should have an accurate knowledge of what he is experiencing. In order to really achieve his aim it is not possible to have the experience of Shakti and call it something else, for in that way, at certain crucial points in the development, his ignorance will defeat him. It is essential for those who aspire to a radical and integral change to know that it is always the Manifest Divine with which they are dealing, who is the doer in any experience, and of whom the aspirant is only the instrument; for the work is difficult, and only in this way can the full transformation be accomplished. To conquer the forces of Ignorance it is necessary to engage in the battle with full knowledge of the powers at our disposal and with the tactics of warfare well assimilated: and in this case the tactics are the key to the workings of *Time*.

The beauty of the Circle lies in the fact that it is only a power of the Spirit, for the spiritual evolution, and has no meaning for those who seek mundane and temporal benefits. The mysteries of the Circle, once revealed, can only be of assistance to those who desire the divinisation of the Earth and of human nature. In the hands of the opponents of Truth it is a meaningless tool, because one of its purposes is the revelation of the Harmony and Perfection of the play. This revelation gives the aspirant the most potent element for the growth of his consciousness into a wider and more divine manifestation, bearing a subtle yet powerful effect upon each of his actions, showing him continuously that he is one with That, whose essence is Perfection, and that in spite of the surface darkness there is a way to see this perfection and be constantly aware of its harmonies. This is the magic potion in the work, that gradually changes the aspirant, moving him in the direction of a new vision and consciousness.

The consciousness of the gnostic being is characterised primarily by the ability to see beyond the appearances, with a vision of unity. But this we know has always been the state of realised souls; yet what makes the difference in today's realisation is that the integral yogi follows the perfection of the unfolding spirit in the events of the world with close precision, recognising the connecting link in the *surface events as well as in those deeply hidden.* That is, he sees the Divine in her full Cosmic Truth, in the state of waking consciousness, not in trance or semi-conscious states, or in the inebriated spasms of divine love ecstasies, from where one can perceive the Beloved in All. The experience is in the ordinary consciousness because this has evolved to a higher level and becomes a permanent state which cognises always in terms of unity, harmony and hence perfection. No aspect of the Earth's life and process is excluded and one need not abandon this creation in despair and seek the perfection on another plane. The gnostic being is capable of perceiving the three modes of action, the Divine Mother's creation, preservation and destruction, and walks in rhythm with her power at all times.

The Planets and the Circle of 9

The Circle of 9 is the best means we have of seeing this harmony, for, as has been stated, it is the atom, the cell, the individual and the Cosmos at one time, and reflects the perfection of the Transcendent in these forms of expression. Through this Circle we can show how the solar system becomes the cell, for it is, in effect, a cell in the body of the Divine Mother, the nucleus of which is the system's Sun.

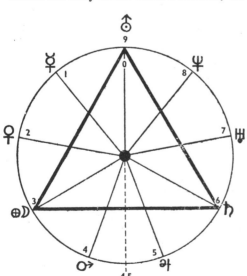

In the adjacent diagram the planets of our solar system are placed around the wheel, at the numbers to which their orbits correspond. Thus, Mercury is the first orbit, Venus is the second, Earth-Moon the third, and so on. The Asteroid Belt becomes the 4.5 orbit, having no crystallised centre. The Circle is completed with Pluto at the 9 point, which is also the 0; 0 in the System is the Sun, therefore Pluto brings the movement back to the Sun and this is the key to the planet's aspect of *transformation* which resides in the fact that it joins two movements, the solar descending light with the vital ascending power.

Further on it will be shown in detail how this joint action is indispensable in the transformation of matter.

In this way, the 9 Circle becomes the *numerical* and *planetary* representation of the symbol of the Serpent biting its Tail. Pluto is the farthest known planet, yet at the same time it is the closest in that its action is to join the two movements; its power is in the union it brings about which is captured in the Greek myth of Pluto, the King of the Dead. Hades is the hidden divine Energy in the Underworld of Matter, and in Pluto lies the key to its transformation. The discovery of the planet in 1930 signified that the time had come when man could begin the full experience of the physical transformation, the transformation of the living cell. It marked also the beginning of the Atomic Age, because that very year the third element of the atom, the neutron, was found, making nuclear power a utilisable reality for earth life. In fact, in all aspects it is in the mysterious third element that the secret of the transformation of matter can be solved.

Pluto (Hades) is the fertility God. His seed is the necessary ingredient in the process of transformation. In the myth, Pluto rapes Persephone who is the Earth and a portion—the soul-spark in fact—of the Divine Mother, Demeter. Therefore Persephone is obliged to remain a part of evolving matter. The marriage of Pluto and Persephone represents the redemption of Matter, which is not complete unless the three elements, Pluto, Persephone, as well as Demeter, become an integrated part of the process. On the scale we have reproduced, this process is found in the Sacred Triangle, consisting of the planets Pluto (9), Saturn (6), and Earth-Moon (3). Demeter, the Divine Mother, is 6, and Persephone, or Kore, is 3. But where Persephone is the Divine Mother is, for they are essentially one and are interchangeable, and this is the significance of the Moon combined with the Earth in the scale. In fact, the satellite of the Earth is a unique phenomenon of our solar system. In astronomy they are termed the *Binary Planets*; and moreover, in this way we can perceive the constant interchange of the 6-3 points. Actually it is only with the appearance of the 3 that the work of divinisation of the Earth is stabilised. Thus the Divine Mother remains *continuously involved* in the process of transformation.

This language may appear somewhat obscure, or perhaps too esoteric, for the student. It will, however, become clearer as we proceed with the study, and the student should especially make an effort to bear in mind what has so far been said about the Sacred Triangle and the evolution. Clarity in the study will be granted by the harmonies themselves. For example, if we speak of the Earth as the planet upon which the Trinity incarnates, for which it is brought into the play of creation, this can be further verified by the fact that the Earth occupies the 3rd point, or the 3rd orbit; hence, the Law of Three, from the Divine Trinity down to the individual's psychic being and to the simple atom, is always the supreme pattern and rhythm of the planet.

The laws of Matter are rigid. If one succeeds in breaking these laws or altering them there can be a new course. It is this way regarding any transformation. There must first be a knowledge which will reveal higher laws; there must be an understanding of existent laws in the light of an occult knowledge. The purpose of the Gnostic Circle, particularly the phase of its 9 division, is to enable us to fully understand the occult laws which govern the structure of Matter, of the subtle and dense physical, for it is only by knowing the laws pertaining to both these realms that the actual transformation can come about. The 9 Circle represents the cell as well as the macrocosm with relation to the Earth. We have seen therefore that the Law of Three is essential to comprehend, and then '3 × 3', which represents the full scale or the fullest possibility of transformation given to the human race at this time. Humanity so far has progressed through two of these triads successfully; it is now time for the last to manifest. This is the deeper significance of the three newest planets. They are the physical bodies which govern the last triad of the Sacred Triangle.

The Cancer symbol is a picture of the protective atmosphere of the Earth, what is termed the Van Allen Belt. Cancer is the sign of Prakriti, gestation and maternity. Its significance and shape is similar to the Belt's, a covering which protects the Earth from the cosmic rays. Likewise Cancer is the protective sack of the evolving soul. But at the same time it is the Ignorance, for it impedes the penetration of the higher light. Therefore Cancer is the ego, and the ego's function is to veil the light of the soul until the time of its birth, just as the Belt is a veil of the Earth until the time of the Earth's Birth when this covering can be safely shed, or at least altered. This is the egg in which we live, and when the moment of the Great Transformation arrives it will coincide with a radical alteration in the Belt, so subtle however that it may not be immediately observable. The Earth will become better equipped to handle the purer cosmic rays which at this point would destroy it but which at a later stage will be essential for the maintenance of the new body, for it is precisely these rays that will be its 'food'. The exploration and release of nuclear energy is one aspect that can lead to this great physical change.

If we consider the zodiac with respect to the Belt, we see that the openings at the poles correspond to Cancer and Capricorn which we have termed the *evolutionary axis* of the planet. The Precession will coincide with these poles in 2,000 years.

The influence of our times is mainly Sagittarius, as has been described previously, and with this comes the impulse of expansion and consequently of travel, which has brought us to the need for exceeding the limits of the Earth through space travel. But there are some problems which face us in this respect: namely, the question of the barriers imposed by Space and Time.

Travelling in space will be a realistic experience for those who are in the voyaging capsule, and in order to travel the vast distances which inter and extra-galactic exploration require, the travellers must break through the same barriers one does in sleep. They would then experience a trip of 9 years as perhaps 9 months, or even 9 days. But the experience on Earth remains what it is according to Earth time, and therefore the races of Earth lose contact with the beings sent into space because they are obliged to remain within the Earth's time cycle. Thus if an expedition had been sent to another galaxy, say during the last Aquarian Age, 26,000 years ago, the travellers who, having had to break through these barriers for the trip to have been at all possible—considering the requirements and limitations of the human Earth body—would have experienced it as one of 25 or even 7 years. They might return to Earth during this Age and if they were unaware of the Age of Darkness that the Earth has lived through since their departure, supposing that at that time the Earth was populated by a superior race, they would be remarkably surprised to find a planet inhabited by peoples who have lost all knowledge of the earlier race's existence. If there was truly such an accomplished civilisation on Earth in the past, it would be possible to regain knowledge and contact with that remote civilisation in this way. That is, in and with the physical body and without the necessity to discard the body, a link with the past and future is quite feasible.

This Aquarian Age can bring many unexpected events and surprises to humanity, things that we tend to look upon as a sort of science fiction.

In order to solve the problem of Time in the adventure of space, which is the real barrier that must be broken, it is necessary for man to evolve a means whereby the experience of the traveller and the place from where he has begun his trip maintain the same relation to time. As well it is necessary for the traveller to be in a condition to withstand the shock of the plunge into the dimension of Time—let us call it the 4th dimension. This can happen if the traveller moves in an element which is already known to Earth beings with occult knowledge; the subtle physical plane where the experience of Time is different, the 4th dimension of Space.

Until now we have not really needed to solve this problem, because man is only on the periphery of actual penetration into space. If the civilisation finds it necessary to continue in its progress a new system will become imperative. At that time there will be the joining of the experience of the Scientist and the Spiritualist because it is the yogic experience which reveals to us the reality of the 4th and other dimensions of space, and it is the scientific experience which brings the necessity to act and create within those dimensions. In the 4th we begin to enter the experience of simultaneous time which gives us the solution to the problem. But both voyager and base man must have the capacity to live the same experience together. Herein lies the difficulty.

In the work in which we are now engaged we are primarily concerned with the experience of Time in Matter, because only by discovering the occult rhythm of its workings can we begin, in a concise way, to break the veils of the Ignorance that encompass the Earth, both psychologically and materially. The question may appear very materialistic and not at all related to the spiritual quest; but it is not so. If anything, it is beyond both the spiritual and scientific quests and reflects the true destiny of the evolution, wherein spirituality as it is now conceived as well as science, will soon appear to us like cave-men gropings, a consciousness old and unreal. There can be no *essential* and *real* breakthrough in the realm of the Spirit unless Matter is carried along in the experience and participates in equal measure. This brings us to a totally new view and possibility of action. When man's consciousness expands as indicated by the Sagittarian 9th Manifestation Time-Spirit, there is automatically the will to expand physically. But in this mankind is faced with dramatic problems. As space travel is being planned and carried out today it is impractical, for scientists who intend to probe the vast distances of our Galaxy, and others as well, are immediately faced with the Time-Space Monster and beyond its iron jaws they cannot penetrate making use of the known procedures. There must be a solution to the puzzle which can obviously come about only by living in the 4th dimension and in that state to unravel the secret, carrying the physical body as well into the experience.

The question is: How is man to surpass the Time-Space Monster in his present structure? He can perhaps come close to the solution by travelling on a 'beam' which is yet new to us, which carries us at a speed that surpasses light and sound: the beam of consciousness. Consciousness is light and light is time: the mystery is unravelled by the key of Time.

Once we have begun to pierce the veils of ignorance the Light will make itself evident and illumine our path. The transformation of matter will itself reveal the means, for when we have touched that 'beam' we are approaching the secret to the transformation of the physical body of the human species.

Nuclear power can serve as a tool in the action of breakthrough. This year, 1974, is the initiation of the Breakthrough; 1975 will call forth a definite measure to resolve the problem of ill-use of nuclear power once a certain 'saturation' has been reached because of the great threat to Earth existence as we now know it. When India became the 6th nuclear power in the world, the time had been reached. With respect to the 9 Circle, the 6th point is Saturn, Kala, which is the planetary ruler of India.

11

The Enneagram

THERE ARE MOMENTS in quietude and silence when for an instant we break through to an all-inclusive consciousness. For a moment in the waking state we identify ourselves with the totality, and by doing so, for that all too brief span, we become That. At the same time then we know that there is nothing but God, the whole of this immense infinite universe is the Supreme—each pulsation, each breath we take is within the Being of God. If the experience prolongs itself we are over-whelmed. It is not possible to live in this consciousness for too long a time, because the realisation of Infinity is too powerful for the mind of man. Yet for that moment, when we went beyond mind, there was the knowledge by identity: one became That.

There is however a way in which the experience of the Infinite and the Eternal can be made permanent in us. If we draw the perception back into ourselves, into the point, the spark of Divine Consciousness, we know that the Soul is in effect the very Infinite and Eternal we perceive beyond. When it is drawn back into the inner Point, we realise that man is truly the image of God, he is the Immortal, the Vast, the Right, the True—the Divine in evolution. In the human soul lie all the secrets of the Absolute, because it is That and this is the core of ourselves. Just as the Circle of 9 is the Cosmos and at once the cell and the atom, so we know that the same proportions pertain to our own experience of God. It is this essential truth that the great spiritual leaders of our known cycles have stressed: We are That. In the experience of that instant we come to know the state of *Sat*, pure existence. It is only this experience brought into every moment of our lives that will signify the full liberation of the Earth from the Ignorance. This is the eternal message of the Avatars, and the secret of Capricorn.

The Circle of 9 can be drawn in the following manner, called the *Enneagram* by G. I. Gurdjieff. He used this means to pass on the knowledge of the Law of Three and the Law of Seven (the octave) to which the Three is related. The symbol is obtained by converting a fraction of the octave ($1/7$) into a whole number, and following the numbers in the order obtained to draw the diagram. They are 0.142857.[1] In the figure the 3, 6, 9 are absent, which are the numbers of

---

[1] The enneagram of Gurdjieff is numbered clockwise, whereas we prefer to number it in the above manner, according to the development of the zodiac, or more precisely as the Sun and planets revolve, eastward.

the Law of Three, the inner Triangle. Thus, by combining the two the
Enneagram is formed, and all the
numbers from o to 9 are included.
However, we have gone further in
the study than Gurdjieff explained
by actually relating these laws to our
cycles on Earth and to the overall
pattern of the evolution of the planet's major organic species, man. .

Gurdjieff, and later P. D. Ouspensky, spoke of the *Ray of Creation*
which this symbol represents, starting
in its descent with the Absolute, then
all the Galaxies, the Milky Way, the

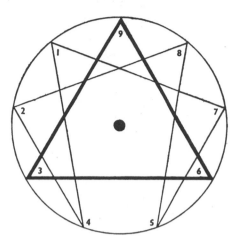

Sun, the Planets, the Earth and finally ending with the Moon—in all, seven rays.[1]
Each of these 'Worlds' is bound by a certain number of laws, augmenting with the
descent until at the level of our planet there are 48. This number would correspond to our Greater Circle, page 25, where, in fact, as far as the Map of Evolution goes there are 48 Manifestations that the Earth must pass through in order
to complete a major cycle. We could call these the evolutionary laws of the
planet which are progressive and at once simultaneous, and the map could be
spoken of in relation to the individual as well, just as we speak of the Circle of 9
as both macrocosmic and microcosmic. The Triangle with respect to this Ray of
Creation would be the intervention points where a 'shock' is necessary to keep a
movement on its proper course, pertainable also to the life of the microcosm. Yet
Ouspensky explains that in the descent the Absolute's will does not manifest beyond
the creation of the Galaxies. He states that in order to intervene the Absolute would
have to break all the Laws, which It would find impossible to do. Further, Ouspensky gives the analogy of man and his body. Man would represent the Absolute
and the cell is the last element in the Ray over which, Ouspensky states, man has no
control or any possibility of intervention in the course of its development. He can
influence the *tissues* of his human body, but nothing beyond that.[2] This is where we

---

[1] In *In Search of the Miraculous*, Ouspensky records Gurdjieff's explanation of the Enneagram
which is the description of the Shakti, though he does not use this term. He speaks of it as the key to
perpetual motion, and the symbol which contains all the secrets of the cosmos. Ouspensky's transcrip-
tion of Gurdjieff's words on page 285 to 294 of the book, reveals an accurate knowledge of the Divine
Mother, and perhaps the Indian origin of the symbol, which he may well have obtained during his travels in India.

[2] *The Fourth Way*, P. D. Ouspensky, Chapter VIII.

must differ with the teachings. The Absolute intervenes in the lower worlds, of which our planet is one of the lowest, and this is accomplished precisely by the Evolutionary Avatars whose lives and essence are attuned in a very precise way to the Will of the Absolute. In this study we shall be able to show this, and also we must show how, in fact, the last phase of Sri Aurobindo's supramental yoga, which the Mother carried out on the *cosmic* level, is to bring about a change *in the cells themselves*, by which man is eventually to be capacitated to intervene in the mechanical laws and bear a pressure of transformation on the cells of the human body, by the experience gained in yoga and the collaborating descent of a higher power which reveals to us the laws of higher planes, termed the 'Supramental' by Sri Aurobindo.

If Ouspensky and Gurdjieff have stated that the Absolute cannot intervene in the laws of the lower worlds it is perhaps because they were not aware of the information we are able to put forward, which makes the study of the Enneagram one of the most fascinating of our times, bringing it from the realm of theory and the abstract into our very lives and into the concrete evolutionary pattern of our planet. We can agree with most of what has been said of the Ray of Creation but our intention is to clarify certain points which we can do by means of the knowledge and experience of the 'interventions'. Without the periodic interventions hinging on the Sacred Trinity, the evolution would have had no hope or possibility of accomplishing its task of self-discovery and of continuing on its predetermined course.

The Gurdjieff system places the Moon at the lowest level and considers it responsible for all man's mechanical actions. This would be Prakriti in our terminology, and her sign is Cancer, ruled by the Moon. She is indeed the force controlling the lower nature of mankind as well as the organisation and functioning of all organic life of a certain level. When this life is to burst into a higher order of things it then becomes necessary to break away from her rule and for this the process of yoga is imperative. Gurdjieff disconnects ordinary humanity from other influences, such as the planets, the Sun and higher ones because, he says, the centre which is the receiving apparatus of those influences is lacking in mankind as a whole. It is through *essence*, Gurdjieff states, that man is able to come into contact with higher influences. It is certainly true that the higher worlds influence Earth primarily in terms of the masses and not individually, and we have seen that the more evolved man is the more in harmony he is with certain laws that undeveloped man never perceives. In this respect the gnostic being may appear to be even more bound by laws than the ordinary man, but these laws are of a much more refined and subtle order and therefore their harmony is easier to perceive once one is in the consciousness of gnosis. The arrangement is essentially very simple and the gnostic being moves out of the influences as recorded in the movement of the planets and Sun in the actual sky, into the sphere of the subtle occult circles that are non-existent for the majority, which indicate the play and harmony of which he is a part.

The stumbling block that one faces in these teachings is that the question of the equality of the macrocosmos and microcosmos is not sufficiently a part of the realisation. This *Ray of Creation*, as well as other systems which explain the process of Creation, goes from larger body to smaller and makes *space* and therefore *time* a major rod for measuring the possibilities of evolution, i.e., the smallest is farthest removed from the Absolute and therefore has the least possibility of falling under its direct influence and laws. Yet this can be misleading, for in the realm of cosmic harmonies the question of space and time can be the experience of another dimension where in us the vast is equal to the small, as the Circle is equal to the Point, as the 9 is equal to the o. In the level of higher perception, the farthest is closest and the closest farthest, and man is particularly equipped with a device, let us say, which is his direct connection in consciousness with the Absolute, and wherein he can find the resolution to this problem of time and space. His soul is the very universe within him. It is in his soul that he can know himself to be equal and one with That in every way, and therefore it is in his soul that he must find the answer to all things—the higher knowledge he is now to achieve. With the full realisation of his soul, which would mean the shedding of the outer darkness and its entire liberation from the veils of ego, man then knows himself to be a cell in the vast body, but equal to it in every way, therefore there is no end to the possibilities of his evolution, just as there is no end to the development of the universes. Through his soul he can enter into a dimension which does away with the accepted concepts of time and space and shows him the hidden reality of things, which he can in no way perceive in the normal consciousness. The psychic realisation is the first step and it shows man that the Absolute is lodged not only in the structure of the vast universes and the galaxies, but it is his fundamental core, and the core of each cell and atom. The Law of Three is the very essence of *all* creation. In the most concrete manner therefore he can transform himself into an 'image of the Lord'. In creation there is no essential reality to *vast* and *small*. These are the terms of the human mind. Man should now be closer to this understanding, having released the tremendous energy in the minute atom which, if handled in the proper way, can bring about the most extraordinary transformation. He knows from the experience of nuclear power that size has nothing to do with potency. In the same way space has nothing at all to do with the experience of oneness.

There is a way in which man can experience this concretely, and it is by passing into a dimension where the laws of space and time are transmuted. This dimension is as real as those we are now aware of and it is only by opening ourselves to that secret dimension that we can truly speak of the unity and oneness of all things.

Transformation of Matter: The New Body

Awareness of this dimension has been restricted until now to certain centres and parts of the being, the spiritual, the mental and perhaps in rare cases the vital. The last, the Physical, appears as yet closed to the awareness of this dimension. But a work has begun which will slowly reveal what is being accomplished in this field, rendering the cells of the body conscious participating elements in the transformation of matter.

And why not? Is not the cell equipped with the very same properties as man, the universe and the Absolute? Size is immaterial and has no meaning when the three elements of the Sacred Triangle are present, which is the determining factor in the capacity to become consciously equal to the Supreme. If the three are not present in any given particle or substance, it only means that in order for that element to realise unity it must join itself with two other particles thereby together completing the triad and evolving as a group toward the realisation of Unity. The same pertains to the evolution of man. It is in the joining of three, thereby producing the phenomenon of $3 \times 3 = 9$, that gives the possibility of the full transformation of the earth nature, from spirit to matter and vice versa. Each element of the Trinity bears within it another triad, and this is the combination of 3×3, the occult Trinity, an occurrence apparently only possible by Earth incarnation. There is nothing in creation that falls out of the structure of the Triad, only we must train our eyes to see in a special way in order to become aware of the law.

Let us observe the laws with respect to the conception and gestation of man in his present structure, as yet too close to the animal. The sperm and the ovum join and these two elements are met by a third which is to be the child but which in the beginning is concealed in the process; one part of the trinity appears to be absent. The soul of the infant is the third element which in fact is tightly veiled until many years after his growth, and sometimes never reveals itself. In the combination there is therefore the Spirit (Father), Matter (Mother), and the Soul (Child) in between, or an outcome of this union of the first two.

From the microscopic sperm man grows, and the process of procreation, when viewed from 'above', with a new consciousness of man's possible evolution, is wholly animalistic, is gross, is the workings of the most unrefined energies, which produce a child that must move through years and years of ignorance, a product of the Inconscience, never fully guaranteed that he will see the light of his soul reality in his lifetime. But there is a way in which energies of a much finer substance can be utilised in order to bring about the manifestation of a soul on this planet which would be freed of the necessity to pass through the Ignorance and the Inconscience, because the means of its manifest origin would correspond to a plane which is as yet far above, so to speak, and which man ignores. For this to come about all the elements of which we have spoken must be there, and the process of conception must be undertaken, but now devoid of animalistic and degrading forces; and though the same elements of the actual procreation process are present, they are experienced in the form of pure energies and are free from the taints of desire, lust and the other propensities of man's lower nature. The sex force is there, but in a totally transmuted sense; it is the root of the movement, yes, but in a completely conscious way it joins itself with the descending power of the spirit and together these unite to bring about the new body, which is a reflection of the higher transmuted energies that have been used in the process. The body that comes about from this union is a reflection of a higher consciousness and an outcome of a manipulation of energies as yet unknown to the races of Earth. It can be termed a body of light because it is born of Light, the light of a higher consciousness and power. It is a body which is conscious of its divine origin and does not bear the stamp of death in its cells, because it has not come about through the desires of the sex nature and act.

The human foetus can only be conceived once there has been the *quickening* by the orgasm in the male which ejaculates the sperm that the ovum receives. The sperm is necessary, as is the ovum. And the *quickening* is an essential part of the process. In the same way sperm as well as the ovum are necessary for the new birth and body, but these must be the *divine counterparts* of the dense body's manifestations. The sperm is pure energy, its quickening process is achieved through the mechanics of breath and is devoid of all desire and lust. The ovum is the transformed gamete, the cells of which live in a state of conscious Immortality. That is, the matter which is to feed this 'foetus' must come from one who has conquered death, whose cells, though they be a part of the old creation, have realised that death is an illusion and sex, which has been needed to bring birth about, is the way of Death. So the new body must take shape in a Mother who is Immortal, a pure and luminous receptacle which must receive a powerful and transformed or transmuted vital force that has wholly given itself to the divine descending light. The vital force now transmuted into *ojas* is the root which joins with the subtle sperm of pure energy from above and these are poured into the receiving womb of the mother. In this process neither space nor time nor any other barrier are of relevance. And the essential factor is that this 'breath of the divine Spirit' is received in the higher vital centre and from there the transmuted vital force comes forth: this is the centre of Breath. The lowest chakra is merely the seat of the energy which by transmutation is passed into the higher vital situated at the navel, a chakra which has the capacities, once released from the veils of Ignorance, to generate a much more powerful and purer energy. It becomes the centre of the life force of the divine man, far from the animal, free of the bondage of the lower nature; and above all free of the illusion of death.

So, by the marriage of more subtle energies man can evolve into a new species. There are substances that are hidden to our eyes and even to the eyes of our most potent microscopes and electronic devices, which when released into and through the human organism can bring about the transformation of the physical into a body of finer substance, immediately reflective of these finer energies. This has proven to be in no way an impossible feat; it is simply that the final stage of the process now underway has not been fulfilled, the time element of this 'gestation' period having not yet been completed; for this is something that is not removed from the whole of evolution. It is not an occurrence that can or will take place unrelated to and disconnected from the conditions of the whole and the boundaries of Time. First it takes place on the cosmic level, a release of power similar to the release of nuclear energy which was unattainable until 1930. The process continuing, there will be further steps which will impose a variation in the atmosphere that will ultimately provide certain terrain for the uncovering of the new light of which we speak. This energy is not yet detectable because its rate of oscillation is too quick —its *speed*, and therefore its constituent matter, is so tremendous that it is only on the subtle plane that one can see the components. There is nonetheless a workable process to bring this substance into the visible and more solid field of Earth life, but for this to take place both realms, the subtle and the more dense, must evolve. That is, the energy that constitutes the gross physical must find a process whereby it can accelerate its oscillations and the subtle physical must be made to slow down its rate of vibration. In this way the two planes can join.

It is this process, reflected in the union of the sperm and the ovum, both captured in the signs Leo and Cancer of the zodiac, that is to produce the new body and ultimately the divine race of men. The fecundation system is similar to that which man now knows only it is necessary to have the being fully open and receptive to planes above, able to contain the descending power, which appears to be too intense for most of humanity. To acquire this receptivity it is necessary to be entirely free from ego and the pull of the lower nature. The sex instinct which is now on the level of the animal must come to know its divine Purpose and Functioning.

For the accomplishment of the work, it is evident that there must be an action from *above* and one from *below*. But this must be nonetheless within the sphere of physical matter. The plane of which we speak is the closest to ours *in a complete way*. Our actual physical bodies may be composed of certain subtler sheaths, but the subtle physical is also complete in itself and is not simply a 'sheath' of the gross physical. It is a physical body only of a more subtle substance. Such a body does not come naturally with birth but is rather formed by the acquisition of finer energies through the process of yoga. The plane exists in itself and there may be bodies native to it alone, but in order for this plane to merge with the grosser physical and imbue the world of the more dense matter with its finer energies, it is necessary for such a work to be carried out while there is a direct connection with both these planes. The work must be done having one foot here and one foot there, so to speak. Moreover, in order for it to be possible for the entity who is doing the transitional work to complete the process, there must be sustenance received from *above* and *below* so that the links with and between these planes are never broken during the process. At a certain point the gross physical may need to be discarded, when the subtle body is sufficiently formed, in order for the other substance to materialise; up to that point the connection is necessary. The dense body is a sort of pedestal for the work until the subtle one is sufficiently concrete. It is an instrument that decays when its function is over. This would not be death it must be understood. In fact, it has nothing to do with the process of death we know. It is a degeneration of the physical cells that have been stripped of their energy which is fully absorbed by the other more subtle body. In our transitional stage this is the necessary process, until matter is fully transformed. Without this 'death' the final and most important stage in the process could perhaps not fulfil itself.

The factor of Time is most important. For this reason our study centres on time. The rate of oscillation of the gross physical cells must be accelerated in order to be in a position to generate energy which is absorbable by the subtle body, or, let us say, which will go to the formation of that body. But there is also the action from above, determined by the laws of higher planes and powers, and these laws work on the energy of those planes, thereby permitting the union of the two, and furnishing the 'seed' of the body.

The action of transformation is going on, and it has not much to do with the evolution of humanity into a moralistically better breed. There is a teaching for each level and a process of development for each level. There is a yoga for larger numbers and one for a reduced group. This latter continues its work irrespective of the pace of the other levels and it is only when the actions of the lower levels threaten to interfere with the higher that destruction of the lower must take place. The world can continue for thousands of years immersed in the Ignorance and left relatively to itself, but when the time comes for the higher worlds to manifest, there is nothing whatsoever *from below* that can interfere with this manifestation.

For the ordinary consciousness this is impossible, and more impossible is it for one in the ordinary consciousness to understand what is obstructive and needs to be removed and what is a part of the process, irrespective of the external appearances. The work of a supramental yoga is the higher work and it determines what the conditions below should be and when the conditions below are obstacles to its realisation. With a disunified vision it is impossible to perceive such a gradation and understand its laws. When the time comes for a thorough breakthrough from the higher plane, then circumstances and conditions below, on Earth, must be such as to not interfere.

Destruction therefore is not based on principles of good, bad, virtuous, or the like. What to the ordinary consciousness might appear bad, in the higher light is the necessary ingredient for the accomplishment of the work. This we cannot know, we can only have faith in the power of the Divine Mother. From the study of certain acts of destruction we can know through their rhythm whether they are for the purpose of the Work and also what the obstacle is that is to be removed. All destruction or disharmony is not the outcome of the Falsehood. Often it is the Power of Truth at work, to secure the successful emergence of its reign. It is evident nonetheless that the closer we come to a pure translation from the plane of Truth, the less destructive methods will be needed upon Earth. We must view Death in the same light, and we must be able to recognise when it is the God of Falsehood at work and when it is merely a dissolution of the body which is being transformed into its finer counterpart. The Gnostic Circle gives us the key and answer to the enigma.

Following the Circle of 9 with the planets placed around it, let us go through all the steps in the process of transformation of the physical in an orderly manner. We will consider that this Circle represents a period of 9 years, and these 9 years would be equivalent to the 9 months of gestation of a human being. To begin with, we can say therefore that 9 years is the amount of time needed to form a new body by means of an occult process which is still new to Earth. Equally new is the quality of this body which shall not be fully known until the first overt materialisation on this plane takes place.

At the beginning of the cycle there is the necessity to become in possession of a certain force that is unknown to mankind. This force is closely allied to breath, or we can say it uses breath as a channel for its workings. A gnostic being who has this energy would have acquired it by a process of yoga whereby the Shakti had prepared the instrument in a certain way in order that it could become receptive of such a power and able to withstand the force without the instrument's being broken in any way. This requires that the subtle centres be fully opened and it pertains to both the *rise* of energy and the *descent* of the power. In both cases there must be a preparation. The entire period needed for such an accumulation is not relevant at this point, since we are here concerned with the action which begins with the gestation of the new transitional body. From X years on it would then take 3 years for full mastery to be acquired which would then produce the 'embryo'. The action however is carried out on the subtle planes while maintaining the link with the dense physical. By the third year the agent is in a position to join this power to the vital energy from

9

below and this combination begins to form the new body. Between the 4th and 5th years the body is built, though in the foetal state—that is, without the consciousness poured into it as yet. The action is still on the level of a 'physical' process. At this time the work reaches a very critical period when it is necessary for the gross physical to be broken down and the full energies are to be entirely directed to the new body. The dense one has fulfilled its purpose. But once this break has been made there must be a feeding still for the physical that remains until the time when it is to be finally discarded. Thus the vital energy must be supplied from without, and slowly the consciousness of the gross physical is withdrawn and the being is able to retire completely into the new body. After the 5th year this occurs, and from the 6th on there is the process on the subtle planes which prepares for the final materialisation. This means that the atmosphere of the Earth must as well be conditioned to accept the new body; or else another means must be devised so as to allow this form to subsist on Earth, such as the preparation of a particular location on the planet which is able to 'house' such a body in isolation from the atmosphere. All this entails therefore a universal transformation. The work on the subtle physical body in transition is not merely a question of the being who is accomplishing the task. It is a cosmic work, of a dimension which embraces the whole planet and the conditions in the cosmos as well. We shall better explain this as the study proceeds, when we will show how in fact the very activities of the solar system are related to the process we have here described.

Man must understand that he lives in ignorance, and this very ignorance obliges him to be utilised for the effects of procreation in a completely unconscious way. For this reason Nature has made use of desire as the stimulating force to accomplish her ends of propagation of the races, which has its seat in the sex centre and from there feeds the ego nature of man. Due to man's egoistic nature procreation has evolved in the manner we know. Man cannot be a conscious instrument because he is centred in his own meagre interests, his own small world, his pleasures, his lusts, his greed, and above all his ignorance. Being thus ignorant of the higher laws which govern the creation, he is incapable of consciously collaborating to be the channel for the descent of a higher humanity upon Earth. The process of which we speak is one that should take place in total consciousness, or in an individual that is at least totally surrendered to the will of the Supreme Shakti. There is no question of one's desires determining such a birth or the formation of such a new being and body. It is a process which depends exclusively upon the growth of a higher consciousness; and as this perfects itself, so will the process become ever more perfect.

The first step in order to prepare oneself for the event is the complete liberation from the lower nature, the total mastery over the vital force and the most absolute control over the desire nature. The vital centre must be thoroughly transformed and purified before there can be the beginning of the transformation of the physical leading to the creation of a new body, and the real condition of immortality. The life force in the body must become conscious of its immortality, that it is one with the source of life, and that there is a means whereby the contact with this eternal Source can be permanently maintained for the sustenance of a more divine physical. This must become the weapon of the Divine Mother to conquer death, and for this reason we see in the zodiac that in Capricorn, the sign of the victory over death, Mars, the planet of the vital force, is in *exaltation*. Mars is here Kartikeya of Indian tradition, the Divine Mother's warrior son, whose *vāhana* is the Peacock, the bird of Victory, the bird of India. The energy of Mars is no longer limited to the lowest chakra, the sex centre, restricted and enfeebled in its workings by the darkness of the ego nature. It is the vital force immortal, which has known the process of continuing renewal, which knows no death. This is the true meaning of Mars, a planet which traditional astrology connects with death. It is not death, for death does not exist in the plan of creation, at least in the form we now live it; therefore it is nonexistent in the zodiac, and Mars becomes rather the very weapon to conquer the illusion of Death.

After the complete transformation of the vital force, the actual transformation of the physical cells can begin, wherein the more intense work of expansion of consciousness is required. For this reason the planet of the expansion of consciousness, Jupiter, is known to be exalted in Cancer, the sign of the cells.

In the formation of the divine body, Mars is the movement from below, and Venus is the subtle physical plane from above. This divine coupling occurs on Earth, where the traditional marriage of the two must take place. In fact, in the solar system Earth is positioned between these two. Until now our planet has turned more toward the field of Mars, and this in ignorance of its divine aspects. And consequently the Earth is a place of violence, of destruction, and the other distorted reflections of the divine energy and power. Mars becomes for us a planet of war, of strife and lust—when its true meaning is the power to conquer Death and be the source of the eternal and ever-renewing divine vital energy; Mars must be the force or thrust of creation for the seed of the Sun, which is the reason that the Sun is exalted in Aries, the sign of Mars.

On the other side there is Venus who offers to mankind the harmonies and perfections of the heavens, the true love, the divine beauty, the new forms that as yet belong only to the subtle physical world which she represents. And therefore the planet is veiled in the sky and has not revealed herself to Earth. When scientists manage to take the first pictures of Venus beneath its mysterious mists, the subtle physical will have completely married the denser plane, or at least have come very close to it. Mars and Venus will have joined, in the true divine way, and not in the way of ignorance and animality that we now know.

In this process we have the key signs, Capricorn and Pisces, the former being the exaltation of Mars, the latter the exaltation of Venus. Thus these two signs signify in their marriage the only possible divinisation of the Earth. It is through their union on this plane that the new body is formed; or rather it is through this *reunion* of Kore and Demeter that the new body emerges, representative of the new creation of divine men, the gnostic beings to come.

We are studying in this section the formation of a new body through supraphysical means, formed within the time cycle of 9 years equivalent to the 9 months of the ordinary gestation. But what will this being look like? What will its condition be when it is materialised? Will it appear in the form of an infant?

The process of birth now carried out on the planet has evolved according to the level of consciousness of the species. A soul incarnates as a babe because this reflects the drop into inconscience that it makes in order to join the evolution of the planet. Such a process must be fulfilled by all beings, no matter what their spiritual destiny is to consist of later on in life. The soul clothes its light and begins from nescience to slowly work through the dim veils of the Ignorance and Inconscience until it manages to regain a part of the light it possessed before its plunge into the density of this plane. And due to the distorting influence of Mind, with the subsequent need of development of its faculties—that is, perception subject to the instrument of Mind and the senses,—the soul is obliged to recede into the background during human growth, relegated to a prison of darkness due to the half-knowledge of the environment into which it comes, sometimes never to fully emerge. Our entire gestation and birth process is reflective of the state of ignorance prevailing which obliges a being to commence life in the form of a helpless and dependent creature, in many ways inferior to the animal, a creature which must learn the most primary and essential functionings in order to graduate to a higher degree on the path of human growth. We cannot expect this to change in any way, given the present conditions of the race. While man is a semi-conscious individual, his gestation and status at birth must be in accord with the consciousness prevailing. It is evident however that if the consciousness is radically and permanently widened, and if there is a more cosmic awareness taking the place of the old views and capacities, this will inevitably have to manifest in the way a soul descends into this plane. The work progresses in a global fashion; if we pretend to alter man's most essential part, the seed of himself, the consciousness to which he owes his very breath, then we are obliged to speak simultaneously of a new body and its 'gestation.' We can see then that the *new-born* will reflect at once this new consciousness, and this makes it possible for us to understand some of its details and characteristics.

To begin with, it cannot appear in the form of an infant, as is now the case. It must be a being who steps into the cycle already reflecting to a certain measure the wide and full truth-consciousness. It can in no way take its place in the Earth's evolution in a manner reflective of the inconscience into which souls are actually obliged to plunge upon birth. As there is no unconsciousness there must be full awareness at the time of birth. This is to be the true New Creation.

Considering this we can fully understand that the body of the new-born must fully reflect the state of its consciousness and therefore it will be a form mirroring this heightened awareness. It must take birth already in a developed way; it can in no way be expected to pass through the infant stage, as we now know it. It can insert itself into the play at any of the ages equivalent to 9 in theosophical addition, or what would appear to us as coincidental with these ages, for reasons we shall specify further on. Whatever the case, the being comes equipped with a body which is a fully conscious instrument, whereby with the flowering of his soul the mental development need not suffer, or vice versa, nor shall his mind suffer as he progresses in his physical. All his development can follow a formidable harmony, each aspect of the being may collaborate to bring about the full blossoming of his other parts. There would not be the long period of childhood and adolescence which are actually reflective of the passage from unconsciousness to consciousness. At the same time the freshness and full vital energy of youth would be a permanent possession of the gnostic being since there would have been a transmutation of the sexual energy which would not need to be spent in youth and adulthood in the present ignorant way. This energy would be the support of the being and be entirely the food of the higher centres. Its awakening would not come about in the adolescent stage, when as well mind comes into the play and distorts the purity of the force and diverts it into the ways of the inconscience: the gnostic being comes in full possession of the Power, for the very building of his body would depend in large part on its utilisation in full knowledge and with the total mastery over the sex energy. Consequently the whole question of sexuality and differentiation of the sexes is revolutionised in the new body of gnosis.

Even within the conventional form of human gestation the human race now follows there have been developments which just a matter of perhaps a decade ago were considered impossible—impossible merely because they had never been successfully accomplished. One such new happening has been the recent transplant of three test tube embryos into the wombs of their respective mothers. In July, 1974, it was announced to the English Medical Society that three such transplants had been accomplished during a period of 18 months; the experiment had been tried repeatedly in various parts of the world over a number of years, but the attempts had never proved successful. Each time the womb of the mother rejected the embryo that was formed of the ovum and sperm outside itself. Finally, in a year and a half period, three cases were successful, and the scientist reporting the facts was sincere enough to state that the successes were in no way connected with a breakthrough in medical technology. He stated that no new procedure had been followed in order to force the womb to accept the transfer. That the three wombs did, the scientist could only attribute to 'luck' and not to any advance of medical knowledge.

The acceptance of the test tube embryos is due to the heightened pressure of the power of Truth in the world to show mankind that sex is not an indispensable means to bring about childbirth, as other experiences of test tube conceptions have proven, and a child can begin its life free from an act of desire. Evidently this is easier for the woman, but for the male the matter is more complex and intricate. It is only one step more however and man will understand that the entire process can be replaced by a more perfect method for both male and female. This accomplishment will as well happen in a very natural way, which perhaps scientists will concede to luck and which they will not be the essential prompters of, but rather the mere witnesses to the powers of Mother Nature and her infinite variety and imagination.

In this light we can relate that in Pondicherry, India, on 4 December, 1973, a creature was born from a goat—half boy, half goat. It lived a very short time and was then displayed in the local general hospital for the residents of the city to see. An impossible occurrence according to science, we say. Perhaps. But such is the sport of Mother Nature when she is being pressured to change her normal and habitual ways. Perhaps also during this millennium we shall come to understand more about the largely disputed issue of virgin-birth, which may prove to be a rather common occurrence and one which has taken place an infinite number of times in the past as well as the present.

We see then how the Cancer influence of these 72 initial years of this Aquarian Age are truly affecting the birth of our children. But we must be audacious enough to accept as well that the transformation is not only restricted to our human way and will bring a truly new system of incarnation on the Earth, and with it a new race of a more divine light, knowledge and power.

The New Planets, the Significance of their Discovery and the Calendar Years

WE HAVE SPOKEN of the Circle of 9 as representing years in regard to the process of transformation of a new type of body. In order to show how accurate the Circle can be in this respect we must refer to the discovery of the new planets, the last triad of the solar system, Uranus, Neptune and Pluto.

In ancient times the Seal of Solomon was a prized symbol for esoterists, occultists and yogis of different orders. This was valid as long as the System consisted of 6 planets plus the Sun. The Seal would have served in a similar manner as the Circle of 9 or the Enneagram. Combined with the duodecimal numerical system, or a system based on six or sixty, as the one employed by the Babylonians, this Seal would have been the most precious design for occultists and astrologers. Saturn, it can be noted, would occupy the apex of the ascending triangle, and the Moon-Earth the apex of the descending one. In this way one can see their relationship and in fact in terms of their orbits, Saturn is equal to the Moon because Saturn takes 29 years to complete a round of the zodiac, or to make one revolution of the Sun, and the Moon takes 29 days to make one synodic revolution; in the system of Secondary Progressions of the analysis of a natal horoscope, the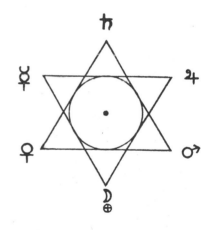

Moon requires 29 years, like Saturn's period of revolution, to make one complete round, meeting in this way the transit of Saturn. The two bodies are intimately linked in time, therefore carrying this link into the lives of the inhabitants of Earth, because the Moon is our satellite. It is for this reason that Saturn is such a vitally important planet in our destinies, both individual and collective.

The base of the ascending triangle is formed of Venus and Mars, which we have seen to be connected in essence, while in the zodiac these bodies rule opposite and complementary signs. In like manner the base of the descending triangle is formed of the orbits of Mercury and Jupiter, which are also linked in essence as well as by their rulership of opposite and complementary signs. Consequently it can be understood how the Seal of Solomon was a formidable key to the mysteries of the zodiac and was no doubt also utilised as a precious means of joining the solar system to the time cycles of Earth by relating these orbits and their numbers to the calendars in use during those times.

The successful utilisation of the Seal would have lasted until the discovery of the last three orbs, after which it became imperative to find another method of working with the orbits, numbers and time. The method we have evolved to is the 9 Circle because it serves the same function as the Hexagram, or the Seal of Solomon: it incorporates all the numbers and it harmonises the novemal number system with the Earth's time cycles. The relation between the planets is equally as interesting as in the Seal of Solomon, if not more so; we find it to be much more subtle and hence richer in significance, requiring a mind illumined by a new light in order to understand its mysteries.

Therefore the Seal of Solomon for our times, the 9th Manifestation and in particular this Age of Aquarius, could be drawn in the following manner.

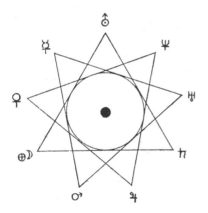

Because the Zero was not employed in the count of the Seal, the numbers ran from 1 to 7, perhaps not at the time that the Seal was initially revealed, but certainly with the decline of knowledge the 7 took the place of the 6. To use the 6 would have implied knowledge of the 0 and if the ancients spoke of 7 as the sacred number it meant that 1 was equivalent to the Sun in the most esoteric teachings, and the orbits were then numbered 2, beginning with Mercury, 3 Venus, and so forth. We can see from this how far the times were from the divinisation of Matter and how far they were from the more perfect vision of unity. We can appreciate through this study just how much the evolution has progressed by seeing the knowledge that it is now possible to reveal.

The Zero came later, introduced by India during our Manifestation, or perhaps the latter portion of the 8th. In the 9th or 10th century the Arabs carried it to Europe. With this simple cypher, this unpretentious Nought, the Divine Mother revealed and prepared the extraordinary revolution that was to take place for mankind. It then became possible for the cosmic harmonies to show the equality of Brahman and Shakti and to create of man a living image of the Lord. Through these observations the occultist is able to see how the evolution is progressing and coming ever closer to the full perception of the Perfection, and for humanity to become a pulsating embodiment of Truth.

With the triangles numbered in the old manner on the Seal of Solomon, the sum of the numbers of the descending one yields 3 (Mercury 2, Moon-Earth 4, Jupiter 6=12=3), and the ascending one gives us 6 (Venus 3, Mars 5, Saturn 7=15=6), thus comprising only two of the occult triads because that was the stage of the evolution then. But the greater perfection came with the 9th Manifestation and the appearance of the further triad, signifying that the work had indeed progressed a great deal, whatever the exterior appearances might be.

The sum of the orbit numbers of the 9 Circle triangles are: 9 (Pluto 9, Earth-Moon 3, Saturn 6=18=9) and 6 (Venus 2, Jupiter 5, Neptune 8=15=6) and 3 (Mercury 1, Mars 4, Uranus 7=12=3). These sum numbers therefore yield the three key numbers of our study, 9, 6 and 3, which are synthesised in the Sacred Triangle of 9-6-3 that adds the 9 to the design, marking a graduation from 2×3 to 3×3.

It is necessary for the student to be aware of all these harmonies, because only in this way is it possible to reach the point of truly understanding the perfection of the Cosmos. Gradually one also begins to see how the number systems and the calendar develop according to the progression of man's vision of the solar system. It is obvious that though our number systems and calendars are arranged for us by men who are not aware of the deeper and occult rhythm of the heavens and their relation to Earth, there appears to be nonetheless a guiding power which sees to it that mankind is furnished with the proper means to understand the cosmic perfection to the fullest extent. The development of one is intimately involved with the other; mankind could not have had anything but a novemal (decimal) system in this Age of Aquarius, to furnish the means whereby the harmony of the three new planets would be rendered perceptible to humanity, and in particular it would be able to discover the link with the calendar we actually use. It could be argued that all this is purely arbitrary; that man could have devised any calendar; that scientists are rapidly approaching the discovery of other planets which could disturb the arrangement of 9. But a point must be emphatically stressed: there is nothing arbitrary. If we use this calendar now it is because it is the only means presently at our disposal to understand the heavens, and surely when we have progressed a further degree we will have also reached the possibility of devising a more perfect calendar. Even as the harmonies now stand the calendar could be altered slightly in order to facilitate the correspondences without radically changing the arrangement. But we propose to show how even with its slight imperfections there is a perfection to be found in the actual system.

As for the discovery of the other planets, this is quite possible, but the discovery of one will not mean much to our development. It would be valid for a re-arrangement of the harmonies only when there are three more, bringing the count to 12 plus the Sun. Until that time the Circle of 9 is our key. For this reason the Seal of Solomon could not be overstepped until the last of the present three was found. Twelve planets would imply a different division of the Circle to give the correspondence with the calendar years, and also a duodecimal number system.

Finally it is necessary to state that the closer we come to a full establishment of the truth-consciousness in the atmosphere of the Earth and within the hearts, minds and bodies of men, the more perfect will the harmonies become to our vision and our ability to consciously work with them. As the supramental force takes greater possession of mankind, the more accurate will our vision become, the more precise shall we become in the art of prediction as well. Man is unable to be fully accurate in his prevision of the future and in his view of the correspondence between the planets, Sun and Earth, and their meaning in the details of his life, only because the Earth is as yet in the hands of the Ignorance. For this reason alone predictions cannot be fully precise and we must grope in the dark regarding what is to be, because the Ignorance is the antipode of Harmony. It is absurd to presume that an astrologer can be totally precise while the Earth is as yet in the clutches of the Lord of Falsehood. Only when it has been entirely liberated can we expect to be sound in our understanding of the past and present as well as the future. In the same light it is evident that even in the best of cases a mystic or visionary cannot be one hundred per cent accurate in his subjective vision about events to come, because this type of vision is also dependent upon the overall condition of the Earth-consciousness. His vision, though he be free from ego, is nonetheless formed of the stuff of his Earth environment. Freedom from ego brings one definitely closer to true knowledge and vision, but it is only the full divinisation or supramentalisation of the entire Earth that can truly reveal to us the harmony and therefore the precise details to come.

The forces of the planes *below Truth* can provoke visions, can imitate voices, can speak of truth, of love and knowledge; the aspirant can be easily misled by these powers and can ultimately find himself a tool in their hands, unwittingly implemented to maintain the reign of a lesser light upon Earth. Until a certain degree of knowledge is acquired by the seeker, it is very difficult to distinguish a power of truth from one of falsehood. However, there is one field wherein the Falsehood cannot impinge, because its power does not include the *seed* of the perfection and harmony of the Time-Spirit. *The very existence of these powers negates such attributes.* And therefore we know that in the study and vision of the cosmic truth, there can be no equivocation, no imitation. The 'seed' of cosmic existence is what determines the workings, and this seed is from the plane of Truth; perfection is inherent in the

Cosmos because the Divine Mother has received the seed from Brahman, and from this fecundation the universes are born. To suppose that the Cosmos is unreal, or is the Ignorance, or is the Illusion, is to deny the very Absolute.

In the harmony of the discovery of the new planets we are brought to see just how close we are coming to the total manifestation of harmony and perfection. That is, where both the perfection that *is* and the perfection of *seeing* are approaching one another. In this light the following study will show how the calendar years are accurately related to the Circle and hence to the planets.

The three newly seen planets, as astrologers know, are higher representatives of three planets in the old scheme. Astrologers know, through identification with the essence of the planets, exactly to which one each of the new triad belongs. Starting with Mercury we are able to feel just what the planet's 'frequencies' are by means of the subtle senses, so to speak. In this way many of the things Mercury is connected with in our lives begin to reveal themselves. The principal one of these is Mind, as well as the vibration of the subtle energies to which Mind owes its being. We know through its study that the stuff of Mind is such that in order for its function to be perfect it must be closely allied to the solar stuff; that is, its energy is very fine and its vibration should be intense, almost appearing to us as non-moving. It has, for this reason, the least *power* of all the planets on the dense material plane. Because Mercury is the closest planet we know to the Sun, we understand that its presence and purpose is to be able to transmit the essence of solar light to the other planets, and man is to make use of the channel which Mercury rules, the mind, to receive the light of Truth. The races of Earth are therefore primarily *mental*, and it is with or through this instrument or channel and its perfecting that mankind can then evolve and experience higher planes.

The first step then is the manifestation of Mind, and the first planet is Mercury, whose colour is a diluted solar gold: yellow, the colour which serves as the intermediary between the force from below, Mars (red), and the heavens above, Venus (blue). The mixture of Mercury's yellow and Venus's blue produces the colour of Earth, green. What this signifies is simply that all our observations and visions on Earth are coloured in this way. It is this yellow that modifies all the other possibilities of 'colour' experience. The better the instrument functions, the more golden does this yellow become; when Mind becomes an instrument of the truth-consciousness it is capacitated to transmit the full ray of the Sun, and the yellow then becomes golden.

What makes this evolution possible in the development of man as mirrored in the solar system is the introduction of the third triad and the new planets that comprise it. The first to appear in 1781 was Uranus, which we know to be the higher vibration of Mercury; or, to be more exact, it is *the power for the transformation of Mind*: it brings with it the full gamut of sound and the whole spectrum of colours. The introduction of Uranus signified that man had progressed to the point where he could begin to make use of Mind in a more intensified yet refined way. He could then be rendered receptive to the pure solar light, the golden light of Gnosis. Therefore Uranus is the initial power of transformation and the instrument for the universalisation of the light of Truth, the higher vibration of Mind.

We know Mercury to be 'exalted' in Aquarius, because this sign provides the perfect terrain for its actual qualities to blossom, and thus we allocate Uranus to the sign of Aquarius, because as it is Mercury's higher vibration, it would naturally have affinity with the sign wherein Mercury is best placed. The signs of *exaltation* can never be fully understood without the revelation of these higher octaves or possibilities.

In this light the first centre that is to feel the power of the great transformation is Mind; thus with this sighting of Uranus, the Descent, as we shall call it, began.

Astrologers have been very accurate in recording significances of the planets and how they affect man's development. We need not repeat here what others have stated so well. We shall only add that for the present Uranus is significant of disruption and separation and break-up because it is the representative of the power that first descends to open the way, break the path, and prepare the channel beginning with Mind, making the being ready for the new force in its descent to the lower centres of the being. Its action can almost be visualised as a piercing instrument that cuts through the skull of man and allows the descending force to enter and fill the being, the first effects of which are felt on Mind. With the initial piercing descent naturally all the values, all the ideas, opinions and myriad mental structures upon which the whole of our present way of living and being are built, are made to crumble and we are faced with the first seeds of a new creation, the first stirrings of a really new consciousness. It can be seen therefore that all the upheavals witnessed in the world today belong to the field of Mercury, i.e. politics, religions, science, communication, travel, language, education,—in a word, the entire structure of 19th and 20th century societies which now strive to experience a truly new way of being. This is the destiny of the Age that Uranus rules.

It is easily understood that since man is essentially a mental being, all of his life is conditioned by mind, therefore the range of Uranus's transformation is vast, embracing almost every action and attitude, since all these depend on Mind. We therefore consider Uranus to be a planet having rapport with all that is universal and all-embracing, and we consider the sign Aquarius in the same light. But the deeper reason for this cosmic breath is that Mind is all-embracing (which is understood by the element Air to which Mind is allocated); therefore Aquarius, the exaltation of

Mercury, works extensively along with Uranus. It is also known to be the planet signifying freedom, which we understand to be the freeing of man from the prison of his mind. It is to break the structures and formations he has created therein and to unravel the ties of conditioning that have become his shackles. This is the action of the descending power as epitomised by Uranus,—the 'electric shocks' that allow man to wake up and *see*, which ultimately will grant him the vision of unity that Uranus promises.

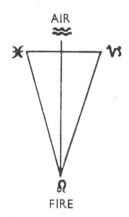

In the diagram on page 42 the work of the Avatars is shown in a combination of the zodiacal signs of the 9th Manifestation, which are Capricorn, Aquarius and Pisces —Earth, Air and Water signs. With the entry of Uranus the element Air is modified through its affinity with that element, and thus the upholding seed of the Manifestation, Leo, is first cast by the descending power onto the terrain of Mind. The Sun of Leo is the generating force, *Tapas*, the energy of which these newest planets are transmitters. That is, the last triad is that which turns the movement back and brings humanity to the possibility of a direct acceptance of solar power. They are to prepare the way, to attune the instrument of man in the most physical sense to the subtle yet potent force which would destroy the race because of its potency, without the work of the new planets or what they represent on the centres of the body.

Thus, to conclude with Uranus, we see that it works through the Air element because it affects Mind and that its action is to allow the descending force to pass through the first centre unobstructed. Along with its action of 'shattering', it carries the first Leo solar seeds, the initial new light into the field of human mind, which is first experienced as a form of cosmic consciousness. The instrument is widened and rendered more capable of perceiving the vast body of the Divine and man as One. With this there is an inevitable turn towards knowledge that helps man in this passage to a cosmic consciousness; consequently we witness the masses turning today toward subjects such as astrology, which Uranus is said to 'rule'. The beginning of the Aquarian Age brought the immediate rebirth of astrology. We see now vast

numbers familiar with a language that until now had been reserved for the élite. Uranus, through the sign Aquarius, is the direct transmitter of the solar seed. It can be said that it is through this channel that the Sun-God fecundates the Earth. An interesting coincidence is that the name given to an important space program which is an outcome of the Uranus impact on the civilisation is *Apollo*, the Sun-God.

The same diagram of the 9th Manifestation can begin to be constructed with this planet, as here demonstrated.

The descent which the symbol of Aquarius pictures ≈ , continues after the piercing sword of Uranus opens the first centre, and so the following planet to appear is Neptune, in 1846, 65 years after the first sighting of Uranus: mankind is made to feel the higher vibration of the next planet in the solar scale, Venus.

From Mind the force passes into the next centre in the process of transformation: the heart, the emotions, as well as the centre of *physical feeling*. The area

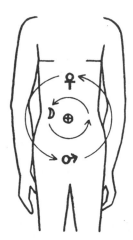

which Venus rules can be situated at the solar plexus in the old order, closely bound to the sex centre which is the domain of Mars. We could picture it in this way: both planets locked in orbit around the navel, the Earth, and veiling the rays emanating from the two would be the Moon, spinning in orbit around the Earth and creating the ego that protects man until he is able to receive the purer force without danger to his instrument. Thus Neptune comes into the scheme and represents the finer vibrations of the emotional nature, the purer energies of a love removed from the taint of animality, of lust, of the coarse and more violent vibrations of Mars; and by this intensely fine quality of Love, the veils of the Moon begin to loosen. Neptune is the planet which has the full power to rid man of his ego. Its subtle action in the pattern of transformation is to give mankind the means by which it can become freed of the ego through Divine Love. For us, on this planet, given the actual conditions, the energy of Neptune is the closest we can come to knowing Divine Love. In the past when this energy was felt, it turned man in upon himself, caused him to flee the world and seek to live exclusively enclosed within for this romance between himself and the inner beloved, because the world proved too coarse for such a vibration. Thus to protect it man sought refuge in solitude, to live his experience of Love in peace, either in a monastic cell, a Himalayan cave, or the lonesome sannyasi road where one can wander oblivious of and ignored by the world.

Today, after the initial work of Uranus, Neptune works to bring this experience into the entire atmosphere of the Earth, to sensitise the generality, rendering unnecessary the escape from the world and society, in whatever of its forms, to a secluded region of mystic paradise—for this is the very power that is to divinise the Earth. The entire planet is to be lifted from the coarse and harsh realm of animality which negates the existence of Neptune, and in this way the mystic can live with his Beloved in the throes of society, in the midst of what is now the Battlefield, generating the force which will help to transform the manifestation.

Venus is harmony and perfection. Her orbit is the most perfect, the most circular. Only Neptune can compare with her: only Neptune as well has such a perfect orbit. Neptune carries the vibration of Venus to its highest pitch and releases it from the clutches of desire, releases it from the old-known marriage with Mars, or, shall we say, has the power to make of that marriage what it is intended to be, raising it to a level which humanity has not yet known. With the appearance of Neptune consequently the many distorted reactions to this power come, as the reactions appear to Uranus's power. Here too the heart centre, like the Mind, must feel the impact of the descending solar light. Neptune prepares the terrain for the descent of the Sun of Truth into the heart of man. All his feelings are affected in the transition; he often loses his way and falls into despair in his quest. Thus Neptune is said to bring the aspect of chaos into the emotional life while the instrument is adjusting itself to the vibrations of the power of Love which it has never experienced on a massive scale. The youth of today have had to work this out; they are principally the ones upon whom the descent is felt, because they are less rigid and more easily open to the Force. Neptune seeks to lift man to the purely spiritual inner state, and the stubborn nature of man can only react by a plunge into further inconscience at first. He seeks these states by drugs, by the experience of so-called free love, only in this way to move away from the delicate vibrations of Neptune. In order to receive the force for which Neptune prepares us, it is necessary to be fully conscious and not dulled in any way, for its vibration is far more delicate than that of Uranus, it can be so easily lost, it is so elusive, and the ego can absorb it for its own interests while making man believe he is in tune with the true thing. This and no other is the 'illusion' of Neptune.

When rightly received Neptune is the power to cast away the veils of ego. It dissolves all illusion, and in this way it is one of the strongest weapons in the fight of the human race for immortality. Neptune is the planet that liberates man from the animality of sex and transforms the nature of Mars, liberating it from the prison of human lusts to become the Warrior of the Divine Mother against the Falsehood, which is Death. It is when these two meet that the true vibration of Divine Love is known and Death is seen as an illusion. Therefore when the Mother lived this experience, as recorded on page 57, she was 84—the 8 of Neptune and the 4 of Mars, a relationship which we shall explain further on in the text.[1]

Astrologers have related Uranus to electricity and Neptune to oil. This may well be but in the sense that these only show the way or passage to the reception

[1] In her natal chart these two planets are 'in conjunction'.

and use of solar energy direct, not diluted in purity due to its alteration by one of the elements such as Air or Earth, which tend to render the power less fine and to densify the vibration. Neptune can be related to oil, the Black Gold of the Earth, only insofar as it is to represent the means whereby mankind can pass to the stage of a direct assimilation and usage of the solar fire of Leo. Oil is in the Earth, locked in its bosom in the same way that the solar light and energy are still locked in the cell and must one day be released. Thus Venus is exalted in Pisces, a Water sign, an element associated with the vital nature, and Neptune rules oil which is the symbol of the solar energy prisoner of the unregenerated vital centre. Neptune is closely related to the vital, it is partly the power needed for the purification of the vital, the emotional nature, as Uranus is the power of purification of the Mind which is of the Air element.

In the diagram of the 9th Manifestation we are building up with the newest planets, the next part of the design is furnished by Neptune, related to Pisces, the

exaltation of Venus, in the same way that Uranus becomes the additional planet of Aquarius through the exaltation of Mercury therein. By now the student can see that the higher triad of planets represents the descent of the Divine solar power, each one opening a centre and allowing the Force to flow through it. Sri Aurobindo has called this the Descent of Supermind, but we can see that it is not only related to Mind as some may believe the term to signify. And we can appreciate also that it is the supramental force as symbolised by Uranus that initiates the descent, which therefore justifies its name. In the Tantric tradition, the way to liberation for the sadhak was by means of the *ascent* of the Kundalini, the power of Mars situated in the lowest chakra, the *mūlādhāra*, to the highest, the 1,000 petal *sahasradala-padma* chakra above the crown of the head. In the present progression of the evolution it is seen through the greater Triad that it is a *descent* from above that accomplishes the task. The appearance of Neptune therefore carries the power a step further along the way in the descent and affects the emotional nature. It frees it from the now accepted vibration of love which is a distortion of the true manifestation; Venus must be liberated from the clutches of the sex centre. Today to feel love means to feel a surge in the lowest sex chakra. But Neptune will uplift the energy, redeem it and free Venus from the prison of the lower nature, free her from the compelling magnetic veils of the Moon which camouflage and distort for her the vibration of Mars.

With the appearance of Pluto in 1930, the last of the Triad, the Descent is carried another step downward and the power is made to penetrate the deepest and darkest part, the lower vital and sex centre, marking the beginning of the actual transformation of Matter. This is by far the most difficult portion of the work because of the obscurity of the plane we are dealing with. When one touches this part there are immediately two possibilities: life or death, creation or destruction. So, in order for the work to proceed in this region it is imperative that a transformation take place in the higher centres, which serve then as 'security valves' that assist the sadhak, and the human race as well, in the right utilisation of the forces released. In this way the supramental yoga is somewhat safer than the traditional Tantric path, because it is a force which passes and cleanses the centres of Mind and Heart and higher Emotional, and then with these accomplishes the more difficult work on the recalcitrant lower stratum. In no way can this area be purified if the others have not experienced the purifying force and light; yet immediately when the two higher centres are worked on, there is the penetration of the power into the lower region.

Pluto rules or represents the energy within the atom, nuclear power, the solar-fire, —in this way completing the scheme of the three principal energy sources for the planet. electricity, the energy captured within the Earth, and solar power. It is to be noted that the artificial destructive element used in the fabrication of the atomic bomb has been called *Plutonium*. It is the product of the fission which occurs in nuclear power generating plants; from this creativity the force of destruction arises —the very nature of the planet Pluto : creation and destruction, the heights and the abyss.

The secret of Pluto is that it is death redeemed; it is the power that brings Mars to the rightful action of being the weapon of Immortality. Pluto is the abyss and the heights and as such, in the zodiac, it rules Capricorn which is the exaltation of Mars, completing the trinity of rulerships by exaltation, all falling in the last quarter of the zodiac, the 9th Manifestation signs, and each corresponding in aspect to one of the Incarnations who embody the new planets' power. Pluto as higher octave of Mars brings this power to its most potent expression, which means—as stated— either an endless process of creation, a continuous and uninterrupted contact with the source of vital energy, the divine breath that feeds the new creation and produces the transformed nature and body, —or it becomes the power of a destruction such as man has never known. With the appearance of Pluto the evolution was given the final ingredient for the complete and radical transformation, for it is with this release of nuclear power that the real transformation of matter can begin, which follows the revolution in the human vital, sex and physical centres. It is Pluto that signifies the appearance of a creation unique for the planet, free of all limitations of differentiation, a fusion of the until now separated parts, the unification of the body senses and the harmonisation of all the levels of being, both for the collectivity and the individual. It is only with the transformation and release of a totally purified vital force, which Pluto represents, that the new creation comes about.

The planet then signifies for the evolution the possibility to raise the centre which draws in energies from the Cosmos from the lowest chakra to the higher vital, the navel area. In this way Pluto serves to replace the Moon at this centre, to marry the Earth as symbolised in the myth where Pluto rapes Persephone and carries her off to his kingdom—Persephone who is the Earth, the third of the planets, the third of the Trinity—and with this pure seed the new creation is fecundated. The Moon represents the veils of the ego as well as the protective maternal sack within which the Earth resides, the Earth's very atmosphere—Demeter, who does not wish to forego her Child. The discharge of Pluto's seed, nuclear particles, and the pollution of that sack can be the means whereby the Earth will be born of it and will express an entirely new being. Thus we can see that Pluto's work is both laudable and deplorable. He rapes Kore and though the Divine Mother mourns for her precious lost child, he nonetheless carries her into the kingdom of the secret and dark cave of Matter and makes her his Queen. In spite of her longing for her Mother and the lost paradise of Elysium, Persephone redeems matter. But the myth ends with the happy union of the Mother and Daughter, because the Moon too must be redeemed, must join in the new creation, the new heaven and the new earth—the Moon must as well be a part of the glorious birth. So, in the reunion of the Two Goddesses the true psychic being of the Earth is revealed and Demeter lifts the spell she had cast upon the Earth and allows the crops to grow once more, eliminates the massive famine and saves the civilisation of the planet. This therefore is the Earth's salvation, this then makes the seed of Pluto the fecundator of Life and not Death. The power of his force must be softened and subdued by the tenderness of the Moon and Earth united, joined in marriage by the Supreme.

In this arrangement we see how Pluto, Saturn and Earth are closely related. Saturn is related to Earth-Moon in time, as previously explained, and Pluto is the power of the new creation, the seed that releases the Earth from the mechanical orbit of the Moon and carries it off to its birth, to the experience of a 'new Matter'. This is the Sacred Triangle upon which hinges the divinisation of Man and his Earth.

Pluto is the most forceful of the newest planets. It is equivalent to Shiva in the Hindu scheme, and to Agni. There is nothing that can stand in the way of its action because it moves slowly, securely, steadily and boldly forward, and is the assurance for the civilisation that the new world has been born. From the time of its discovery the truth of its significance came forth. The revelation of the neutron took place in 1930, when Pluto was spotted. Nine years later, in 1939 the Second World War began which was the power of the released lower forces over the face of the Earth, as the Puranic tale describes in the legend of Durga. Such an upsurge was to be expected since all things come up when one touches the lowest centre to which Pluto is related. There is always the possibility of life or death, as even now through the widespread manufacture of nuclear arms for warfare, mankind is faced with the possibility of life or death. In 1939, 9 years after its discovery, the first fission took place, giving even greater power to the expression of Pluto. With the end of the War a portion of the purification had been achieved. As the higher expression of Mars, Pluto is the fulfilment of the sign Capricorn which it co-rules, the victory of Durga, the Divine Mother.

In the body of man here pictured, the last planet is added at the navel centre to which it belongs. The student can observe that the newer Triad merely raises a slight bit the centres of the planets to which they correspond by octave. Pluto pulls the force of Mars from the sex centre and places it at the navel, which signifies for man that the energy he receives from the Universal Nature which is indispensable for his existence, is filtered, so to speak, rendered less coarse by the simple fact that Pluto has brought about a transformation in the atmosphere of the Earth which receives these forces or cosmic rays and serves man as a filter. This sheath, or filter, has been altered by Pluto through its potent solar power, and in order for man to survive with

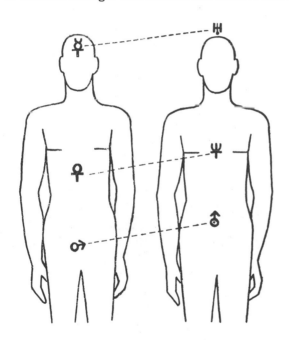

this influx of purer energy he must no longer receive the force from the lower vital chakra but must make use now of the higher vital located at the navel area, the centre of the body of man.

Neptune lifts the channel of Venus from the solar plexus to the heart proper, once more becoming the means whereby man can understand and feel a much finer emotional vibration, —the emotions fully perfected and liberated from the downward pull of the Moon to Mars and the sex centre. Neptune has redeemed the emotional nature of man which is now able to experience and respond to a more divine love.

Uranus lifts the channel of Mercury from the head to above the crown, thus signifying the placing of the faculty of perception and reception of the light above Mind, bringing to mankind the possibility of a more cosmic awareness and a more universal understanding of life. It gives him in this way the ability to rise above his instrument and view matters from a detached stand, free from the little prison of his mind: he is able to identify with the One Consciousness which shows him that he is equal to That, in all ways he is That. This is the new universal awareness, the new perception.

In all there is a mere uplifting, and these positions of the new Triad are the location of the subtle centres which contain the nodi of the more subtle senses. Their higher frequency simply shifts the centre of force a degree upward within the body, perhaps making the new body just that much larger than the one we now know.

The diagram of the 9th Manifestation is completed with Pluto, giving the quality of a *new* manifestation to this fragment of time by the appearance of a higher Triad representing the descent of a higher world whose upholding seed is the Sun of Truth.

Pluto closes the Circle of 9, unites it with the Sun, the o, of which it is the secret representative. Pluto's presence then brings the movement to the Centre and only then is the possibility of the utilisation of solar energy open to the Earth. It would appear that the process of expansion of our solar system as represented by the latest triad would carry the movement farther away, would imply that Matter is moving ever away from Spirit and that the gap grows wider between the two, placing even greater obstacles in the way leading to their indispensable union, *a union which is the only salvation for the Earth.* But the study of the harmonies of the cosmos reveals that the movement proceeds circularly and not linearly. It turns back upon itself in a manner which is only understandable from beyond our actual concept of time and space, because this secret movement is the accomplishment in a dimension which we cannot perceive in our ordinary consciousness. Because of this Great Curve that which is farthest is actually closest.

The Asteroid Belt, the 4.5 Orbit, is the great reversal point, where the brakes are applied on the thrusting movement and the force issuing from the Centre is violently arrested and the curve begins in the sphere of subtle matter and energy, sweeping it back toward the centre once more, uniting it with the Origin from whence it sprang. Therefore the 4.5 Orbit is directly opposite the Pluto Apex. Jupiter is the accumulator of solar energy; because of its size and other particulars, it gives off more energy than it receives from the Sun and in this way serves to *feed* the higher triad. Between the Sun and Jupiter there is a more or less steady gradua- tion in the sizes of the bodies, culminating with the largest proportions of Jupiter. Passing this prime accumulator and expeller of solar power, the sizes of the planets begin to decrease until Pluto is reached, the smallest of the lot, similar to the size of Mercury, the body closest to the Sun. Saturn, Uranus and Neptune are farthest from the Sun and yet in essence and function (because of the indispensable presence of Jupiter who substitutes for the Sun, so to speak) they are experienced as closer; or we can say they are more subtly attuned to the Solar Fire and can capture it and send it back transmuted into the inner zone of the solar system where Earth orbits. By this arrangement we see the essential functional equality of Sun and Jupiter, the orbs which together represent the Truth-Consciousness. The System is a mathematical perfection. The laws are exact so we can understand why Earth is the home of man and the psychic being in evolution, because as it is the third it is upon the Earth that the energies of the higher octaves are projected and culminate.

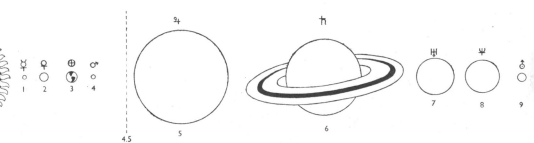

As far as we know Mercury is the first body after the Sun; it shows us the condition of the *old creation*: mental man. Jupiter is the 'Sun' for the outer planets and thus the *new creation* is essentially represented by Saturn, the planet immediately after this 'Sun', the three rings of Saturn indicating the possibilities of the further Occult Triad, and Saturn being the planet of Time is therefore the planet representing the *Cosmic Order*, the perfection of which is embodied in the last and newest Triad. Thus in whatever way we study the System we see the tremendous importance of Saturn, for which reason it rules the Golden Age of Capricorn, holds the key to Time and the orderly unfoldment of the body of the manifest Divine, the Cosmos.

The precision of the laws of the planetary system can be observed in the discovery of the new Triad with respect to the calendar and to their position in the zodiac when discovered. It is an extremely beautiful pattern and offers us the express confirmation of all that has so far been placed before the consideration of the student. Once more we see that the method of theosophical addition is the indispensable formula for understanding the harmony. Without this we would remain in ignorance regarding their appearances, which has been the best means given us in this Age to know the ways of the Divine Plan and its harmony.

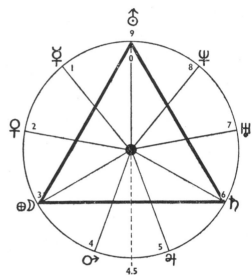

Once more here is the Circle of 9 reproduced with the planets placed around it according to their orbit numbers. We are interested now in discussing the discovery of the last triad, the 7th, 8th and 9th planets, which are the higher octaves of Mercury, Venus and Mars. Consequently the first to consider is *Mercury* whose number is 1. Its higher octave is *Uranus* whose number is 7. These together equal 8. Uranus was discovered in 1781, which equals 8. When it was found it was at 25° Gemini, a numerological 7, the orbit number of Uranus.

The second of the Triad is *Neptune*, the higher octave of *Venus*. Venus is 2 and Neptune is 8, together equalling 10 and then 1. Neptune was discovered in 1846, which equals 1 numerologically. When it was discovered it was at 26° Aquarius, equalling 8; Neptune's orbit number is 8.

The final one is *Pluto*, the further octave of *Mars* whose orbit number is 4. Pluto is 9 therefore together with Mars's orbit number we have 13, or 4. Pluto was discovered in 1930, a numerological 4. At the time of its discovery it was at 18° Cancer, equalling 9, and Pluto is the 9th orbit.

To make the arrangement clearer, here is a chart taken from *Symbols and the Question of Unity*, page 113.

	PLANET	YEAR	COMBINATION OF ORBIT NUMBERS	
9.	PLUTO	1 9 30=4	9+4=13=4	(18° ♋ =9)
8.	NEPTUNE	1 8 46=1	8+2=10=1	(26° ♒ =8)
7.	URANUS	1 7 81=8	7+1= 8	(25° ♊ =7)

The reader is asked to note the graduation of 7, 8 and 9 in the century numbers which coincide with the orbit numbers and the degrees of the zodiac of each of the planets when discovered. And particularly important to understand is the exact relation between the actual calendar and the Circle of 9. The nine division can refer to days, to months or to years, but always the method of theosophical addition must be employed. Therefore 1930, the year Pluto was discovered, is $1+9+3+0 = 13 = 1+3 = 4$, which then falls at the Mars orbit and precisely in that year, as explained, the most important element was discovered which opened the way to the utilisation of nuclear power, truly the higher possibility of Mars. Then, after having passed through one complete round of the Circle from that point, or 9 years later in 1939 ($1+9+3+9 = 22 = 4$), once more at the Mars point, the fission was accomplished.

This is to show the student how the years of our calendar can be followed in this Circle with accuracy.

Each decade there is a shift in number and therefore in vibration. Let us take 1969 for example, the year that Man first stepped on the Moon. That year corresponded in vibration to Uranus, the planet of space travel ($1+9+6+9 = 25 = 7$). Moreover, the feat was accomplished on July 20 when the Sun was in the zodiacal sign ruled by the Moon. (Further on the student can see for himself where this accomplishment, so important for humanity in the symbolic and material sense, falls in the full Gnostic Circle.)

As of 1969 the calendar circle made a slight shift; it moved from the decade of the 60's to the 70's, or from Saturn to Uranus. All during the 70's therefore it is Uranus that is strongly influencing the sub-cycle, particularly acute from September, 1973 to March, 1974.

In 1979 there will be another slight decade shift and Neptune will take first place. It will be the 80's and all that we have previously discussed about Neptune will be felt, with the accent on the late 80's in particular.

In 1989 there is a shift to the decade of Pluto, which lasts until 1998, perhaps the most important singular event for humanity in this millennium. In fact, the millennium draws to an end and the two major shifts and one minor in the Earth's destiny cycle occur. This is the shift of the decade, of the century and—most important of all—the shift of the millennium: an entire new order appears.

A major shift of this type occurred in 999 A.D. We realise that there have been days added to the calendar during the change of 45 B.C., and others subtracted at subsequent periods. But these additions and subtractions are, occultly speaking, for the purpose of bringing the Earth back into the correct time sequence with respect to the Cosmos, since the flow of time is 'imperfect' upon this planet.

In 999 A.D not only was there a decade and century shift but the digit of the first millennium was added, 3 zeroes, or 3 Suns, were opened; this then signified that humanity moved into the sphere of Mercury, planet number 1 of the orbits. In this way we see that at the end of the present millennium we carry the movement from Mercury (1) to Venus (2) and therefore an entirely new order of living awaits mankind. Venus is to us the subtle physical plane, which by that time will have made great strides in its union with our more dense realm. Humanity will then step out of the sphere of Mind of Mercury, with all that it entails, e.g. politics, science, education, all forms of mental conditioning, separative consciousness, duality, etc. By that time Mercury will be brought to function in its proper way. The shift will take us in the 'great body' from Mercury's centre in the head to Venus's centre in the solar plexus, but the newest planets contribute in the work by opening the higher centres in the body so that mankind can actually accomplish the shift to a new creation.

Thus the last three decades in the millennium are extremely important for in the 70's it is Uranus's rule, the 80's are Neptune's and the 90's are Pluto's. The 70's see therefore the even greater awakening to the truths of cosmic harmonies, and they bring before the world a new understanding in this realm; a new light in the mind is revealed. The 80's bring forth the embodiment of Love and the refined higher emotions, while the 90's show mankind the really transformed being, the full realisation and the vivid accomplishment in the transformation of matter, the Power incarnate. As of 1969 we can say we are winding up the millennium, with the help of the new planets, the 7, 8, 9 orbits, rulers of the 7th, 8th, 9th decades.

From 2,000 onward it is no longer Mercury that rules the civilisation, and we shall only then begin to know Venus, the mysterious planet in the sky, sometimes referred to as the twin of Earth.

If we move forward with this process into the future, we see that in 2999 there is a shift to Earth-Moon being, and humanity will be passing through the middle portion of Aquarius according to the Precession of the Equinoxes, the Gemini decanate. In 3999 there is the major shift once more and the Earth passes into the rule of Mars, of which Pluto is the higher octave. According to the Precession the world would be about to enter the Age of Capricorn, the exaltation of Mars. This culmination is beautiful. It would appear that in truth we are now working only to prepare for this coming Golden Age, the rule of Saturn and Pluto.

It is evident that the extraordinary combination of calendar years, orbit numbers and higher octave relationships as described regarding the discovery of the newest planets, may at first sight appear to be very complex, though nonetheless precise and unmistakable in its design. It becomes simple and wonderfully clear only if one has certain formulas, otherwise it is hardly likely that this design can be understood. Without a certain light the harmony of the newly discovered planets could never have been perceived. And thus it is with all studies in cosmic harmonies The zodiac is a labyrinth for those who have not the key of knowledge or the guidance. One can become completely lost in these studies and, what is worse, one can be lost without realising it. It is possible to spend a whole lifetime working with the planets and the zodiac and be totally convinced of having found the way and the light, when in fact we are merely spinning the web of illusion around ourselves, convincing ourselves of harmonies and patterns which may have only slight relevance and may be only subjectively valid, having no bearing on the Great Truth and in no way being able to connect us with the source of objective knowing which the solar system represents.

There is the question for example of the date of the beginning of the Age, about which astrologers each have their opinion, as well as occult, esoteric schools, communities, churches and so forth. Each one has come up with a date that conforms to their idea of when the Age began, but has no objective rapport with the actual beginning. Yet it is imperative at a certain point in the studies to know this date in order to proceed further. Most of the dates considered as the beginning of the Age are again only subjectively valid for the individuals or groups concerned. For them the date is true, because it is evident that most have placed this date at times when for the work of the particular group the Age 'came to them'. Therefore their chosen dates are subjectively valid and must be taken in this light. They do not go beyond but they can be very important for the parties concerned. Also it is dubious whether scientists are accurate in their considerations about what really causes the Precession of the Equinoxes. No doubt the movement is provoked by the magnetic pull of an as yet mysterious centre. Also it is not at all likely that this corresponds to the Constellations but rather to an occult circle, just as our zodiac is an occult but real and not imaginary circle in our sky. One speaks of the wobble of the Earth, and for our purposes at this point we can explain the phenomenon in this way. But the date when the Precession actually moved into Aquarius is one and no other, just as there is only one day each year when the equinoxes cross the ecliptic and the Sun reaches us from 0° Aries, the 0 point. When an individual knows this date it opens up the cosmic harmonies for him, and in no subjective way. It is one's key to the doors of objective knowledge, and it is a piece of information the knowledge of which one must earn, for it is the silent support of one's work.

We say the zodiac is a labyrinth because at any given moment in time if one plunges deeply *all* the possibilities will be simultaneously present. But this has no validity when we try to unravel the progression of the individual and the Earth. In that case we must know rightly what the really predominant harmony is, and its objective reality. Since all the possibilities are always present we can at any moment justify ourselves in our study; we can always find an influence or an indication which will give weight to our particular idea or system. In astrology there are now myriads of systems, each day a further one appears and each of them has its basis in a partial truth and can therefore reveal a particle of the Design, because whatever the new system it is always taken from the zodiac of 12 which will invariably yield a beauty of form and a harmony of pattern. When one is faced with all the possibilities, one must have the consciousness of unity in order to know rightly and to have this knowledge truly serve us and be our guide. Otherwise one is lost in the multiple alone, and one moves along in semi-darkness, believing oneself to be in the full, or at best half, light.

In view of this it is imperative in the realm of the harmonies of the Cosmos to have a synthetic key at one's disposal, an arrangement which we can look to for the purpose of *synthesis*, which will make sense out of the chaos of the Many and show us objective truth and the way to objective knowledge. It must be for us a means whereby we pull all the threads together which Mind has woven of itself and attached itself to in these studies, a key which can open the corridors of a consciousness of unity regarding the Cosmos in which we live and have our being, in which all things live and have their being, out of which or beyond which nothing is because it is by going into this rather than into the non-existent Beyond that we come to the Only Reality.

This key is the *Gnostic Circle*.

The Gnostic Circle

THIS IS THE Gnostic Circle, the design that contains the means whereby it is possible to find one's place in the cosmic vastness. Its components, though they present us with an apparently complex design, are extremely simple to understand the Gnostic Circle is nothing more than the combination of all that we have studie so far. It is the synthesis based primarily on the union of two major divisions of t Circle, —that of 12 with all its sub-divisions, and that of 9 which contains the d sion of 3, or the Sacred Triangle. It is this combination that makes it possible man to join the heavens to his Earth cycles through the calendar years. It per s to the individual, to nations, and the entire globe; it is the chart of the Avat as well as the revelation of the path of development of each individual.

The Gnostic Circle is merely the combination of the zodiac—the occul ircle which contains the knowledge of evolution—and the structural pattern of th solar system. The Circle of 12 is the zodiac, and the Circle of 9 is our actual solar system, each orbit representing one year of Earth life. The joint harmony of these two, superimposed or synthesised in one circle, is what constitutes our key to the evolution and flowering of the seed of the Spirit. In fact we can say that the Gnostic Circle is mainly for this purpose: it shows mankind the ultimate and ideal perfection that can be attained during this particular phase of the evolution, during this great transition point from the animal-mental to the more divine mankind.

The Gnostic Circle can be used in a mundane manner; it can indicate the small details of life, though rather unsatisfactorily, for it speaks neither of positive nor negative, to which the ordinary individual attaches himself. He who still clings to the ego, to preferences and desires, will find little satisfaction in the Gnostic Circle, because it is impossible through its use to continue labelling in this way and to seek to distort the divine plan for one's limited interests. It shows one the way to the harmonious development of being. Actually this is its purpose: To show the utter harmony of life and the subtle occult force that carries all things to the knowledge and fulfilment of their rightful place within the Divine Mosaic.

This is the Divine Mosaic. Each piece is a portion of the Divinity Manifest. Each part is a part of her soul and can reveal a phase of her journey through unending Time. By inserting ourselves into the Circle with the correct understanding, we can learn of the portion of the Divine we are in the process of revealing. *We are that portion, and we are That.*

In this way the Gnostic Circle can be of immense benefit to the seeker, for in its simplicity it reveals to man how he is an integral part of the Manifest Divine, and can in no way extract himself from this Mosaic. Birth brings him to consciously enter the Circle at a particular point, according to his birthdate, and from then on he fulfils his destiny within the eternal round of perpetual motion as established for this planet at this particular time. This is a means whereby the seeker immediately has the understanding of the unity of all things, whereby he breaks through his petty and limited vision of his destiny, as well as that of the entire Earth. He sees in this design the piece that Earth itself is—with relation to the entire System—because today, in this particular Aquarian Age, it is no longer possible for man to ignore the destiny of the Earth itself and detach himself from its unfoldment. We are all here together, on this particular planet, a portion of this solar system, within this Milky Way Galaxy. We are not elsewhere, we are not in the Unmanifest, whatever we believe that to be. Most of us are not at all certain what becomes of us at the time of death. We cannot be sure that we do indeed enter the Paradise we strive for and have been assured of; and even if this be a fact, we know not with accuracy what that paradise is and what its relation to Earth life really is, what the state of Nirvana within the scheme of things truly signifies for the seeker, whether it actually disconnects him from the progressive movement of the evolution. In short, we know nothing, but we have many, many theories, the most accepted of which is that we can disconnect ourselves from the destiny of the Earth, abandon the planet to its own fate while we move off to another more beatific plane. In this illusion, in one way or another, the seeker lives.

The soul that we are is one with the soul of the Earth. This is the knowledge contained in the Gnostic Circle, and captured in particular in the Sacred Triangle. We are the Earth, each of us. We carry within us the veiled psychic being, a particle and spark of the Manifest Divine. Not only do we envelop this spark but each cell of our body is as well an envelope of the spark, and each atom and sub-atom. Our bodies are the perfect and identical representation of the Supreme because each of our cells is like unto the Supreme's cells, the Galaxies. They each contain the Trinity, and all these minute particles spin around and owe their life to the Central Fire in the soul, the psychic being.

In this very same manner the Galaxy is constructed. There is the mysterious centre that keeps all the stars in orbit around itself. This Centre, that Science knows so little of as yet, is located with respect to our Sun and planet in the direction of the Constellation Hercules or the zodiacal sign Capricorn, and slowly, at the rate of 12 miles per second (43,200 miles per hour, 432,000 miles in 10 hours or 1 day for

Saturn) our Sun orbits around and moves ever closer to this Solar Apex, as it is called. That is, at the end of December each year, the Earth is directly behind the Sun with respect to this great Void; our solar system with our planet is being drawn ever closer toward this colossal Magnet. We could go beyond. We could also see how this Centre is revolving around an even vaster one, and finally how all the Galaxies are part of One Movement. But this is unnecessary because as we are presently constituted this knowledge only serves to have us lose ourselves in the immensity of it all, without being able to retain a knowledge of and relationship with our place. On the general scale we are at the point where we can safely know of our place in our own solar system, without this impeding our development. During ages of darkness one loses this knowledge, during times of in-drawn energy such as the Manifestations of feminine force, the even numbers. But of course during those periods the knowledge is somehow retained for the benefit of the future evolution. In one way or another it is always present on the Earth.

Thus, at this time, we are given the means whereby we can know the so-called esoteric truth of our System and its evolution, and the part the Earth plays therein, as well as each of its inhabitants. We can go so far as to know that there is a Great Centre to which we in our System are related and which determines our course, because it is this Centre that finally holds the key to the Precession of the Equinoxes. It is this Centre that makes of the axis Capricorn and Cancer the Evolutionary Axis of our planet. And through our study we know that in ourselves, in our very bodies, we can find the exact reproduction of this Galaxy which then gives us the revelation of the Supreme Herself.

The purpose of our destiny therefore is none other than to become ever more conscious of this 'centrality', and to reveal its essence always to a greater degree. We see that we are being slowly sucked into this Great Cauldron, and the closer we come the greater must our capacity be to reflect and embody this Energy.

As it presently stands we do not even know what this Centre is. To Earth beings who study the matter it appears to be a mysterious hole or point, a solemn Void. To those who enjoy a subtle vision the void seems to be due only to the incapacity of man's eye to register the intensity of the vibration that emits from this Centre. Man is protected by his blindness, for seeing too soon would destroy the possibility of experiencing his growth toward the union with this Great Light. The evolution is for this purpose: the being must progress gradually in all its parts so that it may have the integral experience of God. Man's mind may not plunge forward while his body remains in darkness. This would be as if our Sun were to suddenly accelerate its pace toward the Centre and, irrespective of the condition of its satellites, to plunge into the Cauldron of Bliss, thereby bringing about the dissolution of its denser parts. The Sun can withstand the Fire because it is closer in essence to it; but its *body*, the system of planets with all their cells (organic life on Earth, for example) would dissolve without having had and enjoyed the experience of Union. *The whole of the Universe exists so that each cell and atom and sub-particle may know itself as That, and enjoy the progressive delight of this copulatory Ecstasy.* The process is unending, for each consummation brings about a birth from the combined and fused energies of the elements, like the nuclear fusion in the core of the Sun, and the movement continues in that way into Infinity, into Eternity. The Universe is built of this Energy, this fusion and union is the élan that carries it forward in its unending experience of self-enjoyment and self-expression. Each marriage, each particle of Brahman that bursts into the secret recesses of the Divine Mother and possesses and devours her in a passionate and intense fusion, brings forth a further image of this union. The Child is continually being born. There is no end to this process of reproduction, because there is no end to the thrust of Brahman, to the multiplication of his Seed.

This is the truth of man, the truth of all his longings. This is the secret in his desire for woman and his longing to fecundate her. This is woman's longing for child. Man desires woman, woman wants child and child becomes the father who then seeks the mother, and the mother brings forth the child, and on and on. This is the 9 evolving to the 6 and becoming the 3 who is then the 9. This is Shakti who lends herself so that Brahman can fecundate her womb, enjoy himself in her being and in this way give rise to a further expression of himself. This is the Sacred Trinity, by and within which all the possible relations exist. This is the essence of the Absolute, the essence of the Galaxy, the essence of the Sun and planets, of man, of the cell, the molecule and the essence of the atom. The fission of the atom is the delight of Brahman, casting his seed into the hidden realities and fecundating the creation. This is Pluto's seed, the God of fertility: Shiva. This is the rape of Persephone. This is the Earth, Kore, the Child of the Divine Mother.

The web of creation is Consciousness which spins itself within the sea of Bliss, and brings forth the Existence. These are the three *guṇas* we have been describing, which are also the final Trinity of unity of the zodiac: Capricorn, Aquarius and Pisces, Sat-Chit-Ananda. Sat and Ananda are upheld by Chit: it is a process of the manifestation of Consciousness, a continuous growth of the Light, the Light that is the seed of Brahman. This is the whole purpose of evolution, to be ever-more conscious in order to know this Bliss, this Delight, and then to know oneself as the child of that Union: to be, *Sat*, pure existence—the child of the Trinity. For this reason the centre of our Galaxy with respect to Earth zodiacal direction is Capricorn. Toward this *being* we must each one of us evolve.

This is the joy of the Gnostic Circle: a means whereby man can have the highest knowledge that shows him his place within the Absolute, that shows him through the key of Time, the integral process of the divinisation of the Earth. By the Gnostic Circle one can reconcile the myriad and often disturbing faces of the Supreme. One can see the play of the *gunas* in their rightful measure; one knows the joy of Creation, the stability of Preservation, and the value of Destruction. Through the Gnostic Circle one sees the way of Love, because one can therein perceive that all things are right in the scheme of Time, the Ignorance as well, the sinner as well, —who is but a desperate seeker without the light of gnosis. Each human being is seeking for union with the Divine, each human being is a part of the Mosaic, a cell of the Mother, each human being can find his right relation to Time and therefore have the knowledge of the part he plays in the unfolding of the spirit in evolution. There is a level and a place for all beings.

The Gnostic Circle is the manifestation of Love, for the circle is the symbol of Love. The Gnostic Circle is the supreme mandala.

In this study we can come to know the way in which we may assist the evolution of the race to a finer expression of being, as well as our own individual development. There is a sense to all man's sins which are a distortion of the Divine Truth, a deviation of the Divine Energy. But the Ignorance which allows for this distortion now gives way to allow for the progression in Light, to grow not from darkness to half-light, but from truth to greater truth. Thus we know that now it is possible for man to embody the Energy in a pure way and to become representative of a new humanity, a totally new manifestation.

Before we begin speaking of the minute details of the Gnostic Circle with respect to an individual's life, it is well to show how the Sacred Triangle is the Trinity of Fire of the Map of 12 Manifestations. In the Circle the 9 is 0° Aries, 3 is 0° Leo and 6 is 0° Sagittarius. These numbers are then equivalent to 1, 5, 9. With the superimposition of the Circle of 9 on the Circle of 12—9, 3, and 6 would become the 1st, 5th and 9th signs: the Fire Trinity. So in terms of our number system and calendar, the 1, 5, and 9 would manifest as 9, 3 and 6. In the study of the geometrical circle on page 107, (Diagram C), these numbers, 1, 5, and 9 correspond to the last triad in the planetary system, Uranus, Neptune and Pluto, and would occupy positions from 10° Capricorn to 0° Aries, thus falling precisely within, and embracing, the quarter of unity of the zodiac.

A development begins at the 0-9 point of the Gnostic Circle. From then on it moves through each sign, completing the 12 in a period of 9 years. There are thus 12 stages or steps and phases of development and 9 years within which to complete them, and within each one of these 9 years there are as well 12 steps, or the 12 signs, experienced.

The student must observe the various divisions of the zodiac of 12 that have been incorporated in the Gnostic Circle, because these are the means whereby he is able to join the movement of Time to that of the journey through the 12 stages. All of these divisions come to us through Indian astrology, and still bear Sanskrit names. They are simply various forms of dividing the circle of 360°.

The first circle of symbols encountered after the inner ring of the numbers from 0 to 9 is the division of 12: each sign having 30°. Then follows the division of the circle and signs into *decanates*, or each sign of 30° is divided into sections of 10°, (coloured in orange). In time this would be equivalent to *three months*. Within one year therefore one passes through 4 such decanates.

The next division of the Circle is that of 9, or the *navaṁśas* (coloured gold). This means that each sign of 30° is divided by 9, yielding segments of 3°20' each. It would take *one month* to complete one of these divisions. Thus a navamsa is equivalent to one of our calendar months. It is principally this division that joins the zodiac to our calendar through the number system.

After the navamsa there is the division of each sign of 30° into 12 sections called *dvādaśāṁśa* by the Indians, (coloured in violet). This yields a section of $2\,{}^{1}/_{2}°$, each section comprising $22\,{}^{1}/_{2}$ days.

The last circle division is that of the *Individual Degrees*, the *triṁśāṁsa*, each sign containing 30, which correspond to 9 days in the Gnostic Circle, (coloured in blue)

These are the major divisions of the Circle, upon which we have placed the nine orbits of the planets, each one at its corresponding number. The combination gives us the pattern of the actual planetary system with the occult circle of the zodiac. In this manner we are able to combine the two and see what this produces and indicates in human evolution on Earth.

There is one difficulty that we encounter along the way. Our calendar is not yet perfectly devised to correspond each month with accuracy to this design and consequently there are certain minor points which create a discrepancy in the observation, —namely, the 28 days of February, and the 31 days of some months. Over an extended period this discrepancy works itself out, but it is our wish that a society of knowledge emerges once more and adopts a calendar which will especially correspond in one way or another to this sacred design. It would of course have to be a society that profoundly understands the reason for such a correspondence, the occult significance behind the adoption of any particular calendar, the need of establishing a more illumined manner of recording the passage of time on our planet; one that takes into consideration the gnostic development of being within the solar system.

The ancients apparently had this knowledge. In the major civilisations of the past of which we have record, there was a higher knowledge that guided the peoples in these matters. Two such civilisations that come to mind are the Mayan and the Aztec. Preserved from those times is the great Calendar Stone which is a device similar to the Gnostic Circle, utilisable in the same way. The Mayans and Aztecs in fact were but seconds off in their calculation of the solar year, which has only become precise for today's civilisations because of technical devices which measure the rotations of the bodies involved in the phenomenon: something which the Mayans had done supposedly without any instruments of precision. When the Aztecs were using the perfect calendar based on the accurate calculation of the Sun's year, Europe was still asleep in this regard. But though they knew the true measurement of the solar year, this civilisation as well as others of their kind, maintained calendars which were devised for a period of 360 days which would correspond to the perfect division of the year into 12 equal parts of 30 (or 18 parts of 20 days). The five extra days were considered 'out of the calendar'—and rightfully so, because they correspond to the imperfection of the Earth's orbit. Scientists have much criticised and ridiculed this practice, degrading the custom on the basis of pure surface knowledge without understanding the deeper significance. The five extra days were spent in meditation and concentration, the citizens were withdrawn from all outer activity so that they could go deeply within and prepare for the new calendar cycle which would open up the possibility of a new and greater progress. For those five days the entire civilisation stopped. It was a time of reassessment, libation, sacrifice and preparation, a flushing out of a sort, in order to leave a void and allow the new to take shape. In the spiritual development of an individual this is an extremely helpful and beneficial practice which has especial effect when preceding certain birthdays—for example, when the Apex of the Triangle is reached every nine years. But for the entire society each year these five days would serve to stop all activity and collectively place the group soul at the feet of the Divine Mother and re-new the community's dedication and consecration to her work.

There are two starting points: the first is the 12 months based on the zodiacal signs corresponding to the 0° Aries equinox, and the other is the 12 months of the calendar year, which we count from 0° Aries but which corresponds to the 10th sign, Capricorn. This latter starting point would be considered as the indicator of the world's societies, since it is this method of calculating time that has become most universal; the former would be the shift of the Earth itself, *its* relation to time. Both these starting points are significant, each in its own way. The equinox is the equal division of day and night, and the January solstice is the time when the Earth is closest to the Sun. The Earth marks its time according to the March 21st equinox, and the civilisations on the planet mark their time according to the New Year beginning January 1st, for the major part. There is an interesting correspondence as far as numbers go in this arrangement since January is the first month and Aries is the first sign. February is the second month and Taurus is the second sign, and so on.

Traces of the zodiacal arrangement of the calendar are still evident in the current Gregorian system: the last months of the year bear names which point to the number of the zodiacal signs they correspond to; *Septe*mber derives from the Latin *seven*, being the time when the seventh sign, Libra, commences. *Octo*ber (8) is the month wherein the eighth sign, Scorpio, begins; *Nove*mber (9) is when the ninth sign, Sagittarius, starts, and *Dece*mber (10) is the beginning month of the tenth sign, Capricorn.

In the wheel of 12 the first three signs are related to the last three by number vibration. It can be seen in the diagram that Capricorn is equivalent to Aries, Aquarius to Taurus, and Pisces to Gemini.

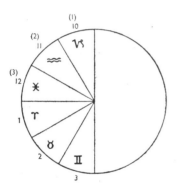

Numerologically when calculating the sum total of any particular day of the year there is a correspondence between the first three months and the last three. For example, 1.1.1956 equals 1+1+1+9+5+6=23=2+3=5, and 1.10.1956 is also 5 in the same way. In this manner many interesting number arrangements occur during the year and have a deep significance based on this uniformity.

The Gnostic Circle can be used for a calendar record as well as a pure zodiacal map. And it is the combination of the two that offers the most interesting results.

The Greeks have left us many clues to the arrangement of the calendar year, the most important of all being the tale that is handed down about the night of January 5th, which was later adopted as the Christian Epiphany. Kore, Demeter's daughter, gives birth to Aeon, the Age, on this night. In bas-reliefs Aeon is shown inside a sort of zodiacal 'egg', with the 12 symbols encircling him. He represents the year that is born of Persephone on that night of January 5th. This legend has a very profound significance because the five days between January 1st to the 5th would be those 'outside of the calendar', and the night of the 5th-6th was the Epiphany, the appearance of the light once more. It is precisely at this time, around January 4th each year, that the Earth is at its perihelion, its closest distance to the Sun. This is consequently known as the Festival of Light. According to the clairvoyant, Edgar Cayce, this was also the real birthday of Jesus Christ.

In view of these and other facts, this appears to be a more perfect arrangement for a gnostic calendar. The year would begin on the midnight between 5th-6th January, after five days spent withdrawn from all activity if one would so desire or feel the need, —to re-assess that which had been and to prepare the being for that which is to come. It is a period of regeneration of the collective aspiration, for the calendar is this: it is the means whereby the Earth civilisation, on a collective scale, unites with the vibrations and rhythm that numbers capture and represent. The calendar we can say is the horoscope of the civilisation from which it has issued.

There is no coincidence. Our present calendar is in perfect correspondence with the beginning of the 9th Manifestation. And it is no coincidence that the count started from A.D. 1, when it did, this being considered the beginning of Christ's reign. In the legend it must be pointed out that the three Persian astrologers (magi) who followed the 'Star' to the new-born Christ, saw him on the day of the Greek Epiphany, the birth of Aeon from the womb of Kore, the virgin-maiden daughter of Demeter. Mary is Kore, St. Anne is Demeter, the Christ is Aeon,— and he had 12 disciples who each correspond to a zodiacal sign beginning with Peter (Aries), just as Aeon is depicted in the zodiacal circular egg of 12 signs which he sustains.

It is most important that the student see these correspondences and understand as well the conditions prevailing around those times, and how the knowledge was transferred from sect to sect, each using its own symbol to pass on the same truth. It must be remembered that all during the first 600 years of the 9th Manifestation, the Eleusinian Mysteries were a prominent influence over the spiritual development of the civilisation, and the 'Two Goddesses', Demeter and Persephone, were the figures upon whom the gnostic tradition was centred. Later on the Gnostic Fathers passed these same traditions and keys of knowledge over to the figure of Jesus Christ, when his worship displaced that of Demeter and Kore.

The Eleusinian Mysteries came to an end in 396 A.D., the numbers of the Sacred Triangle, which in themselves tell us the same story as the myth and indicate the same initiatory process.

In one type of gnostic calendar, if such a development would actually take place, the number harmony would be that the first sign would correspond to the first month almost entirely, remaining therefore the number 1, the second to the second month, etc. The year could begin on the night of January 5th-6th after five days of indrawn period and preparation, and each subsequent month would consist of an even 30 days, each day corresponding to a degree of the Circle. Every four years there would be six days instead of five, or an extra day inserted somewhere in the calendar as would be deemed in accordance with the significance of the fourth. The arrangement for leap years would remain in essence entirely as it is now.

The Leap Years

There is a very beautiful pattern in the arrangement of the leap years according to number study. Leap years would revolve around the number 4. We have already considered the five extra days of the year, so it is 4 and 5 that are prominent. We can study the matter based on Leap Year Day 29 February, 1956—the day the Mother announced in the Sri Aurobindo Ashram that the Supramental Manifestation had occurred. From that year we will study the numerological development of all the leap years until after the millennium.

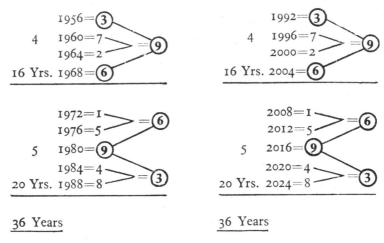

36 Years   36 Years

From 1956 to 1992 there are 36 years. Of these, the first 16 complete the numbers 3, 9, 6, and they consist of a batch of four numbers and four leap years. The next group consists of 20 years which complete the trinity 6, 9, 3, and this group is made up of five numbers or 5 leap years, numerologically reduced. This 4 × 9, or 36 years, is a most important period in a person's life cycle, which we shall discuss further on.

Four is an interesting number for us on this planet. The day is imperfect in time by four minutes, which accounts for the slippage and the accumulation of five extra days each year over the perfect 360, or 4 times 90. And then each four years there is the need to make up a further day because of remaining seconds over these five extra days. After this a further correction is made based on 4 by eliminating a leap year at every century that is not divisible by 400.

In terms of the Gnostic Circle, these numbers 4 and 5 correspond to the orbits of Mars and Jupiter, the ascending power and the descending light. In between there is a huge 'abyss' of 342,000,000 (9) miles, the shattering zone of the Asteroids, the 4.5 Orbit, which may be responsible for our slightly imperfect year. It is, in fact, at this point that in the perfected calendar the leap year day would be most appropriate. There are theories that in the past the year consisted of an even 360 days and that subsequently some natural catastrophe took the Earth in this slightly extended orbit. It is also possible that instead we are evolving *toward* the perfection, that what may have been lost in some aeonic age may as well be regained, and that in the future the Earth will have a time cycle perfectly in accord with the circle of 360° and the even progression of 1° per day. It is possible that the greater perfection will take place according to and in rapport with the manifestation of a more illumined consciousness on the planet, as we move closer to the great Centre.

These are all questions that the student of cosmic harmonies considers as he progresses in his studies, but it is better in these matters to concentrate on the facts of today and find their perfection, rather than lose ourselves in considerations about the future, trapped in the prison of the speculative mind. In the same light we consider only the nine planets of our actual system in our study, because this arrangement is the only one that concerns us at present and can help us in any concrete manner in our quest for truth and the divinisation of the Earth. In any case, whatever the problems we encounter in the use of the Gnostic Circle, the design is accurate as far as is necessary for us at this moment in Time.

Use of the Gnostic Circle

A person can find his place in the Wheel by considering his birth to occur at the 0-9 Apex of the Sacred Triangle. The 9 months of gestation will produce the full development of the infant: at the 9 point one's independent journey begins. This process corresponds to all things, all people. We can see this in the many aspects of our civilisation, some of which we shall discuss as we continue in the study. For example, in 45 B.C. (9) the Julian Calendar was devised and adopted, starting an entirely new cycle for humanity with regard to time measurement. We can say therefore that this was the birth of our calendar which did not break out of the rhythm of the Gnostic Circle, since the starting point still fell on the 9 Apex. Moreover, occurring in a year made up of the digits 4 and 5, it would be the 9 point consisting of the planetary vibrations of Mars and Jupiter and would correspond in cyclic development to the area of the 4.5 Orbit. When considering the development on the basis of the beginning of the 9th Manifestation, the arrangement varies a bit but is nonetheless in harmony with the 9 Apex. Certainly the adoption of the Julian calendar was a turning-point and a revolutionising force in or for the civilisation. We cannot consider the Gregorian Reform, which occurred in 1582, in the same light, for it merely added a measure that affected the correction of every *400 years* mentioned previously. The calendar remained basically the same and a leap year was eliminated at every century that could not be divided by 400. This can in no way be compared to the birth of an entirely new calendar for the Roman Civilisation in 45 B.C. The Gregorian Reform took place in 1582, which would fall at the 7 point of the Gnostic Circle—a reform, but not a completely new birth.

All that which signifies a new beginning belongs to the 9 point, and it is therefore at that point that the human being begins his life cycle according to the Gnostic Circle. Each subsequent year of life would correspond to a section of the 9 Circle within the 12. o to 1, Mercury's position, would correspond to 1 year of life, 1 to 2 would be the second year, falling at the Venus orbit, and so on. Thus we see that the navamsa sub-division (coloured in gold in the diagram) is our means of methodic progression. Each navamsa corresponds to 1 month of life until, after passage through 12, one year is completed. It could be said that the first six months are still under the influence of Sun-Pluto, after which the orbit of Mercury becomes prominent, culminating around the first year, diminishing slowly until it gives way to the influence of Venus around the first year and a half, which in turn would culminate at two years old.

The other divisions of the Circle are also to be taken into consideration when reading the chart, —mainly the decanate division, embracing a period of 3 months, and the trisamsa or individual degree, corresponding to nine days. Studying the very first navamsa in a child's life we see that for nine days there is the full presence of Aries, each of the divisions falling under its influence. After nine days a slight change occurs in the individual's progress by his moving out of the Aries individual degree and into that of Taurus and remaining under this for a further nine days, making 18 in all. Following Taurus there is the Gemini influence for a further nine days, bringing the count to 27 days, equivalent to 3° of the zodiac. And for the last 20 minutes of the navamsa 'month', three days would fall under the influence of Cancer. In this way the first month of life is completed and the next navamsa or month begins, which belongs to Taurus, still in the individual degree of Cancer where a person remains for six more days to complete the nine corresponding to each degree of the zodiac. The individual then swings into Leo for a period of nine days, making now 15 in all, then he passes into Virgo for a further nine days, making 24, and concludes the month in Libra, for six days, making 30 in all.

The Gemini navamsa begins in Libra and lasts for three days; the next individual degree lasts for nine days, Scorpio, making 12 in all; then Sagittarius occupies a further nine days, making 21, and finally Capricorn occupies the last nine days, concluding the cycle of 30.

The first three months of the year of a child's life are recorded in this manner.

At the end of the third another shift takes place and the child moves from the *deca-nate* of Aries to that of Leo, wherein he will remain until the sixth month. During that period he will have passed through three more navamsas, from Cancer to Virgo, or ten individual degrees, from Aquarius to Scorpio.

The sixth month of life begins in the Sagittarius decanate and remains there until the ninth. The navamsas passed will be Libra through Sagittarius, and the individual degrees will be Sagittarius through Virgo. The ninth month of life opens the way for a big change and an entirely new sign is entered, Taurus.

The Circle in violet corresponds to the dwadasamsa division and is another sub-division of time, but it appears to be more relevant for the deciphering of the hours of the day, a division of $2^1/_2°$ corresponding to one hour. In days, $2^1/_2°$ would be $22 \ ^1/_2$. One would need 16 dwadasamsas to complete one year, whereas there are 12 navamsas in 1 year, equivalent to passage through each of the 12 signs, thereby neatly fitting into the calendar year.

The process may initially appear very complex, but in reality it is extremely simple when one has mastered certain basic principles, namely that each individual degree of the 360° celestial circle corresponds to 9 days, each dwadasamsa to $22 \ ^1/_2$ days, each navamsa to 30 days, and each decanate to 90. The count is to begin with the birth of an individual at the 9 Apex and to proceed through the division in the manner here described. For this one must simply make use of the birth date. All counts must begin at that time, that being the 0 or starting point, the 0° Aries of the Gnostic Circle.

Arrival at the Mercury orbit, the number 1 of the Circle, would be on the first birthday. The second would be when the child had reached the Venus 2 point, and so on through the wheel. The 9th birthday would bring us to the Apex of the Triangle once more, back to the 0° Aries point.

The new student of cosmic harmonies or the rigid pragmatist will argue that our measure of time is arbitrary, unreal, of value only for this planet and limited because of the temporal quality of the methods we use to calculate time. It is true that a calendar such as the one called 'World Calendar' would be a somewhat better arrangement and would signify by its adoption that the civilisation had made a certain progress, but the student must bear in mind that we are dealing with a *Divine Consciousness* and not the Ignorance,—an intelligence capable of total seeing and total being. We tend to believe that whatever the human consciousness cannot conceive or cannot do is impossible. We cannot see that this Consciousness moves along with us and upholds our progress. Each step we take is because of a power of light and knowledge that has first issued from the womb of the Divine Consciousness; each truth we see is because this Consciousness has lifted the veil. The pattern of discovery of the new planets is testimony to this action. We *see* when and how the Divine Consciousness wills, and this is determined by a host of factors far too all-inclusive for the human mind to grasp as yet. The more humanity progresses toward total identity with the Supreme, the more exact will be its seeing and hence its method of recording and measuring time according to the Divine Harmony. We are dependent on It, but It accompanies us on our way and arranges things in accord with the knowledge we possess. The more we perceive the perfection, the more perfect will this be revealed in all the ways of our lives.

It must be stated once more that total harmony will be realised when the complete manifestation of the Truth-Consciousness takes place. Until that time we must make do with the means at our disposal to find our place in the cosmic perfection, with total faith that the day will soon be upon us when there will no longer be error and perfection will show its full face. The upholder of our evolution is the Supreme Mother, and she acts according to our needs, intervenes when necessary, determines the patterns we can fit into and can understand, alters these when necessary, reveals new stages as the evolution progresses: in short, she holds the key to our individual and collective destiny and lifts the veils when the time comes to see.

Tibet: Its Destiny in the Gnostic Circle

THE PATTERN DESCRIBED regarding the birth of an individual can be followed for the birth of anything, and its subsequent development. For example, the progress of a nation can be seen in the Circle when accurate dates are known. It is also necessary to discover the particular pattern that the nation or the individual is susceptible to, and how it is to be perceived within the Circle. Tibet is a perfect example of one type of pattern that has been employed, and by the study of its history since the time it became an organised nation—since the beginning of the gestation of its 'group soul'—we can see the clarity of its destiny and we can understand much of the hardships it is now undergoing, in the light of a vision which transcends the small details of the present. We can know, by the pattern of its destiny within the Gnostic Circle, just at what point the Tibetan soul is in its process of birth and affirmation. By this we can see perhaps in what way the movement of this birth can be assisted.

All of the information here put forth is taken almost entirely from the fourth chapter of the autobiography of His Holiness, the Dalai Lama, entitled: *My Land, and My People*.[1] In this book the Dalai Lama gives a brief history of Tibet and supplies us with all the pertinent dates, and above all the *dynasty numbers*, whereby the key to the nation's development can be found. The information is precious to students of cosmic harmonies because Tibet represents perhaps the last of the theocratic rules upon Earth, which alas are also suffering under the pressure of the Time-Spirit, dramatically made to alter their patterns and submit to the new force that is manifesting. In this play there are pawns such as the communist and other materialist powers, and these must not be confused with the ultimate power of the Divine. They are tools and measures which are temporarily needed to carry humanity into a new phase of its destiny; they are the attendants at this birth, and nothing more.

The beginning of Tibet as an organised country, according to the Dalai Lama, was in the year 127 B.C. The first King was thereafter succeeded by forty generations of kings. It will be shown with precision how the dynasties themselves were the pattern used within the Gnostic Circle, which then culminated with the Dalai Lamas.

[1] Weidenfeld and Nicolson Publishers (London).

The destiny of the nation began to take shape therefore with the first ruler. We consider him to occupy the o point, the Apex of the Triangle, embracing the section from o to 1. During the early part of the life of the nation the religion *Bön* was prevalent among the people, which lasted for 27 (3 × 9) reigns. The student can see in the diagram that this brought the nation to the Apex of the Triangle once more and a new beginning of some sort was felt. In fact, during the reign of the 28th (1) King the doctrine of the Lord Buddha began to spread in the country through this monarch, slowly replacing the former religion. If we continue following the wheel we see that, according to the information furnished by His Holiness, it was during the reign of the 33rd monarch that much was done to 'establish the new religion more firmly'. It was he, the 33rd king, who laid the firm foundations of the Buddhist religion in the country: during his period the faith was 'crystallised' in the nation, and his reign would correspond to the Saturn point, where precisely this process of firm establishment is felt. As well, it falls in the sign Sagittarius, the sign of religion and philosophy, among other things.

During the reign of the 36th (4 × 9) king there was war between Tibet and China. In the Gnostic Circle this would fall at the 9 point, indicating a very important time in the destiny and a beginning of a new order: it falls in the sign of Aries and hence there was a powerful influx of the vital force which was intended to sustain the new order that was being established through the cycle that was opening up. But with the influence of Aries—because a powerful influx of energy occurs— we often find that the outcome is war. In the case of Tibet's 36th reign, war did indeed take place and Tibet was victorious. The first 4 × 9 cycle was completed and the new destiny was firmly established.

The next phase is very interesting for it corresponds to the 37th point (number 1) and Mercury's orbit. We see clearly how the influence of Mercury and then of Gemini was felt during that monarch's reign because it was the time that Indian scholars were invited to the country and the major Sanskrit works of the Buddhist doctrine were translated into Tibetan; the Samye Monastary was established and the first monks were ordained in Tibet. Tibetan Buddhism was fully on its way.

In his autobiography the Dalai Lama then passes on to the 40th reign, falling in the year 866 A.D., and tells us that again there was war between Tibet and China, in which the former was once more victorious. It is to be noted that the 40th reign falls at the number 4, the orbit of Mars in the Circle; hence the nation was brought to war again. But the power was strong and much appears to have been done to establish the kingdom. It is stated in the book that these three kings we have mentioned are considered the greatest in Tibet's history, the 33rd, the 37th and the 40th.

For our study the development takes an interesting turn at this time. On the

Circle Tibet would be at the Mars orbit, passing through the Asteroid Belt and moving on to the orbit of Jupiter, the 5th. It is precisely at this time that a 'shattering' occurred in the nation. The 41st (5) monarch, according to His Holiness, undid everything his predecessors had done. The kingdom began to disintegrate. According to our calendar his reign began in the year 901 A.D.; so his was to mark passage through the last century of the first millennium, which is somewhat equivalent to our times, this last century of the second millennium: the old is broken up and room is made for the new, though this appears to be disastrous while it is taking place. In fact, this king was assassinated 6 years after his enthronement, which in his reign would have corresponded to the Saturn point. We shall see further on how this point is again important in the same way for the present Dalai Lama.

The reign of Tibet's 41st king and his assassination left the kingdom divided, split between two of his sons. This, the student must recall, was the time of passage over the Asteroid Belt in the solar harmonies, truly a breaking-up, and the effects lasted for over 300 years. The situation brought the nation through the 4th to the 5th orbit in its development. Then in the year 1253 (2) A.D. the second form of rule took shape and the first of the Priest-Kings was installed, in a sense a preparation for the rule of the Dalai Lamas who were to come later. This arrangement lasted for 96 years and was then followed by another of the same type, lasting for 86 years. In all these 182 (2) years there were 20 (2) lamas of the first order who ruled and 11 (2) of the second—a total of 31 (4). Thus we find ourselves back at the 4 point once more, through more than 1,400 years of calendar time. After this the country returned to secular monarchy for 207 years, 23 (5) cycles of 9 in the Gnostic Circle, and in the year 1642 (4) A.D. the Dalai Lama became the temporal-spiritual leader of the country. He was in fact the *5th Dalai Lama*. The student must note that this falls at the orbit of Jupiter, precisely the planet that indicates this type of rule. It is between the two orbits of Mars (4) and Jupiter (5) that the destiny of the nation is captured and the entire Tibetan civilisation we know today can be described. The rule of the Dalai Lamas embraced the section of the Triangle from Mars to Jupiter to Saturn. It ended (within the country for a time) on the orbit of Saturn, as we shall later point out.

During the 300 years since the establishment of the 5th Dalai Lama as spiritual and temporal leader of Tibet, there have been 9 such subsequent successions. Let us follow the reign of the Dalai Lamas within the Circle and we shall find that it fits into the same section of the Triangle. The first priest-kings and the intervening secular monarchs had revolved around the 4 point, where the very first dynasty of Tibetan kings had stopped, and gradually opened the path to the 5. The Dalai Lamas took charge of secular rule with the fifth in their line. The first venerated Dalai Lama (only a spiritual leader) was an incarnation of Chenresi, the Buddha of

Mercy; he was born in the year 1391 (5). From this first the entire lineage of Dalai Lamas has been maintained and connected by a continual process of conscious reincarnation. Thus we can say that the *seed* of the line began with the number 5 (1391). After this initial one, the fifth Dalai Lama in line then became spiritual and secular ruler and the reign continued for over 300 years. (The incarnation of Gautama the Buddha itself corresponds to the 5. He was born in the 5th century B.C., and possibly in the year 563, a numerological 5, though the actual year in the century is not accurately known.)

In 1933 the 13th (4) Dalai Lama left his body and his reincarnation is the actual Dalai Lama, the 14th (5), back to the original 5 point.

How has the present Dalai Lama chosen to incarnate? He was born...'on the fifth day of the fifth month of the Wood Hog year of the Tibetan calendar—that is, in 1935'. Moreover, 1935 is 9, the Apex of the Triangle: consequently this Dalai Lama was destined to carry out the passage into a new reign, similar to what occurred in the destiny of the country during its last passage through the 900's, the disintegration of the nation, because it is still caught within the sphere of the 4th and 5th Orbits and the Asteroid Belt. The 13th (4) Dalai Lama left his body in 1933, or the 7th orbit of Uranus, and the reincarnation took place two years later when in 1935 the Pluto, or 9th, Orbit was reached, opening a new cycle. But this cycle brings a renovation, and with it all the untold difficulties that the new times entail.

The 14th Dalai Lama was found when he was just under two years old, but it was not until he had turned four that the lamas who discovered the incarnation were actually able to take him to Lhasa, during which time the Dalai Lama was passing over the 4.5 Orbit in his own life cycle. It was in the 9th month after his fourth birthday, on the 14th (5) day of the first month of 1940 (5) that he was officially enthroned.

His formal education began at 6, the Saturn point, where this type of activity usually begins in a child's life and corresponds very much to the influence of the planet. The next most important event of those years was at the age of 13 (4th orbit again) when he was tested and formally admitted into two monasteries; these activities culminated when he was 23 (5) and received the Master of Metaphysics degree. The Dalai Lama was being prepared during those years to take over his duties as head of the country, both secular and spiritual, on his 18th birthday. But unexpected events changed this course. In fact, when he was 15, at the Saturn point in his life cycle, the Chinese invaded Tibet in 1950 (6). They had been cast out of the country in 1912 (4) under the influence of Mars, only to return this time under the more solid influence of Saturn, the destiny point in the Circle. Plans for the 18th year acceptance of his duties as head of state were changed abruptly when he was 16 (7) under the influence of Uranus—the planet of the unexpected, because the country needed the power of his presence as head of affairs for the unity this would bring to the nation in view of the difficulties it faced because of the Chinese menace. All of these events were Uranian in nature. The next nine years signified the end of Tibet as an independent nation and the disintegration of the staunchest seat of Buddhism in the world. This was completed in 1959 (6), when the Dalai Lama was made to flee to India, again an event of the Saturn point, when he was just turning 24 (6) years of age.

It is necessary to go over some of these details further because this case is perhaps one of the most interesting to study from the point of view of the Gnostic Circle. The student can easily see how the entire destiny of the nation was centered around the 4th and 5th Orbits, which encircle the 4.5 Orbit, the abyss of the Asteroid Belt, the disintegrating force or that which brings a profound change in the being, a change in the very depths. It corresponds to the sign Libra[1]. This is the beginning of passage through the higher half of the wheel, the progression back to the Origin and progress through the sphere of light commences. It is evident that Buddhism in the history of Tibet represented this, but it is also evident that the nation could not stop there; in some way it would have to continue on its journey, as all things and beings must, and there would be the need to pass out of the influence of this sphere and touch the Saturn point which would then open the gates to the even fuller experience. This point would be the real birth of the soul. It is clear that the Jupiter point, the 5th, can become a fossilisation in that it may signify the dogmatisation of the religious experience. Therefore when the person or the nation must cross the Saturn point, because we must all continue on our journey and meet the Time-Spirit face-to-face, whatever is crystallised in the negative sense must be broken down. The work starts in fact at the 4.5 Orbit. When the 6th is reached, as happened in the case of the young Lama in 1950 (6), the greater the matter that is crystallised and serves as an obstruction in the passage, the greater will the suffering and the destruction be in order to bring about the opening to a new life and a new future. The 14th Dalai Lama symbolised all that which is the 5th point, and he had to face the Time-Spirit during that fateful period of nine years between 1950 and 1959. Upon his sincerity and enlightenment and the sincerity of his people, the future of the soul of the nation rests.

The student must see how the country, from the beginning of the 9th Manifestation, was carried to its destiny which centred around the 4th Orbit by the first 40 dynasties. At that time it was arrival at the 5th Orbit, the 41st king, that brought disintegration, what has re-occurred now at the 6 point. Then again there is the factor of the close of the millennium to consider. The previous disintegrating period of 5 occurred in that final period of 100 years; this time the disintegrating period of

[1] 0° Libra is the point of *Nirvana*. (See Chapter 17)

6 occurred during the 100 years of the end of the second millennium. What is more, it began precisely when the 5 decade of the century was reached, 1950. There is another relevant point to consider: It has been said that Buddhism will last for 2,500 years or until the 5th period of 500 years after Gautama the Buddha's passing. Or at least some say this implies that at that time there will be a renovation of some sort and a preparation for the coming Lord Maitreya. We are now in that period and the present Dalai Lama is the incarnation who must face this potent destiny, whatever it may bring. (Precisely in that crucial decade of the 50's (1956-57) the Dalai Lama went to India to celebrate the Buddha's 2,500th birthday.)

While the Earth was passing through the Age of Pisces before the discovery of the latest planets, it was obvious that the passage to the last triad would not be so imperative, and therefore Tibet survived during the last shift and simply restructured itself on the basis of a new religious rule, certainly better than what it had known before. But with the new powers at work and having entered into a new Age, this time the test was harder and the nation could not survive in the same conditions. We are precisely in the times when the old structures are being cast to the ground, whatever these may be, and only the truth of the past must live on. Tibet is no exception to the process: it is, in fact, a nuclear element in the big change humanity is undergoing. For this reason the harmonies are so clear in its case and the position of its development is so easy to verify. We have in this unique destiny the image of the two forms of government before each other. There is the rule of Kings, which in the case of Tibet was epitomised in the first dynasties of secular rule and centred on the 4th orbit of Mars, *the power from Below*. Then there was the rule of the Priests, the theocratic reign, epitomised by the Dalai Lamas, and centred on the 5th orbit of Jupiter, *the descending force from Above*. In themselves these two bodies, Mars and Jupiter joined, give us the planetary image of Tibetan or Tantric Buddhism. In between these two there is the strife of the Asteroid Belt and the shattering experience it brings, but which signifies the urge for a *balance of powers*, for it is the sign of the Balance, Libra. This clash, or this working out in the destiny of Tibet, must bring about a third possibility eventually which as yet lies in the penumbra, unknown to the world and the parties concerned, and will correspond to the nation's passage into and through the last Triad of the System. The present ordeal has fully brought Tibet through the second triad and opened thereby the doors of unity. It can never go back again to what it once knew and cherished. Whatever the pain it has moved from the 5th to the 6th Orbit, just as in the 900's it worked its way to the 5th from the 4th. Difficulties arise when we cling to one and try to carry it over to the higher stage. That can take place up to Saturn's point, but no further.

It is believed that if there is a truth in the existence of Tibet, if the nation possesses a soul, as all true nations under the Divine do, this soul shall be victorious. A foreign power may claim territories, armies may invade, there may be treachery, bloodshed, disaster, legal mishaps and jurisdictive fumblings and ineptitudes, but no one, no earthly power can truly stifle or extinguish the soul of a nation. What Tibet suffers now is merely the real birth of that soul. Tibet has now passed through Scorpio in its destiny: it has had to die in the sign of Death, so that it can leave the dead carcass and move into Sagittarius. 1959 is the beginning of the birth of the soul of Tibet, in which the Chinese are the pawns, whatever the outward appearances may be.

What is to emerge? In what way will the soul of Tibet manifest? What will be the new religious-spiritual experience after the ordeal of the 'labour pains' is over? Of this we cannot as yet be certain. But it is sure that the soul of Tibet awaits a *higher manifestation*, a field wherein it can express the higher triad of planets and the quarter of Unity of the zodiac. It could no longer survive under the yoke of Scorpio, imprisoned in the area of the Asteroid Belt, so to speak, —thrust to and fro between Mars and Jupiter, carrying one over to the other and trying to impose this on today's birth; menaced on the one hand by violence and aggression and on the other limited by the dogmas of a religion and philosophy which must now give way to a new experience of the soul, a true awakening of the Spirit in accordance with the times.

And when that time arrives there is nothing that can hold the process back; just as there was no power that could hold the Chinese back, for even with the highest Tantric knowledge and understanding of the manifestation of occult forces that the Lamas of Tibet possess, there was no stopping the fall of the nation into the hands of the enemy, nor was there any assistance received from outside. All elements became mere pawns in the hands of the Supreme Mother. It is she who carries out the birth, arranges everything and knows the secret tactics whereby her designs shall be fulfilled. The actual occurrences are simply details in the long process of the true birth of the soul. If there have been so many enlightened beings born on the sacred soil of that nation, nothing then can stand in the way of the birth of Tibet's new spiritual kingdom.

Endurance is needed, and faith, on the part of those who share in this destiny— faith that the Divine Mother is victorious: the circumstances of today are the means of a greater manifestation of the light. Until now everything was only a preparation. The nation has not known itself, its full face of Truth. And as with Tibet so with all other nations in some way open to the Divine Light. They shall all be born, they shall all have to suffer the labour pains.

The unique circumstance of Tibet's *isolation* has given humanity the possibility of seeing what the religious consciousness can offer the world when its development is not influenced in any way from outside. Tibet is an example of the maximum that can be attained through this mode: it was a monument to humanity of religiosity, with the beauty of its secure stability, but at the same time with the crippling factor of rigidity and stifling of the vast and ever-renewing spiritual breath. We can see just where this experience can bring the seeker today, through this episode of unfoldment in time, frozen within the folds of the sacred Himalayas.

Because we have felt the utter sweetness of the presence of His Holiness the Dalai Lama, because we have seen and witnessed his humility, his pure simplicity, his noble and dignified courage, and his spiritual light, we would like to say: Tibet will be as it once was, and the reign of this pure soul will remain intact, with all his people united once more around him and on his blessed land. But the part in us that knows the march of the Time-Spirit also knows that this is now impossible, precisely because of the sincerity of the Dalai Lama. The Time-Spirit moves on and all that which does not keep pace with it becomes its shadow and must die: the Truth of yesterday can become the corpse of today. The religious consciousness must now give way to the true and new *spontaneous* spiritual expression of the races. Religion is suffering under the pressure of the New Light, and this is the real dilemma of Tibet. Its enemy is not entirely communism; ironically its enemy is itself, its religious consciousness. And its sincerity and holiness are the power of Truth inherent in itself that shall be victorious and shall carry the nation to a fuller being, the birth of Sacred Tibet—something new, wherein only the truth of the past shall live.

15

The United States of America and India

Examples in the Gnostic Circle

THE UNITED STATES of America is of course a very important element in the Earth's evolution at present. Together with India it forms the *evolutionary axis* of Cancer and Capricorn that has often been referred to in the text. Capricorn is India's ancient occult sign, and Cancer is the Sun sign of the United States; these together represent the axis of Spirit and Matter which is now carrying the evolution. It is around these two nations that the future of humanity's growth into a more divine species largely depends. Both must pass through 'labour pains' as described for Tibet. India must become 'materialised' and the United States must awaken to the Spirit. If neither of these fulfils its destiny there is no possibility of a transformation on Earth. It is also essential that the two realise their union and come to the point where they shall work in harmony with one another in order that the new reign upon Earth become established, for it is no coincidence that Columbus in 1492 thought he had reached India in his travels and called the natives of the land Indians; it was a year of Uranus, the 7th Orbit, and certainly brought the unexpected. Also meaningful is that it was an Italian who served to forge the link, Italy having been the principal Centre of the last Age.

Both these nations began their cycles in this present round during number 3 years. For America it was 1776 and for independent India it was 1947. Thus this year, 1974, on July 4th the United States was 198 years old and had therefore reached the 9 Apex, and on August 15th, 1974 India is 27 years old, also reaching the 9 Apex. For both nations a new round commences and both have been preparing for this new beginning.

With regard to India it is nuclear power that has given the nation a new image, and for the United States it is *Watergate* and all that it has brought to light which serves to give a new direction to the nation. For India nuclear power was a breakthrough in material science, for America the recent happenings are to make the nation ready for perhaps a spiritual birth, a purging before the actual transformation.

For the purpose of our study there are three leaders who have had strong ties with these two nations because of their importance in the Earth's spiritual evolution. All three are Indian born: Ramakrishna, Vivekananda and Sri Aurobindo.

In the lives of these three there are significant dates which show us the important role they play. Ramakrishna was born with the Sun in Aquarius, *in opposition to India's new birth sign*, Leo, and he left his body on August 16th, just an hour or so after the date of India's independence, August 15.

Vivekananda was born with the Sun in Capricorn, *in opposition to the sign of America*, Cancer, and he left his body on July 4th, the date of the American Independence.

Ramakrishna's incarnation was necessary for India's spiritual awakening, and Vivekananda brought the *word* to America and planted the seeds of Vedanta in that country.

Sri Aurobindo was born on August 15th, the very date of the foundation of the new India. This places New India in the sign of the *purusa* and America in the sign of *prakrti*, still partners and neighbours in the spirit/matter pole. But neither Ramakrishna nor Vivekananda brought a new teaching to the world. They belonged as yet to the previous Age. It was Sri Aurobindo who showed the new phase of spirituality that was to open before mankind.

The recent happenings in America are important to observe in the light of the Gnostic Circle: we can see just to what extent the movement which is affecting the political structure of the nation is deep in its significance of a process of renewal, and to what forces this process corresponds.

Having recently celebrated its 198th (9) birthday, the United States is at the 9 point on the wheel where the true new beginning occurs. It is interesting to note that all during the Watergate Affair, the nation in its life cycle was passing through the final quarter of the zodiac, Capricorn, Aquarius and Pisces. The fatal Watergate break-in occurred on 17 June, 1972 (6), during the country's 195th (6) year; according to the Gnostic Circle this would fall at the Pisces navamsa just before the 7 point in Capricorn. This, together with the break-in of the psychiatrist's office, was the beginning of the destruction of all that had been negatively crystallised, since the nation was passing through the last 6 point in its second century. The old habits and disintegrating influences would begin to feel a disturbance and entry into the last quarter would mean that a certain cleaning up was to be felt before the cycle could re-new itself at the 198th birthday in 1974. The entire process of Watergate can be followed within the Circle. By the March equinox of 1973 the situation became more grave; this was the time of the famed taped conversations which the President of the country had with his aide. The United States had by that time moved fully into the sign Aquarius in its life cycle and was well under the influence of the power of transformation. All the details of the affair are well-known; we need not repeat them here. To be brief we can only point out certain relevant dates which will show the student how to use the Circle and follow a development within it, the main purpose for offering these examples that the political workings of nations present us with.

The problems the Administration was having from the time of the first leakage began to augment as the cycle progressed within the last quarter, and when the country passed over the Uranus orbit on its 196th (7) birthday, the really strong pressure was applied. But to understand this fully and its importance within the whole, it is necessary to go back a bit in time—9 years before the date of re-election of President Nixon in 1972. We find then that on November 22, 1963 (7), when the United States was passing through the sign Capricorn (just after the 7th Orbit) in the Circle and at the navamsa of Leo, which in this case would correspond to November, President Kennedy was assassinated. Even the numerological sum of the day equalled 7. The event was fully Uranian in nature. This initiated a movement of the unmasking of degenerate forces, but the power was not strong enough to conclude the unmasking by the time the nation reached the 9 Apex in 1965, two years later. It needed another entire round, 9 more years, after which when it touched this very same Leo navamsa in the sign of Capricorn, President Nixon was re-elected in November of 1972, and shortly afterward the Watergate scandal broke fully, becoming more and more complex as the cycle neared the Apex, more and more painful for the nation and more and more revealing of the need of a renovation for the survival of the nation. It can be seen that President Nixon merely took up the work that could not be accomplished with Kennedy, namely because for a work of this order there must be a certain stamina which the Kennedy destiny lacked. It required a type of great endurance, whatever his motivations, so that he would withstand and remain in office during the entire process.

The passage through the sign Pisces from October of 1973 revealed the full nature of the sign on the mundane level and why the ancients have given it the attribute of 'self-undoing'. The entire Watergate Affair and the manner in which it unfolded has revealed this aspect of 'self-undoing', in that most of the problems developed from blunders the accused parties themselves were making, such as the revelation of the existing tapes which then became the meat for the prosecutors, and the gap in the most important of the first nine requested, which was 18 minutes long (9). The initial incriminating files of John Dean that were preserved in a safe deposit locker were 9, and the word 'Watergate' contains itself 9 letters. But these are minor considerations. They occur in this way because this is the rhythm of the times and the entire Affair can be seen continually to reproduce this figure in one way or another. For example, the House Committee voted 27 (9) to 11 for recommendation of impeachment.

The movement to impeach the President seemed blocked during June, 1974; in fact, it looked as if there would be no such thing. The entire process slowed down.

However just after July 4, 1974, when the United States reached the 9 Apex of the Triangle and celebrated its 198th birthday, everything suddenly precipitated and the ball was forcefully set rolling once more, this time appearing to be the final thrust. In fact, exactly 36 days (9) after its 198th birthday, on August 9th, the new President was sworn in. Just prior to this the 37th President gave his final nationwide address, the 37th address in fact, announcing his resignation. President Ford is the 38th head of the country, which falls at the Venus orbit (2), and during his two years in office the United States will make the important shift to the orbit of Venus, lasting for 99 years. Lyndon Johnson was the 36th President, introducing an 'intervention' in the cycle of election, as all 3-6-9 points do in one way or another. His succession was in fact out of the usual rhythm of the four-year terms, just as Gerald Ford's succession is. In President Ford's own life cycle we find that he had just turned 61 in July and that he was therefore at the Uranus point, and of all politicians most unlikely to become president it was surely he—hence his nomination was truly a Uranian event. Richard Nixon was also moving through the 7th orbit, being as well 61, when he was made to resign, and near to the area in the wheel which corresponded to the Kennedy assassination and his re-election in America's cycle. The two Presidents together form the Cancer-Capricorn axis, and when Gerald Ford becomes 63, at the 9 Apex in his life cycle, the new elections will take place, at the time when the United States will be moving into the 'orbit of Venus'.

But the effects of a birthday such as this one, which closes the 1 sphere and opens up the 2, are far-reaching. Mercury, which has been the principal ruler of the country during the last 100 years, is now giving way to Venus in the same way that we have described for the Earth in its millennium shift, based on the calendar progression. This shows the importance of America's destiny with regard to the entire globe at this crucial moment in the planet's history. This coincidental influence is a strong indication of the channel through which the Shakti works.

India, according to its 'new birthday', reaches the 9 Apex also this year, on August 15, 1974, —42 (6) days after the United States. On this date the new independent nation becomes 27 years old. It too will see a form of renewal. The student can see therefore how India and the United States are moving at almost an identical pace. India will be 29 (2) at the Venus point when the United States will be making the shift to Venus from Mercury on its 200th birthday. But now in 1974 events occur which make that shift two years hence possible. The real cycle begins now, for those who know how to look at the harmonies.

Passage through Pisces in the Gnostic Circle is always an end for a new beginning. There are two signs in the zodiac which are concerned with death. One is Scorpio and the other is Pisces (actually three, if Cancer is included). But each presents a different aspect. When there is 'death' in Scorpio it is a first stage which opens the way to the possibility of work on a higher level. Let us say, in Scorpio the process is not complete. It is only the first phase. In Pisces there is a thorough renewal based on life and the truth of what has remained after Scorpio. In Scorpio that which is old and of no more use dies, the useless appendages, but in Pisces it is the new birth from the *already regenerated form.* Pisces is the further complement of Scorpio, as Scorpio is the further complement of Cancer. The new beginning of Pisces sets the pace for the work of the subsequent nine years.

These examples that are offered should be carefully observed by the student, for they give one the understanding of how to use the Circle with regard to the individual's development. The Circle contains the key to development on all levels; the process of growth is proportionately the same for all things, as has been explained, and these details of the life of nations are to be understood as also pertinent to the individual in his growth toward a more divine being.

With regard to India's place within the Gnostic Circle, as determined by its new birthday, we note that on May 15th, 1974, the nation had reached the Capricorn navamsa in Pisces in its life cycle and entered then into the Scorpio decanate of that sign: this was nine months after its birthday in 1973. Three days later, on May 18, 1974 it exploded a nuclear device which made India the 6th nuclear power and appears to have changed the image of the nation before the world, which is one of the factors that the sign Capricorn is concerned with. It must be remembered that India is ruled by Capricorn and that Capricorn is sub-influenced by Pluto, the planet of atomic energy. The presence in its life cycle of the overpowering influence of Scorpio by decanate division, dwadasamsa and individual degree, and the Capricorn navamsa, are most interesting harmonies because both signs are concerned with the energy of Mars, the lower octave of Pluto,—Scorpio by its rulership and Capricorn by its exaltation. This shows us the tremendous destructive power that was released, but which can nonetheless bring India to a destiny of perhaps demonstrating the way to a creative and peaceful use of nuclear energy.

India as the 6th nuclear power occupies a position which places it at the Saturn point in the solar system. Since the land of India (in its complete sense) is the symbol of Capricorn, it is evident that Pluto's power will play an important role in the nation's destiny. A visitor to India has recently pointed out that the cupolas of atomic energy plants have the identical shape of the Shiva lingam. So once more we see the correspondence between Pluto and Shiva, and it is interesting that from the fission that occurs within those plants the element Plutonium is created, the destructive particle utilised in nuclear arms.

The entry of the 6th power shows us through the Gnostic Circle that a critical point has been reached in the question of nuclear power; by the time the 9th country enters the wheel and concludes the first round there will be many, many important happenings regarding the Earth's use of nuclear energy. Each country now until the 9th brings the world a step closer to the imperative need to resolve the question of the pollution of the atmosphere due to nuclear tests, and by the 9th the right use and understanding of the energy will be clear, as well as the necessity to reach a common agreement on the control of nuclear proliferation. The threat of nuclear warfare and the consequent destruction of the civilisation will be understood in its full reality. Since the world enters a very critical period in 1980, which lasts until 1986, (and a minor one in 1975) it appears that the question of the right usage of nuclear power must be resolved before then, otherwise this will be an element of destruction at that time.

The 6 point continually reveals itself to be vitally important, and tremendously dangerous if passage over this point does not serve to open one to the final round of unity and growth on a higher level. It is the point of crystallisation, and matter is energy crystallised. So just as matter equals energy, the 9 equals the 0. We could call the 0 *energy* instead of spirit, but the word spirit adds that something to energy which the materialist ignores: consciousness. It is possible to say that energy is: energy plus consciousness, or the Indian term that expresses the quality of the Supreme Shakti, Consciousness-Force. Matter is this very same energy only less distinguishable. We could go further to say that depending upon the arrangement of this consciousness-force which we call Spirit (energy) there arises the development of beings with varying degrees of consciousness. A stone is conscious, and so is man, but the arrangement or 'formula' of the particular energy (consciousness-force) differs one from the other. In man there is a certain balance which produces self-consciousness, an awareness that turns back upon itself, or that is constantly breaking through a certain barrier in a way that other masses of particles do not experience. This 'curve' is determined, among other things, by interventions in the process of formation of the species at the three points of the Triangle, which create the movement that turns back upon itself, that becomes self-aware. We could imagine this graphically as a person looking at his face in a mirror and seeing the back of his head; or else, —the serpent biting its tail. Thus it can be understood that the variety of arrangements can be infinite regarding the possibilities of development of conscious species, from man to superman and far beyond that. The universe is of infinite possibilities and the possibility of experiencing all these is open to man.

In the Gnostic Circle we see the curve of *becoming within being*, Time in Matter. Time is becoming, Matter is being; they are interdependent, they are One. We see this energy moving into matter in the particular arrangement of the human species, and also through the 12 divisions of the zodiac, we see the field of expression of this

0-9 being. The 12 Circle gives us the various psychological and physiological fields that the being of consciousness-force makes use of for expression. The 0-9 would be the *seed* placed in the 12 division of the earth. The 9 Circle is the subtle essence, the breath flowing through the 'body' of the Earth, the 12 Circle.

In our study the 9 division is the *time-measure*, and the 12 is the *space-measure*; the superimposition of the two reveals the pattern and pace of the evolution. With respect to the globe, *longitude is the time dimension*, and *latitude is representative of the space dimension*. In the full territory of India, —that is, the land that makes up the symbol of Capricorn, the knowledge of this superimposition is contained, which shows us in another way the particular importance of the Capricorn hieroglyph. The land this symbol comprises extends from latitude N 6° to 36°, a total of 30°, the number of degrees in each segment of the 12 Circle, the space dimension. India's longitude would be 61° E, to 101° E., in all 40°, the very segments of the 9 Circle, the time dimension. So India's latitude based on this symbol is the key to the dimension of space, and its longitude is the key to the dimension of time.

The 9 division is Time, but Time as we have seen is inherent in the manifestation. We must recognise the fact that time is matter, however

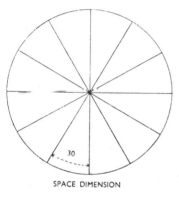

SPACE DIMENSION

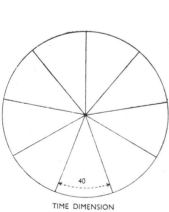

TIME DIMENSION

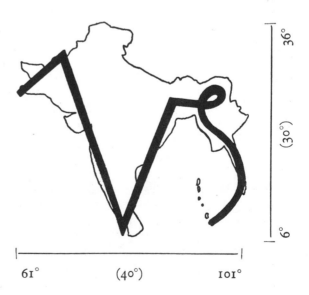

61°   (40°)   101°

ethereal this may be; neither is without the other. Consequently we must admit that Time is energy, or spirit, or consciousness-force, because matter is equal to energy or spirit. Matter is energy crystallised or frozen. Going further in this process of discovery, it is soon found that the entire manifestation can be reduced unceasingly until all things become That One.

This carries us to the conclusion that 'all is only matter, all is only spirit'; but even more interesting is that we have seen Truth to be perceivable only in and within the Manifestation, which shows us ultimately that *Truth brought to its fullest possible expression is Matter.* Thus if we speak of a full reign of Truth, or a divinisation of the Earth, or a full realisation of the Divine, of any order, we must speak of the redemption of Matter, wherein Truth is crystallised in its most complete possible form.

The Sacrifice in Matter

The 'frozen element' within which the crystallised energy of matter is contained is what is sometimes referred to as 'the Ether', the *fifth element*. It can be thought of as a *subtle water*, the mysterious binding energy of the atom, that certain something that keeps mass together and does not allow it to fly off in any direction. It envelops the atom, it envelops the planet, it sustains the System and the Universe, it is the vast cosmic sea, of 'water that is not water'.

What occurs at the 6 point of the Gnostic Circle is comparable to the action of the atom when it converts some of its mass into the binding energy that pulls and keeps it together. This is the crystallisation of Saturn, the brakes that slow down the energy so that it may densify. It takes place on the scale of the minute atomic particle, as well as on the scale of the solar system and the entire universe. It takes place also in the evolution of the species, the 'body' of civilisation, as well as in the individual's development. When speaking of human development, the 6 point can in a sense be termed *the point of sacrifice*. Some part is given up or transmuted, in order to be utilised in another way. There is an element of sacrifice and at the same time of redemption.

186,000 miles per second is the speed of light which becomes the 6 of the Gnostic Circle. It was with this constant squared that Einstein evolved his famous formula $E=mc^2$, the process whereby mass can be converted into energy. When energy is stored in matter it contains a little additional mass. When the energy is released, the mass returns to what it originally was: energy. In the evolution of the spirit through the human races on this planet, the same process is experienced in another way: In the growth of consciousness and the way in which human beings are brought to a higher level. By means of the Gnostic Circle we can see how the legendary crucifixion of the Christ reproduces this drama for us on the scale of human life. The scanty information we have of Jesus begins with his 30th year. He is said to have disappeared at the age of 12, and thus for a period of 18 years, or passage through the Gnostic Circle two times, there was no further record. He re-appeared at the age of 30, when in his cycle he would have been at the 3 point; he 'returns to Earth', in the year which in his life cycle corresponds to the Earth, in order to begin his mission. Three years later, at the age of 33, he is crucified, a sacrifice which was to have been a redemption of matter. The entire legend of the Christ reveals to us the goal of the divinisation, or redemption, of matter. The age of 33 in the Gnostic Circle falls at the Saturn point, and as with the minute atom so the crucifixion of Christ becomes the sacrifice: a part of the divine energy is released from the nucleus (the Trinity) and is converted in the act of crucifixion to become the force that carries the evolution a step further along in its process of divinisation. The event is supposed to have taken place in the spring, around the Equinox, which would then have placed the Christ in the Cancer navamsa after the 6 point, if we consider his birthdate to be in late December or early January. It must be remembered that all these details of dates are ingredients which the Gnostic Fathers added in the early years of the Christian era. It is not at all certain whether they are in agreement with the actual facts. Nonetheless, we are concerned here precisely with what has been passed down in the *way of Knowledge*. The respective ages that were recorded for the principal events of importance in the Christ's life reveal to us the knowledge of the times and the work of the redemption of matter, as prescribed by these men of knowledge. For a very particular reason they wanted the crucifixion to be recorded in this way.

If we study more recent times in the same light we come to an interesting fact which would escape our vision if we did not have the Gnostic Circle in order to follow the events. We could perceive it through intuition and similarly arrive at the same conclusion, but this wheel gives us the precise information we seek. The passing of Sri Aurobindo occurred, according to the Gnostic Circle, at the very time that the crucifixion of the Christ is said to have taken place. Sri Aurobindo was 78 (6) years old, which would fall at the same 6 point, and he left his body four months after his birthday, December 5, 1950, which would fall at the very same Cancer navamsa as the Christ, in Sagittarius. It is particularly important to note that both these passings took place in the sign of Sagittarius, which is the sign of our 9th Manifestation. And it is the sign of the Saviour,[1] who, by the process of the transmutation of energy, brings the movement increasingly back upon itself, ever farther into a dimension it has ignored and which must be discovered within its own being, at the centre of itself.

[1] Vide: *The Magical Carousel*, Chapter IX.

A Gnostic Community in Formation:
the 6 Point Sacrifice and Intervention

Another more recent example can be given with respect to this act of sacrifice, as seen in the passing of two Auroville children.

Auroville is a township founded on the basis of certain ideals contained in Sri Aurobindo's teachings. It is an important centre in the work that is unfolding upon the planet for the establishment of a reign of Truth. Thus the City of Auroville follows the pattern we have described in a most unusual manner. On February 28, 1974, Auroville was 6 years old, therefore passing over the Saturn point and moving into the Sagittarius section of the Gnostic Circle, the same area of the passing of Sri Aurobindo and the Christ. In fact, it was in June of 1974 that the City's cycle had moved to that very Cancer navamsa which corresponded to Sri Aurobindo's passing and the time as handed down for the crucifixion of the Christ. In that month a son of Auroville, *Aurolouis*, left his body. He was the second child to do so in the very short life of the Township, and he chose to leave in the very same manner as the first, who was called *Auroson*, the City's first child. These two events are extremely interesting with respect to our study because not only do they show us the accuracy of the Gnostic Circle but they also afford a clearer view of the power of truth at work, as opposed to the action of falsehood. There is a marked difference in the two processes, which the student of cosmic harmonies must realise.

When the power of truth is at work the action is quite distinct from that of the Ignorance. The difference is recognisable in the process of *inner disintegration* that is evident, which is the work of the pressure from the descending power of truth. An example of this action has been the Watergate Affair as well as political crises in other nations. The number of governments which have either collapsed under the pressure of inner disintegration or by the death or illness of their heads of state, or those that have had to be reorganised for one reason or another, has been astonishingly high in 1974. These shiftings are due to the state of corruption of the seed of politics as a whole, the need ultimately to find another way to carry on the business of state and attend to the needs of the people. The light descends, we can say, and its purity and pressure cause the action of inner crumbling and disintegration. The elements of falsehood cannot bear the pressure of the light and they turn upon each other. When this is in evidence it is a clear sign that the events are produced by the power of Truth.

Falsehood works in a different way, by accidents or sudden calamities, acting upon an element *from the outside*, inflicting a blow which has no bearing on the inner being and which therefore leaves conditions essentially unchanged. Truth always bears a pressure to purify and transform, and to work upon the ingredients so that the ultimate result will be harmony; Falsehood seeks only to destroy, its action bears no thread of unity, no organic and revealing harmony, there is no gradual uplifting process that can be followed because it has no affinity with the hidden light and therefore does not call forth a response from within. Moreover, the action of falsehood is more sudden, whereas the work of truth is a slower accomplishment, and for this reason its ways are often ignored, or pass unnoticed. Truth acts silently but steadily from within, by the force of a pressure which is at once *outside* and *inside*, because it is the descending light from above which awakens and calls to the hidden spark under the veils of ego. Ignorance and falsehood always belong to the realm of superficial, temporary phenomena; truth is stability or 'immobility' in creation, falsehood is that which is transitory or changeful or that which hides the light. All things are moving toward a complete manifestation of Truth, because all things move toward this sacred union of the descending light from above and the aroused inner flame. The clearer the outer garment the more quickly is the action of truth upon the world made possible.

In most children it is known that the soul is very prominent in the early years, and particularly in children who belong to communities such as Auroville or the Sri Aurobindo Ashram. It is usually this part of the being that arranges and determines certain actions. There is hardly any mentalisation. The soul may be disturbed and having no adequate means to express and formulate its disturbance, it can feel itself being suffocated. Since often the outer being is not developed to the extent where it can express its disturbance, the soul may feel obliged to withdraw when it sees that outer conditions are contrary to the development of its essence. Thus the only way open to it—if the soul is not to be stifled—is to leave and perhaps await a more appropriate time for incarnation.

It is a fact that these children are of a somewhat different species. Incarnation is more impersonal, it signifies the possibility of contributing to the establishment of the reign of Truth, rather than for the purpose of solely working out personal karma. In order to accomplish this work and thus fulfil the destiny, it is necessary to keep the soul-power alive, which is the only tool or weapon that can be utilised in the work these children have come to do for the Divine Mother. If the child intuitively knows this power is in grave danger of becoming suffocated and he will then have to pass his entire existence as ordinary humanity, lame and rendered semi-impotent, with the living spark hidden in the darkness of the desire nature and veiled by the ego, he will resolve to leave and perhaps re-enter under more favourable conditions. For these children there is no sentimentality, as there is no sentimentality in the Divine. They are conscious of their immortality and because they are still in close contact with the other worlds, they understand themselves to enjoy the particular capacity of consciously coming and going as they please. They have not taken on the burden of human ignorance which impedes one to knowledgeably take such a decision without breaking the link, based on an essential truth and not the ego. Moreover,—and this is the most important point to establish in our study—leaving their bodies is often the very best means at their disposal to assist in the work of establishing Truth in the atmosphere. This is the offering, *the sacrifice*, and in some cases they come only for this: to be an instrument of truth, the necessary 'shock' or intervention, at times where it is known that such shocks are to be necessary. The quality of the shock is determined by the ignorance or enlightenment prevailing.

Thus in the case of Aurolouis, given the available data, we find that his departure corresponded in the first place to a power of Truth and the action of Saturn, the Time-Spirit, and not the power of falsehood; and secondly, his death was the culmination in a series of difficulties and potential wrong movements in the Township's population and therefore was the necessary shock which is supposed to bring the movement back once more onto its original course.

In the light of our study, the data are the following:

The birthday of Auroville is 28 February, 1968, the full numerological total being 9. In 1974 the City was 6 years old. When its life progression, with respect to the Gnostic Circle, had reached the very point wherein Sri Aurobindo left his body, that is, the Cancer navamsa in Sagittarius just beyond the 6 point, the child left his body. The period recurs once every nine years. Because of its birthday in 1968 (6), Auroville entered into the scheme at the *Cosmic point* of the trinity, and falls under the rule of *Saturn* in this respect. Its sixth year then is extremely important; of all the three 'intervention' points, this would be the most powerful. But let us place the event within the scope of Auroville's entire life span. The first child of Auroville, Auroson, was born on 25-6-1967 (9), before the City was actually founded. In a sense we have to consider him more within the destiny of the Sri Aurobindo Ashram because the field into which he was being called did not in fact exist in the full sense of the word. Thus to call him the City's first son is somewhat difficult. We can look upon him as *the first possibility*. On 4-5-1968 (6) he left his body, not having completed even a year of life, and this occurred just after the foundation, when Auroville was at the 0-9 starting intervention point. Almost precisely 6 years later, and 6 years after the City had been officially founded—that is, when Auroville had entered fully into the wheel of Time on its own independent breath—Aurolouis left his body. The date was 15-6-1974 (6). Moreover, the two children in discussion chose to leave in the same way, by water. They both succumbed to a death by drowning. In India physical conditions are difficult, illnesses abound, but both these children left not by illness but by what must be either considered 'accident' and perhaps the intervention of the Falsehood, or the departures must be considered 'willed'. Seeing how they fit into the scheme of the City's destiny according to the Gnostic Circle, we can say that they willed to leave and that in both cases their deaths served as shocks to attempt to correct the direction of the movement and keep it on its proper course. When an individual or a community fits into the pattern of the Sacred Triangle there will always be interventions at the angles in time for this purpose, and these interventions will be such as to correspond to the needs of the moment. If the movement is proceeding as it should they will be felt as greater influxes of creative force, corresponding to one of the three gunas which the angles epitomise: Aries-Creation, Leo-Preservation, and Sagittarius-Destruction or Dissolution. If there is an element of falsehood strongly in the atmosphere and threatening to overtake the movement, then the intervention is of a more drastic order. In this regard the 0° Sagittarius intervention, the 6 point, is more acute, since it corresponds to the guna of Tamas. Such was the case in Auroville in June of 1974. It must be remembered that June is the 6th month; with the 6th birthday and the intervention point the 6th, it therefore naturally follows that the 6th month would be a culminating one in the year. Between the two passings, the first Auroson[1] and Aurolouis, there were 6 years and 42 (6) days, thus the day count would as well equal 6 and both children left on numerological 6 days. But the element of sacrifice as we explained in Sri Aurobindo's passing and the Christ's is present in Auroville through the death of Aurolouis while the City's progression moved through the same Cancer navamsa in Sagittarius. This shows us the nature of the death, especially when combined with all the other numerological information.

The place in the celestial sphere to which these passings correspond is the 253° or 13° Sagittarius. The lunation of June 4, prior to the child's passing, occurred precisely at this point, the 13° of Sagittarius, and was an eclipse as well. In this manner the two circles, the gnostic-occult and the celestial-physical coincide and join.

Death by water is known to be one of the most peaceful. For the child this represents a return to the element which carried him into the world. It reveals a will to return to the womb of the Supreme Mother, the waters of eternal life, the waters of Ananda. If a soul in a three year old or younger body wishes to leave this plane, this choice of death is the most logical. During the month prior to the child's passing the entire City was afflicted with mishaps regarding the water supply: pumps in the various communities were breaking down, wells were threatening to cave in, many sectors were left without water. We know that water is the symbol of *consciousness*, and this slow and sure pressure on that aspect in the City's functioning was the sign that a drop of consciousness was menacing to take the movement into

---

[1] The soul reincarnated at a later date through his same mother and received the same name once more: Auroson.

a direction contrary to the Truth. The final intervention shock was the death of Aurolouis by water, in a manner and at a time when it would reveal itself as part of the pressure of the power of Truth and not the Falsehood, thus there could be no equivocation that the action corresponded to an inner disintegration and the need for a firm corrective measure. Such occurrences are the assurance that the force is powerfully active and determined to carry the City to its rightful destiny. When studying these harmonies it is necessary to be able to distinguish in such matters. Tomorrow's intervention can be of an entirely different order—one of positive growth, of joy and determined power for construction. The stage of development of the individual or the members of the collectivity determines th's. One can move along with the divine grace, love and protection, from truth to greater truth, from light and bliss to an even more ecstatic communion with the Divine Mother; or one must be pushed along as an ignorant and unconscious animal, knowing only the lesson of disaster and catastrophe. Unfortunately this latter seems still to be the condition of humanity.

The student can see that the Gnostic Circle is not concerned with considerations such as good and evil, creation or destruction, in the sense attributed to such terms. It is concerned with the time factor and the impartial field of expression and the various stages of growth. The sufferings seen that may be experienced within the Circle are simply due to falsehood and ignorance. These it must be stressed are a temporary condition; a human being need not suffer in any way, and this is not the outcome of a detachment from suffering, from that which causes pain, but it is the outcome of a transformation of the very element of falsehood and the field wherein it has its stronghold. This is the ultimate goal as seen in the Gnostic Circle: a total transformation of the Ignorance and the rendering of all the levels of being a tabernacle of the Light.

Re-establishing order and the process of renewal

What is written here regarding the harmonies of the Cosmos is not new. There is perhaps nothing here that cannot be found in one form or another in some ancient scripture or monument. Even the teaching of Sri Aurobindo corresponds to an ancient one and is not an entirely new revelation. He himself has written of the places in old texts where Supermind is spoken of or alluded to. A further example of a modern reiteration of the eternal Word is to be found in Teilhard de Chardin who, like Sri Aurobindo, speaks of the evolution of the Earth to a cosmic Apotheosis. Followers of these great beings like to believe that their masters are unique and bring a teaching that is likewise unique. But we cannot agree with this fully: the uniqueness of one over the other may stem from the fact that the greater the sage the more accurate is the revelation and the more light does he cast on the Truth that is obscured.

There are innumerable places where the advent of a divine race of men has been mentioned, as, for example, in the Puranas where the 'sons of Brahma' are the last, the 9th Creation. Likewise in Hermetic thought there is the same theory and in the work of the early Gnostic Fathers. But what happens along the way—over the many years of accumulation of knowledge—is that the teachings become somewhat clouded over. That is, they are transmitted along with knowledge that is pertinent to the period of revelation only. For the aspirant who enters the play 3,000 or 2,000 years later it is difficult, nay sometimes impossible, to sift out what is eternal in the teachings. Slowly a degeneration occurs in the different schools of thought, reflected as well in the number of sects and cults that spring up around any particular message, each with their own scriptures, each adding something to the original ones, or sometimes deleting important parts because they appear to be irrelevant to their followers. Over the centuries then there is a clouding over of the Truth. It is necessary at certain stages of the evolution to bring about a re-ordering, it is necessary to sift out the truth from the half-truth, the eternal from the temporal. This must happen during any Age of Fixed (Preservation) energy flow, such as the present Aquarian Age. The work then is a mere re-ordering of the eternal word, a process of cleansing and placing of the Truth back into the scheme of the Eternal, or better said, an unveiling of it once more within the eternal harmony. And with this re-ordering naturally the future stage of the work is revealed, evolved from the cleansed foundation of the past, moving toward the pure ideal of the future.

Most of what has been written here, apart from the references to actual happenings in the world, can be found in the scriptures to a certain degree, especially the Hindu. These contain perhaps the most timeless quality, their cosmology is perhaps the easiest to follow and the closest to the truth of the process, their gods and goddesses appear to be the most mature. But even in the Indian tradition this process of clouding-up has occurred and it is imperative to put order therein, because of India's central role at present. This is the work that is being done. It is not a new astrology or a new scheme of cosmic harmonies. It is the same thing made new by the light of actual happenings, if one knows how to look at them, —in particular bringing these facts out of the realm of abstract theory. This is the time of Kalki, the restorer of the Order. In many aspects of life therefore a re-establishing of order must take place. The ever-recurring myths must be revealed in their eternal essence as a part of the present evolution, as the story of our times and not a relic of history, pertaining to millenniums past. We are living the myth right now. We are living and establishing the Age of Truth today. We are not awaiting the Satya Yuga; it is upon us. But unless we bring order into the Knowledge we can never perceive this and see our place on the spiral of manifestation.

From the last Age of Preservation 6,480 years have intervened, —years of darkness moreover, a veritable *kaliyuga*. Thus how can we be sure of what was known and accomplished before, in the previous Age of Leo, 12,900 years ago—or before that, during the Age of Scorpio? We have only the Sphinx and the Pyramid to go by, and some other minor constructions, or else fossils within the Earth, a history buried within the bosom of the Mother. Yet these monuments clearly show us that the Earth was populated at least by a hierarchy, if nothing else, of gnostic beings. We can identify in consciousness with peoples of historic times, know what they were, what they felt. But these lost Ages of Egypt, for example, are completely closed to our present consciousness. We cannot know what they were, these gnostic beings; we have only their monuments to go by which, even with our advanced technology, we can in no way reproduce today.

What shall be left of today, in the event of a dissolution? The Empire State Building? the Statue of Liberty? the Houston Airport? the Vatican? Present civilisation has nothing to show in the way of a monument which reflects the higher knowledge of today, which can show to future Ages the state of spiritual growth, *because the spiritual realisation of today has not yet been completely achieved.* One is allowed to create in matter only that which corresponds to the spiritual essence of the civilisation, even if that pertains to just one person. This is the glory of all the past monuments: these sacred constructions show us the degree of enlightenment of the times in which they were formed.

Today we can show the future only that which pertains to the material, and perhaps in this sense there has been no other civilisation which can compete with us —though even this is doubtful in the light of the more recent discoveries regarding the past. But the times are important in the light of spiritual as well as material growth, more important now than in any past gnostic society, because it is man himself, the species itself, which is to be the revelation to the future. Man's very body is the Temple that shall disclose the accomplishment of his Age in the work of the divinisation of the Earth. Therefore constructions of the order that were carried out in the past so that the knowledge could be transmitted, are no longer essential in the way they once were. Today the body is to reflect the work and be the link with the future. Organic matter is destined to be transformed into the Temple of Light. The entire new race shall be one of Gnosis. And the Temple of today must speak to mankind, now and in the future, of this truth.

Nonetheless, Truth is not a static quality. It is eternal yet dynamic, and reveals always a new face of itself. Because we cling to its old face we must await the perennial Redeemer who will pull aside the veils once more and reveal the ever-glorious Way.

We are now at the point where Science must discover the oneness of Shakti and Brahman: Energy is Matter and Matter is Truth, mobility is one with immobility. These are momentous times because a unity is to take place between the elements of Darkness and Light, and along with recapturing the unity that was enjoyed in the past, we shall now step beyond and in this forward march the new race will be born, the new species, the divine man. We are in the Age of Unity. It is not tomorrow. It is now.

East and West Rapprochement

There are certain teachers in the world, in particular in America and Europe, who find it convenient to criticise the opening America has had with regard to Eastern teachings. They feel this is a false happening and that it is a *Western* way that must be found, an occidental language and terms to express an experience which is supposedly different from the Eastern one. The difficulty with such an idea is that it tends to widen the gap between the two poles that are trying to unite and become the Axis of Evolution for the emergence of the divine humanity. America is the pole of Matter, India is the pole of Spirit; these two must work together and in no abstract or occult way. There is a profound truth trying to express itself in the opening America is having toward Indian spirituality. It was initiated by Swami Vivekananda at the beginning of this all-important and culminating century. The urge for the union of the two poles must not be stifled but all parties concerned must on the contrary make an effort to assist this movement of unification. It is an inevitable part of the Earth's destiny, but it can be brought about consciously or unconsciously, in the midst of suffering, confusion and destruction. A certain basis has been prepared and by recent world events we have been brought closer; merely *closer* however, the union is yet far. Nor is it assisted by elements in the pole of Spirit. There too we find the same resistance, if not more than in America. The Indian spiritualist sits on his throne of detached superiority and sees himself as isolated from the pole of Matter, equal in attitude to the materialist who shuns the light of the spirit. The prejudices reigning in the heart of the most powerful seat of Truth in India against the Western movement are perhaps more seriously hindering than any urge in the West to formulate its own school, to forge its own isolated path. The Indian is suspicious of the Westerner because of the still vivid memory of the English subjugation, and in a host of ways he makes this attitude felt. One point must be considered regarding the problems of the English rule and the residues this has left: It was only during that reign that the symbol of Capricorn was made complete, and also it was only during that time that any form of unity between Indian states was achieved, as well as a unity by means of one common language—

English, which to this day serves as a communicating channel for the people and the government. Upon the departure of the English the symbol collapsed once more, disunity reigned which brought the outcome of partition, and even the effort to establish a common language brought untold strife to the nation. Here below is a delineation of the actual territory of India, compared to the area of the Symbol. The student can easily see how the actual map appears truly to be a figure with its arms cut.

Regarding the map on page 68 of the full territory, it must be clarified that 'unity in the symbol' is not abolition of the independent status of the nations that comprise the area, but that in some way—perhaps in a near future—a union amongst them may come about, or a confederation of some sort, or even an entirely new system of unity among nations; or, more ideally, the nations and peoples that make up the symbol, though sovereign, might understand its meaning and form a *unity in consciousness*, with the knowledge that the area is sacred and that joined efforts directed toward a common goal will carry the Earth into the light of its spiritual destiny. We use the term 'true India' to designate the symbol-territory, since the major portion is formed by the Indian nation, but the name given to a future coalition of this order could be any other, as the name 'Europe', for example, designates an area made up of many independent nations.

In a wider sense the English rule was indispensable, given the state of human ignorance of the Divine Plan, so that during the passage into the Age of Aquarius there would be unity under the symbol of Capricorn, if only for that brief period; and English would become a part of the area's means of communication, not only within the country but more important, it would serve ultimately as the link with the outside and be the channel for the teachings of the age to be transmitted. India was given, during that period, a taste of its true destiny, though diluted and subjected to the ways of the Ignorance. This is a prime example of the impartial development within the Gnostic Circle which can be experienced as negative or positive according to the degree of human resistance. The Divine is not at all sentimental: she uses means which are at her disposal, with thought of neither good nor evil. It is in the human domain that such considerations exist, because we must rule ourselves on these bases. We consider Richard Nixon perhaps an obnoxious element, and yet it was because of his stamina that the process of purification could get under way. Had he resigned at the first difficulty, nothing would have really been accomplished. Yet when the cycle reached the point of change, as seen in the Gnostic Circle, Mr. Nixon 'agreed' to resign, and the politicians are happy, the American people are happy, we all give forth a sigh of relief and feel that our human endeavours, whatever their secret motivations, have finally been successful and have brought about order based on our laws. We ignore *the higher Law*, as we ignore *the real Power* that determines. With a vision based on the perception of these higher laws and their purpose, we come to view evil as a sister of righteousness, because both are simply expressions of the lamentable state of human existence within the ignorance. [1]

The two poles, Spirit and Matter, as epitomised in India and America, must unite in the deepest sense and collaborate to bring about the great birth of our times. India has the upholding force but it has lost the 'arms of Durga', the material power and possibilities; America must become its *matter*, America is the Word, the body of the Ideal. From its land the Word has been born and receives its body.

Experiments are being undertaken to bring this about. Auroville is one. But there too prejudices reign, the split between East and West, spirit and matter, are still evident. The old consciousness has not been fully uprooted, and it is only with the realisation of the consciousness of Truth that the work is accomplished and the unity we speak of is achieved. Whether this will one day take place on the soil of Auroville, where elements have been amassed to make this a reality, it is difficult to say. The seed of victory is planted, but human nature is still a small and limited thing. The light has not yet been fully perceived upon its soil, for Auroville closely follows the pace of the world. Yet the destiny of that experiment is precisely to be the link between India and America, or East and West. If America could turn to this venture and support it, be its 'arms', and if India could truly welcome America and descend from its pedestal of Light and embrace its dark sister of Matter,

---

[1] Note to the American Edition: It is interesting to observe the events concerning the election of Jimmy Carter in the light of these studies. First of all, the United States entered 'the orbit of Venus', as stated, and President Carter is born in the sign Libra, ruled by Venus. Regarding number harmony, the 9 is a fundamental piece in the history of his rise to power. To begin with, his birthdate, 1.10.1924, equals 9; he announced his candidacy on a 9 day (12.12.1974); his campaign lasted 99 weeks; the election date was 9 (2.11.1976); the date he assumed office was also 9, (20.1.1977). Furthermore, the electoral votes he received were 297 (9), while Gerald Ford's were 240 (6).

Of more interest is the fact that Jimmy Carter, in the Gnostic Circle, had just reached the 7th orbit of Uranus in the sign Capricorn, exactly where Gerald Ford was when made president and, oddly enough, where Richard Nixon was when he resigned. Jimmy Carter assumed office just when he reached the $15°$ of Capricorn, the point of the soul of India. He is the president who could easily help to forge the link with India we speak of here. In this his mother has played a role; apart from having lived in India for two years, her birthdate is August 15, — the birthday of Sri Aurobindo and the Independence Day of India.

Every 36 years elections are held in the United States when in the Gnostic Circle the nation passes over the very degree where the Sun was located in its natal chart, $15°$ Cancer. This occurred at the time of President Carter's election. It is clear that such elections are more meaningful than others, given this time/planetary concurrence.

the victory would be immediate. Alone, as she now stands, India cannot fulfil her destiny—because her destiny is to unite with matter, she is the Mother, she is in fact most fully fulfilled in Matter; alone India is powerless, alone America is spiritless, an inert mass. And without the conscious marriage of the two, the Earth cannot be born, or can be born only with great difficulty and destruction.

The breath of Truth is immortality, the capacity of continual self-renewal, not through death and birth, but rather a constant renewal within life. This is Immortality's secret. We know creation is eternal; we know the soul is re-born and the spirit never dies. But we rely on Death to maintain the flow, to give the possibility of a new birth. We have not drunk of the elixir of Life whereby the process knows no death and renews itself always on the basis of a life divine, forever revealing the new face of Truth that is born at each instant, a conscious shedding of the old on the firm stand of the true. We have spoken of Tibet and its problems, that its religious consciousness was its true enemy. It was its own self-undoing. The Dalai Lama himself may believe that because of Tibet's isolation it fell into the hands of the adversary. Yet this was not entirely the case. Its isolation served only to strengthen its religious consciousness to such a degree as is not to be found in any other nation on Earth. Its isolation gives us a picture in these times of what can occur when the religious consciousness we have inherited from the 8th Manifestation, the death of Scorpio, is preserved intact and has not felt the pressure of renewal from outside. We can see the beauty of it, and its death as well.

The religious consciousness is more difficult to transform because its breath is finer and the forms it moulds around itself can appear to us as new. The material consciousness is easier to change because its crystallisation or fossilisation is quicker and it dies a heavier death. Such is the case with communism or totalitarianism or political structures of any order. The life of the movement is already exhausted on a certain level; the ideal has already withered because the State cannot compete with the image and compelling power of the Gods. Totalitarianism is more rigid than the religious consciousness and it has an even greater difficulty at continual renewal. These societies will fall because of their own inner strife, the disintegration within themselves by the death or suffocation of the ideal upon which they feed. Like Tibet these powers will disintegrate, but Tibet can renew itself because of its spiritual light. They have covered the light and therefore have become their own tomb. The corpse will decay inside the very tomb, without the need of any outside intervention. It will collapse by the very law that gave it its short support. The rigidity within the totalitarian countries, the lack of freedom to persue one's own interests, to explore the varied ways of the Divine, the constant suffocation of the spirit inherent in the people, is the seed of their inevitable collapse, more colossal and immediate than any other reign the Earth has known. This rigidity has only served to squelch the only possibility for survival: the possibility of renewal within the field of the Unknown. Truth exists when it can constantly renew itself on the basis of life and not death. Then we can say we have known the full face of God.

On the basis of the Gnostic Circle it is evident that with regard to the governing of the masses and the structure of society a form must evolve which allows for an ever deeper and vaster process of renewal, and for this to come about freedom of pursuit and exploration of the unknown is essential. This pertains as well to the spiritual expression of the new society. The question of the formation of an orthodox religion around a new light is a serious one and must be considered by each true seeker, by each individual who truly wishes to create a new world. The ways in which religions are formed are well known, and in some respects one can have sympathy for those who have been responsible for such a fossilisation of the Truth. No matter how sublime the teachings are, they can become fossilised when the *living experience* is absent, when the seeker creates an insurmountable gap between himself and the master—adoring him as an inaccessible god, or else when a solid body of teachings becomes dogma and scripture for the followers, when the experience must be made to fit into the written or orally preserved teachings, when then the pandits and the priests and the philosophers and scholars arise to 'protect the purity of the teachings', and to assure the growing congregations that the Master, whoever he may have been, is not being betrayed. The pandits and priests are there to assure us that the teachings are being faithfully preserved and not distorted. And over the centuries this process of striving to keep the teachings intact becomes their very death. It is a serious problem and all seekers must face this question because it is only when ultimately the aspirant is able to rely on the truth of his own experience which is ever in a state of renewal, that the Truth can live on. When he needs confirmation from the guru, the scriptures or the commentaries on the scriptures, the Truth has become weakened, his experience loses its power and the movement begins its painful and long and tedious process of fossilisation. Because people have no faith in themselves, in the Divine within them, and seek continually outside support on the limited human level, the world is in need of religions. When each man becomes his Guide, a light unto himself, the reign of Truth will be here, the work of the last Avatar will have been accomplished.

This brings us to the most important phase of our study, the knowledge of *individual development*, because it is only when each person can see his own place within the Gnostic Circle and understand the beauty of its spiral of perpetual renovation as expressed within his own life span, that the human species as a whole, the body of mankind, will be the living monument of the light of Truth for the coming Ages.

the Child **3**
the birth
the Earth's realisation

The Individual

"...*We shall come to feel all the consciousness of the physical world as one with our physical consciousness, feel all the energies of the cosmic life around as our own energies, feel all the heart-beats of the great cosmic impulse and seeking in our heart-beats set to the rhythm of the divine Ananda, feel all the action of the universal mind flowing into our mentality and our thought-action flowing out upon it as a wave into that wide sea....*"

16

The Gnostic Development
of the Individual

THE HUMAN BEING, whatever his state of consciousness, moves in creation along a particular pattern which accords with his rank in and of the animal kingdom. This rhythm is reproduced in the subtle strata in the form of a circle, and by means of numbers and the fields of time and space to which they correspond an individual can consciously observe and follow and experience his growth and journey in the evolution according to this rhythm. To know this subtle circle is to be able to transcend the human plane and merge into the higher consciousness which contains such knowledge. Because there have been beings in the past who have done so, humanity is left with the knowledge of that circle of light, the zodiac, and can make unending discoveries within it that correspond to the ever-expanding and ever-renewing state of man's being. For the zodiac is eternal; the very same patterns which revealed the stage of evolution for humanity 5,000, 10,000 or perhaps 50,000 years ago, pertain as well today. The images of the zodiac recorded by sages who were able to transcend the human limitations of consciousness are so arranged as to be perpetually significant, especially because their arrangement is the very key to perpetual growth and unceasing renewal of being. So long as man has not achieved the direct identification with the Supreme, so long as he needs the aid of symbols along the way, the zodiac can be his guide.

Therefore to study ourselves on the basis of the zodiac, and in particular within the Gnostic Circle, there must be the consciousness that sees in terms of unending growth and the ceaseless possibility of expansion. In the individual there are two simultaneous movements: one is a continuous formidable expansion, the other is a tremendously compelling contraction; one leads to identification with the entire Cosmos, the widening of the consciousness so as to become one with the whole of Creation, and the other is the drawing back of this consciousness into the inner central point, carrying into the centre of one's being the knowledge of the Infinite, so that one may thus evolve into the image of the Eternal and the Infinite.

The Creation itself evolves in the same manner, an unending expansion and a ceaseless contraction. Thus we have two theories in existence regarding matter and the origin and development of the universe. One tells us it is expanding and all things are moving away from each other, and the other formula states that it is on the contrary a movement of contraction: we are slowly being drawn into a great or many great and mysterious centres. The electron is a particle, but under a certain observation it is also a wave; it is contracted into a point, yet it is also spread out as an expanding energy. Truth lies in the harmonisation of the two theories, for in fact we are existing in both expansion and contraction, but we have not yet moved into the consciousness which can perceive the simultaneous movement; we live in the area of perception which cognises in terms of *paradoxes.* So for now we must content ourselves with calling this creation *the paradox of becoming within being.* The symbol of the Sun which expresses this fact, ⊙, for humanity at its present stage would be the image of the paradox of creation. It is possible now to have the knowledge but the consciousness is such that we can only partially perceive the truth, and because of this partial perception knowledge then unfolds in terms of the Paradox. In total ignorance there can be no such thing. It is with the emergence of Mind from Life that paradoxical perception is born. And this is the attribute or the contribution of Mercury. Half perception means paradox, full perception means the sphere which embraces all, within which all things are found to be perfectly and harmoniously in their place.

We can see therefore that Science, which is the child of Mercury, is ever imprisoned within the realm of the paradox. When it perceives a truth, this perception is immediately placed before the fact of yesterday and seems to cancel, though unsatisfactorily, the former's worth. And it proceeds unceasingly in this manner of discovery, —always coming upon a concept and formula which while solving one problem, only opens the way to a greater enigma on another level. Our minds are forever caught within this tide of perception and conflict and rejection and acceptance. We cannot suppose that by this method of discovery we will find the answer to the enigma of the world, because one answer will only give rise to a further question, one possibility only throws another experience into the realm of the Impossible.

In man's life this same process is in evidence. The expansion of one part of the being appears to require the contraction of another, the birth of one centre means the diminution of the force of another. In this way the total humanity can never come about. As for the whole of Creation, so for the Individual: he must become conscious of his movement of expansion and contraction, of his *becoming within being.* He must experience his growth in terms of a complete breath, where each step forward is supported and activated by the measure of the last step, each opening is the outcome of yesterday's birth and in no way contradicts or cancels it.

The first factor which calls our attention regarding the knowledge contained in the Gnostic Circle is that of the absence of negative and positive methods of qualification. Impartiality immediately thrusts us into a sphere of perception regarding astrology or cosmic harmonies which is new to us. For this reason, in fact, we call our study one of *cosmic harmonies*, simply because the term 'astrology' has become crusted over with false ideas and attributes and hence limitations. In order to bring the individual to the appreciation of the full qualities of this study, it has been deemed necessary to call the work by another name, which, though meaning essentially the same thing, liberates the study to some extent from the errors of the past.

And this new vision initially creates a conflict in us: we are suddenly freed of a set of constricting prejudices, but at the same time this signifies the loss of a certain order to which our vision had accustomed itself. The conventional study of astrology was made easy by a host of patterns pertinent to a creation enveloped in the veils of the Ignorance, based on a series of considerations of positive and negative qualities, arising primarily from the relationships between the planets in terms of *aspects*. By this means it was possible to interpret an aspect and sometimes to accurately predict the state of mind for an individual, as well as the events which would occur in his life. Liberated of this, one faces the problem of how to interpret what one sees, and this brings us to the threshold of the most important contribution the Gnostic Circle can make in the effort toward expansion of consciousness: we must accustom ourselves to the fact that the movement of life corresponds to laws which transcend our mental formulations and when liberated from these we must seek for a new way to see and then to express the process of growth we are involved in. This vision is the first concrete aid to the true expansion of consciousness. No longer do we review the small or larger details of our lives as good or bad; we see only the unending process of growth, and the movement from ignorance to awareness and to full knowledge. We see also the myriad possibilities that are at our disposal and how these afford a certain soil wherein we may plant an expanding seed of consciousness and tend to its growth. This simple fact of being liberated from the notion of negative and positive influences is one of the most potent tools for the expression of a new consciousness.

However, it is evident that the vision the Gnostic Circle affords does not condone all and any action; on the contrary, we see that when one has found one's place in the wheel and has seen the pattern of one's development, the disciplining factors become even more acute, because with the loss of the notion of good and evil, we acquire a gnostic vision of the evolution where the Ignorance—which is the realm of so-called good and evil—does not exist. Thus if we transcend the Ignorance and move to a higher realm we must observe that our life, to all outward appearances, becomes less 'free', more tightly bound to laws which, though they correspond to a higher vision and plane, are nonetheless rigid and imposing. But simultaneous with this perception is the understanding of what the purpose of *law* truly is, what is the true value of *harmony*, and where the realisation of *freedom* really lies.

Everything within the Creation is the Divine, but the fact is we have lost the vision of this omnipresence. If we could see the Supreme present in, let us say, our acts of lust, these actions would be entirely different. But in order to see the omnipotence and omnipresence of the Supreme one must be *conscious*, always, and such acts become impossible when one is conscious. It is because man falls into periods of unconsciousness that he is able to be the mechanical tool of Prakriti. Thus these acts in themselves are not wrong; the only wrong movement is the loss of the vision of the Divine. There is no sin other than unconsciousness and hence ignorance. By becoming fully conscious and by retaining this total state of awareness all that which pertains to the lower and animal nature of man falls away. One moves from the lower to the higher laws, from being the instrument of Prakriti to becoming the instrument of the Supreme Shakti; the laws always exist because we are in the manifestation, within the sphere of Time, —but the divine man, by identification with the Supreme, has the possibilities of the entire universe at his disposal, whereas the ordinary human being must abide within the sphere of Earth laws solely. Thus in the wider sense the divine man becomes 'free', or what to the normal consciousness would appear to be free. The idea is prevalent, for example, that when one practises a certain yoga or similar disciplines one transcends the plane of Time and one becomes free of all laws. This is an erroneous concept: one is never free of the Laws whilst one is within the manifestation, it is simply that to the ordinary humanity the realised being is indeed free, because he is identified with a set of harmonies and laws that the man of lesser development can never perceive. In fact when one is identified with that Consciousness the question of freedom does not exist: there is total union, harmony, power, bliss, pure existence, none of which can be without Law. By identifying with That, man never falls into the state of unconsciousness which is the only condition whereby the forces of the Ignorance which presently appear to have rule over the Earth, can enter into the being and bring it to commit acts of so-called evil.

The study of the Gnostic Circle is unique for the individual on the path of gnosis for he learns that his evolution is recorded in the subtle spheres. He no longer needs to look to the actual positions of the planets in the sky, though these have their worth and are relevant on another level. The aspirant to gnosis sees that his growth is determined simply by the *harmonic structure* of the solar system, for in effect the Gnostic Circle merely represents to us the structure of the solar system projected onto the 'screen' of the magical zodiac. If he looks to the sky for precise scientific confirmation, he will find nothing, because he must be able to recognise *the value of the play of orbits*, or the interrelationship of occult circles. There is a 'scale' for each system, and his task is merely to find the *note* to which he corresponds or vibrates, and to become aware of the point in the scale that is his entry into and position within the Harmony. His life is a magnificent symphony which the Gnostic Circle reveals to be a part of the entire heavenly Theme.

Thus man can move out of the 'influences' of the actual sky and the laws which bind him to a destiny overshadowed by the Ignorance, and he can move into a sphere of higher light and knowledge veiled to the ordinary eye, a harmony which is perceivable only to those who have eyes to see in a new way. Like all studies, astrology has different schools or systems. They can be divided into the more materialistic, or realistic, and the more spiritual—those which do not depend upon the actual physical positions of the planets and their ever-changing relation to each other, but rather find their meaning and the answer to the mystery of the evolution into a more divine species by a pure vision of the harmony that the Cosmos is, a harmony which is steady, unchanging and eternal.

Nonetheless, with a penetrating self-knowledge, it is possible to foresee certain precise events based on the Gnostic Circle which may be considered negative in that we become aware of the degree of ignorance prevailing in the individual or community or nation, which then grants us the vision of certain difficulties that will be encountered during progressive growth, viewed as negative only because of the suffering they bring. The problem lies in the fact that when ignorance prevails there is *attachment*, and this is the greatest actual hinderance to one's individual as well as collective development. One must continually die to the past and be new at each dawn, so that the nescience of yesterday does not cloud the possibility of today. When there is too much accumulation, too much baggage, there are certain points in one's development which represent periods when precisely the old is made to die and the truth of the experience alone is carried over, serving as a pedestal for the progress of the future. Hence we can see the disharmonies that can temporarily be caused by such attachment and in this sense only the Circle shows us the negative and the positive, because at the same time it shows us the accumulated effect of the Ignorance.

The Four Cords

The life of a human being on the gnostic path can be seen to take place in cycles, or groups of years. It is much the same as the development within the Greater Circle for the whole evolution. There were periods that corresponded to physical, vital, mental and spiritual growth. In the individual also these sections of growth prevail and they are seen to stem from an attachment of a sort to the Divine Mother.

The human being begins his life cycle equipped with certain channels of energy that attach him to the Mother's being in a particular way. These are virtually to be considered umbilical cords, four in all. The first is the physical, the second the vital, the third the mental and the fourth cord is the spiritual. When one starts life on the planet these four cords are intact, and the initial purpose of existence is to liberate oneself slowly and thoroughly from these cords, a process that is to ultimately signify full liberation. These cords are one's ties with four aspects of the Mother, so to speak. During his lifetime an individual will encounter persons and situations which externally represent the psychological reality of the existence of the cords, and from the beginning of his life by means of these relationships he must strive to sever each cord and be born into a higher level of being, a different and thoroughly new and mature identification with the Supreme. Thus for approximately the first nine years of life the child is dedicated to developing himself physically and during that period he works to render himself physically independent, or at least in a position to face the passage of the subsequent nine years which, at a particular point, will signify the full severance of the first cord. When the physical being is fully established on this plane, the senses functioning as they should with respect to Earth existence, the individual is free to attend to the other parts of his growth. The first cord, the physical, is usually objectivised in the embodiment of the physical mother, —but this role can also be played by one who functions as such and yet is not in actual fact the real earthly mother. The human being will always find some way to fill this position, even if he lacks the presence of the physical mother; and if it cannot be accomplished on this plane, he will take refuge in nighttime experiences to satisfy the necessity of the being in this respect.

After the initial period of nine years, important in another aspect which we will speak of further on, the work passes to a different level of being, the vital-emotional. As described in the section on the Greater Circle, progress in the establishment of the vital being signifies severance of the first, the physical cord. Thus the individual through emotional development, moves from the exclusive dependence on the physical umbilical cord and passes on to a feeding through the emotional cord. This action deadens the first, which becomes a useless appendage, and, in so far as possible, is cast aside. With this liberation the physical being can be considered to have passed into its true independent being. The first secure outer signs of this severance would generally occur around the 13th to 14th year, the full period of adolescence.

If the student refers back to the Gnostic Circle, it can be observed that at the 4.5 Orbit, which is passed during the thirteenth and a half year of life, a *reversal* takes place, which is nothing more than the severance of the first cord. During the first nine years, when the child is fully establishing himself on the material plane, passage over this point in the fourth and a half year signifies the severance with the plane to which he was subtly connected before birth. For this reason children up to approximately that age live in close rapport with the subtle worlds and are often capable of seeing subtle images and personages, or else of remembering experiences on other planes or past lives. Until that time there is still a firm link with the 'other side'. The first nine years of life bring about the severance of that link and the beginning of the firm establishment of roots on the physical plane.

As the individual then progresses through the next nine year cycle, which would bring him up to the 18th year, he would be moving through the subtle sphere of growth which corresponds to the vital being and development or discovery of the emotional self, which has as one of its objects the liberation from dependency on the physical mother or her representative. This is usually accomplished by a substitution process, whereby another 'Mother' comes forward, objectivised either in a man or a woman with whom the individual becomes emotionally involved, irrespective of his or her own sex, and through whom the discovery of the vital being begins to take place. By that time the physical being is well enough established to be able to support the work on the other parts. The physical being throughout one's incarnation on the planet remains as a sort of pedestal or vehicle for the process of growth.

In this light it is easy to understand why there are so many psychological problems plaguing the human race at present, because none of the cords is ever fully severed when it should be. Usually work on the physical, let us say, is carried over to the vital, without the former having been actually and substantially completed. It becomes then a hinderance, an extra and useless weight which the individual carries with him, and as he moves on in life he steps into one phase burdened by the incomplete process of the past: he lives in the present only half there, as it were, because the *un-born* past is clouding over the work of the day. This is the major source of psychological disturbances: one seeks the fulfilment of certain needs when it is no longer possible in the just harmony of living and being to attend to them, when attention should be focussed on a different aspect of growth. One 'carries over' continually. This is well and good if truth is carried over—it usually happens however that there is a partial truth contained in a vessel of much obscurity. And this obscurity accumulates each time passage is made into a further part of the Circle without having fully accomplished the work of the former part. This is the origin of suffering and pain and incomplete living and being. This is the source of ignorant participation in the movement of evolution.

We find that suffering arises when one is attached to and still feeding on the first cord while engaged in work and liberation from the second, or third, or fourth. In short, we rarely live fully in the present; in some way we are always subjugated to the past and therefore to death. We are always demanding of others that they be what they are not, that they fulfil needs which in the light of a further and wider reality are fictitious. We constantly strive to keep all the cords simultaneously, never to move into the realm of true birth and liberation, or, in a word, to become the veritable New-Born.

If each process of liberation were fully accomplished—first from the 'physical mother', then the 'emotional', then the 'mental', and so forth, —there would cease to be any cause for suffering, and what is more there would be the emergence and birth of the true individual, possessed of a light and knowledge and power which it is difficult to imagine at present, because it is very rare to find a truly mature soul who has been thoroughly born of the Four Mothers. Under close observation we find that though some parts of the being are liberated, even in the best of cases there may be one which is recalcitrant and holds back, thereby impeding the integral development of being.

After work has proceeded on the vital-emotional nature a further section of nine years commences, approximately around the 18th year of life and lasting to the 27th. This work corresponds to the mental feeding and concentration on this part of the being which automatically brings about the severance of the vital-emotional cord, possibly around the 22nd to 23rd year. This phase of the work is also personified in some being or relationship, someone who has the power to cause the release from the former bondage and reveal a further part of ourselves. This growth may bring with it an opening to studies or interests of a higher order. It is possible that this be accomplished through intellectual affinity with someone who would then stimulate the development of the mental being and the detachment from the pull of the vital-emotional area. The hold of the senses at this time should give way to the expression of the higher being, or become subject to control from above. But here too we find that there is usually a 'carrying over', so when the vital being still lingers in an unliberated state and comes to interfere with the mental development of being, a perversion of the true function of both begins and the problems of sex arise, with their psychological and physiological nuances; eroticism commences which is a combined mental-vital aberration, and the individual finds himself subject to the suffering which consequently ensues, inflicting it not only on himself but to some extent on the whole of his society.

If the student observes carefully he can see that situations are repeated in a person's life in a most dramatic way in correspondence with the Gnostic Circle, precisely when a certain liberation is not fully accomplished. This may happen several times, but at a certain stage the negative crystallisation is too strong and there is no longer a repetition, which means that in this life cycle there is no further possibility of liberation from that 'cord' and the work is to be carried over into another life, under conditions which will impose a stronger and more determined concentration for that particular liberation. This would be the karmic debt that one has to pay, which comes under the rule of Saturn, and Saturn is the crystallisation point of the System. When a critical juncture is reached in the evolution of the soul from lifetime to lifetime, tremendous sufferings may be experienced because of this accumulation from past lives which needs to be violently broken; for the individual's own good it is sometimes necessary that the circumstances of life be such as to produce intense suffering, for it is through suffering that the Ignorance is checked. Progress while the Earth is under the rule of the Ignorance is most often made possible through suffering. In the gnostic development this is no longer the case. Thus we are our own self-undoing, as the last sign of the zodiac, Pisces, reveals to us, and the way we close one cycle signifies the quality of the next.

In relationships with others as conditions now stand it is rare to find an individual relating to another on the basis of pure un-mixed energies. Bonds are usually formed by a clouding process where we rarely see and recognise the role certain people play in our lives. We are constantly relating to *images* of others which are unreal and in no way correspond to their actual being and worth. The process of relating on the basis of image-making becomes very complex as life goes on, gathering an ever greater momentum and finally smothering the true being with all its parts entirely under a mantle of illusion. We pass our entire life relating to ghost images instead of living entities.

As mentioned it is mostly found that the 'Mothers' are represented by persons who act to liberate us from some past enchainment, if not in the usual terms of relationships at least the entry of these people into our lives, though they remain in the background without occupying an obvious and predominant position, will have the effect of shaking the foundations and releasing some part of ourselves. Needless to say this work can be done on the subtle planes, a direct contact with the Divine Mother and her emanations which serve to carry us through this process of birth and growth without the need of incarnations on the physical plane.

After liberation of the mental being, the period from approximately 27 to 36 years corresponds to the spiritual quarter and this is the time of unity of being, the harmonisation of all the other parts and their centering around the principle of Light. But it too means a liberation from a certain bondage and the severance of a particular cord with the Mother. The being then passes into the highest stratum and accomplishes the severance of the mental cord during the 31st and 32nd years, opening up the possibility of work in the higher realm of unity, or unification of all the other parts, and the final liberation. If this relates to a personification in terms of a spiritual teacher, however this may present itself, the individual who has truly accomplished the former work must, during this period of nine years, sever the last and most difficult cord of all: he must become his own light.

14

In liberation from the fourth and final cord the true liberation comes, the fully mature being emerges, the *individual* is born, and from this point on we can say that there is the capacity for true action, arising from the state of pure, unclouded being.

The spiritual liberation is the most difficult of all because its hold is more subtle and therefore the tie is strongest. It corresponds to the deepest part of the being and consequently it is rare to find one who has actually passed through this initiation and known the real Death and Birth. If this is experienced it is an entirely new individual who emerges, one who has gone beyond the Ignorance and lives in the light of Gnosis.

This would be the classic or ideal development of an individual on the spiritual path, the way of gnosis in harmony with the cycles of Time and the rhythms of the Cosmos. For those in whom the other aspects of being are more important because of destiny, such as the mental or vital, it is passage through these sections which will be most significant and will have the appearance of a sort of initiation. But for those who intend the integral development then the process must work itself out fully and there must be the severance of all four cords, the spiritual as well. When an individual remains involved in the vital or physical being chances are more remote that he will be able to achieve sufficient liberation to pass on to the higher hemisphere of being. He remains forever on the wheel of Prakriti, within the prison of mind or the bondage of the senses. For this reason at a certain stage in one's progress it is necessary to achieve full liberation from sensual living and subjugation. Further along the path it becomes absolutely imperative that complete control over the power from below, the vital force, and the senses be fully accomplished. This, as we can see, pertains to those whose destiny carries them towards a higher level of being For others the life of sensual pleasures, with its accompaniment of pain and suffering, is quite adequate and one does not demand of them or expect them to attempt any further transmutation. The so-called sinner can be viewed with compassion for he is his own destruction, and all sin is merely the obstinacy to remain imprisoned in the lower part of the being, disconnected from the higher. It is consciousness of separation from the Origin of Light which plagues the sinner, creates his suffering and stimulates him to progress. We see, furthermore, that there is no sin for those whose time has not come to work on other aspects of being and to graduate, so to speak, to another world.

At a precise point in one's development the destiny is fully revealed, which corresponds to the Initiation we have spoken of prior to severance of the spiritual cord. Only at that time is the individual granted the vision of himself and his destiny in the fullest terms.

The period of nine years 'gestation' which brings forth the birth of any one of the Four Beings, carries the individual through 12 signs of the zodiac, each of which indicates a field of expression and an area of development. These 12 are to be taken also in four parts divided at the four Cardinal points. Equally important in this passage of nine years is the division into three parts, reposing on the three angles of the Sacred Triangle. We find that this experience of the four and three-part Circle is the most important. During nine years one experiences the union of these two and has passed through their total or full range of possibilities. Thus even within the period of nine years that corresponds to mental development, let us say, the individual passes through a sector which has a sub-influence of one of the other sectors, just as we explained for the evolution within the Greater Circle. It is this complexity of layers or superimposition of strata that may render the study difficult at first, but ultimately profoundly rich and beautiful.

For the first two and a quarter years, in any one of the nine year cycles, there would be passage through the first three signs of the zodiac, Aries, Taurus, and Gemini; this would signify the complete experience of the three energy flows, Creation, Preservation and Destruction. It is not possible in this text to enter into discussion of the qualities and characteristics of each sign in detail. For this purpose the student should refer to a text such as *The Magical Carousel* wherein by means of allegory, images are impressed upon the inner being which contain the significances of all the signs.

Briefly we can say that the first three signs according to this synthesis would represent the laying of the foundations for the entire cycle. The first nine months which embrace Aries are usually intense in nature and bring a definite close to the last cycle and initiate the new beginning, the direction being established with this passage through Aries. In a cycle of major importance such as that which occurs at the 36th year, there is an even greater sense of 'conclusion and opening' in this sector. The seeds are usually planted for a new activity and in some sense a termination of the work of the past. As stated elsewhere, six months before the 9 year culmination and six months after would fall under the rule of *Pluto*, after which *Mercury* becomes prominent for a year, and so on.

The influence of Pluto and the *new thrust* of Aries only emphasise all the more the aspect of an emergence of a transformed part of the being, in particular during certain significant passages over the 0° Aries point, through the 9th orbit of Pluto. If we take human gestation as an example, which this Circle epitomises in a host of ways, we see that this is the *conception* point and following the process according to the development of an infant, the meaning of all the nine years will become clearer. The angles of the Triangle mark the three major zones in the development. The first, the 0 or conception, is when the seeds are planted. The 3 Point, or four groups of nine months later, is when the soul is 'breathed' into the vessel, the breath being the destiny and development of an individual during any of the 9 year cycles, and it corresponds to the third month in the gestation of a foetus. This process of intervening 'shocks' is known to be an essential part in the growth of anything, be it an infant in the womb or a seed and plant in the ground.

Passage over the 3rd Point is perhaps the least spectacular of all the angles, but it is silently important and has a delicate quality about it. The first manifestation of the psychic being should come forth and take the reins of life to assure a smooth and easy course during further progression. But the soul seeks the image of itself which is to be found in the indwelling spirit, and consequently this search is often projected on to a person who represents the quality of one's soul. We seek that which is most like our deepest Self. It can be understood how and why the ego deflects the course at this angle by means of this method of projection: man is to realise his soul within, but because of ego which belongs to the realm of separation from the Reality, he seeks for fulfilment outside himself. The Purusha and Prakriti (Leo and Cancer) within one's own being are here to meet and join, yet because there is not the consciousness of this Subliminal Self, the search is directed outside and satisfaction of this primordial need comes to depend on exterior factors. This need for the unification of soul and spirit is the very stem of life and around this inner union the whole of existence is woven.

If the work is not accomplished as should be during passage over the 3rd Point the subsequent progress becomes obstructed and more difficult. That is, if instead of the soul being victorious the ego comes forth and moulds the life around its illusory substance, the difficulties that will be met during the ensuing three years can be determined. There is the opportunity at this time to live in the soul, or at least to recognise the attempt at projection for what it is, in its true light. Or else there can be the further feeding of the ego with the imposition of its hungers and demands and the succumbing to the clouds it casts over all one's perceptions and actions. The work of this part of the wheel is very delicate and subtle,—it is, as it were, a mere breath passing through the existence which will not impose itself and which can easily become deviated. Therefore this period is best spent in a quiet and indrawn state.

When the student looks at the Gnostic Circle as a graphic image of growth he can readily perceive the process of development. The 9 is the Apex, the peak point, after which the movement apparently dips down and plunges deeply into itself, until at the 4.5 Orbit it is farthest away yet potently linked to the Apex. At this juncture in the flow the Apex exerts its formidable magnetic pull and begins to draw that to which it gave initiation back unto itself. So the period between 0° Cancer and 0° Libra equivalent to the second and a quarter to the fourth and a half year of any 9 cycle, can appear to the student as the most outwardly unimportant, because these years refer to the deep inner work whereby strength is accumulated through the soul realisation. Around the 3 angle, where we find the Moon and Earth and the guna of Preservation of the Sacred Triangle, it is indispensable for the soul to come forward. In the ideal sense this is the silent period of the flowering of the psychic being, the story of which is contained in the myth of Demeter and Persephone, who are these two celestial bodies. The individual may not be aware of what is attempting to become established, but nonetheless the work is being done though he lacks the proper perception of it. The more conscious a person is the more he can benefit from this period. It should be a time of going within, or at least of indrawn attention, though one be involved in outer activities. The 3 Angle is the marriage of the Purusha and Prakriti, the masculine and feminine poles, the outgoing and in-coming breath. The inner being is firmly forged by this mingling, which will become solidified or crystallised at the 6 Angle.

Passage through the sign Cancer can often signify a plunging into the past, which has the effect of awakening one to the true position with respect to one's progress. It can also signify a reorganisation of the cellular composition of the body, because Cancer is concerned with the cells. Thus it is found that this area produces at the outset some noticeable change in health, more marked than at any other point in the wheel, or in some way the need to attend to the physical. The other Water signs also have some bearing upon the physical condition, in particular when one is passing through decanates within them that correspond to Cancer.

When the individual passes over the 4th orbit of Mars there is generally an influx of energy, also in periods of passage through the signs Mars rules, Aries, and to a lesser degree Scorpio; we find then that the Mars energy is most potently felt at the 0° Aries point, where it is present through sign as well as through planet,—

Pluto, the higher octave of Mars.

There is a firm thrust at the 4th Orbit, because in its plunge the movement could lose momentum without being able to complete the trajectory. In fact, it is at the 3 Angle that a shock or intervention occurs in the life movement so that the correct course is kept, after which at the 4th Orbit the energy of Mars is breathed into the movement to further assure the success of the directive. It is at this point, as well as at the 9th, that a truly great influx is needed, consequently Mars is known and felt as a planet of war and aggression. In the planetary harmonic scale it is placed so that the movement from the Apex, the Transcendent, which is in its descent, so to speak, may receive once more the same influx of vital force that gave it its initial momentum and that will sustain it through the further and most intense passage. Mars is perfectly situated in our System so that its energy is ever being thrust when it is best and most acutely needed. The Transcendent Apex is capable of holding the direction up to the 3 Point. Then an intervention is needed to bring about a 'curve' and at the 4th Orbit a new influx of energy, almost equivalent to that of the Apex, is demanded so that the power is renewed.

Following the graphic image of the Gnostic Circle the student can observe that after this powerful intake of Martian force, the individual must 'cross' the Asteroid Belt six months later. And then there is the clash between the power from below and that from above: this is the juncture of the two, as epitomised by Mars and Jupiter, the 4th and 5th Orbits. The movement from above serves as the *pull* to the heights, and the thrust from below is the necessary élan which makes the upward movement possible.

The Asteroid Belt with its enormous 342,000,000 miles of millions of shattered particles is representative of what exactly occurs in the individual in his growth as he passes over this particular point. If left to itself after contact at the 4th Orbit, or year, of Mars, the thrust would be so great that the movement would be compelled to *move away from* the Apex, there would be no definite and radical reversal or curve. To counteract this possiblity and to assure that all things return to the Origin, we find the formidable and hugely magnetic Jupiter next in the scale, the only means whereby the power of Mars is held in check. At this position it is indispensable to have such a large body so that it serves as the Sun in a sense. For the movement of life and growth in fact, Jupiter becomes the Sun,[1] because in the System it is that which catches hold of the Seed in gestation, the movement of life re-vitalised by Mars, and draws and directs it back to the Centre, assisting in the progress of the subtle great curve. For this reason Jupiter is the Guru, whose function in one's spiritual development is precisely that of replacing the Sun, the Divine,—becoming the representative of the Sun on this planet. The Sun and Jupiter together therefore are the orbs of the Truth-Consciousness.

After Jupiter Mars enters once more through its rulership of Scorpio and another revitalisation occurs, after which this 'thrust' is met by the 6 Angle, Saturn,

[1] Jupiter is much like the Sun in the physical sense: the planet has been found to be a huge spinning ball of liquid hydrogen. It has 12 satellites that could be taken as the 12 zodiacal signs or else as the Sun and the orbiting planets which one day may amount to 12. Jupiter moves through the zodiac once every 12 years, thus 1 year for it is like 1 month for the Earth.

and a further intervention takes place, 'curving' the movement. The next two stages fall under the magnetism of the Apex, which is capable of controlling the direction and drawing it back to itself. The Apex thus handles 5 orbits, and the remaining 4 are cared for by the bases of the Triangle. This gives us the image of the Sri Chakra in Tantrism, made of 5 descending and 4 ascending triangles. The planets after Jupiter must necessarily be of large proportions because they must provoke the return of the Great Curve; nearing Pluto the size is no longer important because the Apex is reached.

The student can observe that the base angles of the Triangle are needed for interventions to bring about the indispensable *curves*, and each is supported in equal proportion by Mars, either through orbit or the zodiacal signs which it rules, the 3 by meeting Mars *after* its curve when it is needed in fact, and the 6 by receiving the Mars thrust *before* through Scorpio, just at the time it is needed to pull the movement out of the magnetic field of Jupiter.

In the graphic picture we are studying the student can see the deep significance of passage over the 4.5 Orbit, which occurs at the $4th^1/_2$ year, the $13th^1/_2$, the $22nd^1/_2$, the $31st^1/_2$, the $40th^1/_2$, the $49th^1/_2$, the $58th^1/_2$, and so forth. The period in life which is especially sensitive to this orbit is between the 44th to the 54th year. It is well now to establish certain points regarding the planetary cycles and the years that are sensitive to them:

10th to 19th are sensitive to MERCURY
20th to 29th are sensitive to VENUS
30th to 39th are sensitive to EARTH-MOON
40th to 49th are sensitive to MARS
50th to 59th are sensitive to JUPITER
60th to 69th are sensitive to SATURN
70th to 79th are sensitive to URANUS
80th to 89th are sensitive to NEPTUNE
90th to 99th are sensitive to PLUTO

with the 45th to the 54th sensitive to the 4.5 Orbit, the ASTEROIDS,

after which the cycle is repeated again on the basis of *three digits*. A practical example of a shift of this order can be given in the life cycle of Sri Aurobindo, when he was 99 in 1971 and made the shift from *two* digits to *three* that marked the entry into the third phase of the work which he initiated; that was the period of completion in practical terms of the Sacred Triangle. From then on the work could no longer be studied and understood on the basis of two elements but rather three, and therefore revealed itself to embrace all aspects of the higher manifestation upon Earth, something which does not seem to have occurred before in this phase of human evolution of approximately 300,000 years. We shall have more to say of this cycle further on.

The first years, from birth to 9, belong to the essence of the planets to which each one corresponds by number vibration. Thus the first nine years are for the pure development of essence and therefore they are actually the most important in life, for according to how these years are passed the rest will unfold. It is a time when the ray of each orbit can be firmly established or settled in the being, or we can say, *the seed of each orbit is planted during these years,* which are to bear fruit later on when in the life cycle the individual passes through these orbits once again. The foundations therefore of the entire life are laid during these first 9 years, which show us the fundamental importance in acquiring a just understanding about the manner in which a child is to be brought up who is to take his place in the gnostic evolution of the race, and the understanding of the proper influences to which he must be exposed during these early years.

It is hoped that the student is able to follow the beauty of the harmonic structure of life as here put forth, that he can grasp the idea of *one orbit equalling one year of life,* in the same sense that one day equals one year of life in the traditional study of astrology. It will be necessary to return to this fact in greater detail in a later portion of the study.

Another factor which will show the student the intensity of the 4.5 Orbit is its critical location within the Solar System in its relation to the movement of *ascent* in the individual, and the unfolding *descent* of the Divine in evolution, which can be viewed in terms of the process of evolution and involution.

The 0-9 of the Sacred Triangle represents the Transcendent Divine, the 6 is the Cosmic Divine, and the 3 is the Individual Divine. A human being in his development moves from 0 (Transcendent) to 3 (Individual) to 6 (Cosmic) and then back to 9 (Transcendent). Thus through the portion of 0 to 3 there is the establishment of the individual aspect of the Divine in Manifestation in the human being, which is his very soul. He then moves on to the 6 where there is the possibility of experiencing and expressing the Cosmic Divine,—in his growth he widens his consciousness after passage through Jupiter's orbit which immediately precedes the 6 point and is known as the planet of expansion of consciousness. Thereafter the individual moves through the sector comprising the last three signs which bring him to the possibility of identification with the Transcendent Divine in manifestation, where he meets the 9 point.

In terms of the evolution of the Manifest Divine in the Cosmos the process is reversed: the Transcendent descends, moves into the Cosmic, and then touches the Individual in the descent; the Seed appears to become *smaller* as it plunges, which in fact is the method of Descent. It starts as an all-embracing breath and then becomes intensified or focuses its attention onto or into the Individual after passing through the Universal. For this reason the Mother has said: 'The Divine is for us the 4th dimension.' The dimension of Time is the above described movement of contraction which we experience in the Absolute's descent and manifestation. The movement of the Supreme appears to go from vast to minute, a sort of involution in the process of evolution. The human being, who is the 'focused attention' of the Supreme, has the task of unfolding that Seed and bringing it to the width, breadth, height and depth of the Transcendent. The latter is the outgoing breath which diminishes as it expires out from itself and the former is the ingoing breath which draws an ever greater quantity of itself into its being as it progresses.

These two movements of Ascent and Descent intersect at a certain place in time and space, which occurs in our System at the 4.5 Orbit. If the Asteroid Belt is studied in this light it will no longer be a mystery to the student. It becomes easy to understand why such a zone exists and how it is inevitable that it exist, why Jupiter is of such tremendous proportions compared to the rest of the planets and why Mars must furnish the *thrust*, which is mistaken for violence and aggression at present by Earth beings. Naturally if one approaches the matter from the standpoint of the physical sciences, that is, if one looks at the arrangement of the Solar System in terms of present-day scientific vision, limited to the study of phenomena in a lifeless and disunified manner, the enigma of Jupiter, the Asteroid Belt, Mars, and so on, will not be even remotely solved. Astronomical science does not take into consideration the factors which really determine the structure and flow of the solar system: they do not see the *consciousness* behind the phenomenon, for through Science one cannot perceive the formidable Curve of Consciousness and how all things are compelled to return to the Origin though they proceed at the same time to expand. Though Science has recently come close to the solution, through the formulation of the space-time theory and all that this has signified, the physical sciences cannot see the movement of Becoming within Being, or the *contraction of Time* and the *expansion of Space*. Only with a spiritual vision can one understand that at the precise location of Jupiter a body is needed in the System to replace the Sun in magnetic pull and, in terms of consciousness and its unfoldment, to bring the movement back upon itself. Because of Jupiter the 4.5 Orbit of the Asteroid Belt is where the *farthest bend* occurs in the descent from and ascent to the Transcendent. (See diagram page 217).

In the movement of DESCENT Jupiter holds the force magnetically. There is expansion, which is indispensable after the contraction of Saturn, but at the same time Jupiter would not release the movement unless Mars were next on the descending scale and did not *compel* the flow to continue by its tremendous power.

After Jupiter, in the contrary movement of ASCENT there must be a body of large enough proportions to carry on the flow, possessing a peculiar characteristic which reflects its crystallising capacity, and this is Saturn with its three rings, unique in our System. This body replaces the Earth, so to speak, or its rings represent the first Triad from the Sun which culminates in our planet. Thus Saturn represents the forged psychic being on its voyage 'homeward'. This is the other Angle of the base, and it is the Time-Spirit, precisely he who epitomises the movement of contraction of Time or, we can say, who represents the action of condensation of becoming within being. The point in the sky for our planet which captures the combined elements of the Triangle's base are the Lunar Nodes, representative of the Earth's psychic being, —they are the lunar-solar currents (Cancer and Leo) brought into fusion by Saturn.

It is perhaps well at this point to throw some further light on the Lunar Nodes and their relation to Saturn and to Time. The farther away one is from an object, the deeper is one looking into the past. Space we can say is the measure of the Past; consequently separation and division make our vision one of death, of the past. Consciousness, or identification through consciousness, is the means whereby we can make simultaneous perception. On this basis we can come to understand something of the so-called 'Akashic Records'. To read the past in this manner would mean reaching the point in the ether where the space orbit crosses the time orbit. One would be able to know the details of an event by reaching the point of intersection. There would not be a gigantic book in the ether where all is recorded as some believe, but the ability to read 'akashically' would be the possibility to project one's consciousness to the point of intersection where time crosses the orbit line of the space dimension of a phenomenon. This point would be the Akashic Record for the event. The zodiac is the synthesis of such a process, or we can say it is the celestial book where all is recorded. Each symbol of the zodiac is the synthesis of a particular combination in time and space, where these two have come together and their joint relationship has produced the image of the symbol, containing the knowledge of that particular relationship. So each zodiacal symbol that corresponds to a degree of the celestial sphere reveals the outcome of that particular cross-sectioning. By means of the Gnostic Circle one would be seeing the full synthesis of time and space with all the elements of its potential unfoldment.

Cancer is the sign of memory; it is ruled by the Moon and we can say the Akashic Records belong to this sign, or better, the phenomenon of reading akashically belongs to Cancer. The process can be known by the Lunar Nodes. They would be or would represent the points of juncture of the Time-Space contact. Therefore the Lunar Nodes have a very acute relation to a person's past, for which reason they can also reveal the potential axis of a person's future, because the past is the foundation or seed of the future. Let us say, by projecting oneself to the point in the ether which corresponds to the Lunar Nodes of one's horoscope, one could see oneself yesterday, or in a past life. Another way would be to penetrate deeply into the degree of the zodiac wherein the Nodes of any particular chart fall and these would be one's Akashic records. Work with the Lunar and Planetary Nodes should be approached in this light.

At the birth of an event the time-space orbits are coincidental. This is the meaning of 0° Aries. As can be seen it is here that the Circle of 9 and the Circle of 12 perfectly coincide. The Circle of 4 (the Cardinal points) coincides at 0° Aries with the Circle of 3 (the Sacred Triangle), the only one of all the angles of the Triangle to do so. This point therefore is the true birth of anything, where these two measures, time and space, are one, the point of the Sun's rising. From then on there is a separation and one moves away from coincidence which is necessary in order to become *aware* and to fully explore all the possibilities within the evolution of being. From the birth point one lives out the movement by separating the two measures, but in a period of nine years these two movements have once again rejoined and merged in the point of unity where birth takes place. Thus birth in potential is experienced once again. The fullest possible expression or experience of such a fanning out would be 36 years, because 3, which is the support of the 9 (Time) Circle divides into 36, 12 times, and 4 which is the support of the 12 (Space) Circle divides into 36, 9 times. Thus the 3 Circle has transformed itself into the measure of Space (12), and the Circle of 4 has become the measure of Time (9). One has, in 36 years, gone through the wheel in a manner which makes this interchange possible, whereby the one has become the other or has fully explored the other. Thus 36 years is the true point of return to the birth degree, only on a higher position within the spiral. The same is experienced by the greater evolution which moves in a rhythm of 36 signs (that comprise the 12 Manifestations.)

To see the future one would have to travel reversely, or deeper into the dimension of space, to that point which has yet to unfold, which is locked in the folds of matter. Thus Cancer, a Water sign, would be the fluidic uncondensed movement of the past, and its opposite Capricorn, an Earth sign, is the future. In matter the secrets of the future are 'jelled', just as in symbolic imagery winter has frozen the seed in the breast of the Earth mantled in snow until the spring of a new birth in Aries. Matter therefore holds within itself the future in potential and all the possibilities of the unfoldment of the highest truth. The seed of Truth in fact is buried in the core of the cell and atom, which contain the fullest potential experience and expression of Truth.

Cancer would be the means of perception outside the body, travel in the subtle sheath which carries one to the sphere of time and space wherein the past is recorded; and Capricorn takes one ever deeper into one's shell where the future is contained. Capricorn takes one into the heart of Matter, the point in inner consciousness where simultaneous time is perceived. Hence Capricorn is the realisation of Immortality, the Divine Mother's victory over death, the redemption of Matter or the unveiling of the seed of Truth which reveals the hidden light, —or the sign wherein the Dark God unfolds the golden child of Light.

Perhaps once more we have gone into aspects which are too esoteric for the student concerned with his individual development, but it is necessary to know the precision of our System with respect to the various angles of the Circle and to the Transcendent, Universal and Individual development, and though this may seem irrelevant regarding the details of one's life as reflected in the Gnostic Circle, it is actually the best means to convey a deeper understanding of what can be expected when in his life cycle a person passes over the orbits we have discussed. This manner of explanation may appear abstract, but in reality it is the only way to awaken one to the occult meanings and workings of the zodiac and the solar system.

Returning to Saturn, the deep significance of the 6 point has already been fully discussed. The student must take the information given regarding the Transcendent and Cosmic manifestations that have been delineated and he must apply this information to his individual growth. To further specify we can state that passage through the sign Scorpio would ideally bring about the death of that which served as a pedestal to the growth but which has no place in the higher evolution of man. In a word, when there is ego during passage through Scorpio, the individual must become liberated from some of the 'excess baggage', otherwise it is not possible to advance further. In that case the being remains caught in the wheel of eternal rebirth in ignorance, stopping in his development at Scorpio, much as we have described in the case of Tibet and its painful efforts to go beyond and meet the orbit of Saturn in a cleansed condition. To experience the higher sphere it is impossible to carry the seeds of the old consciousness into that realm. The gnostic being who has the realisation of immortality has experienced the true meaning of Scorpio, which is to have died to a certain sheath of ourselves, to have become rid of the protective sack of the Mother and to have the psyche come forward and become the beacon of light during the further progress. For this individual the symbol of Scorpio has become the Eagle, a transmutation which merely means that he has realised his immortality and become rid of that which is death, the illusion of his ego.

In Scorpio all that which is no longer of use falls away, the truth alone remains. Scorpio is the birth into the higher hemisphere, the plunge through the void of death into the fire of life of Sagittarius, the very process the entire races of Earth are actually living through in this 9th Manifestation. Most of humanity has never lived through such a birth. With a subtle vision one sees that individuals proceed through life enshrouded in the maternal sack, their auras are thus clouded by this stuff and the light which they carry within never manages to show itself. They are the living dead, for all that which has not become born exists within the kingdom of Death. The illusion of Death is only the fear and the reluctance to shed the veiling Sack and become born a light, full and pure, upon Earth.

To assist the student in better understanding Scorpio and its relation to death we must summarise the signs from the beginning, and briefly explain the process of creation captured in the zodiac.

The Zodiac and the Creation

The zodiac begins with the manifestation, with the first projection of the Supreme into manifested being which is shown in the sign Aries—after which the wheel is the representation of the progression and endless process of becoming within being. To truly understand the creation in the zodiac the signs should be observed preferably in groups of three, and there are times when it is difficult to actually speak of which one precedes the others, for they are often only comprehended when meditated upon simultaneously, when their unfolding is seen as a total and simultaneous action.

Therefore the first three signs together give us the understanding of the manifestation of inorganic matter. Aries, a Fire sign, is the undifferentiated energy which Mars rules, wherein the Sun is exalted. Taurus, an Earth sign, is condensed energy or matter such as that of the mineral or the stone, and this is the home of Venus, the planet of form, and the exaltation of the Moon. Gemini, an Air sign, is the principle of Mind. Considering the signs as part of the body they would govern the head, the throat and the arms, respectively, for which reason we say that this primary Trinity is the Speaker, Voice and the Word. Gemini, the last of the triad, shows us the intellectual capacities of human creation, in contrast to the other species. Taurus is the organ of speech whereas Gemini is articulate language, the ability to express oneself through the word, written or oral. The arms which it governs, for example, are indicative of the power of expression which the mental instrument and faculty grant the human species. The ape and the monkey come close to this similar human ability to utilise their arms and fingers and we find that in the scale of animal life they come closest to man in many respects. The connection between mind and the arms and fingers is evident, for which reason in Indian mythology in order to establish the power of expression of any particular deity, he or she is given a certain number of arms, each holding a particular implement or object which reveals to us their especial attribute or power. The fingers are also important, for so many arms and hands equal so many fingers and so many numbers or digits which also indicate their power. When the Earth was passing through the 8th Manifestation according to the Precession, the first sign met along the way was Gemini and these images of the Hindu Gods and Goddesses became a part of the religious experience of the people, transmitted to them by sages who had the capacity to see these Gods in the overmental plane with all their powers, which they then transcribed in the form we know today, of many-armed deities.

In Gemini therefore we find that the faculty unfolds whereby man is able to perceive and formulate intellectually, but this is achieved by *separation*, for which reason Gemini is the sign of duality. There is the knowledge by division not identification, precisely the determining quality of Mind. Thus when taken as a whole, the first triad of the zodiac reveals to man the process of creation in terms of the separation from the Source by the initial explosion or diffusion which Aries represents, followed by the accumulation or preservation of released energy under Taurus, and then the breath of Mind, which renders the creation conscious of its separation. Gemini is the knowledge of the division, the tree of *good* and *evil* of the Bible, which opened the way for the Fall of Man. In fact, the first three signs are the state of the creation before the Fall: Aries, a masculine sign, is Adam, the first man; Taurus, a feminine sign, is Eve and the Garden of Eden, the earthly paradise where creation is not yet aware of the separation, where Nature fulfils herself in contentment on the basis of unawareness. It is Gemini (Mind) which arouses the consciousness by means of division, or the knowledge of good and evil, the opposites and paradoxes, the faculty to project outside itself, to see itself as distinct and divided, preparing the terrain for the Fall of Creation which occurs in the next sign, Cancer. Gemini and its opposite sign Sagittarius, the 3rd and 9th signs, form the axis of the development of the species from Mind to Supermind, or the planes above Mind. For this reason these signs are considered the exaltations of the Lunar Nodes, the axis of the Earth's soul unfoldment and the indication of the ultimate goal of the evolving species, its past as well as its future.

The dominant note of the first Triad is the Cardinal point Aries—Fire—the secret reality of Matter. Hence though the first trinity be initiated by the fire of spirit, it is the *Triad of Matter*. It is Fire that is the support of inorganic matter, the gaseous energy of the Sun for example, the first term in the process of condensation of energy; consequently the Sun is exalted in Aries.

The second Triad is introduced by the Cardinal sign Cancer, which is of the Water element, therefore following Matter is the principle of Life and the formation of the living cell. The aspect of rapid and continual change is introduced and the rigidity of inorganic matter is broken down. Cancer is the sign of gestation and the beginning of Life, but at the same time it is the *end of life*, for growth in terms of the cell implies decay as well, more rapid than in any other formation of Matter. Cancer is the womb of the mother and the grave which is the womb of Mother Earth where the decomposition of the tissues and cells is carried out: she who gave life is the devourer as well. The *womb* that gestates becomes the *tomb* of matter. In the human gestation the same process is carried out that takes place on a universal scale. The embryo arises in an endless and limitless sea, where it abides in enjoyment of the experience of infinity. For it the physical mother's womb, which Cancer symbolises, is the very Cosmos, the waters of the cosmic sea contained in the womb of the Divine Mother. But this womb feeds it and thus brings about its growth, which is then its own condemnation. The body of the foetus begins to occupy the totality of the womb and that which was its infinity becomes its imprisonment, the walls which will one day contract about the foetus to force it to plunge into the void beyond the mouth of the womb that was its infinite bliss. In the Gnostic Circle the 4.5 Orbit is the place where the reversal occurs. Until then the embryo and foetus live in the ecstasy of infinite space. At the Asteroid Orbit the space begins to diminish, its growth signifies the death to that experience and the remainder of the term is spent in the final preparation of its form for the new world. In the last sign or month the foetus dies to that other world and the womb ejects it amidst its waters and the infant begins life at 0° Aries as we have previously described. This entire process is the dominion of Cancer, the physical birth, just as the spiritual birth is the dominion of Capricorn, its opposite sign.

Water, the principal element of the body of man, gives suppleness and plasticity to form. To keep the cells and tissues in a constant state of regeneration food is needed and therefore Cancer represents the breasts, the first channel of nourishment for the human being, as well as the stomach wherein digestion takes place.

It is the element Water that is the soul in evolution, hence Cancer is the Fall or the imprisonment of the soul, the root of the Life Principle and the process of continual rebirth. Jupiter is traditionally considered in exaltation in Cancer, which indicates that consciousness is the upholder of the cells that Cancer rules, as the Sun is the upholder of the energy Mars of Aries rules. The sign is ruled by the satellite of Earth and so we know evolution of the psychic being takes place on this planet in the System. As ruler of the second Triad, Cancer makes the Water element predominant in the human species, and is joined by Leo, the indwelling Purusha, the partner of the soul or the secret aspect which quickens the element and breathes life into it, the masculine contribution. Leo is then followed by Virgo, or the body of mental man built of these three principles—matter, life and mind—for Virgo, an Earth sign, is ruled by Mercury the planet of Mind. This is the final product of the lower hemisphere which Prakriti rules, the realm over which the Ignorance has hold for the present.

In the first triad Fire initiated and Air terminated; in between was the Fixed sign Taurus, an *Earth* sign, Matter. These two outer energy flows of Cardinal and Mutable signs, Aries and Gemini, orbit around the Fixed sign Taurus, or they give rise to the principle of Matter. Taurus is that quality in matter which makes it solid and not etheric, which makes it occupy a definite place.

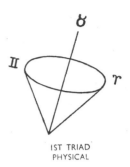

1ST TRIAD
PHYSICAL

In the second triad Water initiated and Earth terminated; in between is the Fixed principle of *Fire*, the Spirit and sustainer of forms. The energy flows of

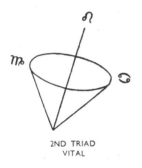

2ND TRIAD
VITAL

Cardinal and Mutable, Cancer and Virgo, orbit around the Fixed sign Leo which gives us the full principle of Life.

These two triads are the terms of the lower hemisphere.

Progressing now to the third triad we encounter the Air element in the sign Libra which initiates the Trinity and therefore the principle of Mind predominates through this element. It is here that the upper hemisphere of being begins, where it is possible for man to liberate himself from the hold of Mother Nature, accomplished by the factor of *union*, or the joining of that which was divided in Gemini, the last Air sign which brought about the Fall. The redemption of creation can begin in the third triad by the awareness of unity or the reversal which initiates the return to the Origin for it must be remembered that 0° Libra is the 4.5 Orbit, where the evolution through man is reversed and made to turn back upon itself, so to speak. Man can become liberated from the Ignorance through union or *yoga*.

After Air there is *Water* and the Fixed sign Scorpio is reached that must bring the death to all that bound man to Mother Nature, the death of the ego. The power that is Scorpio and that brings about the liberation from Prakriti and the freedom of the soul, carries the being soaring to the heights of the Spirit in the following sign Sagittarius, where the power is cut from the lower bondage and the arrow which was the tail of the scorpion, is free to rise and join the descending light.

The possibility of everything that is to manifest is present in the first triad. If Gemini did not precede Cancer, the Life Principle, the latter would not carry within it the principle of mind, with all that it signifies for the human race, and we can appreciate the predominant position of the Life Principle which is, as it were, the fruit

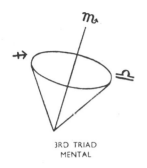

3RD TRIAD
MENTAL

of the first triad. Scorpio, as the Fixed sign of *Water*, around which the initiating Cardinal and terminating Mutable energies orbit, shows how Mind is contained in the Life Principle, just as we have seen by the Fixed sign of Leo that the Fire element, the secret of matter, was contained and brought forth in the triad which Cancer dominates. The student can see therefore that the Cardinal initiation of each trinity becomes the Fixed Principle of the trinity that succeeds it, showing us that that which is contained emerges at a later point in the development. Spirit is contained in matter, in matter life is inherent, in life mind is involved and in mind supermind, or the truth-consciousness, or spirit, or whatever one wants to call the higher principle above and beyond mind, is contained. The symbol of the Sphinx is precious to humanity for this knowledge: the Fixed signs hold *the secret of the unfolding of the inherent principles*.

The fourth and last triad is dominated by the Cardinal sign Capricorn of the Earth element, wherein the realisation of the highest possibilities for the species is revealed, the complete divinisation of man.

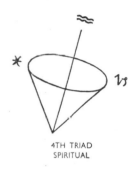

4TH TRIAD
SPIRITUAL

By the central Fixed sign Aquarius, an *Air* sign, we see that Libra is fulfilled in this triad or that the Mental Principle has given birth to the higher principle inherent in itself, the supermind, which signifies the spiritualisation of the species.

The three signs or Energy Flows which comprise any one element in the zodiac will always represent a process of birth, or, we can say, they represent the *flow* of creation and the steps toward the maximum fulfilment of that particular element. The four Elements as such are the *components*, the ingredients, but the three Energy Flows show us the working of the divine breath. The way the elements and energy flows or Qualities are arranged in the zodiac is essential and reveals the real process of evolution. Particularly important to note are the angles of the Sacred Triangle which are the fusion of Life and Spirit, Water and Fire. This fusion of Life and Spirit is the end and beginning of all created things.

This is, in part, the knowledge the zodiac gives to man about the process of creation and the evolution of the species. It shows him that he may remain in the lower hemisphere for as long as Mother Nature is content with him in such a condition. But the goal of evolution, as far as man is concerned, is more complete and will one day collectively move toward a fuller experience; then the present species of mental man may remain, as the monkey remains to remind us of other remote stages, or the entire species may be replaced by a finer specimen; the in-between link in any case may not remain.

In his individual development the aspirant cannot expect to stay imprisoned in mind and the processes of intellectual perception. He must become aware that now the System is no longer arrested at the 6th orbit of Saturn. Consequently the harmonic life span no longer concludes at 69 in terms of the average of the race, which would be the full and final period of the 6 orbit Circle. (In fact, the symbol of Cancer is formed by what appears to be a 6 and a 9, and Cancer is known as the end of life period.) While remaining in the lower hemisphere this could hold; once having passed into the further development that the upper hemisphere of the zodiac promises, it is difficult to suppose that the movement can be arrested in terms of time and the expansion of consciousness at that point. As the System expands so will the life span of man expand, and along with it his consciousness.

With Uranus, Neptune and Pluto in the System the species can never remain permanently what it is. This would mean cutting the evolution off from its cosmic oneness, which may be accomplished in terms of the individual but not in terms of the species in general, the races of Earth. We may individually lose the consciousness of our oneness with the System and the entire Cosmos, but this does not interfere with the work of the Divine Mother and the facts as they stand supported by the growth of the System by a further triad, or the re-acquisition of the knowledge of their existence in the System. The last three planets signify the expansion of our experience of the time-space reality, the conscious passage into that last stage of gestation, by far the most important, where the foetus is made fully ready for birth. Until now, with the System of 6 plus the Sun, the races of Earth were never fully gestated, never fully born, because mental man was never intended to be the final term. And in all sincerity we cannot say that the so-called Superman will be the final accomplishment.

The individual must consider this extra triad the zone wherein he is prepared for the coming birth and therefore each time that he passes through this portion in his own life he will experience a 'drawing together' of all the threads of being. He must consider this the term of unity where he is *made whole*. It is the true process of conclusion which alone can carry one to a new birth. We are literally compelled to arrive at such a collective fate. There is nothing that can hold the process back. There is no possible way that we can remain what we are. The day the last planet of the new triad was spotted marked the death of mental man, and it is significant that this was also the year the Atomic Age was initiated, the major threat of extermination that hangs over the races of Earth, for it is possible that if the collectivity does not fulfil the destiny of expansion in the intended manner, awareness of the further Triad will be removed.

The final triad of planets and the passage into the last three signs brings a widening of the collective and individual consciousness, thus it is evident that man should be capacitated to understand the process and cooperate with the work at hand instead of obstructing and perhaps causing the destruction of a major portion of the human species. On the collective scale there is no such consciousness in evidence as yet, equipped by the fullness of its vision and experience *to act* in the realm of matter, a group in full possession of the power of transformation. It is difficult to say whether even individually we can be certain such a power exists. That is, individually and collectively to a very limited extent the understanding may be there, but the power to act in the field of matter is not yet in evidence. We can say that the new consciousness is still in gestation, or that the child has not yet fully manifested, because for it to manifest means to a certain extent that there must be a fertile terrain to receive it. The soil still appears unready.

The zodiac does not end at the sign of Scorpio and the triad of mental being. The experience is a series of 12 steps and the full 12 produce the divine man. We have lost the light of this knowledge because, it must be remembered, we are emerging from the 8th Manifestation, —that very realm of Death. We have come through a dark, dim Age, beyond which we have no recollection. We do not know who we were 10,000 years ago because we have, the races of Earth, lived through the death of Scorpio. We cannot suppose that collectively there would have been no loss of light therein, because we do not as yet know the conscious death. So the knowledge of our origin and our goal was necessarily lost. By this it is not meant that the birth we are now to know has taken place in the past, but only that at least the knowledge was there which died in Scorpio; or better said, was put to sleep.

The 8th month of pregnancy is ruled by Neptune. It is the heaviest period, when the foetus is completely prisoner of his space. Births occurring during this month are said to be the most difficult, for the term does not have natural affinity with birth but rather with death. Yet by approach to the 9th orbit of Pluto the being is ready and birth can take place.

As we have described, the 36th year brings the liberation from all the cords, or from all the props man needs to help him along the way. He then stands nude before his God and has drawn all the lines to the core of his being, has realised the Divine Mother within his soul, has unveiled her light therein and this light can then be his beacon and his power throughout the rest of permanence on the planet. This is the ideal birth, but failing to accomplish it the individual is then given other opportunities, sometimes in his actual life, sometimes requiring further incarnations. Whatever the case he will one day achieve his total liberation in his very body, on this very Earth, for this is his destiny. And if this destiny is to be fulfilled according to the harmonies of the Cosmos, making man consciously one with all that surrounds him, it will be accomplished during a precise time span, in accordance with the actual boundaries of the System. In fact it can be said that the real purpose of existence is to find ourselves within the whole of things, or to find our place within the Harmony. The whole of Creation is nothing but *the manifested urge of the conscious experience and realisation of Harmony.* This urge is epitomised in one planet: Venus, the twin of Earth. Venus is the ruler of the first sign of the higher hemisphere, Libra, and she is the exalted planet of the very last sign of the zodiac, Pisces. She is the beginning and she is the end, for it is Divine Love that she symbolises, which alone can carry the Creation. She is Love, she is Union, she is Harmony, and all the things that are born of this sublime trinity.

A Gnostic Pattern in Life

We have often spoken of Sri Aurobindo and the Mother, his co-worker, in this text and it would be good to use them once more as examples because of the harmony manifest in their lives. Yet the student need not rely solely on this information for his comprehension of the Wheel: he can and must find himself within it, and his environment, for in this way only can he carry over the principles of cosmic harmonies into his own life and circle and only in that way can they have any true meaning for him. But to show the accurate function of the Gnostic Circle, this is best achieved by the lives of those who are intimate with the plane from where the Harmony extends. As we have so often spoken of the importance of the 36th year, we find that in both the lives of Sri Aurobindo and the Mother, these years marked turning points.

Sri Aurobindo was born in 1872, a 9 year, placing him at the point of the Transcendent in the Gnostic Circle. The Mother was born in 1878, a 6 year, falling at the point of the Cosmic Divine which she embodied, containing within herself the Transcendent just as the Transcendent holds within itself the seed of the Cosmic Divine, for all parts of the Trinity complement, complete and *are* the other parts. Between their dates of birth the three sixes emerge. Sri Aurobindo's month was August, hers was February, with therefore 6 months in between. The day of the Mother's birth was 21, his was 15, with 6 days in between as with the year count—1872 to 1878—a period of 6 years. When the Mother left her body there were exactly 6 hours between her passing and Sri Aurobindo's,—19:26 to 1:26. (The official count is 19:25, off one minute from the perfect 6, perhaps due to an inaccurate recording.)

Furthermore we find that all the events of importance in their lives regarding the fulfilment of their missions occurred at one of the angles of the Sacred Triangle. After Sri Aurobindo's birth there was his return to India in 1893 (3), occultly speaking perhaps the most deeply significant event in his life for the Earth. The next important year was his 36th, 1908 (9), when in May he was imprisoned because of his political activities which, at that time, formed the axis of his life. It was during that year of imprisonment that Krishna, the previous Avatar, took Sri Aurobindo fully to himself and transformed him, revealing to him his mission and drawing him away from the activities which he felt obliged to participate in for the sake of his country. In his 36th year the Beloved Vasudeva (Krishna) and he became One, radically altering the course of his life and drawing him entirely towards a path of yoga and away from the call of social and political reform. At the same time Swami Vivekananda from the occult planes revealed to him certain fundamentals pertinent to his work regarding the *Supermind*, the rudiments of his future work. That 36th year was the true new beginning in the fullest sense of the word; the firm roots were grounded for the whole of his life's work, never more to recede. This is the essential meaning of the birth at 36; it is not a completion or a culmination in the activities: it is the veritable beginning, but on the sound basis of truth and with one's feet firmly in the ground, so to speak. The Indians would call it having the 'four feet of the cow on the Earth', as they speak of the Satya Yuga, being a measure of four kaliyugas just as the 36th year is four times nine.

In February 1914 (6), 6 years after Sri Aurobindo's new birth, the Mother was 36. In March after this birthday she arrived in Pondicherry where Sri Aurobindo had established himself. The first meeting with him was to radically alter the apparent course of her destiny; it laid the foundations for her future work and in the same way that Sri Aurobindo's 36th year signified the rooting of his destiny, so did the Mother's 36th.

Obliged to leave Pondicherry in 1915, she returned in 1920 (3), 6 years after their first meeting, to settle herself permanently by the side of Sri Aurobindo. Once again, 6 years after this return, in 1926 (9) Sri Aurobindo retired into seclusion to carry on his work; the Ashram was officially begun under the Mother's guidance.

We have spoken of other dates in the text regarding their work which the student can locate within the Gnostic Circle; but whatever dates of importance are to be found in their lives, they will be seen to correspond to the 'intervention' points of the Triangle. Their lives epitomise the attunement to the higher power which guides the course of the evolutionary work in the manner described in the text. They are, as it were, antennas which capture the light of the higher planes. The interventions continue in this same manner during the third phase of work, corresponding to angle 3 of the Triangle.

On page 182 we spoke of Sri Ramakrishna and Swami Vivekananda and their involvement with this work. All those who are aware of the real meaning and import of Sri Aurobindo's teachings and the significance of his coming know as well of the intimate link between him and Ramakrishna and Vivekananda. The 36 year time span again figures in their regard. Sri Ramakrishna was born in 1836 (9); 27 (3 × 9) years later in 1863, Swami Vivekananda was born, and in 1872 the 36th (4 × 9) year after Sri Ramakrishna's birth, Sri Aurobindo came. It can be said that these three beings form almost one body and the appearance of any one of them could not have come about without the appearance and preparation of the others. Their births in fact all took place in years of the Transcendent seed (9), and Sri Ramakrishna and Swami Vivekananda were preparations for the advent of the New Age and its messenger. Together the first two prepared the birth of the third. For this reason it was Swami Vivekananda who revealed the fundamentals of Sri Aurobindo's future work.

The 36 years' establishment would be the ideal of a harmonious attunement with the cosmic law of truth. For some, however, it takes a longer period to come to the realisation of the full being, which would put one into the category of a conscious and active participant in the bringing down of a new creation. Yet it is not possible to fool ourselves in this respect: the results of a full birth are discernible in the very course the life takes in the inward sense. That is, there may be difficulties in the exterior orbit of the destiny but the inner reality promises the change and therein the foundations are laid which externalise themselves in some definite accomplishment or event or meeting, revealing of this reality to those who can see in this deeper and far-reaching way.

This marks of course only the beginning in a life of participation for the aspirant who desires a full and integral transformation of the Earth life and nature. The sea of ignorance within which the Earth is submerged is thick and the task is long and tedious to try to establish a new way for oneself and one's fellowmen. But in order to do this work the inner 'triangle' must be forged. There must be the soul realisation, which is the accomplishment of the 3 Point and corresponds to the years between 30 and 39. In terms of numbers 36 is the first time that the Triangle is complete because 3 touches the three angle, 6 touches the sixth, and the sum of the two makes 9, equalling the Apex. All of this points to the possibility of the full establishment of the *individual being*. It signifies a concentration on the personal realisation which then renders the aspirant capable of participation in the larger work and able to branch out into a wider and more universal area. First comes the Individual realisation, then the Cosmic and finally the Transcendent, in terms of the harmonious development of man. One may shoot to any of these without first having accomplished the steps before, but whatever the case this is the integral realisation of man, no matter ultimately what the rhythm is.

The 60's can centre around some specific work of cosmic importance, as has been shown in the lives of Sri Aurobindo and the Mother when the ages 66 and 60 brought them into involvement in the Cosmic War of Durga. Moving toward the 90's in the full span the Transcendent aspect is established in the Earth atmosphere, or the fully realised trinity reveals its power, the highest truth is unveiled and the transformation of matter can begin. According to the Gnostic Circle the full life of the physical is 90 years, after which its transformation can start according to and in harmony with evolutionary laws and not sporadic miracles. It is at that time that the 0 and 9 become one again, the Sun and Pluto join, the Light God and the Dark One; the Circle is completed. In terms of the cosmic harmonies after this point the transformation or the formation of a new physical begins.[1] The student can see that in order to complete the work of transformation in its most complete sense, a long life is needed because of the present conditions in the atmosphere. This can vary greatly with the eradication of the Ignorance and its hold over the Earth.

When a being on this path cannot bear the full pressure in all of his parts and centres, or else when he has crystallised certain aspects of the Falsehood within himself in such a way as to render an integral progress impossible, it is often necessary for the being to withdraw prematurely in order that a new vessel be formed and the cycle can begin fresh under more appropriate conditions. All of this demands a profound sincerity of being. If one has asked for a total transformation, then the events of life will guide one in order to bring such a transformation about. The soul will arrange matters in such a way that conditions will always lead one closer to the integral realisation.

If dissolution of the physical is necessary, then the soul will also arrange for this to occur when the moment is propitious for a new beginning in more favourable circumstances. Sometimes the physical vessel is weak and therefore only a part of the work can be accomplished in such a vehicle. The full pressure necessary for integral transformation could perhaps not be withstood. Consequently for that being work on the mental or vital alone is possible, but in any case it is always the soul that knows the correct moment for departure and when the required progress for any given lifetime has been completed. For a full transformation a very sound physical is needed, and eventually when the soul knows the time has come for a complete work, it will arrange the adequate physical vessel.

There are cases when the mental instrument is not sturdy enough and cannot bear the pressure of the descending power. In various ways this is discernible, as, for example, when the individual tends to lose consciousness frequently and passes into trance states without retaining the memory or knowledge of what happens in

---

[1] See: *Symbols and the Question of Unity*, 'Transformation of the Body and the Cosmic Rhythm'.

such a state when he returns to normal consciousness. He leaves his physical sheath without awareness, often due to a descending light and power, and the loss of awareness retards the work because it is a process which must be lived in full consciousness and is intended to widen the consciousness in fact, and render the individual aware rather than not of what happens usually only in trance conditions.

The soul must decide the course; for an integral transformation it is necessary moreover to accommodate the mental instrument in such a way that it not become deranged by the power. When the possibility of derangement is too prominent this may also necessitate a withdrawal and a return under more adequate conditions if the aspiration is strong. Many cases of mental imbalance of various degrees and levels are the result of an intense inner battle between the aspiring soul and the predominant ego. Such cases often signify the individual's desperate attempt to bring about a breakthrough, but all the centres not being joined in the task and each pulling for its own end, derangement in some cases occurs and the task is postponed.

The mental instrument is the most easily damaged today by the descending power, especially in the youth who have weakened the mental being (and dangerously opened the vital) by drug taking. For the integral transformation a work in full consciousness is sought, not one wherein the being is violated by the intake of chemicals and narcotics which dull certain parts and forcefully open others. Such a yoga can only be successful in one who is in complete control and whose consciousness has naturally awakened to certain planes and states, whereby full benefit can be attained through such mutations. These experiences then become the means for a true growth and not an illusory burst into a state which has not been gained through sadhana, which does not belong to us but rather to the chemicals we have ingested, and brings us therefore no substantial benefit. When the soul is awakened it is that part which brings the experiences in the order in which they can be useful. To violate this natural rhythm creates a serious problem and no sound accomplishment can come about on this basis. The soul is the protective valve of our endeavour; it is the Divine Mother within us who is our guide and who carries us through the various phases of sadhana which may otherwise be perilous.

Work on one part of the being allows for the flowering of another,—it is a closely knit and unified process of growth and not an unconscious plunge, irrespective of the condition of three quarters of our being. Impatience will increase today because the channels from above are opened, shall we say, and the forces are freely flowing—at least compared to what they have been in the past; but human nature is feeble and ignorant and man relies often on his own mental judgment and not on the dictates of the soul which is the Divine Representative within him. Thus the calamities resultant from an untimely pulling down of the forces will be more noticeable and the 'casualties' more numerous. This is also the reason for the 'descent' of so many 'world saviours', avatars and immature teachers today: when the higher forces come into an impure and ill-prepared vessel, the ego can use them for its own ends and it distorts the descending truth. In the individual's ascent he must first pass over the 3 point, wherein his soul must come forward and guide him the rest of the way. Any passage over this point brings the strengthening of the soul for the subsequent task that lies before the individual; in the last analysis, it is only upon this inner divine spark that one can rely.

The Triad of Unity and the Initiation of Being

IF THE WORK is properly cared for passage through the last three signs of the zodiac is usually the most fruitful period of the life, in any of the rounds. It is indeed the time when all the threads are there and the individual is fed from the planes of higher consciousness, being and bliss. It is often then that the higher centres open and receive the descending light, met by a purified vital force in ascension. We can say that up to the sign Scorpio this is the process: the physical and vital are prepared so that the higher centres will find support in the firm vehicle and the purified ascending power. Sagittarius, preceding the final trinity, is the journey into 'no man's land', the period between death and resurrection, which is perhaps the most accurate statement of our 9th Manifestation: we are in the solitary 'King's Chamber', suspended between the death of the Ignorance and the resurrection into the light of Gnosis. When a being passes in full consciousness through this sign in the wheel, this is the process that is experienced: one is as though caught within a realm between these two planes, or possibilities. It is entry into, and penetration of, the unknown plane after death that is experienced. It is the realm of the Immortal Exploration, and when this stage is passed in full consciousness of one's immortality, when this death is lived either in the waking state or the state of conscious sleep, that period of life is most important and the most radically transforming. It is suspension between two possibilities, or two realms, and one can see oneself in both and experience the two powers in an entirely conscious way, from below and from above. It is this process that opens the gates to Supermind and the possibility of reaching the highest planes of consciousness available to man in his present stage of evolution. Sri Aurobindo has described the phases leading to this more total reality: 'First is the psychic transformation, in which all is in contact with the Divine through the individual psychic consciousness. Next is the spiritual transformation in which all is merged in the Divine cosmic consciousness. Third is the supramental transformation in which all becomes supramentalised in the divine gnostic consciousness. It is only with the last that there can begin the *complete* transformation of mind, life and body, —in my sense of completeness.'[1] These three phases are the ascending aspects of the Triangle, 3 to 6 to 9.

[1] *Letters on Yoga*, CE page 95.

Physical death occurring near or in the sign Sagittarius leaves one in a state suspended between two realms, and if there is sufficient consciousness continued action in the atmosphere of the Earth is possible.

The sign Sagittarius marks the beginning of the Initiation, a process which, according to the harmonies of the universe, should last for nine months. Starting at the 6 point it would mean that the culmination of the process would occur in Capricorn, the fourth and last Cardinal pillar; truly the 4 cardinal points are the pillars of the universe.

What occurs during this period is the true and authentic initiation, which is the being's preparation for the commencement and practice of a yoga which transcends the paths of old and proposes to carry the sadhak into even deeper, wider and higher regions of growth. It is not to be thought of as a ritual or ceremony, as those in use in occult societies. The initiaion we speak of is one wherein the Shakti comes into the person and starts the initial process of purification, prepares the vessel and being for the coming stages of sadhana, for it is this preliminary cleansing that assures one of the victory and the ability to receive the power. It is the point where the necessary props of the past, with all their vital and mental formations, are broken down in order that the being be in a condition to absorb the descending light and power in its fullest form. The individual becomes consciously involved in the process of witnessing the two powers, from below and from above, and their collision, so to speak. His sincerity and dedication to truth are at that time his only safeguard, and his reliance on the awakened spark of the Divine within him, his soul. His innate sincerity and truthfulness are his protection.

The Great Pyramid and the Mutation of Consciousness

It is believed that an initiatory process of the type described above was held in the Great Pyramid, in both the King's and the Queen's Chambers. This may be only a part of the truth, for the Pyramid had as its function the transformation or alteration of matter as well. But in its role of initiation site there is no doubt that the location and the dimensions of the construction were appropriate for bringing about a mutation of consciousness at a time when the cosmic forces were not present on the Earth to induce such a state anywhere on the planet. That is, at that time conditions were not *universally* available and they had to be fabricated artificially, shall we say, —a structure had to be built which would attract certain forces and create an energy field that existed no where else on the planet but that was known to be necessary for the process of transformation. The ancients before historic times, were aware of the need of such cosmic forces on the Earth for a real transformation to come about, because they knew that such a work could only be accomplished in conjunction with the Cosmos and its rhythms and harmonies and their resultant effect upon Earth. There was at that time an élite which had advanced remarkably in the process of transformation, but it was a process reserved for the élite, due to a host of considerations which we have delineated throughout the text. In short, the time had not yet come for the universal transformation. It was the Age of Leo, the privileged Age of the kingly and priestly class, who were to prepare the ground, to some extent bring down the knowledge and power and leave monuments for future ages which would indicate the line of action and the process of transformation in harmony with the forces of the Cosmos. As far as the Earth was concerned it was an artificial happening, but one that was necessary in order to allow for the full descent of the powers which are actually in play around the planet. The work that was done then, during the Age of Leo, is the one most directly in rapport with the transformation of our times. Thus today such an initiation can take place in any corner of the globe, in any room—that is, any room can become the King's Chamber because it is the inner being that is now able to open to these available forces and become attuned to their vibration so that such an awakening can come about. In fact, the King's Chamber is virtually symbolic of this 'inner space' which is the soul and all the many secret dimensions of being, wherefrom the process of initiation has its flowering. The Divine Mother is revealed therein and she carries out the process with the aid of the newly manifested cosmic forces and occult powers that are freely at work upon the Earth and available to its inhabitants. Because of such an influx of cosmic forces we have the deranged habits of the masses in so many different fields: economic madness, drugs, sexual indulgence, war hysteria, and the like, because these forces are of a powerful order and in impure vessels they destroy instead of create. Our times are interesting because perhaps for the first time in our Great Circle the masses are exposed to powers which they previously ignored or which were reserved for the enlightened few, the aristocratic spiritual élite who alone knew how to attract these forces and possessed the secret knowledge. The clear sign of this universal participation is the availability of the true knowledge now, which only until just recently was kept secret, be it either regarding yoga, cosmic harmonies or occultism of different orders. Perhaps never before has so much been revealed to so many.

When we look at the Great Pyramid today, or some of the minor pyramids around the globe, not only in Egypt but in Central and South America as well, we are struck by the desolation that surrounds them. They are instruments which are no longer needed; in particular the Egyptian pyramids impress us in this way, reposing on dry barren expanses. It is evident that their function has ceased and they no longer are the pivot for the attraction of the forces that gave them their value and life. In meditating on the spiritual fate of the planet, the pessimist regards this as an indication of the backward pace of civilisation, but this attitude is erroneous for the pyramids are no longer used simply because their function has been surpassed. What they contained and signified is now universally present and any initiate incarnated today who lived during that period knows this fact to be true. Those who cling to the magnificence of the Pyramid often miss the greater beauty of the present manifestation, and this is the reason why it is necessary to almost ruthlessly ignore certain data of the past during one's present search, because the past has the tendency to absorb our interest to such an extent that we lose the conscious vision of the present when it is most necessary for our development. It is a fact, for example, that occultists thoroughly engaged in the 'deciphering' of the dimensions and meaning of the Great Pyramid are those most uninterested in the work of the present Age in a positive and dynamic way. Their work may be necessary but for the gnostic being of today it is proven that one can come by the same knowledge and obtain not only the same but infinitely greater results by a positive and dynamic and conscious participation in today's Work. Man, with his body, on a vast and total scale has become the Pyramid. He has the capacity at this time to be his own initiatory site, he carries the King's and Queen's Chambers within his body and this instrument is now ready, because of the movements of the cosmic bodies and their interrelationship and link with the Earth, to become the field for the juncture of greater forces of a higher frequency. The Queen's Chamber is the ascending power and the King's Chamber brings the descending light of the spirit. They are the Purusha and Prakriti, Leo and Cancer, the zodiac's 'king and queen' in fact. The same arrangement is to be brought about in a fused manner today, a joint chamber which we shall discuss further on.

In any case, the shape and structure of the Great Pyramid brings about a 'cross current' of forces which is able to produce a breakthrough into a state of consciousness where occult phenomena of a certain order become a living and conscious reality. The symbol of the Pyramid, the Triangle, is one of the principal images of Capricorn—the mountain, and in Capricorn the neophyte moves into the 'inner mountain' and penetrates the Sacred Chamber that will unveil his Self to himself, and will bring him to the portals of the consciousness of immortality on this Earthly plane. It is in this sign that Death or the powers of degeneration are finally and fully conquered, and it is in this sign that the contact with the Supreme Shakti, she who stands above all the occult forces and uses them for her designs, is established. This merging of the ethereal with the material, the surreal with the real and the bringing of certain planes usually inaccessible to us into the ordinary level of perception, is the purpose of the crossed energy fields as found in the King's Chamber. This same process is today translated in 'form', which represents the same *mountain* of Capricorn, in a manner which corresponds more directly to the sign's ruler, Saturn, and is being constructed in India, —the Matrimandir.

There is a rather romantic notion of Initiation prevailing among the masses, due perhaps to the unsound influence of esoteric societies that abound upon the face of the planet today, and also the heavy flow of gurus who freely 'initiate' by means of a mantra whispered in the disciple's ear, or some brief ritual. There is no doubt that such a practice, when coming from a guru who in truth possesses the knowledge, can set off an inner process similar to the one we are describing, but such cases are rare nowadays, and also the initiation we are speaking of is somewhat different both in its process of unfoldment and its goal. A real initiation, such as that of Egyptian times, is one wherein the disciple is taken up by the Shakti and is revealed the totality of himself and his destiny, —a process which in most cases is far from being romantically pleasant, because the being is revealed in its real and truthful state, without any veils and pretenses, the dark part as well as the bright, and the disciple must live with and bear this sometimes horrendous self-exposure. All of himself is thrust open and he must *see himself*, which will then enable him to reject what is false and belongs to the realm of ego and retain that part of himself which is true. It is his soul that must come fully forward and embrace the spirit, and it comes forth and stands side by side with the ugliness of his ego so that the disciple positions himself in the centre and from there accomplishes the task of death and rebirth. The major reason for an initiation is that the disciple may *know himself*, as the ancients have described, —above all so that he may know just what he can expect of himself in his future sadhana: he comes to know of what stuff he is really made. He lives the moment of Truth and knows just how far he can go and what he can rely on in himself. It is not a process of exposure for the benefit of the Divine or the Guru; the Teacher knows the pupil when the pupil knows nothing of himself, so it is for the purpose of *showing the disciple what he is*—that the initiation takes place. The neophyte is given the opportunity to uncover his most hidden recesses and view all his potentials; he deals with his energies in their most potent and purest form. During that period he must become aware of every power and force that he embodies or attracts or is open to, down to the condition of every cell in his body that must become aware of its immortality. The disciple must come through the initiation with the knowledge that he is both immortal and a child of Truth; during the process he is made to take his stand on one or the other side, the Light or the Dark. If the Light in him is victorious, it becomes his support during the whole of his lifetime.

Some go through the experience in a condensed, recognisable manner, where for the required period of time they are swept into this other world and made oblivious of the surrounding realities. For others it is a series of life circumstances which thrust the secret self into the vision of the sadhak. Whatever the case may be, it is always for the purpose of knowing oneself and of knowing the deep, bottom-less pit that is one's soul, the infinite unending pool wherefrom all knowledge can be extracted and all bliss. The neophyte comes to know what is real in himself, the Infinite and Eternal of his being, the Divine Mother who is his sole reality, and at the same time he dies to his ego, his false self, the sack which protected him and veiled his soul until the moment of its birth. From that time what remains of his ego is merely a ghost formation, void of any power to truly impede the progress and influence in any decisive way. But the difficult part for him to accept is that this sack, this ego, this falsehood *is as well a part of the Mother*: she is the Dark and the Light—everything, all things are within her being, a realisation which cannot be given to everyone. It is only the sturdiest of beings that can come face to face with the full truth: the Dark and the Light are one. And this is Capricorn, the Divine Mother revealed in the fullness of her being, a revelation which demands the highest powers of discrimination in order that the disciple discern which is the dark and which is the light, for both are contained in the one. Yet he must discern, for in this discernment lies his salvation. This is his initiation, the very first step on the path of integral being.

The solitary chamber is the place where he symbolically reaches the moment of 'suspension' between life and death, truth and falsehood, the birth of the soul and the death of the ego. The 9th sign is the chamber, between Capricorn and Scorpio, Life and Death, the Mother of Light and the Mother of Darkness. It is the chamber of truth where the moment of truth is lived, where the neophyte is either victorious and the soul is born, or he falls a helpless victim to the even greater delusions of his ego. It is precisely this experience of total abandonment and isola-tion, accompanied by the apparent paradox of dark and light oneness and the impos-sibility of discerning that which is real from that which is false—or the utter and stark stillness of that moment and the experience of seeing them as one—that is the most difficult for the pupil. The isolated, bare chamber, —this is its meaning.

The Great Pyramid and the Mutation of Matter

The creation of a zone wherein the acceleration and deceleration of energy could be brought about was also the purpose of the Great Pyramid. This monu-ment was devised so that cosmic energies could be used in a certain way in order to bring about a process of materialisation or de-materialisation, resulting from a particular crossing or intersecting of forces. The work would bring the subtle physical plane in evidence in an area which was congenial to this finer matter and wherein it could manifest or persist in a constant state of renewal. Such a process when known could give a leader of a gnostic society the possibility of physically remaining in the Earth's sphere to carry on his or her work, where not only psychic or subtle intervention would be possible but the power of *action in matter* would be retained. Such a task could only be successful when those who proposed to accomplish it worked in strict harmony with the cosmic laws of a higher nature, because the alteration of matter is not fully possible without the conjunct knowledge of Spirit (Transcendent) and Matter (Cosmic) brought to realisation in the Individual.

We can understand what took place in the Pyramid to a much greater extent if we study the facts in the light of the formation of a new body. There is a period when literally the old body can be laid to rest when its support is no longer needed, during which time the other body is being prepared to precipitate into the denser field. For a period of years it could be sealed off from the Earth atmosphere. If this process had been worked out then—that is, one of transformation of the body—it is equally understandable how when the knowledge was lost, the pyramids came to be thought of as tombs for the Pharaohs, and the preservation of these bodies was looked upon by subsequent civilisations as a mere superstitious or barbaric custom. It is possible that during the Age of Leo, 12,000 years ago, such a transformation or materialisation based upon a body yoga did occur, but hardly likely in more recent times. If we study the matter today on the basis of what has been found in the tombs it seems rather that during *historic* Egypt there was the knowledge of how to *preserve* a body, to leave it in such a condition that when a soul wanted to 're-possess' it, the body cells would come to life once again, awaken from their slumber as it were. This has been proven in recent times by the observation of the cells of some of the mummies that were found to be in a living condition, deep frozen we can say. Such a process however is quite different from what we have discussed because it is the preservation of a normal body, maintained in the same unenlightened condition; whereas the transformation is a work on the cells to evolve them to a higher manifestation, for the cells themselves to participate in the work, to become conscious to such a degree that they reveal their hidden light. Such a work implies a totally revolutionary aspect of matter. But the fact that in some rare cases the Egyptians wanted to preserve the body and then perhaps resuscitate it thousands of years later is interesting because it shows us that, whatever the case, they attached great importance to the body-consciousness and understood that if a truly conscious passage was to be effected, from one life to the next, the body itself would in some way have to take part. That is, fully conscious reincarnation would depend also on the retainment of the same body-consciousness. As conditions actually stand this is one of the major reasons for the loss in the link between one incarnation and the next, which imposes a long and tedious work in order to awaken the soul to its past achievements and take up the work from that point on. The body has its memory too, and the early Egyptians wanted that corporeal remembrance intact, so that there would not be the veiling interference of a newly-formed physical.

The tombs of the more recent Pharaohs that have been violated by modern investigators do indeed maintain an occult field around them which is able to produce a certain phenomenon, though perhaps one no longer capable of bringing about a body transformation or resuscitation. These tombs have undeniably the presence of occult forces, but possibly of a more degenerated form during our historic times, for Egypt too has passed into and through a dark age.

The Great Pyramid appears to have been not only the place where the gnostic being was laid to rest when the time of dissolution or transformation of his physical came about, but also the temple wherein he was initiated into the full knowledge and passed through the necessary experiences recorded in the zodiac and the solar system as previously explained; for which reason it was constructed in a manner which remarkably captures and reveals the harmonies of the cosmos and in particular the zodiac. The Sphinx resting before it would be the key to the time such a transformation could take place in harmony with the position of the Earth with respect to the heavenly bodies and orbits, and above all with respect to the great centre of our galaxy, which is why it was so necessary to determine accurately the precession of the equinoxes and incorporate this knowledge in the construction. It becomes evident from the Sphinx that work on the full transformation of matter is best achieved during passage either through the Age of Leo or the Age of Aquarius, the Lion and the Man of the zodiac. Between these two points there is the period of 'sleep', or the loss of knowledge, the 8th Manifestation of Scorpio—and therefore the ancients of Egypt, with this very precise knowledge, worked to erect the Great Pyramid and the Sphinx not only to make a place propitious for such an initiation and transformation but constructed in such a way as to preserve the knowledge throughout the millennia, which they knew would otherwise be lost and was to be essential for the progress of the civilisations of the Earth toward a more divine manifestation. Egyptian art and architecture reveal a race that lived in the consciousness of immortality, not only of the soul but of the body as well.

Historians and archaeologists maintain that these ancients were selfish and exploited the population for their own egoistic glory, compelling it to construct huge monuments which required extraordinary labour and skill merely to house their bodies so as to satisfy worldly desires and ambitions. In actual fact theirs was the act of self-giving for the benefit of future races, stemming from a profound wisdom and knowledge of the goal of creation. Their purpose in constructing such monuments was for the ultimate good of evolution and mankind, whose destiny they knew through the knowledge of the Cosmos and the zodiac.

Whether the Egyptians were successful in their work on the mutation of matter for the transformation or the formation of a new body in the sarcophagus of the Great Pyramid is unknown to us today; however, it is more than clear that the King's Chamber was not a tomb in the ordinary sense, as found in other pyramids of later date. The vestiges of a traditional burial site were never found, nor any traces of a decayed or preserved body. The enigma certainly has not been solved by scientists and never will be, at least not until such a transformation takes place in our times and will show scientists the process in a manner that their physical eyes can follow. It is quite probable that this site was used for incarnation by subtle means, overpassing the demands of gross physical methods, as well as for the de-materialisation of a body, its re-absorption into the subtle plane from where it had come.

Since the Age of Leo was the time of the *élite* and this present era is the universal transformation, the split between science and spirituality which is characteristic of our times would prove valid; such a radical move might indeed be the only possible means for the knowledge to reach the entire Earth, and this would be the only way that the whole of the earth-consciousness could be transformed, as well as the structure of the species' body.

The occult experiences which many have recently had in the Great Pyramid, and the smaller pyramids as well, can be easily explained by the fact that the mutation of matter as we have described rests primarily on the formation of subtle physical forms which do not decay with time as our more dense ones and can be preserved for long periods since they do not depend on Earth substance and food, which suffer decay more rapidly. They maintain themselves by the play and intake of cosmic energies directly, that are freer from the process of decomposition or degeneration and regeneration of the atoms and cells in the manner we experience. In fact, the cell is the major block in the work of transformation; the dense body must transform the element of Water, its principal constituent, and a more gaseous substance must be achieved, closer to the more refined energy of the atom, the more rarified particle. For this work the sign Cancer comes into prominence and the Ignorance must be transformed *together with the cell*; that is, the ego must die and the experience of the cell must pass from water as we know it to a more subtle water. Likewise the subtle physical atom must become denser. There must be the marriage of heaven and earth, the transformation of our entire atmosphere, its rarefication, the lift of the dense gravitational pull we are now subject to, —in a word, the 'atomisation' of our entire planet and all its inhabitants, the foundation of a new heaven as well as a new earth.

In this light one can better understand the scriptures of old, for it is not only the Earth that mutates: it is, '*a new heaven and a new earth*'.

Into the Dimension of Simultaneous Time

With the establishment of the foundations in Capricorn, the portals are opened to the last quarter where the realisation is brought down into Matter, on this Earth. A Cardinal, Earth sign, Capricorn is *Sat* of the trinity, Sat-Chit-Ananda. Within this sign there is the orbit of Uranus and thus the realisation of Capricorn opens the possibility of the contact established firmly with the descending power. This is achieved by penetration into the realm of simultaneous time that we have referred to so often in the text, the particular feature of Capricorn. That is, the process of Initiation culminates with the experience of simultaneous time. The individual is plunged into the sphere of oneness of time, the experience of which is rendered possible by the orbit of Uranus in the scale which facilitates the 'breaking of the barriers' that impede our perception of this unity of time. It can be said that from Sagittarius the experience of the simultaneity of time begins, and both Sagittarius and Capricorn are the journey into the region of initiation which brings this enlightenment, the fundamental piece for the acquisition of the consciousness of immortality. To understand some aspects of the unity of time it is necessary for the student to become acquainted with the relationship between certain measurements of time, their interrelationship and harmony, for the entire art of astrology is constructed upon the knowledge of these seemingly abstract equivalents.

To begin with, it is necessary to understand that *one day equals one year*. This is the first equation of importance to be grasped. Traditional astrology bases its art of prediction in large part on this principle, called, the method of Secondary Directions, and on this basis it has become possible to follow a person's life through its development after birth: the positions of the planets the day after birth give the details of the first year, the positions on the second day would be the second year, and so on. Those who have studied the matter can vouch for the accuracy of the method.

The fact is that 24 hours for the Earth is indeed equivalent to 1 year of the Sun or, let us say, the experience of revolution of the Earth is attuned to Sol in this way. The Sun is the measure of time for the System and each planet adjusts its rotation upon its axis according to its relationship with the Sun. The Sun is in fact the ticking mechanism. We understand this by studying its proportions in conjunction with the ticking of a clock. In the section on the Indian Yugas we spoke of the 'Measure of Unity' which is the radius of the Sun, or the measurement which unites the central point to the outer circle or sphere. This is 432,000 miles (the figure of kaliyuga). The same figure is the number of ticks that a precision clock gives in 24 hours; there are 5 ticks or beats per second, which amounts to 432,000 in the 24 hours. In the same relation the Sun is our pulse or our ticking mechanism, and the Earth adjusts its 'clock' or its workings to this Central Piece. Everything on our planet therefore is in harmony with this great Machine. As a matter of fact, we can say that the Sun is our heart-beat, and the perfection of organic life is found when it adjusts itself to this great Heart. Thus in astrology the Sun belongs to the sign Leo which is said to rule the heart in the human organism, hence the student can understand the connection between the heart, Leo, the Sun, the kaliyuga and the Age of Truth, as described in the section on the Yugas, —its beginning at 0° Leo. Truth is unveiled when the Earth has found its harmony with the Sun, physical and subtle, which occurs when in each individual the barriers of time are broken and the experience of simultaneous time is achieved.

The same measure of a watch and the Solar Heart-beat can be carried over to other aspects of life, namely to the mechanics of breath which are the means of keeping apace or in rhythm with the Sun. But before discussing this aspect it is necessary for the student to understand the different time measurements of the Sun. There is the day, the month, the year. The year of the Sun, according to a certain view, would be four signs in the precession of the equinoxes, or 8640 years for Earth. Consequently in the Map of the 12 Manifestations we find that the full 36 signs which comprise one Great Circle in terms of the Solar Heart-beat (which is its radius, 432,000 miles=4 signs=1 solar year) would be 9 solar years. In this way the student can understand the importance of the 9 year cycle, as recorded in the Gnostic Circle, and then the 36 year cycle. These periods of time are the human being's harmonisation with the Sun. Within that span he lives a full Sun year and also experiences all the dimensions of being of the Sun, 12 in all. In terms of consciousness he can, in fact, travel into these planes of 12 solar dimensions.

So, one Sun year is equivalent to four signs of the Precession, or 8640 Earth years, and one Great Circle is equivalent to 9 Sun years and within 9 Earth years the human being experiences the same dimensions of being as the Sun.

In terms of the regeneration of the human organism through the mechanics of breath, the same relation exists. The individual takes an average of 18 breaths per minute, or at a rate of $3^1/_3$ seconds per breath. Therefore in 24 hours he would have taken 25,920 breaths. In terms of respiration in 24 hours he would complete one round of the zodiac, or he would have experienced the 12 dimensions, or better said, the organism would experience the 12 solar dimensions. In terms of degrees the $3^1/_3$ become 3°20, the navamsa division of the zodiac. Three days then is the period of regeneration ($3 \times 25,920 = 77,760$, or 1 Great Circle) and it is said that three days after the crucifixion the Christ resurrected. In like manner in the Gnostic Circle, three years after the death of Scorpio the regenerated form emerges, the three years of unification of all the parts, the first of which brings the entry into the dimension of simultaneous time. The student is to remember that the basic equation is one day equals one year.

All these figures are based on the *sphere of perfection*, the circle of 360°, and this perfection, when translated into Earth time, becomes not 360 days but 365, the extra five being the imperfection of the Earth, so to speak. Actually it is this 5 that we call the number of Earthman, for which reason the geometric pentagram has been such an important design for seekers of the past; man is 5 days, or 120 hours, behind the experience of the Sun. The number that is to replace this one for the species is 9; the human evolution goes from step 1 to 5 (our actual level) to 9. In between are the various intermediate levels which disappear when the goal is reached.

Therefore, at the 5th orbit in the System there is the planet that strives to become a Sun for Earth beings, for the purposes of the Earth's evolution. Jupiter accelerates the experience for man (and it rules the 9th sign) because Jupiter is the planet representative of the Divine, it is the companion planet of the Sun, giving off more energy than it receives from the Fire King, for which reason it is also the planet representing a person's guru or spiritual perceptor.

These figures of imperfection accumulate over the years and the centuries and the millennia, which is why the aspect of destruction exists in the trinity of evolving being. *Destruction is the means whereby humanity and the planet are kept in rhythm with the Sun.* Every so often it is necessary to accelerate the pace and during a certain time span the Earth lives through an accumulated experience. In terms of the calendar as well there are a number of days eliminated or added every so often, for the same purpose. The same occurs in the life of an individual: the Initiation we have described has as its purpose the acceleration of growth and the placing of the being in harmony with the Time-Spirit.

To better illustrate, Capricorn is the *Cosmic Midday*, or when the Sun is directly overhead, casting no shadows, the illusory forms equivalent to the Ignorance. The Shadow of Time is the Falsehood and in Capricorn the Sun is experienced at its peak point, or the being is placed directly under its rays, —another way of expressing simultaneous time.[1] It is the point when the imperfection of 5 days is broken through. When man reaches the 5th orbit of Jupiter he is capacitated to begin his adventure into the realm of perfect time, the harmony of the Sun. This is inexorably connected with the Manifestation, with Earth life. The experience of Nirvana, for example, is located at the 4.5 Orbit, the 0° Libra; that is the first entry into a sphere of higher consciousness, but it is not the total manifestation. It is the beginning of the return Curve. Its goal is Scorpio, the 8th sign, for which reason perhaps the number 8 figures so strongly in Buddhist teachings, as well as

---

[1] See: *The Magical Carousel,* Chapter 10.

the number 5 which is Jupiter, the orb that most fully expresses the Buddha and Buddhism. Sri Aurobindo expresses the same fact:

'I don't think I have written, but I said once that souls which have passed into Nirvana may (not 'must') return to complete the large upward curve. I have written somewhere, I think, that for this yoga (it might also be added, in the natural complete order of the manifestation) the experience of Nirvana can only be a stage or passage to the complete realisation. I have said also that there may be many doors by which one can pass into the realisation of the Absolute (Parabrahman), and Nirvana is one of them, but by no means the only one. You may remember Ramakrishna saying that the Jivakoti can ascend the stairs, but not return, while the Ishwarakoti can ascend and descend at will. If that is so, the Jivakoti might be those who describe only the curve from Matter through Mind into the silent Brahman and the Ishwarakoti those who get to the integral Reality and can therefore combine the Ascent with the Descent and contain the 'two ends' of existence in their being.'[1]

Five days is the extra period that must be reconciled, but in the experience of gnostic being the harmony is of 360 and the body can as well be brought to this perfection. Hence all the figures we are using, and which come to us from remote gnostic societies, are based on the perfect sphere, translated into the perfect Earth year, conscious of the fact that in a thorough experience of yoga the disciple will inevitably find himself attuned to this harmony at a certain stage of his growth. The gnostic being is the product of this finer solar rhythm; in his very essence he *is* perfection, he *is* one with the Sun in all ways. By this the student can better appreciate the long-time practice of placing the five extra days out of the calendar. During that time the disciple brought himself into harmony with the Sun.

Considering one day equivalent to one year a human being would pass through one round of the zodiac, 25,920 days of the precessional rhythm, in 72 years. In the life of Sri Aurobindo we find that at 72 he had moved according to the Precession through one complete round. It would take 6 years to traverse 'one sign', equivalent to the 6 hours of the Sun through a sign; therefore by his 78th, which is when he left the body, he would have gone through 2160 days or 6 hours of the Sun according to the relation of one year for one day. This would have placed him at the end of his life span at the sign of Aquarius, the very sign of our times, and the very degree where the Precession now stands.

Each degree of the zodiac in the Precession is 72 years; for man it would be equivalent to a fraction of his day since the average pulsations in the human body are 72 per minute.

The movement of the Earth on its axis is the synthesis of the solar year. Those

[1] *Letters on Yoga*, page 59 CE.

24 hours are equivalent to 360 days with 5 to be absorbed during the progression by means of the process of yoga. Over a period of nine years, the first stage in the dimensional experience of solar being, 45 days are accumulated ($5 \times 9 = 45$). During the same period of nine years 2 more days are accumulated, the leap years every fourth year. This would take us 5 times around the 9 clock and then to the orbit of Venus. This would be the equivalent of eight years with their 47 days of accumulation. But more interesting for the human being is the remaining year of the cycle, the 9th, which accumulates $1/4$th of a day more, bringing the total accumulation to $47\,1/4$th days for a period of 9 years. In terms of the Gnostic Circle we see that from the orbit of Venus, this $1/4$th would signify a further progression of three more signs (three months) and we find that the 9 year cycle with the absorption of all the imperfections brings us exactly to the 0° Cancer point which is the Moon's reign, the term of gestation, the beginning of cellular life and the commencement of the psychic evolution on Earth. These $47^{1}/_{4}$th days bring us to a position in the Gnostic Circle which epitomises man's imperfection and the plunge of the soul into inconscience.

Therefore in terms of breath the human organism is attuned to the Sun by the count of the precession of the equinoxes: 24 hours in breath is one complete Round. But in terms of the psychological experience of man, 24 hours is equivalent to one year, and this is synthesised in the movement of the Earth upon its axis: this is the beat of the Sun reduced to human psychological experience. The revolution of the planet on its axis is precisely like the cog and wheels of the interior of a clock which spin around their own centre but are motivated by a major central pivot; though their outer wheels may have a faster motion it is nonetheless dependent upon the central one. As previously expressed, the System with its mechanics can be best understood when reviewed as a gigantic clock of which the Sun is the central and principal piece that sets the pace for all the cogs and wheels of the instrument. In terms of Earth time we find that the *year* is the Sun's point; the *month* and *day* belong to the Moon and Earth. Saturn takes the place of the Moon in this working; the synodic period of the Moon is 29 days and the same period of Saturn is 29 years. Therefore between the Moon and Saturn there is the same harmony of one day for one year, just as between the Earth and the Sun. Thus the Moon is to Saturn what Earth is to the Sun. Together all these form the Sacred Triangle, upon which the mechanics of Time rest.

(It is interesting to note that the first mechanical clock was made in 996 AD (6), a year that would fall at Saturn's orbit, the last time in the millennium in fact, during the decade of the great shift to the four digits where a further dimensional experience was added.)

Concerning beings whose incarnations are important for the entire Earth, whose destinies are more cosmic than individual and embrace the mysteries of the evolution in their being in some way, the *year* is the count which is primarily important. Also for events which mark turning-points in the evolution for the whole Earth. Not all beings therefore can be considered on the basis of the year count solely, nor all events. When an individual becomes one with the Cosmos, totally identified with the Cosmic Divine, he becomes a solar (year) man. Until then his incarnation partakes of the experience of the Sun *from below*, he moves along within the wheel of Time as a part of the Sun whose beat is translated into Earth time, which he joins by means of days, months and years. Whatever the case, these are the three terms, years, months, days, —all of which are made up of hours or minutes or seconds or ultimately of 5 beats per second which is the heart-beat of the Sun. If we want to reduce the experience of Time to a fraction perceivable in the most normal consciousness we must consider this to be the measure of 5 ticks to a second, the Measure of Unity, the 432,000 mile radius of the Sun. And this brings a surplus of 5 days to a year, $47^1/_4$ days per 9 years, 189 per 36 years, and so on, —all of which points out to us our distance from the One, our separation from the Centre and lack of identification in consciousness with the Heart, the barriers we must break through in order to achieve Unity.

This is the process of Capricorn and Uranus, the 7th Orbit, for it is the 7 notes of the scale that Uranus epitomises; thus the 'music of the spheres' belongs to the 7th Orbit, or the circle divided into 3 and into 4, superimposed in the following manner. The intervals are seen to coincide always with the 0 point, the 'Do', one between Mi and Fa and the other between Si and Do, and to occur always in the section embracing the quarter of Unity.

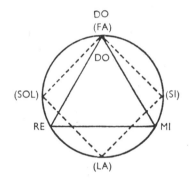

The true music of the spheres shall descend upon Earth once the gnostic being has shed his light on the matter, for the music we speak of is one which will incorporate the laws of cosmic harmonies into the composition. This work has been partly accomplished in historic times, but some amount of widening must also come about in this field due to the expansion of the System and our consciousness. Regarding cosmic harmonies, Indian music comes closest to the reality of incorporating such laws into music in a conscious manner, but Western music is yet very far from this realisation. The channels are opening however which is the phenomenon behind the explosion of music of a certain order in the West among the youth. Young people being more sensitive to these planes, they naturally absorbed the inspiration, but the impurity and unpreparedness of the vessels damaged the flow and brought forth a great amount of distortion. In the way of dance we have the same phenomenon. The shift from the age of Pisces, ruled by Neptune, to Aquarius, co-ruled by Uranus, was immediately noticeable in the dance expression of the populace. Neptune is grace and rhythm in the body, but Uranus seems to have thrust an 'electric shock' into human beings, as far as objective observation of recreational dancing shows.

The Indian *rāgas*, or the 72 scales, are constructed on the basis of the harmonies we have here detailed, and the compositions are also prepared for execution only at certain times of the day, each composition corresponding to or blending in influence with the influences and positions of the heavenly bodies. The composer not only takes into consideration the laws of higher harmonics but he sees these laws also as a part of the moment of execution and therefore carries the listener into a dimension which is usually closed to him. Music in India becomes a means for entering into direct rapport with the Cosmos, and through the Cosmos with the Transcendent.

The last truly productive period of music was when the Precession was passing through the last decanate of Pisces, but music then centred almost exclusively on the emotive centre or played upon the feeling aspect of man, only rarely reaching through to other centres or planes. There was not a work upon all the centres, nor did the music come into being that when heard would have an impact on the whole of the being simultaneously which is to be considered the task of the true music. According to the cosmic rhythms we are entering the period where something substantial can be accomplished in this field.

In the section on the new planets the centres they rule were explained. The student can incorporate that information into the study of himself and his passage through the final quarter of the zodiac, with which these planets have affinity. What occurs in this latter portion is in fact the bringing down into the vessel the force and light and bliss that these final bodies represent. It is a period which tends to consolidate the work and crystallise the higher forces in the physical vessel, much as the last three months of gestation are the solidifying period for the foetus. Aquarius is the image of this action, where the very vessels, the 'jars' or 'jugs', are prepared in such a way as to be able to withstand and embody the force, after which it is spread abroad and universalised. Capricorn is the inward preparation of the proper and sturdy physical: the Light conquers and overtakes each cell and tissue, and in Aquarius that Light can pour forth from the perfected 'jars' and become the transforming power upon Earth, for it is the individual himself who must become the agent on the planet for the action of the universal transformation. He must be the receptacle, the receiver attuned to the higher planes, and through his instrument the breath and the Word spread to redeem the Earth. Each one must become conscious of the Divine Mother within, must become one with her, identified in full with her consciousness, being and bliss, —and then we can truly begin to speak of a New Creation, the consummation toward which we move, epitomised by Pluto.

Before Pluto and the close of the Circle, there is the orbit of Neptune which gives to the universal and wide aspect the intimacy of oneness with the Mother. The consciousness is cosmicised, spreads wide and becomes truly all-embracing, but at the same time Neptune gives to it the sweetness, tenderness and bliss of the Mother in her most intimate and personal way. The individual must bring this unity and oneness with the Mother into his universalised movement. He must not lose touch with the reality of this inner oneness and of the unique and totally personal relationship he holds with her. His realisation must bring him into the integral sphere where the Mother becomes the entire creation for the seeker, while at the same time she is intimately and wholly himself. He must reconcile the two relationships, losing himself in neither one nor the other, and finally he must bring the Mother in her Transcendent aspect into his life: she must be himself, the cosmos and that which upholds the entire play, the very support of creation, for she is all three. It is the trinity that he must forge in gold within his being, by knowing the full divine in all the manifested aspects. He must see her as the support as well, for this support is also 'manifest'. To know what is beyond the manifestation the individual must experience it here, bring it here, and he can experience it in his body because the Transcendent does make himself known to man through the Divine Mother, the Supreme Shakti who becomes all aspects of Himself and of whom all creation is a part.

According to the harmonious superstructure of the planets upon the zodiac we see that there is truly a mutual collaboration between the two for the benefit of the growth of man. We have stated that Jupiter is the replacement of the Sun for man, but to be really accurate we must say that all the planets replace the Sun, for all of them exist so as to carry the 'message' of the Sun throughout the System; they are apparatuses of diffusion of the solar creative impulse, and each one translates this received message in a different way, unique in comparison with the rest of its companions. The zodiac is the way in which this captured solar energy and consciousness reaches the Earth, or works on the consciousness of man. Depending upon where the planet falls in the harmonic structure, that is, within which sign of the Gnostic Circle it reposes, we can know the function of that particular planet for the growth of man and the civilisation. Just as we have spoken of Neptune as giving a deeper intimacy to Aquarius, because Neptune falls in this sign, we can speak of the other planets.

Mercury's orbit falls in the sign of Taurus, which becomes simply *mind in matter*, and it is the quality that 'softens' matter. Venus is the planet of harmonious form in evolving matter and is responsible for the actual forms and patterns of molecules and cells, and in the Circle it combines with Gemini, an Air sign of Mind, to complete the work of establishment of Mind in Matter, as well as the ranges beyond mind with which Venus has affinity, the planes of unity and harmony and love. The two are in a sense companions in the work, and they are called the *interior* planets. In the new translation of cosmic powers due to the further triad, it is found that Venus is no longer the sole planet of Art, but Mercury too has great affinity with this aspect of human expression. In fact in the arrangement of the Gnostic Circle, Mercury falls in Taurus, the sign of Art (along with Libra). In the same manner, Venus is seen to be a sensitive point in the field of Science and the year which she rules in a person's life may bring one to such studies. In effect, Science is becoming an Art and Art a Science; in this way the real expression of both will soon come forth.

Then there is Earth-Moon in Leo (cusp with Cancer), which brings the solar transcendence down onto this planet, and the unfoldment of the soul-spirit becomes a part of Earth life.

Next is Mars in Virgo, precisely the sign that could experience a lack of the vital force and its rejection, because of the sign's character; but the harmonisation is accomplished by the positioning of Mars precisely within its 'house'. Thus Mars gives to Virgo what it would normally lack, for the evolution of the species; it awakens the life-force in the physical, which Virgo represents.

Jupiter is found in Libra, at the point where consciousness must awaken and must begin to recall the Origin, the Sun, and strive to curve back to the Centre,—for which reason the most direct representative of the Sun is found in the sign. Next Saturn appears in Sagittarius (cusp of Scorpio) to crystallise the movement, which Sagittarius would gladly disperse and spread wide, so far abroad that it would ultimately dissipate itself in the far reaches of the dimensions of consciousness. Saturn contracts the expansion of Sagittarius. But in Capricorn, Saturn's home sign, Uranus is found which tends to widen and universalise and break up any undue or excessively contracting rigidity that Saturn might be responsible for. It makes the being aware not only of Self, but of Self in All. After which Neptune must intervene to grant the intimacy with the Divine Mother, but on the basis of a thoroughly cosmicised consciousness.

The Water signs have no planets in them because they essentially represent the quality which is the essence of Creation, Love, the ocean in which all this has its play. The planets transmit the solar fire where they are needed. Love can multiply itself unceasingly on its own breath which it offers to the Sun, Water to Fire, the cusps of the Sacred Triangle. The last trinity of planets brings one to the culmination of this marriage in Pisces, the ocean of Divine Love, that Pluto will grasp for his design and purpose.

This is the final trinity and the final quarter of the zodiac. With this firm foundation the sadhak can begin his real participation in the new creation. Pluto is the creation, but Pluto is the ruler over the kingdom of Matter, and it is finally there that his work must be centred, or, shall we say, find its fulfilment. The vessel of ignorance must become the chalice of bliss, of consciousness, of being, the immortality of the Supreme upon Earth.

This is the destiny of man, not one alone, not a few, but the destiny of each individual. All destiny is one. There is no real separation between one man and another. All have in fact only one goal, and this goal is what the Gnostic Circle reveals. Everyone can find the point wherein he or she enters the wheel and begins the journey to the final full realisation; but the journey is the very same for all beings, there is no one with a different destiny. *The destiny is One for man is One.*

In this light it can be understood how preoccupation with the small details of life—those illusory happenings that make us believe we are on a different road than our fellowman—belongs to a lower realm. The study of astrology in that light is the study of the Ignorance, or at best the half-truth. Cosmic harmonies must as well reveal the lower consciousness because they speak always of the totality for any given moment in Time. Therefore within their body there must be a place as well for the lesser knowledge. But it must show this lesser knowledge for what it is, and this is accomplished by the individual horoscope whereby man isolates himself from the totality and views himself, his life, his destiny as unique, separate though mirrored for him in the vast cosmos. This separative consciousness is the greatest obstacle to the study of the Cosmic Truth as reflected in the Gnostic Circle. Those in the lower hemisphere of knowledge refuse to see that man is one and the destiny is one. This is the greatest offense to the ego, for the ego clings to its 'uniqueness' which is only the loss of identity with the One. The individual who concentrates on these studies with an eye for the personal and an interest in the small details of life loses the opportunity—one of the most sublime given to mankind—to see himself as a part of the superb oneness: and to see that his destiny is the destiny of the evolution of his species and that evolution's destiny is the essence of Creation, of the entire Manifestation, of the universe, of the Divine.

Each human being is a particle, a child of the one Divine Mother, and the Gnostic Circle is the revelation of her being. Within it one cannot see the petty details of life, which are the fluctuations and ever-changing ripples on the sea. To identify ourselves with them, to see ourselves and to seek to find our inner truth through these events, to project ourselves into them and expect to discover the Way through the personal destiny, is an illusion. The personal view belongs in fact to the sign Cancer, the Cosmic Ignorance for the present, because this Ignorance too shall one day be transformed. Its nature is change and through its very nature it will become the higher part of itself, or it will find its complement in its opposite pole.

The zodiac rests upon four Cardinal points which are the pillars of the destiny of creation; in the Gnostic Circle the student can observe that these are the only points which have only one influence. Two are out-going masculine signs, the movement of exhalation, and two are in-drawn, feminine signs, the movement of inhalation. The masculine is the manifestation of Space, the expanding dimension which with regard to the Circle becomes the division into 12, the fragments of 30° or three, the uneven number. The feminine element is the manifestation of Time, the contracting dimension which within the Circle becomes the division of 9, or fragments of 40°, four, the even number. Two signs, Aries and Libra, being masculine belong to 'heaven', and the other two pillars, Cancer and Capricorn, being feminine belong to 'earth'. The four together make the whole: Aries, Fire, is the ejection, the *explosion* or thrust of the particle, the planet, the sperm or any body, and its opposite Libra, Air, is the *equilibrium* of forces that compel a particle to remain in orbit around a magnetic centre, a Sun. Aries is the exaltation of the Sun, the principle of *expansion*, Libra is the exaltation of Saturn, the principle of *contraction*.

Cancer, Water, is the *living* particle, the fluidic, ever-changing state which finds its 'sun' in Jupiter, the principle of consciousness exalted in Cancer; and Capricorn, Earth, its opposite, is the *crystallisation* of this changeful fluidity into the substantial tower of form, the veritable Temple of Life—thus the planet of the life-force, Mars, is in exaltation in Capricorn.

The four pillars are the pillars of every living man. He is ejected in Aries, he grows in Cancer, he becomes conscious of his 'orbit' in Libra and his relation to the central spirit which is the pivot of his being, and then he realises the full worth of being and becomes the solid creation of light, an immortal temple of the spirit, in Capricorn.

To identify oneself with the personal, with that which is ever-changing and pivoting around the principle of Ignorance, is to suffer endlessly. To identify oneself with the ever-stable, the one Reality, unchanging within the change, the support of all that occurs in the outer orbits of life, is to know the way of Truth, is to begin the great transformation. The Gnostic Circle shows us just this: It shows us *the change that is constant*; it shows us the deep and hidden part of the Manifestation which is the Secret Constant. It shows us what is, and yet it shows us the road of becoming. It shows us the being and becoming of all manifested things, for it shows us the truth in both, the truth in change, the truth in stability, it shows us the face of Brahman reflected in the being of Shakti. It shows us the one Divine Mother who is all these things.

18

The Earth

THE EARTH IS in a depressed condition at present. It abides in the Ignorance, therefore it looks above and beyond through the eyes of a sickly being. The vision from the planet is one similar to that of a vitally infirm human being. In the System, if we are capable of regarding it as a being, we see that the Earth is like an infected organ: a part of this being is ill, and this is our planet. We are a tumour in our solar system. The illness cancer is an accurate way of understanding the condition of our planet within the System, and for this reason the illness was named after the sign Cancer which rules the cells and for this cycle is an indication of the Ignorance under which all organic, living matter abides—the subjugation of the cells to the illusion, to decay, to death. In the illness cancer a group of cells breaks away from the central rule to set up its own autonomous one. They carry the body toward disintegration and death because they have lost all contact with the centering light. The Earth is in a similar state. It is separated from the rest of the solar system by the veils of the Ignorance, its *cancer*, and the planet is in the hands of Death, the living particle has lost the consciousness of its immortality or the means whereby it can renew itself on the basis of Life, conscious and uninterrupted. Death has become the sovereign Lord. We believe Death cannot be conquered; we believe cancer cannot be cured, in the same way that we say the Ignorance cannot be redeemed: Creation is a part of the Ignorance and is therefore an illusion, an unredeemable, doomed chaos.

While subjected to such an illness the patient can rarely see the light and retain faith in the all-powerful capacity of the Divine Mother to heal her 'wound.' Earth beings have simply adjusted themselves to this state of affairs, religions have explained the creation on the basis of visions through the Falsehood and through the veils of illusion. Humanity has moulded its vision of the Divine and the universe according to the state of its sickly being. Illness became *the reality*, and in order to reconcile the ill state of affairs, the savants, sages and illuminati constructed the theories of the impossibility of the redemption of the flesh and the salvation of the Earth from its cancer, for which it was necessary to spiritually abandon the patient to the slow and sure process of disintegration, decay and finally death. In order to keep man's faith in the Divine it seemed necessary to convince him of his unredeemable condition and the inevitable need of escaping the planet and finding his Lord and Redeemer in the Beyond, because his Lord could not possibly be within the folds of sickness and decay, the hell of material creation. Death then became the reality of life, the only certainty in this uncertain existence, the Dark King reigned and the Earth became his Underworld, whereupon he imprisoned the Soul-Spark Daughter of the Divine Mother. The Earth was the cancerous tumour, entirely disconnected from the harmony of the solar system, unable any longer to perceive the oneness of itself with the Perfection. It passed into a torpid, chilling sleep, the unconscious slumber and the loss of the light and knowledge of the truth of things. And so, it glorified Death and erected numerous schools of thought around a mere Phantom.

Death, suffering, illness, pain and strife do not *exist*. They have no reality for they are there only so long as the Earth's cancer is there. When the tumour is healed these things to which we have pledged the whole evolution of our planet and for which we have placed its destiny under the rule of the Dark God will fade away as early mists before the piercing rays of a morning sun.

The Earth follows a cycle of six years in its progression; each cycle signifies a portion of the being which is to be cared for, and each portion makes up the whole and can therefore affect the entire functioning. We are now in the portion of the being that is concerned with the *economy of energy*, simply because we are approaching the time of the actual birth and all energies are needed for this great Becoming. The energies must be channeled into their proper quarters because until now we have been wasting the power. The Divine Mother draws her energies together during these six years, accumulates her force so that after 1980 she can give birth to the Child, the new race, the new society, the new world. Each day that passes brings the process clearer to our vision: each day inflation mounts, costs increase, production lessens or sometimes wildly expands—and each man, as each nation, closes himself within his shell. He fears the movement and so he seeks to preserve what he has. He sees it is a time of economy but he cannot realise it is merely a re-organisation of energy which he has until now wasted by misuse; some parts have been overflooded, others depleted and drained. He does not realise that in fact he need not fear because the Divine Mother is more than generous regarding the needs of her being, humanity; but mankind suffers from the sin of waste and extravagance. We say: the Earth cannot support the weight of over-population. What we mean is, the Divine Mother is bulging with a great Child within her womb, larger than the Earth has memory of, but the Child must simply co-operate and know *the balance of in-coming and out-going energy*. It must know when to give and when to take. And in moments of economy it must not become closed within itself but must merely learn the right use of energy and where to turn for power. It must find the answer in harmony, a harmonisation which is all-embracing, not separative, isolating and petty.

One of her tools to bring humanity to this has been an image of the very Dark God himself, black gold, the fossilised power of the Sun that the Earth clasps within her breasts, because this Dark God is finally her servant as well. Through him she can bring the Earth to turn her eyes to the Sun. The dark power can lead man to the light of the Sun. All life is her tool, even the Ignorance is herself, even the darkest means can be the ways to her light, even the ego is ultimately at her command.

The Dark God is the tool as death has been the tool, and like death he can be the power of destruction and disintegration. He can devour the Child as it is being born. The Dark God is also nuclear power, the hidden force and energy of limitless possibilities. From 1980 to 1986, particularly heightened during June of 1985, the Earth will pass through the birth and we shall know either the god of destruction or the power of creation and regeneration. This period that lies in front of us is the time of accumulation: the coming thrust depends upon the quality of the work accomplished in this six year period.

Man identifies with the decaying sack that envelops the Earth which the Mother will cast aside and away from her once the birth has taken place. The Earth lives within this sack that will become poisoned the moment it is no longer needed. Based on the vision from within these veils an entirely false image of the Earth's destiny has been created, as well as the destiny of each of its cells, the human beings who contribute to make up the organic matter of the planet. The remedy is that each cell, each human being on the planet, awaken to the reality and return to the rule of the Central Being. This each one can do by realising his soul: it is this process that can cure the organ, Earth, and dissolve the tumour that afflicts it. Each inhabitant of the planet is a conscious cell. Man is the only species that has the power to heal the wound. The rest of organic life is incapable because it is not self-aware. Only man can cure his planet, only man can redeem the organ and cast aside the veils of illusion, only man can take away the mask of Death, can know that death and illness are illusions and are valid only until the 9th period of birth. And then the sack must be shed. The cells themselves have become identified with the outer strata of darkness. Their inner light sleeps as it were, and for this reason they know illness. They themselves have become convinced of the ignorance and loss of the light of truth. Illness will vanish from the experience of Earth existence the moment the cells no longer identify themselves with darkness, when the inner light becomes once more the guide and pivot of their existence, their sun of life. As consciousness awakens, as man's soul comes forward, the very cells of his body will also awaken. The condition of our bodies is a pitiable affair, but we believe them to be marvellous machines simply because we have become accustomed to accepting the state of

17

illness and decay. Man cannot as yet imagine that there can be a body which though retaining its capacity of perpetual renewal, knows no illness, no decay, to which these conditions are as foreign as the neighbouring galaxies, thousands and millions of light years away. He devises endless amounts of cures, diets, medicines—natural and allopathic—and each of these methods only brings him into a greater conflict. None of them solves the real problem because each such attempt merely deals with the outer strata, however profound it may seem. Such research can often be a greater deviation because it signifies in consciousness a greater identification with that which is an illusion. The way to transform illness is by the dawn of a new consciousness that knows no illness, that is immortal, that has conquered death.

Our times are magnificent. Man is awakening from his 'sleep' and he can begin to see. From this planet he has extended his eye into the Universe. When Galileo constructed the first telescope in 1609, a year belonging to the rule of Uranus, it became clear that man was ready for the great transformation, the universalising of his consciousness, the expansion not only inward but outward as well. This truly was Vishnu arousing from his sleep, opening his eyes so that the creation could begin. He became actually physically capable of seeing the creation and growth and destruction of other worlds, he became capable of looking into time through space, he could take this telescope and scrutinise the body of the Divine Mother. But all of this will have ultimately only the effect of overwhelming him unless he learns that to see he must realise his soul, he must cast his vision outward from the realised Centre of Light, wherein he can know that the immensity that surrounds him and appears to consume him is his very self; the consciousness that is the stuff of the universe, this colossal Divine Being, is his very being. He is not only one with That, but *he is That*, infinite and eternal.

Pondicherry,
January/September, 1974

the Womb
the cradle
the upholder

0

The Centre

"*...This unity embracing all mind, life and matter in the light of a supramental Truth and the pulse of a spiritual Bliss will be to us our internal fulfilment of the Divine in a complete cosmic consciousness.*

But since we must embrace all this in the double term of the Being and the Becoming, the knowledge that we shall possess must be complete and integral. It must not stop with the realisation of the pure Self and Spirit, but include also all those modes of the Spirit by which it supports, develops and throws itself out into its cosmic manifestation. Self-knowledge and world-knowledge must be made one in the all-ensphering knowledge of the Brahman."

Sri Aurobindo
The Synthesis of Yoga

Matrimandir and the Cosmic Truth

To BRING THIS study a degree further into the reality of our lives, on this planet, at this time, it is well to conclude with some discussion of the *Matrimandir*, the 'Temple of the Mother' that is being built in Auroville. South India; because this temple, according to certain dimensions and instructions given by the Mother of the Sri Aurobindo Ashram for its construction, is a synthesis of all that is herein contained.

It is showing the reality of the Centre, the Zero, and how it is taking shape today, that can best reveal to the student the extraordinary meaning of our times, and the new and totally unique way the force is now manifesting. The Matrimandir is being created in a way which differs from other centres of the past—a way more subtle, more intricate, deeper in meaning and more revealing of the cosmic truth and the forces upholding the Earth's evolution than any other Age has experienced. Every Age has a Centre—its 0—an area on the globe which must serve as the generator, the receiver of forces and the expeller of new transmuted energies. Such a centre therefore must reflect in the most precise way the truth of the Age to which it owes its being. Thus the Centre in discussion is a product of the fusion of cosmic forces of a particular order, which we are now in a position to understand better, after having lengthily dealt with the subject of the characteristics of the present era throughout this text. It is known that we are in the Aquarian Age, moreover that we are in the 9th Manifestation. The *guna* of this particular Age is Preservation (Sattwa) of the three modes of the Manifest Divine. And being a part of the final quarter of the zodiac, it is the section that refers to the plane of Sat-Chit-Ananda, the sign Aquarius corresponding to Chit, or the aspect of Consciousness.

Consequently a Centre of today, in the fullest sense of the word, must embody *par excellence* this aspect in some way. It must be a point on the Earth that will be a cauldron of a sort, wherein the particular new aspect of Consciousness of this Manifestation must be 'brewed'. To complete the descent of a new consciousness in the Centre of the Age, it will as well be accompanied by a newly revealed knowledge, for Knowledge is the child of the second mode of the creative essence. Divine Knowledge is the fruit of a manifestation of a higher consciousness. A centre of the Aquarian Age must be therefore the seat of the widest, deepest, highest understanding of the Divine Creation that has yet to manifest on Earth. It must be the cradle of a new consciousness which reveals an entirely new body of Knowledge. This is the Age of *the victory of Knowledge*; such a centre must offer the Earth the way to this victory; its very being must reveal the reality of this victory; its very being is the indication that the time has come for the fulfillment on Earth of all that the planet has been promised in the way of its destiny.

The Centre is the 'Temple of the Mother', and the Mother is the 6 of the Sacred Triangle whose planet therefore is Saturn, the 6th orbit in the heavens; the very place wherein it is being constructed belongs to this same 6, Auroville, India. It is only appropriate therefore that Saturn should be the fundamental key to the Matrimandir's existence. And the manner in which this heavenly body is 'descending' upon Earth is the most awesome and inspiring fact of this Aquarian Age.

It is also to be noted that the temple's *soul and inner body* were conceived by the Mother just when the Sun was in Capricorn, during the first five days of January of 1970—when the Earth is closest to the Sun, —in Saturn's zodiacal month.

The planet that represents the *Cosmic Divine*, or the Mother in manifestation, is also the key to Time. Holding the key to Time it therefore encompasses the fullest mystery of *matter*. For this Age that is to reveal the divine consciousness in matter it is essential to understand this planet's hidden aspects and all their implications, since in itself it holds the secret to the structure of matter. Auroville's full birth number is 9 (28-2-1968) which the Mother, the City's foundress, has described as '*Creation in Matter*'. The creation is consciousness, Consciousness-Force, the Divine Shakti, or simply, the Mother, and it is Divine Consciousness that is to find its point on the globe where it can reveal the greater mysteries of itself.

For the Matrimandir 1974 is an all-important year; the first dynamic stirrings of its soul come forth in this year, and for this reason certain details about its past are now coming out, in order that it be able to take its place as the Centre in a more conscious way. It is necessary therefore that some things be revealed regarding the significance of the dimensions and instructions the Mother gave and what their relationship is to other centres of old, in order that they may be understood in their fullest meaning.

The 12th Latitude, and the Radius of the Earth

The first item that must be discussed is the latitude of the construction (and of Auroville itself). We cannot say that the situating of the Matrimandir was a human choice. Certain things had to be arranged very long ago in order to have the Temple so placed, principally because the 12th latitude has certain properties which make it notably different from the others. It is the latitude which most harmoniously coincides with certain solar positions in correspondence with our planet, which indicate the work of our Age and confirm the message of Sri Aurobindo. Moreover the 12th is intimately and beautifully related to the latitudes of other important areas on the globe which are, or were, *in essence* a part of this movement. These are Egypt, Greece and Rome, points that, in one way or another, were established for the greater spiritualisation of the Earth.

Egypt is the oldest of the three and its true gnostic history is so remote that it is now lost. We have only the Pyramid and the Sphinx to go by which however more than amply indicate to us what we need to know from there of the cosmic harmonies. In the Great Pyramid, as explained elsewhere in the text, we know that work was done to carry the disciple into certain states of consciousness unattainable outside its walls, because at that time the cosmic forces needed to produce those states for a being evolving within the manifestation on Earth, were not freely available to the planet. They had to be artificially produced. Also the inner chambers were areas wherein the structure of matter was altered. This has lately been proven because experiments with the pyramidal shape of the proportionately reduced dimensions of the Great Pyramid, have shown the capacity to alter the state of matter, to dessicate meat, sharpen razors, etc. However that may be, we know that such a work could only finally be accomplished by creating a zone perfectly established on the basis of cosmic laws and harmonies centred upon the Earth. The Cosmos was not excluded from the spiritual life of the individual; on the contrary, its essence of truth was incorporated into the experience, for it was known that no real transformation of the human species, whether physical or psychological, could come about in isolation from the cosmic body, from the All, though the spiritualist may believe himself to be separate from the Cosmos. The complete transformation of the human being into the god-man, as was the intention of those early initiates, was known to be a process which would necessitate the complete marriage of *heaven and earth*.

This refers to remote times, over 10,000 years ago, during the 7th Manifestation preceding the Great Flood, two Manifestations prior to our present one, times of which we have no record in matter except the monuments mentioned above. We have now only the degenerated truth captured in the Egypt of historic times, where the pyramids became burial tombs for the Pharaohs, and these were god-men only in name. However, these are distortions of the truth because the ancient leaders were in fact gnostic beings to a certain degree and the tombs were for the purpose of the de-materialisation or the breaking down of matter, or the crystallisation of energy of different speeds into the forms serviceable for Earth existence and its process of higher evolution.

As concerns latitude, the purpose of this analysis, the Great Pyramid was constructed on the 30° north.

We move northward 6°, and some 6° westward, and around 36° latitude north there is Crete,[1] the area where a cult is said to have had its beginning which was later to develop into the most powerful initiatory rite of our era. It was in this area that the Divine Mother began the preparations for her descent, the descent of the Trinity, by adding the pieces of the mosaic in the most human terms; and finally toward the end of the 8th Manifestation the cult formally established itself at Eleusis. The initiation that took place in the Divine Mother's name and that of her daughter Persephone (Kore) on this site, was the dramatisation of the history of our times. It was there that the masses and not just the high and priestly caste were offered the possibility of attaining the state of immortality, or at least its first secure glimpses. They were made *to see*, which was the object of the *epopteia*, when they saw the divine Daughter, the most secret part of the initiation which has never been revealed. To this day the vision of her has remained secret, but it signified the culmination of the Mystery, and this seeing was the assurance of the victory over death and the salvation of the human race.

The Mystery rites in Eleusis were of the 8th Manifestation and a portion of our 9th, and the difference with Egyptian times is precisely that of the universalisation of the phenomenon, which is the major characteristic of our times.

It was in Eleusis that the Divine Mother revealed herself and commanded that a temple be built on the site in her honour, which the inhabitants of the town promptly set out to do. They called the temple the *Meteroion*, which in Greek means *Temple of the Mother* (Matrimandir), after which she retired in mourning for her lost Kore and withdrew her grace from the Earth, symbolised in the grain, the lack of which brought famine to the Earth and threatened to bring civilisation to an end—much the same as the present condition of civilisation on the planet, when once again a *meteroion* is being built and the Mother has withdrawn from the Earth, so to speak, the grain is lacking, floods and droughts abound, and other forms of catastrophe threaten humankind's very existence.

At the Temple of the Mother in Eleusis initiations were held for over 1,500 years, until they were abolished as previously predicted by the Temple's own hierophants, in the year 396 A.D. the three most significant numbers for the Earth and for our times.

In *Symbols and the Question of Unity* much is said of Eleusis and the Demeter

---

[1] Eastward on the same 36th latitude there were the very advanced civilisations that were the cradles of initiatic schools of a very high order, those of the Tigris and Euphrates valley, on through to Persia, then Afghanistan and finally leading right into the 'tip' of India which begins at latitude 36°. Greece, and then Europe, intensely absorbed Knowledge from this area which served as a channel between the Far East and Europe, in particular during the last 1440 years of the Piscean Age. All of this 'contribution' of the 36th latitude has been concentrated in the study in Greece, because of the Mystery rites and the myth of Demeter and Kore which have particular connection with our times.

and Persephone (Kore) story, and how it corresponds to the Indian myth of Durga. In fact, *kore* means 'maiden', as does *kumārī*, the principal way Durga is addressed.

From 36° north we move again upward 6° and some 6° westward and there is Rome. This city has a very particular connection with Auroville which has been briefly described elsewhere in the text, but it is well to add here that at the time of its establishment Rome was to Greece what America is now to India—that is, matter to spirit. Rome was the power in matter, the ability to construct and render concretely established in the Earth the power of the Gods. It was a society primarily created upon the materialistic consciousness, which was the necessary step to bring the higher realisation radically into the Earth. Rome epitomised today's split between Science and Spirituality, which has been indispensable for the evolution toward the full spiritualisation of the Earth. This particular aspect of the work became more evident during the Renaissance, particularly centred upon the incarnation of Leonardo da Vinci, a figure that Sri Aurobindo has spoken and written of frequently. Another incarnation of deep interest to him was that of Augustus Caesar, also a native of Italy, and Sri Aurobindo has extensively explained to his disciples the importance of that manifestation, and expressed the wish to write the history of Rome based on his understanding of that incarnation.

Rome was born with the Sun in Taurus. Auroville is of the same sign by *ascendant*, and though this correspondence signifies in Rome's case the 'mature essence', for Auroville the same sign on the ascendant rather refers to the early years of the Township's life—and this signifies the ability to bring down into matter the forms of the subtle planes of Venus, the ruler of Taurus.[1] Venus, as Earth's twin, represents, as it were, the higher possibilities of Earth's manifestation, the greater harmony which our planet can achieve. In Rome there was a separation from the real work because of the Time-Spirit. The sacred aspect of the task was sacrificed for the glory of conquest. The power was too strong to bear in its purest form, yet much was done then and during the Renaissance—which had as its support Rome of the Vatican—to guide civilisation toward the road it now travels. It must be remembered that the emblem of the city was the Eagle—the higher symbol of Scorpio, the sign of its opposition—and this is also the emblem of the United States today; the American continent even bears an Italian name, from Amerigo Vespucci who extended the original discovery of the New World. The culmination of this process was the establishment of the Christian Church on the site, because Christ's symbol and the meaning of his crucifixion in the esoteric sense is precisely

---

[1] It may be pointed out that Aeneas, the founder of Rome, was said to have been born of Venus (Aphrodite).

the *divinisation of matter*. This is the meaning of the sacred drawing by Leonardo, the Man in the Square and Circle. Previously in the text it was pointed out how the Crucifixion and Sri Aurobindo's passing occurred exactly at 'the same point in time', as also Aurolouis' recent passing. This is the occult tie between Rome and Auroville, the divinisation of matter and the solid power of construction which could bring the supramental truth and power and light down into this Earth we inhabit. One can understand through this connection why it was an Italian—Columbus—who discovered America, thinking he had found a 'new route to India', and called the natives of that land 'Indians'. In effect he had found a route to India because in the occult sense India and America are one, being both extremities in spirit (energy manifestation) of the same axis-pole, as well as opposite poles of the globe itself. Being a centre of the Piscean era, Rome became the shelter of the Incarnation's followers of that Age, he who was the embodiment of Love, the aspect of Pisces in the trinity Sat-Chit-*Ananda*,—Capricorn, Aquarius and *Pisces*.

And finally the connection between Auroville and Rome lies in the fact that Rome was a mere *city* which materially ruled a major portion of the civilised world. From this tiny dot a vast area was conquered and ruled—an act unknown to any other ancient or modern civilisation. Even to this day the power that succeeded the Roman Empire, the Vatican, remains a 'city-state', apart and independent from the Italian nation.

The Mother's intention was that Auroville too should be a point of influence —with the Ashram as its guiding spirit—a city which is supposed to rule but not primarily in the material sense: it is supposed to be the combination of spirit and matter, the point where these two poles join. And it is a city like Rome, having the same essential influence of sign, planet and colour.

With these three points we have three latitudes:

1. 30° North   (numerologically 3)
2. 36° North   (numerologically 9)
3. 42° North   (numerologically 6)

The three numerological sums, 3-9-6 are the numbers in their proper sequence of when the Mysteries came to an end, as well as another more profound significance which we shall presently explain. Let us see how these numbers combine with Auroville's latitude:

1. Between Auroville (12° N) and 30° N there are 18° (9)
2. Between Auroville and 36° N there are 24° (6)
3. Between Auroville and 42° N there are 30° (3)

In this order, 9-6-3, the numbers form the lotus of Sri Aurobindo as here reproduced, which stands in the centre of his symbol, whose petals are 9, 6 and 3 in the descending order. The central part of Sri Aurobindo's symbol in fact is a precious design. It is the reproduction of the *enneagram*, using the form of lotus imagery, which in India is a symbol of the avatar. The flower rests on 7 waves, and itself is made up of 9, 6 and 3 petals. The 7 waves are the 'Scale of Creation', the numbers 0.142857, and the lotus is the Sacred Triangle of 9-6-3.[1] This is the deep, mysterious and profound beauty of Sri Aurobindo's symbol. The 'enneagram' is contained in its heart, within the Square that Sri Aurobindo has said is the symbol of Supermind; the Square's number is 4 and the segments of the enneagram, or 9 Circle, are based on the number 40, or 4.

We see through this study that certain points on the globe are sensitive in a special way, but more important to note is the connection between a determined number of points, and that only with a vision of the whole can this relationship be fully understood. We see that three points existed in the past which were all intimately related among themselves, but these find their culmination by the entry of *the fourth poise,* which is capable of explaining the true meaning of the former three; the fourth is needed to make the happening 'solid', to bring it into manifestation, as it were—because in order to make a solid body four sides in fact are indispensable. As far as numbers are concerned this is easily demonstrated once the fourth is known, because the silent fourth itself is the pivot and therefore must furnish the answer to its existence. Thus Egypt to it is 9, Greece to it is 6, Rome to it is 3—and the silent fourth is *the 0*.

These four numbers are the magic keys to the supramental manifestation, to the Earth's evolution, and to the appearance of the Incarnations who are the pulsating spirit manifest of the planet's own soul. The 'o' is the point on Earth where these Incarnations centre their work, the receptacle of higher forces. It is the 'cradle' or the Womb manifest of the Supreme Mother.

The civilisations spoken of can be shown in the adjacent diagram. During the time when the three angles of the Triangle were influencing the world, the o was truly the Void, the unknown factor. It existed in potential within the transcendent womb of the Divine Mother, who becomes incarnate upon Earth

[1] See page 123.

through the Trinity, the Triangle. It must be remembered that at that time the o was not current in mathematics. It was India's later contribution, a factor in numbers which is radically important for the understanding of the Cosmic Truth and its translation into the Earth's evolution.

And finally the factor that is the most exact confirmation of all that has here been stated, that is in effect the expression in its most perfect sense of the reality of these points, these Incarnations, and the Earth's destiny, is *the radius of the Earth*.

The importance of the Sun's radius has been explained, the 432,000 miles that we have called 'The Measure of Unity', being as it is the Heart-beat of the whole System, the determinator of the System's *time* and therefore the key piece in the structure of matter of different degrees.[1] The Sun, by its emission of energy particles, sustains the System and at the same time determines the time for its orbiting bodies, which determines the type of 'life' that will find its abode upon each of these planets; as each body revolves upon its axis and then around the Sun, so will its own nature be. But we must now speak of the Earth and its radius, for if the Sun gives us the indication of time and matter manifestation for its whole system of orbiting planets, the Earth must likewise do the same for itself and its satellite, the Moon. The Sun is equivalent to the *spirit*, and the Earth is equivalent to the *soul*; the Earth we can say is the synthesis of this work just as the Matrimandir is. Its radius, or the relation between its *core* and its *outer manifested body*, we call the 'Measure of the embodiment of the Earth's psychic being'.

Our planet's radius is *3960 miles*.

The student can now verify why these numbers have been the foundation of our entire study—how, by adding the o we now have the fullest appearance of the avatars, and moreover we can see where their work has been centred in the past, and where it is centred today. We can also see the years which were the points in time of the translation of these numbers into our pace of civilisation, by means of our method of recording time.

Thus we have the possibility of constructing several diagrams each of which takes us a further degree into the heart of the matter, revealing to a greater extent the manifest psychic being of the Earth and the very precise way in which it is embodied. These in fact also reveal to us that it is upon Earth, the third planet in the solar system, that such a work is carried out—this being the only planet that has actually the possibility of expression of the 'soul', which in the full sense means that it is only here that the *essence* of the Sun, spirit, can manifest, the companion of the soul. This process is reflected in the zodiac in the signs Leo and Cancer, the Wheel's Purusha and Prakriti, ruled by the Sun and Moon respectively. The relation between Sun, Moon and Earth is captured in the 18 year cycle of the Lunar Nodes,

---

[1] It has been pointed out that $432^2 = 186,624$, or approximately the speed of light.

the linking point in space of these three bodies. These are degrees we can say in the process of the 'squaring of the circle'—the reality of this process in manifestation, not a geometric puzzle or formula which is devoid of pulsating reality. For the human being in his evolution the process would be considered the 'circling of the square', since the human being moves upward, *ascends*, or works from denser manifestation or matter—the Square—to finer, more spiritual substance, the Circle. The Incarnations work reversely; it is rather a 'squaring of the circle', the rendering of matter a finer expression of the divine light and truth. The process is here expressed in its realistic sense by this series of diagrams. The 0 is the fourth, or the element which makes the 'squaring' possible, and it is the Upholder. The Incarnations appear under the numbers 9, 6, 3—or starting from the Earth and continuing to move in the manner of the 'descent', the numbers flow as 3-9-6, and with the 0 we have the radius of the Earth, 3960 miles.

All together these numbers equal 18 (3+9+6+0=18), which is the Saros Cycle of the Lunar Nodes mentioned previously, the celestial phenomenon that reveals the Earth's incarnate psychic being, numbers which are contained in the Moon's own radius, 1080 miles. It was in fact 18 years after the third entry in 1938, a 3 year and therefore touching the Earth-Moon angle, that the supramental power became a concrete reality upon the Earth. And this offers us another way of bringing to the student the understanding of the 0 and its aspect of silent, secret fourth and its relation to Supermind whose symbol is the Square and whose number is 4. The Supramental Manifestation, as it is called by the Mother, occurred on February 29, 1956, the leap year day of that 3 year, which in terms of the calendar is *the zero that shows itself only every fourth year.* 1974 is now a further 18 year cycle completed.

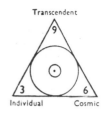

This is the first stage in the study to show the importance of the 12th latitude by its relation to past areas of concentrated cosmic forces for the purpose of assisting the spiritual evolution of the Earth, or, we can say, for the purpose of assisting the Earth to fulfil its own destiny. Above all we must understand that the secret of these places has been—or is presently—this work and not what historians and archaeologists relate about their meaning and purpose of existence in the scheme of evolving civilisation. By studying them in relation to the Cosmos we can know their truth, and it is to this truth that the serious student must adhere.

Let us now observe how the 12th latitude is joined to the Cosmos from the Earth in a special way at this time—through the annual movements of the Sun, or better said, through the movement of the Earth in its orbit around the Sun and the time and manner in which certain points on the globe receive the solar rays. Since the principal feature of the Matrimandir is the penetration of the solar ray directly into a central crystal globe this part of the study becomes fundamental.

Being within the Tropic of Cancer, the 12th latitude north receives the Sun's rays directly overhead two times during the year; one on April 22-23 (there is a slight variation each year because of the unequal speed of rotation and the excess of 5 days over the 360), and the second time is August 22nd (21 to 23). The first thing that strikes our attention concerning these dates is that the first time in the year when the Sun is overhead and piercing the heart of the Matrimandir is the birthday of Rome, April 21[1] and the second time, August 22nd, is especially important for the following reasons:

> The Mother's birthday is February 21st,
> Auroville's birthday is February 28,
> > —between these two there are *seven* days.

> Sri Aurobindo's birthday is August 15,
> Matrimandir's 'Solar Day' is August 22,
> > —between these two there are *seven* days.

From this alone we can see that there must be something particularly important about the last date. But what is its relation to the celestial sphere of 360°, the 12 signs of 30° each?

The Sun on each day of the year touches or reaches us through one of these 360° as is known in astrology, and by studying them on the basis of the zodiac of which they are a part, it is possible to know the meaning of any one of the degrees; the

---

[1] Ancient and new. During the Fascist reign this date was reinstated as the foundation day of new Italy, because it was the ancient birthday of Rome.

Sun can then speak to us, for without the revelation of the zodiac the Cosmos would have no real relation to man, other than a totally abstract or at least a blandly material one, such as in the study of astronomy. Man could in no way understand the detailed psychological way of the Divine Mother, for the zodiac is the map of evolution and the veritable language of the Cosmos. It speaks to us of the trajectory of the Earth and its evolving races, of becoming within being. It is the revelation of the *consciousness* behind the workings of the Cosmos with relation to Earth evolution, a factor which is wholly ignored by modern day astronomy. Many things are taken for granted by the seeker in the work on the expansion of consciousness, but it should be understood that much of what it is possible to incorporate in our sadhana and utilise for our development today depends entirely on what the sages of the past discovered or had revealed to them about the Cosmos in this way.

It is necessary to give this brief explanation because without this understanding the numbers we shall discuss which the Mother has given for the dimensions of the Matrimandir's inner chamber will remain abstract terms, and therefore the meaning of the Matrimandir as a possible concretion on the Earth of the cosmic truth will not be clear.

The birthday of Rome is one time when the Sun shines directly into the *mandir*, casting its rays onto the central and all-important translucent sphere. That is, the Sun reaches exactly 12° N. on or about that day. It corresponds to between 1°30 to 2°30 of the sign Taurus, or the 32° of the celestial sphere of 360°.

On August 22nd again the Sun pierces the temple, being at 12° N. once more, and this corresponds to 29° Leo, or the 149° of the celestial sphere. This is the important point in the Sun's trajectory with respect to the Matrimandir, because 29° Leo (and its opposite 29° Aquarius) is the very position of *the axis of the Age*. This is perhaps the most beautiful 'harmony' of the Matrimandir.

To discuss the Matrimandir in an orderly fashion, it is necessary to recapitulate certain points which are of importance for the comprehension of the central shaft of the temple. The Earth has several motions, each producing a particular count of time. There is the revolution on its axis which constitutes our *day* of 24 hours; there is the revolution with the Moon around a common centre of gravity which gives rise to the *month*; and then there is the Earth's revolution around the Sun which constitutes our *year*. These three movements are our principal or obvious measurements of time.

Besides these three there are the others we know: the motion of the Earth in the form of a cone as it orbits around the Sun, tracing a circle of $23^1/_2$ degrees radius which produces the receding or backward motion of the equinoctial axis that makes a complete shift in 25,920 years, the *precession of the equinoxes* that has been extensively discussed in the text. It is necessary to speak in detail of this once

again because this is the measurement of importance for the Matrimandir regarding August 22nd.
On this day in fact the Sun will penetrate the
Matrimandir on precisely the actual Precession
Axis which now falls at 29° Aquarius and 29° Leo,
while journeying backward through the zodiac,
so to speak. The equinoctial shift, shall we call it,
is a diagonal line through any particular degree
of the zodiac to its opposite: it would be the
Earth's present Ascendant and Descendant. 29°
Aquarius is the Ascendant, for which reason we
say that we are in the Aquarian Age, and 29°

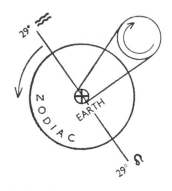

Leo is the Descendant, being the opposite degree to this Aquarian rising point.
Since it takes 25,920 years for the full movement to be completed, passage through
each degree of the 360 takes 72 years. It is this movement that determines, as
stated, what Age the Earth is in, and the Precession has moved into Aquarius
during this century and will remain in the 29° of the sign for 72 years from the beginning of the Age.

There are other time measurements; for example, the shifting of the poles
themselves which is connected with the movement of our entire solar system around
the galactic centre, and takes about 225,000,000 years to be completed, a full spiral-
ling circle. The Centre of our galaxy is situated in the constellation of Hercules
with respect to Earth-Sun alignment, at the 277° of the celestial sphere, or in the
zodiacal sign of Capricorn, the sign of India. Our solar system, the Sun with all its
orbiting bodies, is slowly being drawn into this Centre—or is moving ever closer or
into the sign of Capricorn, we could say. And there is finally the fact that according
to the theory of geologists the age of the Earth—from the time it formed a hard crust
—would be equivalent to approximately nine revolutions around the galactic centre.

For the present, however, the measure that interests us most in this detailed
study of the Matrimandir is the precession of the equinoxes, because it tells us the
most about our evolution and its goal. Thus on August 22nd the Sun is at the zenith
on the 12th latitude north, therefore directly overhead, which corresponds to, or
occurs on, the 29° of Leo. A simplified diagram as follows can make this clear.
It can be seen in this design that the ray pierces the Matrimandir and forms a veritable axis between the Sun and the Centre that determines the movement of Precession. The Aquarian Age zodiacal point is on the exact opposite end of the Axis. It
is as if the Sun's rays were drawn down into the Matrimandir, through the belly
and nucleus of the Earth, and then joined to the magical magnet of the Age. It
becomes then a physical penetration of the Sun of Truth in and through the body of

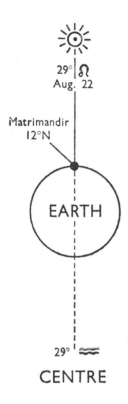

29° ♌
Aug. 22

Matrimandir
12°N

EARTH

29° ♒

CENTRE

the entire planet, a rooting of its power and force in the Earth itself, precisely because it falls on this powerful magnetic axis. We have here a marriage of the two dimensions, —time and space.

On April 22 the same movement takes place, yet this corresponds not to the Axis of the Age—which it does not touch at that time—but coincides in a rather interesting manner with the birthday of Rome.

There is another date when it touches the Axis of the Age and the same thing occurs as in the diagram, but in the reverse form. Such a position occurs on February 18, yet the rays of the Sun do not pierce the Matrimandir directly because it is a time when the Sun is in 12° latitude *south*. The interesting point is that it falls nonetheless on the Axis of the Age, when the Earth's 12th latitude is aligned with this point, but this occurs at a moment in time which coincides with Ramakrishna's birthday. When Sri Aurobindo had done some experiments in automatic writing in the early days, he had contacted Ramakrishna's spirit that communicated to him merely these words: 'Build a temple.' Sri Aurobindo explained that he later understood this to mean 'build a temple within'. But it is a fact that a temple *is* being built and certainly one which Ramakrishna would approve of since the only temple that would have interested him was one to the Divine Mother, a *matrimandir*.

Thus on 17-18 February, Ramakrishna's birthday, the Sun's rays touch the Axis of the Age once more, but on the 12th latitude south—and it appears that Ramakrishna's wish has been fulfilled. Certainly it is well to honour this great sage who paved the way for the descent of Durga and who is intimately connected with the work of this centre, for as was mentioned earlier in the text, it was Vivekananda who revealed certain fundamentals of the work to Sri Aurobindo in

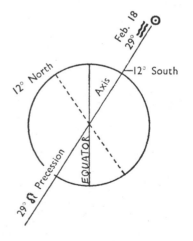

Feb. 18
29°

12° North

Axis

12° South

EQUATOR

Precession

29° ♌

18

the Alipore Jail during his one-year confinement.

The four signs, or two axes, would give us this form in a diagram that seeks to reproduce the events and positions simultaneously, corresponding to latitudes 12° north and south; note that they all fall in the four Fixed signs of the zodiac,

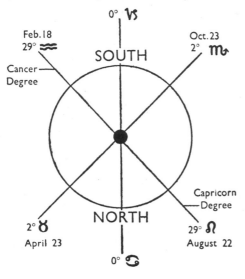

Taurus, Leo, Scorpio and Aquarius —the Bull, the Lion, the Eagle and the Man (Woman), that are mentioned continually in the Book of Revelation and other older occult and esoteric documents and spiritual texts. Of these four signs, the Man and the Lion are the Sphinx of Giza, 'guardian' of the Great Pyramid. As can be seen from the diagram, the Sphinx of Giza represents the same axis of Leo and Aquarius, or August and February, the birth months of Sri Aurobindo and the Mother, which is the important axis of the Matrimandir. August is naturally the Lion and February the Man, but in fact in ancient times the Sphinx was most often portrayed in its human part as a Woman, particularly in Babylonia and then in Greece.

If we look at the existence of the Matrimandir from a certain level we see that it is possible for future Ages to know much about the happenings around the time of its construction just from its position on the 12th latitude, by the pole this would form in conjunction with the penetrating ray of the Sun. This axis would be its sensitive pole, and this pole is the same one symbolised in the Giza Sphinx.

The Age of Leo, when the Pyramid was built or conceived, was a time of kingly, élite rule. The Age of Aquarius, our present era on the scale of Time, stands directly opposite to the former and is the time of universal transformation; the movement descends into the masses and there is a general uplifting. The level of consciousness of the Earth's entire population widens and deepens, no matter how great the cost, how painful the process. Consequently it is a time when those working on a building such as the Matrimandir can be conscious of what they are constructing, or else it becomes a repetition of the past—an élite, gnostic though it may be, imposing its knowledge on the Earth without the conscious support and participation of the masses other than their entire devotion or coerced efforts.

Some interesting points about the 12th latitude have been shown, why it is in a certain sense special, why therefore the *mandir* had to be built exactly thereupon, how it is the completion of work of perhaps 12,000 years and the outcome of three civilisations. It is more than this—it is the culmination of happenings in time which for thousands of years appear to have been mere preparations. We have reached a moment of culmination in the present cycle of 311,040 years for the entire Earth's population and society. A central point for this work is latitude 12° north, and further on we shall see how the longitude gives us the conclusive information, pinpointing the Centre to latitude 12 north and longitude 79 east.

The information given here can be considered 'exoteric', that is, it is all rather obvious to one who decides to fathom the meaning of a temple constructed on the 12th latitude north. But there is a deeper part to the study which takes us into regions of more subtle depth and dimension, not easily seen by the unprepared or untrained eye—and this more subtle dimension reveals to us the real seed of the Matrimandir.

In the celestial sphere made up of twelve equal segments, not only does each segment of 30° have a meaning, but as we know through study of the Gnostic Circle, each *individual degree* of the sphere does as well; and what is more, in each single degree of the sphere one can find the entire circle of 360° reproduced, like a musical note that contains the full scale of the 7 notes and intermediate tones within its vibration, though we have not the capacity to hear it as yet. Each of these individual degrees has as well a sign of the zodiac allocated to it, which forms the most important part in the study of cosmic harmonies. By this method of deeper analysis we come then to know the *seed* of an event, or its true beginning and future purpose—for the individual degree is in truth the seed or the core.

In the case of the Matrimandir the special degree which reveals its seed is the 149° of the sphere, or 29° Leo. And the particular zodiacal correspondence of that degree as the student can observe in the Gnostic Circle is *Capricorn*. It is this sign that is the essence of the Matrimandir, in the most profound sense. Let us see how this fits into the diagram on page 278, where the Sun's motion with respect to the 12th latitude was shown. We find that between 32° (or 2° Taurus) and 149° (or 29° Leo) there are 117°. The midway point between these two diagonally crossing poles would fall at 0° Cancer for the North (celestial South); the same would occur for the South (celestial North) and the midway point between 2° Scorpio and 29° Aquarius is 0° Capricorn. The zodiacal correspondence of 29° Leo is *Capricorn* and of 29° Aquarius is *Cancer*. Therefore we see that the 29° Leo and Aquarius axis belongs to the *seed* of the midway points between these two diagonal shafts —or Capricorn and Cancer, the present *axis of evolution* (not Axis of the Age). Not only in the occult sense, for Capricorn and Cancer are in fact the very axis of the Earth's orbit around the Sun, the points of perihelion and aphelion, when the Earth is either closest—as in the case of Capricorn—or farthest away from the luminary, as occurs in the month of Cancer, considered the Fall of creation and the birth of the ego. This all-important axis of evolution is the secret seed of the Matrimandir, and above all it must be remembered that Capricorn is the ancient occult sign of India. It is the sign of the conquest and crystallisation of the light in matter, or the sign of the victory over Death. It is the 10th sign which corresponds to the 10th Book of *Savitri*[1] where the Goddess conquers Death, for each Book of *Savitri* follows the same progression as the zodiac. It is the 10th day of the Durga festival, the 10th Day of Victory, as it is called, the Vijayadashami, and above all the soul of the temple was conceived during the month of Capricorn.

Now let us consider Auroville's *horoscope of birth*. What do we find there, on that very 29° of Leo? We find therein Jupiter, precisely placed and in the fourth 'mundane house', considered the *roots* of the chart; and Jupiter is the planet governing our entire Manifestation of 6,480 years. Above all, it is the planet of 'temples'.

All of this and much more is captured in the 12th latitude north.

Auroville in its progression through the solar system according to the Gnostic Circle will reach this point, the *beginning degree of the Matrimandir*, 0° Capricorn, on November 28, 1974[2]; as the student can verify, this occurs once every nine years. It is interesting that this information comes forth now, for on that date Auroville reaches the Matrimandir in its life cycle, so to speak. This will have a deep meaning in the course of its destiny. The date occurs in the Gnostic Circle nine months after its 6th birthday of 28 February, 1974, which means that being six years old it had progressed to the orbit of Saturn, the sixth planet of the System, the ruler of Capricorn and India. Nine months from that birthday Auroville touches this very 0 Capricorn degree that Saturn so fully rules, and the gestation of nine months is over. The soul of the City can begin to be born.

It seems to be working toward a conscious birth, and it does not appear that the Matrimandir can live and take its place on Earth as a centre of life, the soul of the planet, in ignorance. Perhaps for this reason only this year certain essential information about its conception has come forth, and based on such knowledge we can better understand what it is to signify.

What does all this mean in terms of spiritual development and collective sadha-

---

[1] Sri Aurobindo's epic work. Sri Aurobindo Ashram Trust publication.

[2] The sensitive period for the Matrimandir in the near future would be from 0° to 15° Capricorn, or, in time, from 28 November 1974 to 18 April, 1975, according to Auroville's cycle. But the Temple also follows its own cycle. Its foundation occurred on 21 February, 1971, thus in February 1975 it reaches the 4th Orbit (Mars) and the very important 4. 5 Orbit on 21 August, 1975.

na? We are well aware that this knowledge is thought irrelevant by some. This is not a phenomenon of our times solely; it is a remnant of the Middle Ages, the Dark Ages, and it is interesting to note that those who have no understanding of the matter are the first to express that such facts and knowledge are irrelevant for one's spiritual growth, or that the Matrimandir has nothing to do with 'astrology', and so on. Some feel that a revelation of this knowledge can only serve to stifle the psychic opening, if it be there, and that the measurements for the inner chamber— which we shall discuss next—were given on the sole basis of a mediumistic intuition, and that this capacity signifies the higher realisation. One wonders then what in fact is gnosis? What is the point in trying to bring down the Supermind on a universal basis, or any such principle of higher knowledge, for any medium can receive such dimensions in an unconscious fashion. The inner chamber of the Matrimandir could have therefore been arranged by a simple opening of a mediumistic nature which has nothing to do with the widening of consciousness and the understanding of the harmonies and laws that govern our life on this planet. The human being thrusts what he cannot comprehend of the creation into the category of the 'unmanifest', that which is far beyond order and harmony and law—because for him *law* is only that which he has knowledge of. Whatever is outside his mental grasp must be for him beyond his 'universe'—at best he calls it the supernatural, at worst it is the 'void', or extinction and liberation from all manifestation. It is evident that a higher power can break the laws that govern the planet, to all outward appearances. But from limited mental perception this seems to be 'going beyond' laws, only because we have no understanding of higher laws to which the lower are subject; and the lower can only be broken or altered *according to a higher manifest principle*. Lower laws are transcended only to insert a movement into a wider, more subtle, more finely evolved scheme. If one speaks of Supermind as being Unity, Harmony, Truth, then for these there must be manifestation, and for manifestation there must be Laws; and the essence of this higher truth is what is to be captured in the inner chamber.

To better understand all this one must realise that a temple which is to be the centre of the Age must be the perfect representation of the Cosmos as enlightened man is able to *see* the Cosmos at that particular point in time. A temple in the truest sense of the word is, in fact, a microcosmic reproduction of the universal truth. It synthesises for man the entire Cosmos and becomes the revelation of the higher laws that can assist his species to attain its greater fulfilment in evolution. The knowledge of these laws is essential for what is to occur in the future. But humanity appears ever ready to bring down to its own level that which it cannot understand or that which is new—for this knowledge, as it is contained in the Matrimandir, is newly revealed and has not, in the complete sense in which it is now coming forth, been a part of gnostic societies of the past; or at least the manner in which it is taking shape reveals a more interesting precision and harmony. Two elements must combine in its creation, an enlightened leader and a receptive community. The inner chamber is the fruit of knowledge; the outer part of the temple is the revelation of the power that has descended and is influencing mankind.

For a fuller conscious participation it would appear that the first step would be to attain a cosmic consciousness, without which any aspiration for the true knowledge is difficult. It is not mentally given, as most think; it is the outcome of a widening of the consciousness to such an extent that it embraces the whole of manifested divinity, with which one identifies. But today man finds fault with such a widening and calls it inferior knowledge, superstition, in his own fashion. The fact is that still, even in the centres dedicated to the spiritualisation of the Earth, or the revelation of the divine light in matter itself, there prevails the idea that all that which pertains to the Cosmos is basically the Ignorance. Because one is not able to see the cosmic truth, these things are labelled the lesser realisation or the Ignorance, even when this truth is revealed. It is difficult and rare to find a true believer and worshipper of the Divine Mother, because in one breath man claims he is devoted to the Mother and in the other he rejects the knowledge of the universe which is her Body. These are the leftovers of the Buddhistic-Mayavadist consciousness which every seeker still bears within him.

And this is the very reason why the Matrimandir is supposed to be constructed in such a way as to reveal the Cosmic Truth, to show the very perfection of Matter but in an entirely new way, a way much deeper and wider than in the past. Science has already come to the point where it accepts the influence of all cosmic bodies on each other, yet in spiritual circles one hears of the imperative need to transform the body, but at the same time there is a rejection of the occult laws that govern this process of transformation. And then one can ask: what is it the seeker knows of matter if he does not know the Cosmos, where this matter comes from and to which our bodies respond that are made up of this matter that we seek to transform? The Ignorance is still predominant precisely because man refuses to see the Cosmic Truth and makes either an absolute god of Science, or else one of Spirituality. He cannot reconcile the two because he fails to see the third poise; and above all he refuses to accept the power of Time.

All of this is part of the ego, the veils are still drawn too tightly. These veils were to have been drawn aside in June of 1974, symbolically and physically enacted by the passing of Aurolouis. This was the famed 'second death' in initiation, as revealed by the cosmic harmonies. The first death which is the plunge into matter, or incarnation in the world governed by the Ignorance, was symbolised by the passing of Auroville's first son, Auroson. This occurred in fact just immediately after the official foundation of the City. The City's soul, as represented by these children, had taken the plunge and its first son was the symbolic sacrifice of this shoot into the world of ignorance for its redemption. The 'second death' occurred exactly at the point in time which represents the shedding of the veils that one acquires with the first death; at the second death the ego is supposed to be cast aside and the soul comes forth that had died to its light in order to join the evolution at the time of physical birth. Aurolouis' passing represented, in Auroville's 6th year, this very *second* death, which is a birth, the birth of the soul. After that it is no longer possible to cling to the Ignorance or to prefer to remain unconscious in a land that is by destiny to be 'the cradle of truth-consciousness'.

In the last six chapters of *The Life Divine*[1] what is to be expected of a gnostic society is detailed. If these are read there can be no conflict over the issuing of knowledge, for this knowledge shows that the Matrimandir corresponds in the occult and physical sense to this vision of Sri Aurobindo and its issuing in no way should lessen one's devotion or stifle the psyche but rather enhance its flowering or progress hand in hand with it.

The mathematical harmonies and magnificent poignant exactitude of the passing of these two sons of Auroville has been described elsewhere in this text, their roles as the symbols of the sacrifice in matter.[2] When seen in this light their passings become almost sublime and one ceases to look upon such events in a personal and limited sense. One sees them as the initiates in the great purification of Auroville, enacting the parts of the neophytes in face of the Blazing Fire. Both chose to leave by the element of water, which in the zodiac is the corresponding plunge or death, the waters from which one is then born. It is necessary only to point out again the importance of the 6th year, 1974, wherein the Second Death occurred, which is Saturn's year, and the 9th month after the birthday which is Capricorn's point and the initial coming forth of the Matrimandir soul. Later on in this study it will be possible to show how the Mother has captured this soul in a very special way in the core of the Matrimandir. Which brings to mind the similarity of the word *core* or heart, and the Greek word *kore*, the daughter of the Divine Mother of Eleusis, her soul and most precious part. All these things may find their meaning and their sense in the Matrimandir, even the language we speak.

[1] Sri Aurobindo, Sri Aurobindo Ashram Trust publication.
[2] Page 242.

The Inner Chamber[1]

On the basis of information recently placed at our disposal during the month of September, 1974, it has become possible to speak with precision about various details of the Matrimandir. These data are certain comments the Mother made regarding what might occur in the temple, and then finally the instructions and measurements she has given for the inner chamber which prove that this room was to contain for her the dimensions of Time converted into the dimensions of Space. In this room she has captured some essential elements of Time as it is experienced on Earth—that is, the Earth with relation to the Cosmos. These two dimensions that we have extensively discussed in other chapters are transcribed in the following way, the 12 Circle—SPACE Dimension, the 9 Circle—TIME Dimension:

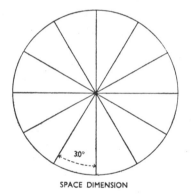 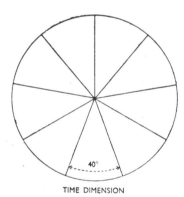

SPACE DIMENSION   TIME DIMENSION

It is possible to show how these two essential divisions of the Circle are captured in the core of the temple, for it is the superimposition of the two, one upon the other, or the simultaneous vision and understanding of the Circle divided into both 9 and 12 that tells us what we need to know about the evolution of our planet, and though this might make one feel insignificant in the light of the cosmic vastness and transcendent beyond, it must be remembered that this very vastness, this

1 It must be mentioned here that all the arrangements and measurements spoken of herein are taken from the original plan given by the Mother that she had drawn up by an engineer, and from her recorded talks on the subject. The correct measurements have not been incorporated in the temple built in Auroville, thus everything we discuss in this portion of the book deals with the *ideal vision* of a Room that exists eternally, in the plane of Truth. The significance of the deviation from the correct and harmonious measurements have been discussed to some extent in *The Hidden Manna,* and, because of its importance for the Earth, the subject is thoroughly treated in, *The New Way,* Aeon Books, P. O. Box 396, Accord, New York, 12404.

Cosmos reduced to the Circle of 9 and 12 is the very core of man. He is That in all ways, and the details of his Earthly life follow the very same patterns of the Cosmos in all its vastness. The macrocosmos and the microcosmos are indeed one.

In giving the measurements for the room the Mother has started from a certain premise in astrological-occult studies that has been detailed in the chapter on Simultaneous Time, i.e., that *one day equals one year*. This is the essential equation and she has captured it in the central shaft of the room. The diameter of the chamber is to be 24 metres; in this she has given the time division of the day, the number 24 being the 24 hours. The revolution of the Earth on its axis (24 hours) is equal to its revolution around the Sun (365 days), because in 24 hours the Earth has experienced all the 'dimensions of the Sun', expressed in the 12 zodiacal signs. It has revolved upon itself and turned the face of its eastern horizon to each of the 12 signs. In the year it experiences the actual rays of the Sun from the 12 signs, not only the reflection upon its axial rotating body, and this is the time period of 12 months which the Mother has captured in the 12 walls of the Chamber, as she explained to her disciples—namely that the 12 walls were representative of the 12 months. Thus the walls are directly connected with the zodiacal signs.

The solar year, 365 days, has been captured in the central shaft, precisely where the ray of the Sun is to pierce through the chamber and shine upon its soul or core directly. In this the Mother has given us *the measurement of the solar ray*, as it were.

If the Earth were a perfect sphere or its orbit around the Sun were perfectly circular and at a quicker speed, the central measurement to the pedestal supporting the globe which is 15.20 metres, would have been 15, because 15 metres is equal to 360; in that case the Sun would move a perfect 1° per day, and the year would consist of 360 days. As it now stands the experience is 'imperfect', the orbs are not symmetrical, the speeds vary and so the overall picture is that the solar year is over 360 by 5 (and 1/4th) days which, when divided by 24 metres (hours), the diameter of the chamber, results in 15.20. Thus the extra 20.20 centimeters are those 'five days of imperfection'.

One day is always equal to one year, no matter how one calculates the year or day, either in terms of months, or hours or minutes or seconds. Therefore in the 12 walls which are equivalent to the 12 months of the year, there is once more the formula: 1 day equals 1 year, but the year of 12 months. The figure 8.65, which is to be the vertical measurement of the 12 walls, is a very important number because it corresponds to the *diameter of the Sun*. But before entering into this discussion, it is necessary to point out how one comes upon 865 centimetres based on the 12 months.

Each month is equivalent to 30° of the celestial sphere; this 30° (30 days) month is broken up into an important division of three, yielding 10° (or 10 days) each. The *decanate* division of each month is most important because it signifies that in one month each of the three modes of the Divine Mother are experienced, her three major energy manifestations: *creation, preservation* and *destruction*. Each year therefore the Earth passes through 36 such energy flows. If one day is equal to one year, and the month is made up of these three divisions, then 24 (one day) × 36 (1 year) gives 864. The month of three divisions of 10° each, which make the totality of 360°, or 36 such divisions, is contained in the 12 walls measuring 865. The figure 865 is like the figure 1520 which takes into consideration the imperfection of the year of the Earth. It can be seen that the actual diameter of the Sun contains the correct division of the month, the Moon's period by its rotation around the Earth; but at the same time it varies from the truly perfect form which would be 864,000 even. As it now stands scientists have the measurement of the Sun's diameter as 864,949. The 949 are usually rounded off to 865,000. But in studying the perfect sphere of the Sun, or *the perfect Sun* and hence the cosmic truth, the hidden reality, the measurement is 864,000.

In the wall measurement the Mother has given, through the digits of the Sun's diameter, the key which determines the month's accurate division as well as that of the seasons which are also manifestations of the three energy flows of the Divine Mother. And this division is essentially zodiacal rather than calendrical.

This is part of the matter. In continuing to summarise we see that the Chamber contains the major time divisions of our planet: hour (floor diameter), month (wall vertical measurement), and year (central shaft height). Apart from this there is another face of the chamber to discuss which relates to the Precession of the Equinoxes, the Earth's greater evolutionary year. The movement is balanced by the Moon, no matter to what prime Source of magnetic energy it owes its being. The Moon serves to keep the Earth in the right rhythm with respect to the mysterious centre which provokes the Precession. The Moon is the sacrificed 'dead weight', hanging onto the Earth for the benefit of its evolving civilisations. The walls, the Moon's measurement in

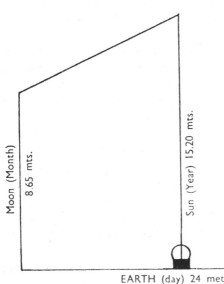

Moon (Month) 8.65 mts.

Sun (Year) 15.20 mts.

EARTH (day) 24 metres

the chamber, are thus the sustaining power of the construction of the room; but the Moon is further represented by 12 pillars which we shall discuss further on.

Whatever the precessional movement corresponds to, it takes place at a rate of 50 seconds per year. That is, per year the equinoctial poles, the Axis of the Age which is now at 29° Aquarius and Leo, moves backward through the zodiac at a rate of 50 seconds per year. The 0° Aries point has come to express itself through 29° Aquarius at present, or we could say, this 29° Aquarius is now the 12 Point of the Cosmic Clock. Thus these *50 seconds are equivalent to one year*, just as 24 hours are equivalent to 365 days. The beauty of it is that we find this figure also captured in the central shaft because 15.20 metres equals *50 feet*. So the central shaft wherein the solar ray joins with the Precessional Axis on August 22nd, furnishes us also with the figure 50 of the annual movement of the Greater Year. It is well to point out that in occult studies the novemal (decimal) system is the correct measurement for the calendar and its equivalents, and the system of Feet based on 12 is the accurate method of measurement for the Earth with respect to the zodiac and the precession of the equinoxes and all their equivalents. Once again it can be seen that the systems correspond essentially to the two divisions of the Circle, 9 and 12, and to the dimensions of time and space.

It is now possible to see how the Precessional movement is also captured in the 12 walls. If one takes 12 into 865 the result is 72 (plus a fraction). It was explained previously that the entire Circle is completed in 25,920 years, and it therefore takes *72 years* to move through one of the 30° that make up a 'month'. This amount of time for the Greater Month—or one sign in the Precession—is equivalent to 1 day on Earth.

The original measurement given for the walls of the Chamber is 30 centimetres; with each centimetre taken as one degree, the 12 walls would produce the complete celestial circle of 360°, from which all these figures are extracted.

There are many ways in which these all-important numbers can be captured in a monument. To give an example, let us briefly examine an extraordinary structure which stands in the central plains of Java—the Buddhist Borobudur Temple[1]. The origins of this prime piece of Indian-inspired architecture are unknown; it is known only to have been constructed during or before the 9th century A.D. There is no doubt that it was a product of that first millennium which was such a rich period for Indian cosmology, astrology and mathematics, as the temple itself reveals.

Here we have roughly reproduced the floor plan of the building—that is, giving merely its essential pattern—which is constructed upon a hill, each level leading up to a solitary *stupa* at the apex, that corresponds to the central Dot in

[1] *The Art and Architecture of India*, Benjamin Rowland, Penguin Books, U.S.A.

the plan. The construction is thus in the symbol form of the Mountain, or the triangle. In all, with a subterranean level, there are 9 storeys, —6 of the storeys are square (one underground and not visible) and 3 circular. In the central triad of circles there are 72 stupas which are drawn as dots on the plan, each stupa enclosing and rendering semi-hidden a figure of the Buddha.

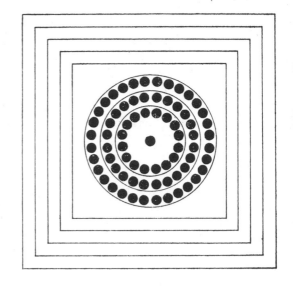

The temple is basically constructed around the principle of the four Cardinal Points, —much the same as the Matrimandir that is sustained by four great pillars—as almost all other gnostic temples old and new. Therefore this number 4 has been used in the inner circles in the Borobudur temple in an interesting and special way, which, we shall see, give us the figure 864.

If the student observes carefully it can be seen that the outer circle, the first, contains 32 stupas, or four times 8; the next circle contains 24, or four times 6; and the inner circle has 16 stupas, or four times 4—in all making a total of 72.

Thus in the heart of this magnificent temple we find once again the number 8-6-4, and finally the total of 72, the number to be captured in the walls of the Matrimandir. It is evident that these figures can be reproduced in a variety of manners, and it is further evident that it is One Truth which is invariably displayed in all gnostic temples throughout the world, because such a temple is for the very purpose of capturing the cosmic truth and consequently results in the creation of an area perfectly in tune with the cosmic forces. But the manner in which the truth is reproduced in stone is what is interesting to observe, because each Age brings a new vision, a fuller scope—and by the manner in which such a building takes shape, we can know much about the Knowledge of the times, the quality of the race of enlightened men who built it, and consequently the stage of the evolution during any particular period.

The topmost Point, or the Apex of this 'mountain' Triangle is the 0. In fact, there is a 'void' stupa there in contrast to the 72 others; this principal stupa is entirely sealed off and hides whatever it is reputed to have once contained completely from the view of the pilgrim[1]. In this way we find that here also the o and the 9 are considered equal—the 9 being in the ground, covered up by the earth and thus hidden from view, and the o by being exposed but hidden and *void* of any form. Here is an exquisite means of reproducing in stone this basic cosmic truth as captured in numbers.

So in this sublime temple-mandala of Java we find that the core of this work, this synthesis of cosmic harmonies, is beautifully preserved—the equality of the o and the 9, as well as the reality of the Precessional rhythm and its importance for the Earth evolution, for in the temple we find as well the numbers 8, 6, 4, and then 72, the period of years necessary for the Earth to move through a degree of the zodiac, the same figure as the walls of the Matrimandir, only here incorporated by the 8th, 6th and 4th multiples of 4.

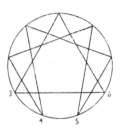

The value of the number 4 regarding the cosmic manifestation can be shown in a simple manner, taken from the *diameter* and *radius* of the Sun, the perfect Sun of 864,000 miles.

4 × 864 (the numbers of the Sun's diameter)=3456 the numbers corresponding to the section of *the base of the Sacred Triangle* in the 9 Circle.

4 × 432 (the numbers of the Sun's radius)=1728 the numbers corresponding to those *surrounding the Apex* in the 9 Circle, those needed along with 3456 to complete the numbers from 1 to 8. Only the o and the 9 are missing, the Apex itself, and this is obtained by the sum total of all the numbers: 1+2+3+4+5+6 +7+8 which equal 36, or 3+6=9, and once more the Sacred Triangle, 3, 6 and 9 (o).

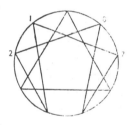

Thus if one counts in this way in the plan of the Borobudur there is a fine synthesis of the universal harmonies: the sealed off and once empty central stupa at the Apex is the o; then follow the three circles which are the numbers 1, 2 and 3; after which there are the five levels in square form, or the numbers 4, 5, 6, 7 and 8; finally there is the subterranean number 9, which in its own way is equal to the Apex in that it too is entirely hidden from view, the former being sealed and devoid of form and the latter entirely immersed in the world of form and therefore completely obscured.

---

[1] It is considered that the statue lately found in the Apex was not original to the construction and was a later addition, that in fact the space was void, which would seem to correspond more accurately to the Buddhist philosophy.

It is of supreme interest to note that the monument, being Buddhist, reflects so perfectly the Buddhist concept of the creation, or existence in material creation. The 9, Matter, is the seat of ignorance, because the 9th subterranean storey is found to consist of bas-reliefs which depict the world of desires, the hell of material creation, whereas all the storeys above the ground (out of the Earth or the material creation or manifestation) contain scenes from the life of the Buddha, where the pilgrim is made to seek refuge in enlightenment to become free of the wheel of karma and death and re-birth, until finally at the Apex—the o—even the Buddha is no more and the final fulfilment and liberation is achieved, liberation from this Earth with all its pains and woes. But in these studies we have seen that essentially the o and the 9 are one, that it is not in fact a linear movement as depicted in the terraces of the Borobudur, but is rather circular, and in the manner of the Serpent biting its Tail these two expressions of the Supreme meet: the Void and the Manifestation are one. We must bear in mind that the Borobudur is a monument of the Age of Pisces, when precisely the tendency was to lose oneself in the Void. Yet this is the revolutionary experience of today's spirituality, the spiritualisation of the Earth and its Birth, and the rendering of the manifest creation visibly an expression of the Transcendent Divine.

In the Borobudur when the pilgrim reaches the Apex he finds Nothing. In the Matrimandir when he reaches the core, he finds the Sun wherefrom all these numbers are derived, or shall we say, where all these figures of our solar system have their culmination and synthesis. In the heart of the Matrimandir we find the source of Matter of our System, and the structure represents the marriage of soul (Earth) and spirit (Sun).

This variation between the two temples shows us the fundamental difference between one realisation and the other. It is for the student to understand which is in accord with the times—this Aquarian Age—and which is basically of more urgent value for the Earth and its present ailing humanity. Because spiritualists of the past have satisfied their quest in this way, by an escape into the o, disregarding the 9, its equal counterpart in Matter, mankind has not been able to stand 'face to face with the Sun', or directly under its Ray, suffering the consequences of all that this simple fact signifies for the evolution of the spirit, unable even to make use of solar energy in the way that is necessary for mankind's survival, needing to depend on inferior sources of energy to supply the planet's needs. We are now paying the price for 2,000 years or more of 'withdrawal'. In this Age, in this 9th Manifestation, Matter —the 9—is redeemed.

Whatever the ultimate message of the Borobudur, one is struck by its magnificence and its deep meaning and the splendid way in which the message has been captured in stone. The terraced 'pyramid' has been preserved as a further proof to mankind of the exactitude of the sages' vision regarding the flow of Time and its significance for the evolution of spirituality for humanity.

It is possible to go on and on in this way, because the information contained in the inner chamber of the Matrimandir is unending, but to conclude this portion it may be said that whenever this knowledge has been lost in the past, religions have formed. Where it was kept intact either by an élite that guided the masses along the way—as was the case in the Ashram where Sri Aurobindo and the Mother consciously possessed this knowledge—or else by an entire society enjoying the capacity to *know* as well as *be* and *feel*, religions did not form. The presence of a gnostic being and guide, or a population of gnostic beings, is the only means whereby the knowledge is kept alive, for in the religious consciousness the knowledge is maintained through dogma—that is, the faithful repeat and carry out certain rituals, or construct temples, which they know not the meaning of, merely on the basis of faith and devotion; and they build churches and temples according to dimensions the priests and pandits give who also have lost the living knowledge. It is evident that the quality of knowledge contained in the Matrimandir is not for the majority, because it is very difficult for the common man to relate to God, the Cosmos in its entirety, not embodied or personalised. Man needs the props he can recognise and relate to his personal limited life, and in this process religions are formed. It is good to participate in the creation of a cosmic temple—or all the work that is in one way or another connected with it—on the basis of devotion and love, for the purpose of widening the consciousness and realising the soul; but the danger is always there that when there is no knowledge there is religion. If one goes over the history of all the major religions this is found to be true. Whereas if one looks to the places where the knowledge was kept alive it can be seen that when the time came for the knowledge to be occulted because of the dangers of a progressively hostile humanity toward such things, or because of the secret demands of the Time-Spirit, the sages preferred to let the truth they captured fall into oblivion and not entomb it in a religion. Such was the case in Egypt. Such was the case in Eleusis. On both sites we find barren, sleeping ruins— but also we find no religions. Whereas in Rome the conscious knowledge apart from Greece never existed in the full sense of the word, and after the fading of the last of the gnostic fathers, the knowledge faded as well, and then the Roman Catholic Church came into full being. It is naive to think that this cannot happen today; it is man's vanity that makes him believe he is different and that under his superior guidance things will be different. Evidently for this reason the Mother has expressly insisted that there be no photographs of herself and Sri Aurobindo in the temple—only their symbols which contain the knowledge here put forth, and the dimensions and specifications of the inner chamber which could, by their harmony and unity with the Cosmos, carry the being into states of consciousness perhaps otherwise closed to it, or at least remind man of his mission and the way leading to its fulfillment. The Matrimandir, as the Mother has arranged it, is not a church of devotion; it is a Temple of Gnosis—and when that knowledge is lost or is thought irrelevant, it will follow the same pattern as the Pyramid and other such monuments of the past. Religions and churches may appear to be eternal because they are kept alive by artificial means—the power of money, even military power at times. But sites of true knowledge seem to die along with the gnostic beings who created them. Yet this is only the superficial appearance of things. Gnosis does not die, it renews itself on the basis of life, for its very existence depends upon the conscious participation and the life that is poured into it. It falls asleep in one centre only to flower in another, taking on different outer forms, continually revealing a wider, greater and deeper aspect of the Divine and the possibilities of realisation open to humanity, never denying what was done yesterday, only embracing and fulfilling the ever greater need of the Earth to know the Creator in an increasingly more complete sense. There is the possibility now, at this point in the evolution, for Knowledge to become a universal achievement and for the human race to truly evolve into a more divine and enlightened species. In this case the patterns of the past may be changed, whereby it may not be necessary for the centre to sleep, or for *pralaya* of any degree to occur. Pralaya is precisely when the knowledge fades and mankind becomes unconscious, loses contact with the Cosmos and the higher powers, and must start a long and blind journey, groping through the corridors of Time, trying to recapture the light of the Sun once more. Pralaya is the sleep of *the 'eye' that sees.*

The Central Portion

Let us consider now the central portion of the floor where the Mother's symbol is to rest, and the dimensions she has given for that all-important portion. Her symbol is to hold the most important part of the Temple, its core or nucleus, the globe which is to receive the solar ray. Embracing the sphere itself will be Sri Aurobindo's symbol which, combined with hers in the particular manner she has indicated, contains the 360° of the celestial and global sphere. Her symbol is projected as 300 centimeters, and the inner square which is made up of Sri Aurobindo's is 60. Thus 300+60=360, the celestial as well as the global sphere, the way in which our very planet is divided. Therefore the two symbols combine in the heart of the Matrimandir to contain the full circle of the Earth and the heavens.

12 pillars were projected to encircle these symbols, in an area of diameter 1350 cm. This would give us the symbol of the Mother as the floor plan of the *man-*

dir, which is composed of three concentric circles, those all-important energy flows of the divine Mother, —creation, preservation and destruction. In this manner, calculating numerologically on the basis of cabbalistic reduction, the radii of the three circles form the numbers 3, 9, 6, once more in the same order found in Eleusis— perhaps the last site of the authentic matrimandirs built in the Western world—and in particular the radius of the Earth. *Theosophical addition* is of prime importance in these studies because it is the *mathematics of unity*, since it merely means starting the count from the last multiple of 9 that a figure contains, and then counting the numbers beyond that multiple. For example, 24 would be: 18—which eliminates itself because $1+8=9$ is equal to 0; after this '9', one counts to 24 and there are 6. Hence 24 is 6 with two 9 multiples eliminated on the basis of 'mathematics of unity', whose main principle is: 9 and 0 are equal. The central globe (the soul) is the 0, the point. Here is the detail:

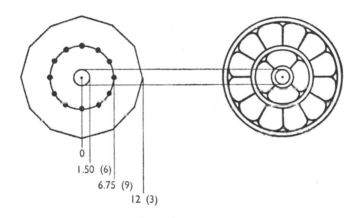

Also it can be seen that in this way the Mother's symbol in the Temple's floor plan occupies what would be the central or inner circle of her own symbol. This central portion of her symbol is ⊙, in astrology the symbol of the Sun. Hence exactly where the solar ray is to fall she has combined her symbol with Sri Aurobindo's and placed them onto the area where the symbol of the Sun lies. The pillars form the next concentric circle of her symbol, the division of 12 petals, and the outer walls are the third and final concentric circle. The dot in her symbol is the central crystal globe. If one knows that the entire unfoldment of the evolution is contained in the Mother's symbol then its reproduction becomes tremendously important, primarily because such pure forms are known in these studies to be indicative of divisions of space which have a subtle effect on the consciousness; these studies are unfortunately not a part of modern architecture and certainly we are far from being a society where higher knowledge is the foundation of architecture and sculpture, and not aesthetics, or comfort, or other such considerations. Evidently this aspect of life must also find its way once more, from darkness to light.

All of this points to the extent of receptivity of the human race at present, and what can be accomplished without the conscious participation of the individual, to show us, in a sense, how far the study of architecture has taken us on the basis of— let us say—a materialistic consciousness toward the union with the same expression based on a higher knowledge. Obviously the problems of creating gnostically perfect forms in matter are many and there can be numerous reasons for the need to alter certain dimensions and designs. In most cases the basis for change, however, has been merely a question of aesthetics, a criterion limited to a fragment of time only.

The Core

We come now to the nucleus, the truly sacred core of the *mandir*.

The 360° of the combined symbols of Sri Aurobindo and the Mother are to uphold a globe of 70 centimeters. *In those 70 centimeters the entire area of India is contained.* It can be stated that the core of the Matrimandir is the land of India, Mother Durga herself, and therefore the soul of the planet incarnate. It is here that the essence of the Sun, the spirit, meets and weds the essence of the Earth, the soul. It is here—captured in the core of the Matrimandir, a centre of the Age—that the union of heaven and earth takes place; this is the new temple for the new Age, the new expression of the eternal cosmic Truth.

On page 187 there is the map of India and the full territory, with the symbol of Capricorn, India's sign, superimposed upon it, delineating the area. The only other area on the globe that comes close to this manner of graphic geographical symbology is *the boot of Italy*, for Rome was the centre during the Piscean Age and Pisces rules the feet. The two territories have many similarities, being surrounded on three sides by water and topped on the fourth by high mountain ranges that separate them from their northern neighbours. (Both these symbols, water and mountain, are used to represent the Divine Mother, or the feminine principle.) Both have an island at the country's lower tip. Both consisted formerly of city-states which have only recently become united. Both countries are essentially 'religious' and devoted to the Divine Mother—Italy through its devotion to the Blessed Virgin, Mother of God, and India to the Shakti, the Power of God. Both names in English are composed of five letters, beginning with 'I'. (As for the number of letters a name contains, we could consider this a purely arbitrary coincidence, and no doubt it is so; yet regarding the work of this centre these 'arbitrary' occurrences seem to happen continually. On the Triangle Sri Aurobindo occupies the 9 point, and his name in English contains 9 letters. The Mother occupies the 6 point and 'Mother' is 6 letters. Every time one writes 'Sri Aurobindo Ashram'one is writing 3, 9, 6 really; every time one writes 'Auroville' one is writing 9, which is also Auroville's birth number and which is equal to the o. And so, these are the amusing coincidences one encounters. They happen because of the harmony of the seed.)

Returning to geographical coincidences, apart from Italy and India, no other two countries today seem to offer such close connection with the zodiac in terms of their actual shape and territory—in particular India, formed as it is of the ancient symbol of Capricorn, the so-called 'Name of God', better called perhaps the 'Name of the Goddess'.

But how is the territory captured in the central crystal?

If we look on the globe we find this symbol and the land it envelops to begin at longitude 61° East and to extend to 101° East, a total of 40°. In terms of latitude the area comprises from 6° North to 36° North, a total of 30°, beginning with the tip of Sri Lanka and ending at the top of 'the lion's head'. It is to be recalled that these amounts of degrees are the segments of the 9 and 12 circles, 40° and 30° respectively, and that they accurately correspond to the dimensions to which their respective circles correspond, the dimensions of Time and Space on the globe. Therefore the central globe of the Matrimandir, with a diameter of 70 centimetres (40+30), captures the entire territory of India which is the symbol of Capricorn, known to represent the soul of the Earth, ruled by Saturn,—a planet which holds the key of Time. Thus in the temple where the gnostic key of Time is contained, *the core is the very land of the Time-Spirit upon Earth.*

The soul of India rests on the globe of the Earth (300+60) of the combined symbols and is the core of the Matrimandir. Moreover, starting from 61° longitude, if we count each degree until we reach the Centre and the Matrimandir, there are 18°40′ approximately, the Saros cycle of the Lunar Nodes in fact. At the juncture with latitude 12, the Matrimandir comes into being.

The Geometry of Time

Finally the most interesting fact about the central globe is the manner in which it captures the days of the Matrimandir's conception, the solstice period traditionally considered the 'Festival of Light', when the Earth is at perihelion—with January 1st, the beginning of our calendar year, falling at exactly the centre of the Globe.

As the globe measures 70 cm. diameter and rests upon a square of 60 cm. length and 30 cm. height, this leaves 55 cm. of the globe visible above the supporting pedestal. It has been pointed out that the central shaft of 1520 cm. is equivalent to the year of 365 days. Thus we have the Solar Ray visible and falling upon the globe for 1520 cm., combining with the pedestal of 30 cm. to give in all 1550 cm. However, the important dimension regarding Time is 1520, because this is the measure of *the visible solar ray*. Since these 1520, plus a fraction, are 365 days, or one year, we can find the days of the year that sweep down this ray, as it were, and when we reach the globe it is possible to locate the point *in time* at which the juncture of the solar ray and the globe occurs, by the conversion of metres into days.

It was stated previously that the 20.20 over the exact 15 metres corresponds to the 5 days of 'imperfection' of Earth/Solar time experience. Thus in the central shaft of the Matrimandir the 15 meters would fall at precisely the centre of the globe. This then would be the perfect solar year, the perfect sphere, the perfect Sun. Then from the central point of the globe to the pedestal there are 20 cm., and this brings the count from ceiling to pedestal, or the fully visible ray, to 365 days. These 365 days embrace, or consist of, the celestial sphere of 360 degrees.

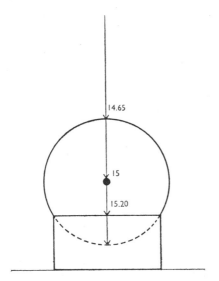

To sum up: in this 'geometry of Time', as it were, we see that the ceiling to the tip of the translucent globe measures 14.65 metres; the central point of the globe is 15, and to the pedestal is 15.20, the visible Ray ending at the symbol of Sri Aurobindo. In calendar time these figures would be as follows: if we consider the year of the Sun calendar to begin at 15° Capricorn, equivalent to 5/6 January, the night Aeon is born, a descent down the solar ray brings us to December 22/23 exactly at the top of the globe, or at 14.65 metres. This is the solstice, or 0° Capricorn of the celestial-zodiacal sphere. From 14.65 to the centre of the globe there are 35 cm., or 8 3/4 days, bringing us to 1st January or 9° of the celestial sphere; continuing to the base are 20 cm., or 5 days, which take us to 5/6 January, or 15° Capricorn, and the birth of Aeon, the Solar Year God. It was during the period captured in the globe from the central point to the beginning of the pedestal that the Mother conceived the Mandir and drew up the exact plans for the construction of the Inner Room as here described.[1] Moreover, this is the land of India, ruled by Saturn and Capricorn, whose period in Time is captured in the core of the Temple, just as the entire territory of India is also contained in the core, the globe. More interesting to note is that in Sri Aurobindo's natal horoscope Saturn is found *at 15° Capricorn*. Thus the Ray ends at the pedestal of his symbol at 15° Capricorn, the very position of his natal Saturn which is the planetary essence of the Matrimandir and of India.

The solar ray of the central shaft, from the ceiling to the centre of the sphere, is 360 days, the 'perfect year'. From ceiling to pedestal is 365 days, the 'imperfect' year but the perfect celestial sphere of 360 degrees. Thus in the shaft the two methods of time/space demarcation are harmonised. In the Gnostic Circle this area, 0° to 15° Capricorn, is the journey into the Matrimandir, with all that it signifies for the sadhak in terms of the expansion of consciousness, or the initiation that the Chamber can offer. 0° Capricorn is the entry, we can say, while 15° Capricorn is the culmination. This area is the birth of the soul, its crystallisation in Matter, the conquest over Death. This portion of the Gnostic Circle, which is the Matrimandir, corresponds to the 10th Book of *Savitri*, by Sri Aurobindo, wherein he describes the conquest of Death and the Victory of the Divine Mother. And it is the perihelion of the Earth.

The entire globe, considering also the part which is concealed by the pedestal (15 cm.), embraces a period of 18 days, from 22/23 December to 9 January; hidden from view are four days. The number 18 we have frequently discussed in the text, in particular the importance given to this time-cycle in India.

The radius of the Earth is contained in the radii of the concentric circles of the floor: 3-9-6-0, and it should be noted that this measurement is found in the dimension of the Chamber which captures the 'day' period. The day comes about by the Earth's spinning upon its axis, therefore to find the planet's radius in the 24 metres, or the day count, of the Chamber's floor is noteworthy. The calendar demarcation is determined by the Earth's revolution around the Sun, and in the Chamber we find that the Solar Ray presents us with the full year of 365 calendar days.

The pillars and the walls have a joint function in the Chamber. First, the 12 walls each correspond to a month or to a zodiacal sign, hence they are the Moon in the harmony, since the Moon's orbit determines the month. The Moon encircles the Earth with its orbit, and so do the walls encircle the Room. As representatives of the walls, the Pillars stand mid-way between the central symbol area and the walls—just as the months stand between the year (central shaft) and the day (floor). These two elements of the room serve to give it balance and support, just as the Moon serves to 'balance' the Earth's spin, thereby maintaining—among other things

---

[1] The first few days of January, 1970.

—the harmony of the Precessional rhythm. The pillars stand as spherical sentinels before the walls. When the Sun goes down lights are to be projected from the pillars onto a reflector in the central shaft to form a single ray that descends to the globe—so that the ray will be constant, day and night. Thus they become reflectors of the solar light, just as the Moon serves to reflect the light of the Sun; and their function comes forth at nighttime, the period of the day considered the 'reign of the Moon'.

It is the day, however, that harmonises all the elements involved in the play —or, we can say, the day is the time-field within which and by which all the rhythms find their place. Just as in the Chamber it is finally the floor dimension that upholds the rest, from which all the rest comes forth. By the ratio of one metre equalling 24 days, the floor diameter is seen to 'contain' 18 months. That is, the floor space of 24 metres would give us 576 days, or 18 months completed. The central shaft is 12 months, and the pillars should be the height of 8.80 cm., which would be six months completed. In all, therefore, 36 months are contained in space/time within the Matrimandir's inner chamber. And we see that the bodies involved which produce this harmony are Sun, Moon and Earth, that all together can be said to form 'the core of Saturn'. We shall presently see how the outer sphere of the Temple gives us the 'outer crust' of Saturn, and in its own way captures this same 36. 36 months, or 3 years, is the amount of time we have seen within the Gnostic Circle to be needed for the work on the subtle planes to be completed regarding the densification of finer matter, rendered suitable for Earth existence, as described on page 132, and the amount of 'time' from Saturn in the Gnostic Circle to the Sun-Pluto 0-9 Apex is 3 years.

In this manner, by the thorough study of the core of the Matrimandir, its most essential part, the student is initiated into *the geometry of Time*.[1]

The Outer Shape of the Temple

We come finally to a most beautiful aspect of the Matrimandir, which concerns its outer shape. It is thought by the architects to be the 'egg of Vishnu' (Sanskrit: *śālagrāma*) and was designed according to the dimensions of that form transmitted to us by Tantric tradition, which states that the creation, or matter, is contained in and has issued forth from this 'egg'. In fact it is from Vishnu's navel that the creation (Brahma) comes forth, once Vishnu has been aroused by the Gods from his sleep, or once the sleeping 'eye', the *I* of consciousness, has awakened —for creation is eternal, it is awareness that is lulled or heightened. In the Trinity

---

[1] The measurement of the height at 15.50 is incomplete. The necessary further addition is being thoroughly discussed in *The New Way*.

Vishnu corresponds to the aspect of Preservation and would be *Chit*, or Consciousness—hence it is an appropriate form as a basis for a temple of this Aquarian Age.

It is possible to show how this form has become a part of the Tantric tradition through the 9 Circle with the planets. In this diagram we can see that Saturn, India's planet and the essence of the Matrimandir, falls at the 6 point, the Cosmic Divine, or the very 'egg that contains the creation'. If one looks through a telescope at the planets, there is only one that corresponds with great precision to the dimensions of the Vishnu *śālagrāma* and consequently to the Matrimandir. It is Saturn, the only planet with such a dramatic flattening of the poles. Jupiter comes next in line,

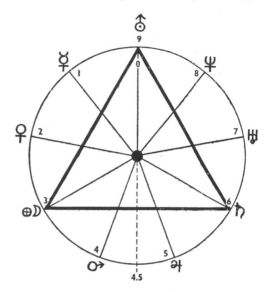

but Saturn's oblateness is even more accentuated and immediately gives the impression of the Temple itself. Moreover, 12 outer 'petals' have been added to encircle the Salagrama. The truth in the inspiration behind the outer petals is precisely *the rings of Saturn*, three in number. (This also recalls the Borobudur—the inner Point with three circles around it.) From a certain angle if one looks at the model of the Matrimandir one cannot help but be struck by this beautiful correspondence. In view of all that has so far been pointed out regarding the meaning of Saturn and India and the central globe and Time and the Cosmic Divine, it is hoped that the message trying to come through to Earth is clear and that this shall be allowed to take shape somehow with the minimum of alterations during its realisation. The three circles, or spirals, combined upon the 12 Circle divided into 4 major sections is what we have called the 'Map of the Evolution'. It is the diagram that has opened the mysterious gates of the Cosmos with respect to Earth progression[1]. It can be seen that this is the symbol of the Mother (page 293), given a dynamic aspect by adding to it the lever of Time in the adequate manner. Her symbol has the four inner petals and the 12 outer, which are all contained within three concentric circles; another version of the same 'Map'. Thus the rings of Saturn are essential to the deciphering of Time and the cosmic truth and the evolution of the Earth. So the

[1] Page 19.

design of the Matrimandir has this 'unknowing' seed behind it: the planet Saturn (the Vishnu Salagrama) with its outer rings that make it sometimes appear to be floating in the cosmic sea, only half visible, precisely like the Matrimandir. And the dimensions are, proportionately speaking, practically the same as the planet's.

Here are two views of Saturn taken from actual photographs of the planet. Its oblateness is more pronounced than that of any other body in the System. The rings are inclined 27° to the plane of Saturn's orbit and their total diameter is 171,000 miles. Because of its rings Saturn is naturally considered unique in the sky, and there are many correspondences between it and the System as a whole which do indeed make Saturn unique for us on this planet, correspondences which affect the Earth in particular. There is the fact, for example, that Saturn is the least dense of all the planets in the System, while Earth is the most dense. This lack of density, or the fact that Saturn would actually *float* if it were placed in a body of water large enough to contain it, is an extremely interesting characteristic; it is no doubt this factor that has something to do with the formation of the rings; in any case, we know that Saturn is lacking in density to such an extent that it would float in water, and the fact is that the existence of its rings truly makes it appear to us to be floating in the vast cosmic sea. We have seen how the actual body of the planet has given us some clues as to the progress of evolution within the scheme of time on Earth, and continuing in this investigation we find as well that Saturn's equatorial diameter which astronomy now places at about 76,000 miles is very close to the 77,760 years it takes for the Earth to complete one *Great Circle* according to our 'Map of the 12 Manifestations'. We shall see how this is also contained in the shape of the Matrimandir. Saturn's size is 9 times the Earth's.[1]

Another factor of interest to us is that Saturn in a certain way appears to be a synthesis of our Solar System—or better said, it is a representation of the *zodiac*, its meaning for the Earth and the reality of its existence, in terms both of development of consciousness and of physical expansion. Thus its rings merely present the Earth with a reproduction of the zodiac—and more particularly, with the *zodiacal light*—the band of 9° on either side of the ecliptic of the Sun, within which all the planets orbit.

As far as astrology is concerned, what are some of the significances of Saturn that would make it of such importance as to have an entire monument come forth under the light of its power?

Before all we must consider, as expressed in the diagrams on page 273, that the

[1] It is also interesting to note that the Earth's circumference is about 25,000 miles, which is very near to the 25,920 years Precessional movement of the Equinoxes, or one Round of the Map of the 12 Manifestations.

MODEL OF THE MATRIMANDIR

According to the Mother's original plan the entry into the Inner Chamber of the Temple is indicated as an ascent through the floor via 15 steps; these 15 correspond to Saturn's position in the Gnostic Circle (6). Moreover, the position of the opening shown in her plan falls at exactly what would correspond to between 0 to 15° Capricorn of the zodiacal circle, in perfect harmony therefore with the essence of the Chamber. The seeker enters into the Time-Spirit's sanctuary precisely at the angle of the Room that corresponds to his month, and in the zone of the Room—between walls and pillars—that belongs to the month count. The floor is the day count.

In the new plan, entry into the Chamber is to be by two doors that pierce the walls at different points.

Mother's manifestation corresponds to the 'position of Saturn' in the celestial harmony, and that she in fact conceived the *mandir* during Saturn's month. And then we must consider that Saturn rules Aquarius, therefore being as we are in this Aquarian Age, it is only logical that the construction synthesising the times should capture in some way the qualities of the Age's prime ruler. We speak of Uranus as the ruler of Aquarius today, but it must be understood that the co-rulers never entirely displace the planets that have basic affinity with the signs they rule—i.e., Jupiter and Pisces, Saturn and Aquarius, Saturn and Capricorn. The co-rulers, Neptune, Uranus and Pluto, merely serve to open a further passage; they give their assistance we can say in order that the sign, or the Age belonging to the particular sign, may be able to express itself fully and more perfectly. They are valves that open a passage of a higher order, or allow for a greater frequency to be experienced of the sign's potential energy because of their assistance. It can be stated, moreover, that Saturn is doubly important in this case because it not only rules Aquarius but it is the ruler of Capricorn as well, the Age for which we are now preparing, for in the last analysis it is the Age of Cardinal (Creation) force, the time of Brahma of any of the 12 Manifestations, that is the period of *culmination*. The Cardinal signs are the fruits of the labour of the previous Mutable and Fixed signs. The Mutable, which in the case of this Manifestation was the Age of Pisces, must serve as the force that breaks down the achievements of the last Manifestation, so that the new can take shape. It is usually a period of 'death', in a sense, a time when Shiva's force is felt in his aspect of *dissolution*—for the Mutable signs do indeed correspond to Shiva and the *guna* of Destruction. This is factually demonstrated by Genghis Khan who appeared under this name in 1206[1], somewhat a representative of Shiva's power of destruction. He arose in fact together with the last decanate of Pisces, when the full guna of Destruction came into being. Through this figure and his descendents a vast empire grew and served, among other things, to throw India wide open to the onslaught and entry of forces and influences of many different types. It was India's full period of 'sleep', from which she only awakened at the dawn of the Aquarian Age. It is now that the awakened soul of India is to fulfill its destiny of *unifier*, in this 'Age of Unity', and for this reason Genghis Khan's destructive force was necessary to break down any barriers she might have felt inclined to construct around herself—as was the case in Tibet. Thus India was forced to give shelter to a host of influences she would ordinarily have chosen to remain closed to, culminating finally with the English rule that brought Europe into her lap, with all that that has signified, which terminated the guna of Dissolution, ending the reign of *Tamas* over the land. The Mogul holocaust is the best proof

---

[1] 1206 (9) was a year of Pluto, Shiva's counterpart—but it was a 'clouded', as yet invisible Pluto, manifesting only its aspect of destruction instead of transformation.

of the degeneration in the Indian spiritual power—that allowed such an occurrence—which must now surge through the nation once more in this present Age.

After Mutable the sign of Preservation follows which in this present era is the Fixed sign Aquarius, and the new reality of the times comes forth, the new is firmly established when the Vishnu *avatars* come to reveal the phase human evolution is entering and the work that is to be done. These are our times—today. And we are in turn preparing for the culmination of the Age of Capricorn.

Since the Middle Ages Saturn has been considered a 'malefic' planet. In fact, it is the most benefic of all planets—in the deeper sense we can say it is *the only true benefic*, for it irrevocably and implacably brings man to the knowledge of himself, the Cosmos and God. It does not release man until he is *aware*, until he has gained full and authentic self-consciousness. Man is forever bound by the wheel of Time—Saturn's crushing power—until he has transcended that Wheel, which can only come about by God-realisation, of whatever order we wish to call it, of whatever school, system or cult. This is Saturn's work. He is negative, as Time is a binding force until liberation from the Ignorance comes; then the individual knows an entirely different aspect of Saturn, as well as a new and revolutionary vision and experience of Time. He is then prepared for the experience of unity of Time, or what we have called: *simultaneous time.*

For those who are not aware of the Mother's exact connection with the *cosmic divine*, the 6 point as expressed in the solar system by Saturn or, for that matter, of Sri Aurobindo's connection with Sun-Pluto, the 9 point and orbit in the System— the rooting in the Earth of a monument which speaks to us of this planet's place in the scheme and its essential meaning and importance for the Earth can have no value. But finally another point to be stressed is that: Saturn is to the Moon what the Sun is to Earth. Thus Saturn and the Sun are equal as far as Earth evolution is concerned—that is, they both combine efforts to keep the movement on its proper course, Saturn by 'being in time' with the Moon, and the Sun by 'being in time' with Earth.

We come now to the aspect of the full dimensions of the outer shape of the sphere. The diameter is 36 metres, and here the student can verify that in the entire form of the Matrimandir the number of the signs of any Great Circle is contained: 36, the magical 3×12 or 4×9, both of which constitute our 'key to Time', as the Great Circle of 77,760 years is contained in the very body of the planet itself.

The polar or axial diameter (height) of the sphere is one of the most important of all the measurements because in terms of numbers it captures the sidereal revolution of Saturn—that is, the polar diameter, 29.40 metres, is the time in *years* that it takes Saturn to orbit the Sun (29.46). Thus the central inner shaft where the Sun's ray is to fall, measuring 15.20, is the translation of the Earth's solar year, or the time it takes the Earth to orbit the Sun, and the height of the entire build-ing gives us the same movement measurement for Saturn. However, not only of Saturn, for this number 29.40 is also the synodic period of the Moon. That is, in this amount of time (in days) the Moon returns to the same point with respect to the Earth and the Sun. Therefore the Matrimandir reveals in its axial diameter and central shaft that Saturn is to the Moon what the Sun is to Earth. We see through this that Saturn is in effect the crystallisation of the psychic being for Earth evolution, just as the Earth is the point whereupon the spirit (Sun) is allowed to manifest in the solar system. And we see once again that: one day equals one year.

Conclusion

What do these dimensions signify regarding the experience of the seeker within the Matrimandir? This would be a work for the future though much has been put forth in this synthesis that is related to the 'experience of the Matrimandir'. To summarise and conclude, however, we may discuss once more the relevance of Time as well as the significance of Saturn in cosmic studies.

Regarding the Matrimandir, regarding the work from 'below' and from 'above', the stress has been on Time and this has revealed itself to be a prime factor in the Supramental Yoga. This stands to reason because any yoga which seeks to alter the state of matter must perforce find the key to the process in Time. Most disciplines of *hathayoga*, which control and radically change certain physical functions, do so by means not only of *āsana* (exercises and postures) but primarily by *prāṇāyāma* or 'breath control'. This is because ultimately it is breath that regulates the 'time' of the body in its cells and molecules and finer substances—at least on this plane of manifestation. *Breath is to the body what time is to the Cosmos; breath is the power of time in the body.* By means of breath and the manner in which it is regulated, the physical of a human being can be altered. But these yogas of the past did not envisage a process of total transformation, whereby the cells themselves would become transformed, or whereby the cells would be made to 'awaken' let us say to a new light, a new rhythm, *a new time.* They aimed at *control* not transformation. The same as the Egyptians who aimed at *preservation* and not transformation,—at least the Egyptians of historic times. In this light it can be understood that suspen-sion of breath in certain yogic practises would apparently take the sadhak 'beyond time', or out of the dense material manifestation, and would ultimately produce his withdrawal from the body and the mergence of his consciousness into the 'Void'. The realisation of today implies rather a *harmonisation of breath* instead of its sus-pension, the reverse process as well as the opposite realisation.

From her *Notes on the Way* we know that in the Mother's experiences breath was considered by her an important factor in the yoga of transformation. But in what manner is breath to be used for such a transformation?

It is necessary to stress that whatever the process it is imperative to have the key to, or work in harmony with, Time, and with this power the work can be accomplished. Science knows that in Time lies the real key to work on energy—its comprehension, its manipulation, its alteration; only Science uses material means for material ends. The Supramental Yoga uses spiritual force, or the force of Consciousness, to achieve its purposes, because it is evident that in order to bring about a radical transformation of the human species it is this direct power that must be brought to bear pressure on the denser material creation; and this 'power' can awaken the particle of itself, the *light* as it is referred to, which is hidden in matter. Thus this would be the union of Heaven and Earth—but an apparent union and no more, because essentially the polarity lies only in our manner of perception. By breaking through the dimensions of consciousness one ultimately reaches the point of perceiving this oneness, that there is only one energy and the means to discover this point of unity is by breaking the barriers of Time, a process which is done by an increasing expansion and contraction of consciousness—or rather a simultaneous experience of what may appear to be two opposite and contradictory experiences.

For all this Time is the mysterious factor, and the way. But it is also the obstacle, just as Saturn in an individual's life is the restrainer and the limitation until, through unity of being and crystallisation of the soul-power, it becomes the Ally.

Sri Aurobindo ended his *Synthesis of Yoga* with the chapter, 'Towards the Supramental Time Vision'. We know that the work is incomplete and that he intended to continue. It is interesting nonetheless that the formulation of his Yoga reached that point, and it is also known that with Sri Aurobindo's work things are cared for with a detailed exactitude and precise vision. The Mother has written to a disciple: 'For Sri Aurobindo "coincidences" do not exist. All that happens is the result of the action of the Divine Consciousness. The Force which is at work at this moment is a Force of harmony, that makes for unity, —the unification of all the symbols that express the Divine Truth.' (This was in answer to a sadhak's inquiry about the 'coincidence' of the August 15 Assumption of the Virgin Mary of the Catholics—a feast which Sri Aurobindo explained to be esoterically connected with the divinisation of matter—and his birthday.)

The Synthesis indeed would have ended there because this appears to be the bridge that must now be crossed. In fact, when Sri Aurobindo left his body the exact time—1:26 AM of 5 December, 1950—placed Saturn *exactly on the Ascendant.* Had his passing occurred a few minutes earlier or later this would not have happened and it is known that his only concern in those last hours was 'what time is it?' He would come out of his so-called 'coma' only to ask this. Moreover, Saturn as explained is at 15° of Capricorn in his natal horoscope, the very peak of the Golden Age sign and the position which reveals the third phase of the supramental manifestation. When the Sun reaches this degree the Earth is at its perihelion.

The cells, or any particle for that matter, vibrate at a certain rate which determines their density. The subtle physical 'cell', which would be the finer specimen of the Earth cell (or a particle of more revolutionary features, perhaps of the order of the 'new particle' that Science has recently observed),[1] vibrates at a quicker rate which renders it invisible to us and approachable only by entering into the dimensions of consciousness in time which will heighten our perception and vision, accelerate our vibrations, so to speak. With the subtle cell a deceleration must occur in order for the particle to become visible in the Earth's dimensions, and this entails as well a breaking of the barriers in the reverse order. In one case it is the acceleration, in the other the deceleration—but the two processes can join, and their union, from below and from above, must ultimately constitute the new Matter.

The beauty of the working of the Force today and its harmonies is that they are imposed neither by the Supreme nor by man, no matter how divinely he be inspired, nor how high his realisation. We can see that along the way in this creation, the Matrimandir has been a unique occurrence: the Supreme has planted the seed from above (through the vehicle of the Mother) and the extent of receptivity of awaiting humanity has been the measure to decide what could and would be accomplished. There has been no rigid power forcing its subjects to follow its dictates, or even to move along in unconsciousness. There has been no secret process, no knowledge that is hidden from the masses and is not within the grasp of the whole of humanity. The Supreme has shown us in these first years of the Matrimandir's existence just in what condition the collective humanity is, the human race in general. We are faced with the fact that a beautiful jewel, a veritable Cosmic Timepiece, in harmony with the most sublime cosmic rhythms, can now take shape, without the population really understandi· as yet what it is they are giving rise to. It is done in this way so that the Matrimandir can be *a living image* of the Age, so that it can capture in its body the level of receptivity of the human race.

It is only logical that it be so, for the Temple is a monument to evolution, to man. There are some points which may fail, and they show us the truth of our times: they represent the imperfections of man and his resistances. When one first looks into the matter, one is struck by these facts: in our hearts we feel that the structure must be exact—in all ways it must be a perfection. But then, plunging deeper into the work and its significance for the Earth, we realise that the perfection

---

[1] November 11, 1974.

of the Matrimandir is perhaps greater than this, for it shows us the truth of what is, at this instant, as it is today. This is the perfection, for Perfection is a continuous growth and a constant reflection of what is, the beauty of each moment being fully and sincerely itself. Truth is that which speaks to us of this reality, as it is in Matter, but the deepest essence of this reality—and that can never be or pretend to be other than what it is. Falsehood can pretend, imitate, masquerade itself, but Truth must always be merely itself, with all sides—the deep abyss, the dark night, as well as the sublime heights, the Everlasting Day.

So the perfection of the Matrimandir—the 'Sanctuary of Truth' as it was once called—we can say lies in perhaps its perfection and its imperfection. Just as the Earth, Saturn, Jupiter and even the Sun are perfect yet they are not geometrically perfect bodies. None of them is a perfect sphere, yet together they all contribute to give us *the harmony of the spheres*: the evolution on Earth is what it is because each of these heavenly bodies is perfectly and fully itself.

There are a few bodies in the heavens with nearly perfect orbits: the third in perfection is the Earth, the second is Neptune, and the first is Venus, an orb with a quasi-perfectly circular orbit around the Sun: Venus, the morning star, the star of the coming race,

> 'I saw the Omnipotent's flaming pioneers
> Over the heavenly verge which turns towards life
> Come crowding down the amber stairs of birth;
> Forerunners of a divine multitude
> Out of the paths of *the morning star* they came[1]
> Into the little room of mortal life.
> I saw them cross the twilight of an age,
> The sun-eyed children of a marvellous dawn,
> The great creators with wide brows of calm,
> The massive barrier-breakers of the world
> And wrestlers with destiny in her lists of will,
> The labourers in the quarries of the gods,
> The messengers of the Incommunicable,
> The architects of Immortality.[2]

Yet Venus is cloaked in dense clouds and mists and man has not been allowed to see her perfection, because the perfect Perfection is not yet ours, that Perfect Sphere.

The Divine has given humanity the Matrimandir: man has taken it and builds it according to his capacity; he is translating the temple of God into the temple for

[1] Italics, PNB.
[2] *Savitri*, Book III, Canto 4.

Man, and in the process he is revealing the deepest part of himself. This is the truth of Initiation,—*to know oneself*. This is the initiation of all the great temples, and of the Matrimandir; the very building of it reveals to man an intimate part of what he is.

We have seen that a monument has been given to humanity which speaks of the highest cosmic truth. It has been given through instruments who were unaware of the true meaning of the work, of the exactitude of the structure that was planned with respect to the Cosmos, Nature and Man. We have seen that it has been possible to work in this way because not only has man become universally more receptive, but the Divine herself has descended upon Earth and has pierced by this descent the veils of ignorance that cloak the planet. Not only has the opening occurred below and the aspiration echoed to the heavens rendering possible the Descent, but the Supreme Mother herself has bent down over and onto the Earth, and the marriage of heaven and earth has taken place. The Book of Revelation speaks of the New Jerusalem, a city built on the plan of 12, the new heaven and the new earth. Where is this city? It is on the 12th latitude and the centre is named *Peace*, which is the meaning of *Jerusalem*—and in that centre called Peace a temple of the Age is being built. It is constructed in the soul of India, the soul of the Earth, the soul of man. When the soul is revealed the knowledge comes, for it is contained therein.

Finally this knowledge is given forth out of love, a passionate and intense love for this Body of the Supreme that is the Cosmos, this Cosmos that is veritably the Truth, and it is love for this Truth that will be victorious.

Of the sincere seeker's compelling attachment to Truth, Ramakrishna says,

"...If man clings tenaciously to truth he ultimately realises God. Without this regard for truth one gradually loses everything.... After my vision of the Divine Mother, I prayed to Her, taking a flower in my hand: 'Mother, here is Thy knowledge and here is Thy ignorance. Take them both and give me only pure love. Here is Thy holiness and here is Thy unholiness. Take them both, Mother, and give me pure love. Here is Thy good and here is Thy evil. Take them both, Mother, and give me pure love. Here is Thy righteousness and here is Thy unrighteousness. Take them both, Mother, and give me pure love.' I mentioned all these, but I could not say: 'Mother, here is Thy truth and here is Thy falsehood. Take them both.' I gave up everything at Her feet but could not bring myself to give up Truth."

Pondicherry,
September/December, 1974

Index

action-in-non-action (see also Tamas), 55, 69.
Adam, 46, 76fn., 226.
Aeneas, 269fn.
Aeon, 166, 167, 296.
Agni, 148.
Air (element), 15, 44, 63, 71, 143, 146, 228, 229.
Akashic Records, the, 222-23.
America, 70, 181-88, 197, 199, 269, 270.
Amerigo Vespucci, 269.
Ananda (see also Bliss), 82, 87, 97, 162.
Aphrodite, 269fn.
Aquarian Age, 8, 51, 52, 74, 83, 86-102, 105, 113,
      136, 155, 198, 245, 265, 276, 278, 290, 303.
Aquarius, 7, 8, 35, 36, 37, 42, 52, 64, 70-74,
      88, 95, 97, 99, 142, 154, 229, 250, 275,
      278, 279, 287, 303, 304.
Aries, 15, 16, 43, 63, 67, 76fn., 163, 165, 170-71,
      174, 215, 217, 223, 225, 226, 227, 257, 287.
Arjuna, 38.
art, 255.
Art and Architecture of India, 287fn.
asana, 305.
ascendent, 306.
Ashram (the Sri Aurobindo), 291.
Assumption, the, 306.
Asteroid Belt, the (see also 4.5 Orbit), 118, 150,
      175, 218, 219, 221, 227.
astrolabe, 18.
astrology, 4, 5, 12, 15, 43, 84, 143, 164, 207, 209,
      247, 256;
      purpose of, 3-11;
      in India, 4-5, 164.
astronauts, the, 10.
Asuras, the (see also Falsehood, forces of), 52, 53,
      54, 111-13.
Atlantis, 20, 24, 27, 29, 30, 32.
Atomic Age, the, 119, 230.
Augustus Caesar, 269.
Auroville, 190-94, 199, 242, 265, 266, 269, 270,
      273, 274, 280, 282, 283, 295.
Avatars (see also Incarnations), 33-41, 42, 47-48,
      49, 50, 54fn., 60, 66, 68, 81, 83, 84, 85, 91,
      101, 109, 110, 115-16, 123, 125, 143, 159, 304.
Aztecs, the, 165.

Balarama, 39-40.
Bali, 34, 37.
beast, the, 54.
Being (see also Sat), 8, 72, 94, 162, 186, 206.
Bhagavad Gita, the, 38, 64fn.
Bhakti Yoga, 97.
Bible, the, 226.
binary planets, the, 119.
bindu, the (see also Centre), 10.
birth (see also childbirth), 23, 40-41, 44, 54-55,
      56, 110, 113, 134, 135-36, 148, 160, 173, 185,
      214, 223, 227, 229, 230, 231, 261;
      of the individual being, 214, 234.
Bliss (see also Ananda), 82, 87, 161-62.
body, the (see also physical nature), 10-11, 16, 70,
      71, 72, 87, 88, 96, 97, 101-02, 120, 121, 122,
      124, 127-36, 149-50, 161-62, 196, 227, 241,
      243-46, 261-62.
Bön, 174.
Borobodur, 287-91, 299.
Brahma, 15, 53fn., 56, 68, 298.
Brahman, 67, 82, 108, 110, 111, 138, 141, 162,
      197, 258.
breath, 128, 131, 251, 305.
Brindavan, 38.
Buddha, the, 48, 84, 174, 175, 176, 178, 288, 290.
Buddhism, -ist, 4, 5, 249-50, 282;
      Tibetan, 173-80.
bull, 38, 52, 53.

Cabbalistic reduction, see theosophical addition.
calendar, the, 105, 139, 141, 152, 153, 164-69,
      250-51, 273, 287, 297;
      Gregorian reform, 166, 169, 170;
      Julian, the, 169.
calendar stone, 165.
Calvin, John, 35.
Cancer, 15, 17, 32, 75, 78, 88, 89, 90, 120, 125,
      136, 181, 217, 222, 223, 226, 227, 228, 229,
      246, 257, 259;
      Tropic of, 274.
cancer, 89, 259-60.
Cancerian Age, 29, 32, 33, 89.
Capricorn, 8, 15, 16, 17, 46, 47, 56, 60, 61, 68-69,

77, 97, 114-15, 123, 134, 143, 181, 187, 197, 198, 223, 224, 229, 241, 243, 247, 249, 253, 255, 266, 279, 280, 283, 295, 296, 297, 307.

Capricornian Age, 8, 29, 32, 61, 154, 304.

Cardinal energy flow (see also Creation), 14, 16, 54, 55, 68, 78, 100, 101, 228, 229, 303.

cardinal points, the, 14, 15, 16, 32, 33, 43, 223, 226, 239, 257.

cardinal signs, the, 37, 54, 55, 100, 228, 229.

Carter, Jimmy, 199.

castes, of India, 17.

Catholic Church, Roman, 81, 291.

Cayce, Edgar, 29, 166.

cell(s), the, 10, 14, 15, 88-90, 101-02, 105, 119, 120, 125, 126, 127, 128, 130, 133, 162, 217, 227, 307.

Centre, the (see also bindu), 10, 78, 160-62, 205, 252, 257, 258, 265, 266, 294.

centers (see also Chakras), 142, 145, 146, 147, 149, 150, 154.

Chaitanya, 35.

Chakras, the (see also centers), 33, 128, 133, 135, 146, 149.

Chamber, the Inner, 284-98.

Chandi, the, 53, 68.

Child, the, 23, 27, 41, 56, 60, 85, 111, 127, 148, 162, 224, 256, 260, 261.

childbirth (see also birth), 88-89.

Chinese, the, 177, 179.

Chit (see also Consciousness-Force), 8, 162, 265, 299.

Christ, the, see Jesus.

Christianity, 73, 76-77, 78, 79, 80, 82, 269.

Christus, the, 98.

Circle, the, 8, 10, 11, 12, 13, 16, 108, 110, 126, 159, 163, 164, 205, 284, 293;
    divisions of, 164;
    Great(er), 18-31, 43, 47, 300.

Columbus, Christopher, 181, 270.

comet (of 1973-74), 56.

Consciousness-Force (see also Chit), 4, 10, 186, 188, 266, 306.

contraction, 205, 206, 221, 222, 257, 306.

Corinthians I, 76-77.

Cosmic (Universal) Divine, the, 5, 18, 27, 51, 220, 232, 252, 266, 304.

cosmic harmonies, 4, 11, 12, 207, 256.

cosmic midday, 249.

cosmic sunset, 90.

Creation (see also gunas, Rajas), 14, 15, 16, 17,

40, 51-52, 53, 54, 55, 101, 163, 205, 206, 208, 225, 226, 229, 232, 255, 256.

Crete, see Greece.

Cronos, 12, 112.

Cross, the, 14, 18.

Crusades, the, 78.

Dalai Lama, the, 173-80, 199.

Dark Ages, the, 46, 63, 78, 281, 304.

Dean, John, 183.

Death, 44, 45, 54, 55, 56, 57, 59, 60, 76-77, 78, 80, 90, 97, 98, 102, 113, 114-15, 128-30, 131, 133, 145, 184-85, 193, 194, 199, 214, 224, 225, 231, 238, 239, 241, 243, 259, 260, 261, 280, 282, 283, 297.

decanantes, 75, 76, 78, 90, 164, 170, 171, 286.

Demeter, 22, 119, 134, 148, 166, 167, 217.

destiny, 256, 286.

Destruction (see also gunas, Tamas), 14, 20, 29-30, 52, 56, 78, 100, 101, 130-31, 147, 249, 303-04.

Devaki, 39.

Devas, 111, 112.

Dharma, 34, 48.

Divine, the (see also Mother, Father, Child, Supreme, Brahman, Trinity, Transcendent, Cosmic, Individual, Love), 16, 18, 22, 27, 33, 39, 46, 50, 60, 73, 86, 99, 111, 114, 116, 118, 123, 159, 171, 198, 208, 220, 221, 238, 259, 262, 265, 306, 308, 309.

Divinisation, 69, 73, 74, 100, 102, 110, 127-36, 140, 144, 148, 163, 169, 189, 229, 270, 306.

Dot (Point), 12, 110, 126, 293.

dreams, 96.

drugs, 236.

Durga, 22, 39, 52, 53, 54, 61, 69, 83, 149, 199, 235, 269, 277, 280, 294.

dwadaśaṁśa, 164, 171.

Dwapara Yuga, 61-68.

eagle, 269.

Earth (element), 15, 44, 63, 223, 225, 228, 229, 257, 260.

Eden, Garden of, 226.

ego, the, 7, 20, 59, 70, 89, 96, 97, 120, 126, 140, 144, 148, 216, 228, 236-37, 242, 243, 256, 282-83.

Egypt, 65, 89, 196, 240, 244-46, 267, 268, 271, 291, 305.

Eighth Manifestation, the, 39-41, 48, 66, 99, 111, 112, 200, 226, 231, 245.

Einstein, Albert, 188.

elements, the four, 15, 44, 75, 229.

Eleusis, Eleusinian Mysteries, 167, 268-69, 283, 291, 293.

Elysium, 65, 148.

emotional nature, the, see Vital nature.

energy, -ies (see also solar power), 3, 15, 110, 119, 127, 128, 129, 130, 135, 141, 162, 163, 188, 189, 197, 206, 217, 225, 243, 260, 306.

energy flows (see also gunas, Cardinal, Fixed, Mutable), 14, 75-76, 215, 228, 229, 286.

English language, the, 198.

Enneagram, the, 123-36, 137, 271.

Epiphany, the, 167-68.

epopteia, 268.

equinoxes, the (see also Precession), 16fn., 22, 155, 165, 287.

Essenes, the, 80.

Eternal, the, Eternity, 45, 123, 162, 194, 205, 243.

Ether, 188.

Eve, 46, 226.

even number, the, 161, 257.

Evolutionary Axis, the, 161, 181, 279-80.

expansion, 47, 70, 71, 72, 79, 205-06, 207, 221, 230, 257, 306.

Fall, the, 226, 227, 280.

Falsehood, forces of (see also Asura), 89, 97, 131, 140, 190-91, 194, 235, 249, 308.

Father, the, 27, 41, 53, 127.

feminine force, the, 161.

Festival of Light, the (see also Epiphany), 15, 17, 166, 295, 296.

Finger of God, see Yod.

Fire (element), 15, 44, 63, 76fn., 163, 225, 226, 228, 229, 256, 257.

fish, 56.

Five, 163, 165, 168, 169, 175-76, 177, 178, 249, 250-51, 252.

Fixed energy flow (see also Preservation), 14, 16, 54, 55, 68, 83, 195, 228, 229.

Fixed signs, the, 37, 48, 52, 54, 55, 228, 229, 278, 304.

Flood, the Great, 32, 89, 267.

Ford, Gerald, 184.

Forty-second latitude, 269, 270.

Four, fourth, 63, 69, 109, 110, 168, 169, 174, 175, 176, 177, 178, 215, 217, 218, 223, 252, 257, 271, 273, 288, 289.

4.5 Orbit, 118, 150, 151, 169, 177, 219, 220, 221, 249.

Fourth Way, The, 124fn.

freedom, 114.

galaxy, the Milky Way, 9, 18, 22, 122, 160, 161, 162, 276.

Galileo, Galilei, 262.

Gautama, the Buddha, 84.

Gemini, 67, 174, 225, 226, 228, 255.

Germany, 53.

globe, the, see Sphere.

Gnosis, 98, 101, 196, 214, 292.

gnostic being(s), 16, 17, 40, 55, 59, 63, 97, 98, 101, 113, 117, 118, 125, 131, 134, 135, 196, 224, 241, 291.

Gnostic Circle, the, 13, 43, 120, 131, 159-72, 173, 186, 189, 198, 207, 208, 209, 216, 224, 256, 257, 297.

gnostic societies, 4, 196, 243, 250, 282.

goat, 56.

God, see Divine.

Goddess, the, see Mother.

Golden Age, the (see also Satya Yuga), 115, 151, 154, 307.

good and evil, 46, 194, 198, 207, 226.

Gopis, the, 38.

Greece, 65, 267, 268-69, 271, 278, 291.

Greeks, the, 43.

gunas, the (see also Sattwa, Rajas, Tamas), 54-61, 68, 162, 163, 193, 215, 286.

Guhaka, 34.

Gurdjieff, G.I., 123, 124, 125.

Hades, 119.

Hanuman, 34.

harmony, harmonies, cosmic, 3-11, 66, 73, 80, 90, 105, 108, 117, 118, 125, 126, 138, 139, 140, 141, 152, 154, 155, 172, 191, 207, 209, 232, 252-53, 260, 267, 281, 292, 306, 308.

heart-beat, the solar, 248.

Hercules (constellation), 160, 276.

Hermetic (thought), 195.

hexagram (see also Seal of Solomon), 138.

Himalayas, the, 68.

Hinduism, 5, 49, 50, 61, 81, 82-83, 84, 148, 195.

Hitler, Adolf, 53-54.

horoscope, 24, 43, 256, 280, 297.

Ideals, the Ideal, 6-8, 13, 199.

Ignorance, 5, 7, 17, 20-22, 67, 73, 78, 87, 89, 96, 97, 113, 117, 120, 123, 132, 140, 141, 190-91,

194, 207, 208, 259, 261.
illusion, 17, 59, 62-63, 66, 80, 113, 114, 141, 225.
Immortality, 59, 101, 102, 113, 128, 133, 147, 224, 238, 247.
Incarnations (see also Avatars), 27, 33, 34, 40, 60, 66, 84, 101, 109, 115-16, 147, 251-52, 271, 273.
India, Indians (see also Hinduism), 4, 5, 49, 55, 60, 65, 68-69, 99, 181-88, 197-99, 268fn., 269, 294-95, 297, 303, 309;
    music in, 252-53.
Individual Divine, the, 5, 27-28, 51, 53, 220, 224, 234, 244.
Indra, 40.
inertia, 4, 5, 55.
Initiation(s), 59, 98, 214, 239, 240, 241, 242-43, 245, 247, 249, 268, 309.
Inquisition, the, 78.
In Search of the Miraculous, 124fn.
Integral Yoga, see Yoga.
Io, 218fn.
Ishwarakoti, 250.
Isis, 22.
Islam, 74, 78, 79.
Italy, 181, 269, 270, 274fn., 294, 295.

Jatayu, 34.
Java, 287, 289.
Jerusalem, 309.
Jesus Christ, 35, 73, 74, 76-77, 80, 82, 115, 166, 167, 189, 190, 193, 248, 269.
Jivakoti, 250.
Jnana Yoga, 97.
Johnson, Lyndon, 184.
Judaism, 79, 80.
Jupiter, 42, 79, 80, 151, 168, 169, 177, 179, 218, 219, 220, 221, 249, 280.

Kāla, 12, 46, 61, 111-18.
Kali, 12, 46, 61-62, 63, 112, 113, 116.
Kaliyuga, 61-69, 109, 196.
Kalki, 49, 50, 65, 66, 82, 85, 195.
Kansa, 39.
Karma, 53, 213.
Karma Yoga, 97.
Kartikeya, 133.
Kennedy, John F., 183, 184.
Ketu, see Nodes, Lunar.
Khan, Genghis, 303.
King's Chamber, 239-41, 246.

Kore (see also Persephone), 119, 134, 148, 162, 166, 167, 268, 269, 283.
Krishna, 34, 35, 36, 37-40, 47-48, 50, 61, 63, 64fn., 66, 82, 85, 233.
kumāri, 269.
Kundalini, 95, 146.
Kurukshetra, 38.

Lakshmi, 53fn.
language, 66, 94.
Law of Seven, see Seven.
Law of Three, see Three.
leap year day, 168, 273.
Leboyer, Frederick, 89.
Letters on Yoga, 34, 238fn., 250fn.
Lemuria, -an, 5, 20.
Leo, 37, 42, 50, 53, 56, 63, 64, 65, 83, 84, 89, 143, 182, 227, 228, 229, 248, 255, 278, 279.
Leo, Age of, 36, 196, 240, 244, 245, 278.
Leonardo Da Vinci, 11, 269, 270.
Libra, 15, 36, 90, 95, 177fn., 178, 228, 229, 249, 255, 257.
Life, 60, 88, 133, 199, 226, 228, 229, 259, 292.
Life Divine, The (Sri Aurobindo), 283.
Līlā, 82.
Line, the, 63, 110.
lion, 52, 64, 245, 278.
Love, Divine, 39, 57, 82, 144, 145, 154, 163, 23., 255-56, 270, 309.
Loyola, Ignatius, 35.
Lunar Nodes, see Nodes, Lunar.

Magi, the, 167.
Magical Carousel, The, 189fn., 215, 249fn.
Mahabharata, The, 64fn.
Mahakali, 53fn.
Mahalakshmi, 53fn.
Mahasaraswati, 53fn.
Mahdi, the, 74.
Maheshwari, 53fn.
Maitreya, 39, 74, 178.
Mamallapuram, 38.
man, 64, 162, 245, 278.
manifestation, manifest(ed) Divinity, 5, 15, 16-1, 47, 66, 67, 96, 110, 114, 116, 117, 160, 18, 208, 281, 290.
Manifestations, the (12), 18, 22, 27, 28, 32-41, 4, 50, 54, 62, 68, 71, 76, 100, 124, 163, 248.
Markandeya Purana, the, 39, 53.
Mars, 38-39, 133-34, 144, 145, 146, 152, 15,

168, 217, 218, 219, 221, 255.
Mary (see also Virgin), 167.
Matrimandir, the, 242, 265-309.
Matter, 3, 11, 14, 15, 43, 46, 65, 67, 69, 72, 88, 94, 101, 102, 110, 111, 119, 120, 122, 127-36, 148, 181, 186, 188, 189, 196, 197, 199, 226, 228, 229, 243-46, 266, 270.
Maya, 17, 68.
Mayans, the, 165.
Mayavada, -ist, 4, 282.
Measure of Unity, the (see also Radius of Sun), 62, 247.
Mercury, 141, 142, 151, 152, 154, 174, 206, 255.
Messiah, the, 74.
meteroion, 268.
Middle Ages, the, see Dark Ages.
Milky Way, the, see galaxy.
Mind, mental being, 15, 27, 31, 43, 44, 46, 67, 72, 73, 93, 96, 141-43, 225, 226, 228, 229, 236, 255.
Moon, the (see also Lunar), 9, 22, 119, 144, 148, 251, 286, 287, 297, 298, 304, 305.
Mother, the (see also Shakti, Supreme), 4, 10, 12, 41, 46, 50, 51, 52, 53, 56, 77, 94, 98, 99, 102, 108, 109, 110, 111, 116-17, 118, 119, 125, 127, 141, 145, 168, 172, 221, 224, 233, 235, 236, 243, 254, 256, 258, 260-62, 265, 266, 268, 270, 271, 273, 274, 275, 278, 282, 283, 284, 285, 286, 291, 292, 293, 294, 295, 296, 304, 306, 309;
    quotes from, 57-58, 91-92.
Mother India (nation), 68, 69.
motion, perpetual, 102, 107-08, 116-17, 160.
Mt. Meru, 39.
Mountain, as symbol, 294.
mūlādhāra, 146.
music, 252, 253.
music of the spheres, 252-53.
Mutable energy flow (see also Destruction), 14, 16, 44, 54, 55, 68, 100, 101, 228, 229, 303.
Mutable signs, the, 44, 228, 303.
My Land and My People, 173.

Name of God (see also Capricorn), 295.
nature, see Prakriti.
navamsas, the, 164, 170.
navel, the, 11, 128, 144, 148, 149.
Nazism, 53.
Neptune, 80, 137, 144-45, 146, 149-50, 151, 152, 153, 254.

Nine (see also Enneagram), 12, 13, 14, 44, 51, 63, 94, 105-11, 117, 118-20, 123, 124, 159, 169, 187, 223, 249, 284.
Ninth Manifestation, the, 22, 27, 28, 36, 40-41, 42-69, 70, 76, 84, 97, 122, 238, 290.
Nirvana (see also 4.5 Orbit), 49, 177fn., 249-50.
Nixon, Richard, M., 183, 184, 198.
Nodes, Lunar, the, 64fn., 110, 222, 223, 226, 272, 273, 295.
Notes on the Way, 94, 306.
nuclear power, 122, 126, 129, 147, 181, 185-86, 261.
number, its meaning and nature, 12, 105-08.

Oedipus, 63.
ojas, 128.
One, 154, 163, 249.
One, the, Oneness (see also Unity, Union), 4, 46, 47, 51, 62, 66, 67, 69, 114, 115, 150, 186, 188, 256, 288.
Ouspensky, P.D., 124fn., 125.
Overmind, the, 99, 112, 113.

pain, 87, 88.
Parasara, 39.
Parvati, 53.
Peacock, 133.
pentagram, the, 249.
perfection, 5, 65, 87, 113, 117, 139, 140-41, 151, 159, 169, 172, 260, 308;
    sphere of, 249.
perpetual motion, see motion, perpetual.
Persephone (see also Kore), 119, 148, 162, 166, 167, 217, 268, 269.
Pharaohs, 224.
philosophy, 43, 80, 82.
physical, the, physical nature (see also body, matter), 24, 28, 71-72, 87, 97, 210, 235.
Pioneer II, 71fn.
Pioneer 10, 218fn.
Piscean Age, 4, 48, 70, 75-85, 86, 100, 268fn., 270.
Pisces, 4, 50, 56, 57, 70, 75, 76fn., 82, 97, 114, 134, 184-85, 213, 270.
Pluto, 118, 119, 137, 146-50, 151, 152, 153, 154, 162, 185, 215, 256.
Point (see also Dot), 12, 110, 123, 126, 205, 206, 299.
Pondicherry, 233.
power, see Shakti.
Prakriti, 29, 30, 55, 89, 120, 125, 182, 208, 214, 216,

217, 241, 272.
Pralaya 101, 292.
pranayama, 305.
Precession of the Equinoxes, the, 17, 18, 22, 32, 51,
    63, 76fn., 100, 120, 154, 155, 161, 245, 250,
    275, 276, 287, 300fn.
Preservation (see also gunas, Sattwa), 14, 37, 48, 54,
    68, 75, 76, 83, 100, 101, 163, 195, 299, 304.
psychic, psychic being (see also Soul), 110, 115, 126,
    148, 151, 160, 217, 238.
purification, 6, 146, 149, 239.
Purusha, 50-51, 55, 56, 182, 216, 217, 227, 241, 272.
Pyramid, the Great, 24, 30, 32, 65, 66, 89, 196, 239-
    46, 267, 278, 292.

qualities, see energy flows.
Queen's Chamber, 239-41.
quincunx, 50.

radius, of Earth, 272.
Rahu, see Nodes, Lunar.
Rajas (see also gunas, Creation), 54, 56, 68.
rakshasa, 34-35, 37.
ram, 37.
Rama, 33-37, 38, 40, 50, 66, 85, 89.
Ramakrishna, 35, 82-83, 116, 117, 181-82, 233-34,
    250, 277, 309.
Ravana, 34.
Ray of Creation, 124, 126.
redeemer, 196.
religion (s), 49-50, 74, 78-79, 99-100, 112, 113, 177,
    179-80, 199-201, 259, 291-92.
Renaissance, the, 78, 269.
Ressurection, the, 76.
Revelation, Book of, 54, 278, 309.
Rig Veda, the, 62, 65fn.
ritual, 79.
Roman civilisation, 170.
Rome, 267, 269-70, 271, 274, 275, 277, 291, 294.

Sacrifice, the, 188-89, 190, 192, 193, 283.
Sagittarius, 42, 43, 44, 45, 47-48, 52, 70-74, 120,
    122, 189, 224, 226, 228, 238, 239, 247.
sahasradala-padma, 146.
Saros Cycle, the, 54fn., 64fn., 273, 295.
St. Anne, 167.
St. Francis, 35.
St. Paul, 76-77.
śālagrāma, 298, 299, 300.
Sat (see also Being), 8, 56, 110, 114, 123, 162, 247.

Sat-Chit-Ananda, 8, 16, 47, 162, 247, 254, 265, 270.
Sattwa, -wic (see also gunas, Preservation), 34, 35,
    36, 54, 55, 56, 68, 69, 76, 101.
Saturn, 12, 13, 18, 38, 46, 95, 111-18, 137, 151, 188-
    89, 213, 222, 230, 242, 251, 266, 295, 299, 300,
    303, 304, 305, 306, 307.
Satya Yuga, the, 29, 61-69, 84, 109, 114, 195, 233.
Satyavan, 45.
Saviour, the, 15, 77, 189.
Savitri (Sri Aurobindo), 45, 280, 297, 308.
science, scientists, 10, 43, 46, 61, 72-73, 78, 91, 93,
    94, 95, 121, 122, 197, 206, 221, 255, 269, 282,
    306.
Scorpio, 38, 66, 75, 76, 77, 83, 184-85, 224, 228,
    231, 238, 248, 269.
Seal of Solomon, the, 13, 137, 142.
seasons, the, 14-16.
secondary directions, 247.
seed, 50.
seeing, 6.
Serpent biting its Tail (see also Nodes, Lunar), 110
    119, 186, 290.
Seven, 138, 181, 183, 252, 271;
    Law of, 123.
Seventh Manifestation, the, 33-37, 38, 40, 267.
sex, sex centre (see also Vital nature), 11, 128, 129,
    132-34, 135, 136, 144-45, 146, 147, 149, 150,
Shakti (see also Mother), 4, 5, 51, 56, 66, 82, 94, 99,
    102, 108, 110, 111, 116, 124fn., 162, 186, 241
    242, 254, 258, 266.
shastras, 81.
Shiva, 30, 39, 53fn., 55, 56, 68, 148, 162, 185, 303-04,
Siddhi Day, 48, 52.
simultaneous time, 12, 46-47, 71, 114, 115, 121,
    247-58, 304.
Sita, 36.
Six, 13, 18, 51, 54, 108, 109, 119, 139, 163, 186, 188,
    190-94, 217, 220, 230, 260, 266.
Smith, Joseph, 35.
solar plexus, the, 144, 149, 154.
solar power, 141, 143, 146, 147, 150, 254, 256, 290,
soltices, the, 16, 29, 165, 295.
Soul, the (see also psychic), 109, 110, 119, 123, 126,
    127, 134, 159, 160, 161, 191, 216, 217, 220,
    234, 235-36, 237, 242, 243, 244, 261, 290, 294,
    295, 297, 303, 309.
space, 10, 62, 65, 71, 120-22, 126, 187, 205, 221, 222,
    223, 230, 257, 262, 284, 293, 295, 297;
    space travel, 120-22.
Sphere, the (globe), 11, 249, 279, 285, 286, 294,

295, 296, 297, 299, 308.
Sphinx, the; Egyptian, 30, 37, 48, 62, 64, 65, 66, 83, 89, 101, 196, 229, 245, 267, 278; of Thebes, 63.
Spiral, the, 18, 22, 23, 299.
spiritism, 80.
Square, the, 10, 11, 14, 63, 69, 109, 110, 271, 273, 295.
squaring of the circle, 273.
Sri Aurobindo, 5, 10, 36, 48, 50, 51, 52, 53, 54, 69, 125, 181-82, 189, 190, 194, 219, 232, 233, 234, 235, 267, 269, 271, 274, 277, 278, 283, 291, 292, 293, 294, 295, 296, 297, 304, 306; quotes from, 34-35, 238, 250.
Sri Chakra, 219.
Sugriva, 34.
Sun, the (see also solar), 8, 9, 10, 12, 13, 17, 28, 42, 51, 62, 64, 69, 84, 86, 105, 109, 114, 115, 118, 143, 162, 203, 235, 247-49, 250, 251, 252, 272, 274, 275, 276, 277, 285, 286, 290, 293.
Superman, the, 40, 98, 230.
Supermind, Supramental, 42, 47, 69, 113, 125, 140, 146, 229, 233, 238, 271, 273, 281, 306.
Supramental Manifestation, the, 54, 57, 168, 273.
Supreme, the, 7, 33, 69, 115, 123, 160, 161, 172, 205, 208, 221, 225, 256, 307, 309.
swastika, 53.
symbol, Sri Aurobindo's, 271, 292, 293, 294, 296.
symbol, the Mother's, 292, 293, 294.
symbols, symbolism, 8, 9-11, 12-13, 15-16, 33, 68, 69, 72, 110, 114, 187, 222, 271, 292, 293, 294, 295, 296, 299.
Symbols and the Question of Unity, 39, 51fn., 56, 235fn., 268.
synthesis, 95, 156, 159, 222, 272; of yogas, 97.
Synthesis of Yoga, the (Sri Aurobindo), 2, 104, 204, 264, 306.

Tamas (see also gunas, Destruction), 30, 54, 55, 56, 59, 68-69, 193, 303.
Tantras, Tantric (see also Buddhism), 5, 101, 146, 147, 219, 298-99.
tapas, 143.
Taurus, 38, 53, 67, 83, 225, 226, 228, 255, 269, 278.
Taurian Age, 37, 39, 61.
Teilhard de Chardin, Pierre, 77, 81, 194.
temple, see Matrimandir.
theosophical addition, 14fn., 105-06, 108, 152, 153, 293.

Third Person, Principle, the, 50, 93, 273.
Thirtieth Latitude, the, 267, 270.
Thirty-sixth Latitude, the, 268, 270, 295.
Three, 13, 51, 63, 108, 109, 119, 120, 123-24, 139, 159, 163, 215-16, 217, 220, 223, 237, 273; Law of, 109, 119, 123, 126.
Tibet, 173-80, 199-200, 224, 303.
Time (see also simultaneous time), 10, 12, 13, 18, 32, 35-36, 46-47, 59, 62, 63, 64, 66, 67, 68, 71-72, 88, 111-18, 121-22, 126, 130, 163, 164, 186-88, 205, 208, 221, 222, 223, 230, 257, 266, 272, 275, 276, 282, 284, 291, 295-98, 304, 305-07.
Transcendent Divine, the, 5, 27, 51, 66, 118, 218, 220, 232, 244, 254, 290.
transformation (see also Divinisation), 10, 44, 70, 72-74, 86, 89, 120, 122, 125, 127-36, 137, 147, 148, 154, 234-36, 238, 239-40, 243-46, 254, 262, 278, 305, 306.
Treta Yuga, 61-69.
Triangle, the, 13, 14, 63, 65, 109, 110, 119, 124, 127, 139, 148, 159, 160, 163, 169, 186, 193, 215, 219, 220, 222, 229, 234, 238, 241, 251, 256, 266, 271.
trident, 52, 53.
Trinity, Triad, the Divine, 5, 13, 28, 51, 67, 68, 109, 110, 119, 125, 146, 150, 163, 226, 227, 228, 229, 230, 232, 235, 238-39, 254, 256.
Trinity of Fire, 28.
triṁśāṁśā, the, 20, 51, 164, 170.
turīyam svid, 109.
Twelfth Latitude, the, 266-70, 274, 276, 277, 278, 279, 295, 309.
Twelve, 159, 163, 164, 186-87, 215, 223, 231, 284, 287.
Two, 63, 110, 154, 184.

uneven number, the, 257.
Union, 191, 208, 228, 232.
Unity, 8, 9, 17, 47, 49, 56, 62, 63, 90, 93, 94, 95, 110, 118, 127, 197, 199, 223, 228, 272, 303, 306.
Universal Divine, the, see Cosmic Divine.
Universality, Universalisation, 99, 142, 150, 262, 278.
Uranus, 12, 47, 86, 137, 141-44, 146, 150, 151, 152, 154, 230, 252, 255, 262, 303.

vāhana, 52, 53.
Van Allen Belt, the, 120.
Vasudeva, 39.

Vatican, the, 196, 269, 270.
Venus, 38, 39, 67, 118, 133-34, 141, 144-46, 149, 154, 225, 232, 255, 269, 308.
Vibhishana, 34.
Vibhutis, 35.
victory, 54, 61, 297.
Vijayadashami, 280.
Virgin (see also Mary), 294, 306.
virgin-birth, 136.
Virgo, 95, 227, 228, 255.
Vishnu, 37, 39, 40, 48, 53fn., 56, 68, 83, 262, 298-300, 304.
Vishnu Purana, the, 39, 40.
vital nature, force, 16-17, 24, 27, 28-29, 128, 131, 132, 133, 135, 146, 147, 148;
   vital body, the, 96.
Vivekananda, 83, 181-82, 197, 233-34, 277.
Void, the, 48, 59, 66, 67, 82, 114, 161, 271, 289, 290, 305.

Water (element), 15, 44, 63, 70, 75, 76fn., 146, 217, 223, 226, 227, 228, 229, 246, 255-56, 257.

Watergate, 181, 182, 183.
witness (consciousness), 72.
woman, 22, 25, 162, 278.
womb, 128, 227, 260.
World Calendar, the, 171.
World Wars, the, 52-54, 148-49.

Yashoda, 39.
yoga, -ic (see also synthesis, Bhakti, Jnana, Karma), 10, 50, 57, 90, 92, 97, 114, 121, 130, 131, 228, 236, 239, 250, 305;
   integral or supramental, 97, 125, 130, 147, 250, 305-07.
Yoganidra, 39.
yugas, the, 61-69, 83-84, 106.
Yugas, the Mysterious, 62.

Zero, 12, 13, 14, 84, 105, 107-10, 126, 138, 150, 186, 220, 265, 271, 272, 273, 290.
zodiac, the, 3, 7, 14, 24, 32, 33, 36, 45, 56, 63, 64, 66, 78, 83, 84, 85, 97, 110, 138, 155-56, 159, 163, 164, 165, 166, 186, 205, 215, 222, 225-31, 254-56, 257, 272, 274-75, 300.

Additional Titles by Patrizia Norelli-Bachelet:

☐ **The New Way**, Volumes 1&2 A study in the rise and establishment of a gnostic society. Ppbk., foldouts, photos, maps, diagrams, index, 601 pp., 1981. ISBN: 0-945747-06-03 Price:-------------------------$24.00

☐ **The Magical Carousel and Commentaries** A zodiacal oddesy with text on the story and symbolism. (Two volumes) cloth, slipcase, illustrated, 153 & 152 pps., 1979. ISBN: 0-945747-30-6
Price-- -----$19.80

☐ **The Hidden Manna** An interpretation of St. John's *Apocalypse* 1975 385 pp. hardcover, ISBN: 0-945747-99-3 Price---$9.00

☐ **Symbols & the Question of Unity** Nine articles on various subjects related to the Integral Yoga. 1974, 157 pp., hardcover Price---$6.00

☐ **"Agni in the Core"** (poster) The New Way Frontpiece photograph 40X50 cm.
Price--$6.00

☐ **September Letters** For young people interested in working for a better world order, 1974, 63 pp., paper.
Price--$1.50

New Titles Forthcoming:

The Tenth Day of Victory   **Time and Imperishability**
The New Way, Volume 3

☐ *The VISHAAL Newsletter* is a serialization of Patrizia Norelli-Bachelet's unfolding vision of the Supramental Creation established by Sri Aurobindo and the Mother of Pondicherry. In its pages she shares her insights about contemporary world events as well as the developmental processes of Indian culture and cosmology. It is published six times a year.   **India   USA**

	India	USA
(6 issues per year)	Rs. 180/yr	$18.00/yr
Back issues:	Rs. 30	$3.00

To Order, check the appropriate box and send this order form to:
Æeon Books
P.O. Box 396
Accord, N.Y. 12404

Bill my: Visa_____ or   MasterCard_____
Card #_____
Expiration date:_____

Signature:_____

Name_____   Book Total $_____
Address_____   Postage & Handling: $2.50
City_____   Applicable Sales Tax $_____
State/ZIP_____   (NY,NJ,PA,CA,)
Total Amount Due $_____

You may also place your order by calling Æeon Books at (914) 687-0639